THE HUMANITIES IN CANADA

The Humanities in Canada

F. E. L. PRIESTLEY

A Report prepared for the
Humanities Research Council of Canada

PUBLISHED FOR THE COUNCIL BY
UNIVERSITY OF TORONTO PRESS

PREFACE

LIKE ITS PREDECESSOR, published in 1947 and prepared by Watson Kirkconnell and A. S. P. Woodhouse, this volume might more properly be called "The Humanities in Canadian Universities." If in 1947 they found the universities as much as they could handle, without seeking out the humanities in the larger community, the enormous expansion of institutions in size and number since then has made me content to do no more than follow their lead. Some parts of their work I felt need not be imitated: I saw no point in repeating or in trying to expand their historical chapters; the history of higher education and of particular institutions can be found, by those interested, in the works named in the bibliography Principal Harris has kindly supplied (Appendix A). Nor did I feel it necessary to give as many tables of statistics; statistical information is now readily available in up-to-date form in the publications of the Dominion Bureau of Statistics, of the Canadian Library Association, and of the Canadian Universities Foundation.

This survey makes no attempt at a full description of the functioning of every institution in Canada; different institutions provided very varied amounts of information, and I have much more personal knowledge of some universities than of others. But my main concern was neither to provide a mass of information much of which would almost at once be out-of-date in a rapidly changing situation, nor, even more emphatically, was it to introduce comparisons and qualitative rankings of institutions. I have been concerned with the general situation and with general problems, and have used illustrations from particular institutions which I took to be typical. As fits a report for the Humanities Research Council of Canada, the main emphasis is on research in the humanities. This gives greatest importance to the bibliography of publication and research, and here there is an attempt at a comprehensive survey, limited generally only by occasional failures to respond to the request for the necessary information or, more rarely, by an over-zealous response which forced some selection on my part.

What I have chiefly aimed to do is to assess the main developments in the humanities in the Canadian universities since 1947, to describe roughly where we stand now, and to suggest the nature of the problems facing us today and in the immediate future. The most powerful evidence

of progress lies in the bibliography of publications (Appendix B), as anyone who compares it with its 1947 counterpart will see. The main moral of this book is that the relatively flourishing structure of research we have managed to erect is in serious danger of collapsing unless its growing needs are met.

In preparing this survey, I have had the most generous help of the university librarians, registrars, administrators, and faculty, who have nearly all responded cheerfully and promptly to yet another request for information, for bibliographies, for statistics. Without their patient co-operation the work would of course have been totally impossible. I am deeply grateful to them, and to all those who received me so hospitably on my travels across Canada, from Newfoundland to Victoria.

I must also thank the President and Board of Governors of the University of Toronto, who generously gave me half a year's leave to do my travelling. My thanks are also due to the Canada Council, who aided the Humanities Research Council with a grant, to the Humanities Research Council itself and Dr. J. R. Kidd for entrusting me with an interesting if taxing duty, and to Messrs. John Willoughby and Harvey Kerpneck, who gave me valuable clerical assistance. Mr. Kerpneck also wrote much of chapter 2. I can only hope that all these assistants will find the result worth their pains.

I owe a special debt of thanks to the Editor of the University of Toronto Press, Miss Francess Halpenny, and to Mrs. Magee, who sacrificed their own convenience, and often their own leisure, to ensure production of this volume for the Council's birthday. That they achieved unusual speed without compromise of quality is a tribute to their skill; that they achieved both without loss of cheerful good humour is a tribute to their characters.

F.E.L.P.

CONTENTS

THE HUMANITIES IN CANADA

1. THE GENERAL COURSE

At the beginning of any discussion of the humanities in Canadian universities, one is confronted with problems created by the system of secondary education to which students entering the universities have been subjected, and by the limitations on entrance requirements that system imposes. These are not new problems, and they have not changed in essence since the 1947 edition of *The Humanities in Canada*.

The most fundamental problem arises from the apparent loss of faith in academic training as education among those who like to call themselves professional educators, as distinguished from the talented amateurs who staff our universities. The universities are still dedicated, particularly in the humanities, to a belief in the value of a rigorous intellectual discipline, of the cultivation of a careful and penetrating scholarship by acquiring a degree of mastery of a subject. They believe in the value of such a degree of mastery for its own sake, and for the ordered habits of thought its pursuit inculcates. These beliefs are obviously not shared by the architects of the secondary school systems. For them education is partly vocational training, partly a vaguely defined process of "moulding the citizen." For them the academic becomes one type of vocational training, applicable only to the minority who intend or will be allowed to go on to the university.

The effect of this divergence of views on the fundamental process is that students receive little preparation for university in academic subjects, and, what is of more importance, arrive at university with little or no understanding of the nature of an academic education. In English, they have been exposed partly to a functional approach, with an emphasis on the mechanics of communication, and partly to an attempt to popularize literature as a form of amusement or of ethical uplift. They have been offered, in their curriculum, a miscellany of oddments chosen for a miscellany of reasons, which they have tried to "appreciate" in an historical vacuum, and in samples too limited to develop any notions of critical principles or of standards of literary form and structure. In history, they have been exposed to what is still "social studies" rather than history; they have been given no notion of how a historian works, what sort of sources he uses or where he finds them, what sort of problems he faces and how he tries to solve them. They have been taught as if history is certain, unambiguous, and settled. In nearly all subjects, they have been given no sense of the excitement of inquiry, the thronging of open questions, or of the techniques by which the professionals seek endlessly to resolve them. Perhaps I may be allowed to cite an example, a typical one, from my own experience. I expounded an interpretation of *Hamlet* to a quite good class of freshmen, and as soon as I had finished went rapidly through the whole play again, giving a very different interpretation. As soon as I had finished, a student asked, "Which of these are we to accept?"

It is true, of course, that in spite of the system, and in spite of the limitations of the curriculum, good teachers still send some well-prepared students to the university. But good teachers are rare, and even in provinces like Ontario which confer a special teaching certificate on the honours graduate, and where this certificate commands a higher salary, the proportion of specialists teaching a subject is extremely small. And in some provinces no premium is paid the honours graduate in secondary teaching. At best, the nature of the high school course, and the nature of the matriculation examination, both place pressure on even the good teacher towards a type of instruction remote from the needs of the university.

In the second place, the subjects offered by the high schools are not related closely to university needs. In Saskatoon, for example, German is available as a school subject in only one high school, and there only as an extra Saturday class. Greek is now offered in very few high schools in most parts of Canada. Much of the elementary instruction in languages that ought to be done in secondary schools is consequently forced on the universities, to the detriment of their proper function. It is perhaps a sinister sign, for example, that universities are spending so much money and devoting so much of their staff's time in modern languages to language laboratories. It might be thought that the skills of proper pronunciation and reasonably fluent conversation could be taught in the schools, leaving the university free for concentrated study of the literature. Some provinces are now beginning some foreign language instruction at an earlier stage; Alberta is starting French in some junior high schools, to give six to eight years of French before university. Developments of this sort, if extensive, would considerably change matters.

But the old pattern of accepting the high school leaving examination as also university entrance is being widely attacked. In many parts of Canada, the senior matriculation year was developed in the high school system as a replacement for the first year of university. During the depression, it was more economical for parents to have their children educated locally for a further year, and it soon became more economical for some universities to drop the first year and insist on senior matriculation for entrance. But as this first year became absorbed simply into the high school system, and as that system changed, senior matriculation has tended to become less the equivalent of first year university. The University of British Columbia has been advocating a separation of the high school leaving examination and the university entrance examination; this would probably be the most effective way of asserting the university's control over preparation of its entrants, but it is not without its own complications, political and administrative. In Manitoba, a Royal Commission recommended changes in the secondary school system which allow "streaming" and the separating of matriculation classes; the University of Manitoba now hopes to review and tighten the matriculation requirements. In Ontario, experiments have been carried out with special examinations in certain subjects to supplement the ordinary Grade XIII papers, and it is possible that senior matriculation will come to include special papers of this sort, more closely related to university requirements. The ordinary examinations are in many provinces put through a process known as "scaling," to bring the marks into conformity with what is called a "normal distribution curve," derived originally, I believe, from the statistical theory used in thermodynamics, of distribution of molecular velocities in a gas. The scientific basis of relation has always escaped me, but the effect is to limit the number of failures, no matter what the performance of the students. The students are thus allowed to set their own standard.

The experience of those universities which still allow entrance with either junior or senior matriculation is not simple evidence for or against either. At British Columbia, the records suggest that the better students come in with junior matriculation; those who do not get a good enough standing to enter with Grade XII (in which there are no supplemental examinations) stay on in school to do Grade XIII. Dalhousie also finds that the junior matriculation students are at least as good as the seniors. The one exception, at Dalhousie, New Brunswick, and Manitoba, is that students from Ontario who have failed the Ontario Grade XIII enter on their junior matriculation, and these are inferior students. It seems likely that they may be refused admission in the near future. There has been a general tendency towards requiring senior matriculation for entrance, and those universities which still admit junior matriculants will either have to conform to the general pattern or erect defences against the failures. Many universities have demanded a higher standard of performance on the senior matriculation examinations than a mere pass, and this has had some effect in lowering the rate of failures in the first year. But it does not remove the chief objections, which relate both to the curriculum and to the nature of the examinations themselves.

II. THE GENERAL COURSE

Some large changes have taken place since 1947 in the organization of general courses. One of these is the disappearance of the General Honours course at Toronto. This was unique, in that it demanded an honours standard, and was made up entirely of courses from the honours prescription, but was designed on a broad basis to give four years of relatively advanced work in a number of disciplines. It was potentially an excellent and unusual course, but it never received full support from the science departments, and tended eventually to become a refuge for discards from the honours courses. It attracted some, but few, really good students. It was abolished simultaneously with the creation of a new three-year General Course to replace the old Pass Course. The new course introduced a principle called "concentration" (for want of a better term) whereby each student chose from the five subjects taken in the first year one in which he had been reasonably successful (60 per cent or better) as his subject of "concentration" in the next two years, taking each year two courses in the subject. To pass his second and third years, the student must average 60 per cent in the two courses of his concentration. This system has worked well in some departments, particularly those, like English, which created special courses to make a co-ordinated pattern of the five courses in the three years. In other departments, and particularly in the science departments, the scheme received little support and in practice collapsed, some departments simply refusing to offer courses for concentration. The science departments then proposed the establishment of a General Course in Science, in which the humanities are represented by a course in English in the first year, one in philosophy in the second year, and a choice in the third year of Greek and Roman history, modern European history, or "Literature of the Western World 1920–1960." For the humanities and social sciences, the "concentration" General Course continues.

At Alberta, too, the general course in arts has been separated from that in science. That these moves do no harm to the humanities is evident; for the first time at Alberta there are now more candidates for the B.A. than for the B.Sc. Alberta is planning a new system for the general course; it would replace the present system, which requires "concentration" of a minimum of five (maximum of six) courses in one department, with a new one requiring a major of four courses and a minor of three. The major and minor subjects may or may not be related. Fifteen courses are required for the degree, and a maximum of five in the major, four in the minor subject, would be permitted. Alberta is also discussing the possibility of extending the general course to four years.

One problem faced by the universities in the Prairie Provinces is the competition presented by the Bachelor of Education degree, which has become the qualifying degree for high school teaching, and which consequently gets more official support and subsidy. In Manitoba and British Columbia the B.Ed. is taken after the B.A., so that its competition is chiefly with the M.A. In Alberta and Saskatchewan, it can be taken as a first degree; it is also possible at Saskatchewan to take both degrees in a five-year combined course if the subjects are properly selected. At Alberta, it was pointed out to me that a B.Ed. student takes only two fewer Arts courses than a B.A. (thirteen instead of fifteen), but since a B.Ed. must take six additional courses to get a B.A., it is clear that the courses are not very closely equivalent. One suspects that few of the thirteen Arts courses for the B.Ed. are in the humanities. It is a comforting thought that a majority of the students now take a B.A., followed by a B.Ed. (145 as against three taking the B.Ed. first).

One area of Canada where radical changes are taking place is in the Province of Quebec, where the tradition of the *collège classique* (described fully in the 1947 survey by President Kirkconnell) has been under somewhat critical examination. The tendency of the universities in Quebec, both old and new, to develop strength in the social sciences and in science pure and applied has naturally led to a reassessment of the *collèges*. The main discussion has centred on the relation of the *collèges* to the secondary school on the one hand, and the universities on the other, and on the relative inflexibility of the curriculum. The most important proposal is to treat the last two years of the course as essentially different from those before, as belonging to the university, rather than the high school level. What is needed, to judge by the advocates of change, is a strengthening of staff to university quality for these two years, and an adoption of teaching methods more like university methods and an approach to the subjects less like the school approach. One gathers that the problem is very much like that of junior colleges, which tend simply to become extensions of high school, staffed by teachers with the training and approach proper to the high school rather than to the university. Whether changes in the *collèges classiques* will strengthen or weaken the position of the humanities in Quebec by comparison with science and the social sciences I am in no position to judge, and it is perhaps not easy for anyone to judge at this time.

McGill introduced a new curriculum for the General Course in 1959–1960, which prescribes in the third and fourth years compulsory "Faculty" courses, defined as "synoptic ones which will enlarge and synthesize the various more specialized studies . . . made in departmental courses." The Faculty course "will deal with the successive conceptions of the nature of man and of the world in which he lives; with the relation between these conceptions and actual institutions, economic, political, and religious; with theories of freedom and authority and their social and political implications; with the chief intellectual and imaginative works of man and with the changes in his standards in these matters; with traditional ideas of knowledge and the effects on them of the empirical findings of modern science."

One of the new universities in Ontario is engaged in a somewhat similar approach. York has established both an "ordinary programme" of three years, and a General Honours one of four years. In the "ordinary programme," the student takes a total of fifteen courses, four of which will be in one department, and will constitute a major; four others, taken in the first two years, must be "comprehensive courses" in humanities, natural science, the social sciences, or "modes of reasoning." Titles of some of these comprehensive courses indicate their nature: in the humanities, "The Roots of Western Culture," "Modern European Civilization." In the first, particular attention will be paid to three periods: classical Greece, the age of St. Augustine, and Europe from the eleventh to the sixteenth century. The aim of the whole prescription is to combine the breadth of area studies with a degree of concentration. The General Honours programme will combine courses from the specialized honours programme with, in the third year, "an opportunity to study an alien culture such as that of the Soviet Union, China or Islam," and in the fourth, "study of selected contemporary problems such as that of world population, the growth of metropolitan centres, and international organization."

Trent University plans a "single-major" programme not unlike a "concentration," and a "joint-major" of five courses in each of two subjects, a total in each case of fifteen courses. The novelty is not in the plan but in the method, which will be predominantly by tutorial and seminar. Students will be expected to do a good deal of work outside the regular term. In other words, Trent is attempting a close approximation of the English method.

The general courses have been extended since 1947 in many universities by the creation of new departments, or by the extension of work of departments. A good many universities, for example, are now offering Russian, often to large numbers of students, and Russian is tending to replace German as a chosen foreign language in general science courses. In many, the Slavics department offers a fairly wide range of languages— at Saskatchewan: Russian, Ukrainian, Polish, and Old Slavic; Manitoba the same; British Columbia: courses in comparative Slavonic philology as well as Russian and Polish; Alberta: Russian, Ukrainian, and Polish, and comparative Slavonic philology. British Columbia, and more recently Alberta, have added Italian to the Romance languages offered. British Columbia also offers one course in Portuguese. British Columbia has also added Asian studies, courses in Fine Art (available both for the B.A. and for the B.Ed.), a department of Theatre, and courses in music leading to the Mus.Bac. These extensions are typical. In 1947, Mount Allison was the only institution to offer a degree of Bachelor of Fine Arts, and Manitoba, for example, had "no organized course of study in Fine Arts leading to a degree." It now offers a B.F.A., and Alberta expects shortly to do so. It now offers a B.A. in Art. At Queen's, students may combine courses in Fine Art (Art, Music, Drama) "to make up a group towards the General B.A. degree." There is perhaps a general tendency, illustrated by the reorganization of music at Toronto into an academic faculty distinct from the Royal Conservatory, to give greater emphasis to the academic aspects of the arts, to musicology, history of music, history of painting, as studies in their own right, rather than as adjuncts to performance. This is paralleled in a number of universities by expansion of these sections of the library, and by accumulation of edited texts of composers in addition to secondary material.

University thinking on the general course is clearly in a stage of experimentation. The extension in number of courses and number of subjects offers more opportunities to the student, but at the same time increases the dangers of free choice. The problem of making the course "general" but not a smattering is the persistent problem of all universities; some of the recent experiments will be watched with interest.

UNDERGRADUATE EDUCATION in the humanities is divided today, as it was in 1947 when A. S. P. Woodhouse and Watson Kirkconnell published *The Humanities in Canada*, into general and honours training. Though it may no longer be possible, as it was then, to say categorically that the distinction between the two kinds of B.A.'s tends to rob the general or liberal arts courses of gifted students, causing them "to be regarded as the refuge of those who lack the gifts requisite for honours" and depressing the standards in these courses, the gulf between the two kinds of training remains. And with the development of additional honours courses, such as Slavics, which cater to interests the high schools in some provinces have begun to develop, the gulf seems, unfortunately, to turn into a chasm.

The premise underlying the distinction between general and honours training remains Newman's in *On the Scope and Nature of University Education*: "Knowledge . . . is the indispensable condition of expansion of mind, and the instrument of attaining to it. . . ." The complete honours course prescribes four full years of study for the degree, with few options—though these options are no longer so severely restricted as they were in 1947. It requires concentration in depth on a narrow area of scholarship, though not necessarily in one humanities subject only, and it aims to impart discipline, proportion, and system such as will fit the student for the professions, especially teaching and, increasingly today, university teaching. In distinction from the general course it requires the student to engage in detailed and independent research and, at Toronto, especially in the senior years to produce a number of essays each of which may be equated, not too fancifully, with projects like the Harvard Senior Thesis.

The complete honours course is an exacting course and yet rewarding. As a result, where it flourishes a high proportion of the best students are attracted into it. At Toronto, of 4,237 full-time students in the humanities, 2,012 or 47.5 per cent are enrolled in honours courses. But the honours course is demanding not merely for the student but for the university as well. Since it places such emphasis on research (and therefore on teaching) in depth, it requires a substantial undergraduate library, adequate to support such teaching, reading, and research. It also requires a large and appropriately trained staff, large enough to permit the division into lectures, classes, and tutorials which characterizes most Toronto honours courses.

Such a staff and such a library are found nowhere else in Canada but at Toronto. And as a result the situation described by Woodhouse and Kirkconnell remains substantially the same today. The only complete honours course in Canada is to be found at the University of Toronto. There students do honours work, and are required to maintain honours standards, quite apart from the general course students, from their entrance with senior matriculation. Elsewhere, there still are only three variants on the Toronto honours programme. In the first case, as at McGill, students take a common first year (after senior matriculation) and begin to do honours work in their second year if they have qualified for it (with at least second class standings) and are approved. The emphasis here is on "quality rather than quantity." In the second case, as at Dalhousie, students "may obtain Honours in four years from Grade XI" (the same length of time required for an ordinary degree), by taking advanced and special classes and passing a comprehensive examination on the honours work in fourth year. At Dalhousie 22 classes are needed for the degree with honours, and the student must make an average of not less than 65 per cent in his honours classes. In the third case, as at Bishop's, students begin honours work in their third year, do a certain amount (at Bishop's a considerable amount) of specialization in their third and fourth years, and must maintain a high average to stay in honours. At Bishop's a student must make 70 per cent or he reverts to the pass list. He must also, in some cases, write a senior thesis in the department of his specialization.

A comparison with the report by Woodhouse and Kirkconnell will reveal the heartening fact that, though none of the other three types of honours training is as rigorous as Toronto's, the distinction between honours and general courses elsewhere in Canada has become more sharply defined. The third category of variant on the Toronto honours scheme is generally much superior to what it was in 1947 when one university offered an "Honours B.A." in three years from junior matriculation. And a fourth category of variant may emerge from the experiment at York University in Toronto, which accepted its first students in 1960. York proposes to give two types of Honours B.A., a specialized degree in four years which resembles the Toronto degree, though specialization is not begun until the second year, and a general degree in four years, which includes "area" studies such as the 1947 report envisaged but also study in the fourth year of "selected" contemporary problems such as that of world population, the growth of metropolitan centres, and international organization."

Yet both the factors mentioned before, access to a large and suitable staff and the provision of an adequate undergraduate research library, operate to render the general picture in Canada only a little less dark in 1963, though it is gloomier in some areas than in others. In the Maritimes, for example, of nine major institutions only five, Memorial, New Brunswick, Acadia, Dalhousie, and St. Mary's, offer honours work. In Western Canada, at least one institution with an enrolment of 1,000 students offers no honours courses. In Ontario, one new university, Assumption University of Windsor, had in 1963 fewer than 15 per cent of its students enrolled in honours, and Carleton had fewer than 5 per cent in honours. At many institutions the numbers of students in honours in the humanities in proportion to those taking honours in other subjects seems disproportionate, even embarrassingly low. At the University of Waterloo, for example, only 41 students took honours in the humanities, as against 92 in science and social science; that is, fewer than one-third of the honour students at Waterloo took honours in the humanities. At Waterloo University College, 285 students were enrolled in honours in Arts but 336 were taking honours in the social sciences alone.

From the point of view of the development of research in the humanities, and of the production of future academic staff, the importance of the honours courses can scarcely be exaggerated. Many universities are preparing to offer Ph.D.'s in the humanities, and to establish a full range of graduate work, but few seem inclined to ask where the prospective Ph.D. students are to come from. At Dalhousie, of a total enrolment of 2,500, 23 were in 1963 in honours in the humanities; at Memorial, of 22,000, 26; at Western Ontario, of 6,000, 229; at Windsor, of 1,600, 54; at British Columbia, of nearly 13,000, 147; at Manitoba, of 8,000, 93; at Carleton, of 2,000, 17; at McMaster, of 2,300, 248. The only really large honours schools are at McGill, Western Ontario, and Toronto, with 246, 229, and 2,012 in the humanities respectively in 1963. And when one looks at the most impressive of these figures, Toronto's, and realizes that for each discipline in the humanities the 2,000 will provide only a good handful of the first quality in each graduating class, one recognizes how scanty is the supply. Toronto represents possibly something like the maximum production in relation to total enrolment. The honours course operates there under exceptionally favourable circumstances: it has acquired over the years a prestige that attracts good students; it is heavily favoured in the system of entrance scholarships (often with free fees for the first-class student throughout his course);

and it is given preference through a specialist's teaching certificate in the
school system. Elsewhere there may be none of these inducements to
attract students into honours. The government of the Province of Saskatchewan offers a five hundred dollar scholarship to good students, tenable
in the fourth year of the honours course, but this is clearly not enough to
offset the expense of the added year, at least in the humanities, as the
enrolment of 22 in the fourth year shows. Yet this is more than most
provinces offer. Other provinces (Alberta, for example) have made
various provisions to subsidize graduate students, but not to subsidize
either the fourth year of honours or the necessary year of make-up
courses the pass student needs before full M.A. work. What is clearly
needed is an energetic programme of recruiting for honours, combined
with subsidy on a generous enough scale to encourage good students to
choose the four-year course.

Again, there seems, to a Torontonian, something backwards in the
haste to establish Ph.D. courses before a thorough honours course.
Certainly the strength of graduate studies at Toronto, as at places like
Harvard, Yale, and Chicago, has been built on a very solid undergraduate course. I am not for a moment suggesting that other universities
in Canada should delay graduate work until they have successfully imitated the Toronto honours courses. I hope I may be forgiven for thinking
the Toronto system the best in Canada if I hasten to add that it is not
the only possible system, and not readily imitable. For one thing, unless
it can be sure of a reasonably large number of honour students, it is an
extremely expensive system. It is also a system that has to be installed as
a totality, since it involves its own pattern of relations between departments, its own system of examinations (based on a whole year's work
rather than individual credits—and no supplemental examinations), and
its own kind of inflexibility (movement from general course to honours
or back from honours to general becomes impossible after the first year
except by repeating a year). For these reasons I do not expect to see
any extension of the Toronto scheme to other institutions.

But some at least of the advantages of the scheme could be obtained
fairly simply. If in some respects it seems inflexible, in others it is
admirably pliant. In those institutions which work on a fixed credit
system, the requirements that each course should count for the same
number of credits (or hours), and that each student should take a fixed
number of courses in the year, make difficulties in planning honours
courses. At Toronto, general courses are of the usual three-hour-a-week
pattern, but honours courses are an hour, an hour and a half, or two
hours a week. Something of this flexibility could easily be introduced into

the more rigid system by requiring, say, students in honours English to take in each year a three-hour-a-week course of unspecified nature, which could be broken by the department into three one-hour-a-week tutorials, each given by a different member of the staff on a different area of the subject, or into a two-hour-a-week lecture and one-hour tutorial, or seminars, and so on. The late Professor Sedgewick used a system something like this with great success at British Columbia.

In general there seems to have been a tendency since 1947 across Canada to move towards separate honours courses. So, for example, at the University of British Columbia, where in 1947 honours depended "primarily on concentration and standing," candidates for honours now are usually required to take certain prerequisite courses in first and second year, are generally segregated from the stream of general students, and may even take honours during the last three years of some courses. At Alberta, where in 1947 there was a common first year in the field of concentration, some humanities departments, for example Classics, now offer a first year honours programme. The problems of libraries which are usually not as nearly-adequate as Toronto's, of undermanned staffs so that it is impossible to provide the individual work with students which is required and departments desire for an honours programme of merit and substance, of the tendency at newer institutions to ignore specialization in an honours programme or to develop honours work in other areas at the expense of that in the humanities, remain as impediments to a full honours programme.

II

The honours courses within the humanities at Toronto are now 16 in number, if one excludes such Arts courses as Political Science or Sociology, but includes Philosophy and Fine Art. In general, they offer four years of honours work, with outside options in related studies, within a literature, as in English Language and Literature, or within an area fairly closely defined, as in Islamic Studies, or within the broader context of the development of one or more national cultures, as in Modern History and Modern Languages. Though theoretically students are accepted into some of these courses from Grade XIII with 60 per cent over-all in at least nine papers, in practice different departments tend to ask higher qualifications—and some of the federated Arts colleges of the University, Victoria, St. Michael's and Trinity, have their own interpretations of the entrance requirements. Modern Languages and Literatures, for example, advises candidates with "lower than 66% in two languages" not to seek admission to the course. And all the departments concerned here anticipate that in 1964–5, at least 64 per cent in nine papers will be the minimum standard for entry into the course. The Department of English already requires a minimum of 64 per cent in nine subjects of Grade XIII for entrance to its course in English Language and Literature. Modern History and Modern Languages also stipulates that 66 per cent is required in at least two languages. And Social and Philosophical Studies, a common first year for students intending honours in Modern History, Philosophy, and similar subjects, now requires a minimum of nine subjects, with an average of 64 per cent.

The courses founded on this grounding in Grade XIII are at different stages in their development. Some, like Slavic Studies and East Asiatic Studies, are just now beginning to establish a programme and a philosophy; while others, like the old-established English Language and Literature, though still changing and strengthening, are rich in tradition and finely articulated. An analysis of E.L. & L. first will demonstrate what the typical Toronto honours course looks like.

English Language and Literature. The course provides, in the words of A. S. P. Woodhouse in the 1947 survey, "an introduction to the historical study of the English language," "a thorough study of the principal periods, authors and works of English literature," and, through essays primarily, "considerable practice in critical and historical writing," with an "optional course in creative writing." Classes in Greek and Latin literature (in translation) are prescribed each year, and generally conform to a principal emphasis in the course. In the third year, for example, a course in Ancient Epic parallels the course in Spenser and Milton. Latin and another language (Greek or a modern language) at matriculation level are required for entrance to the course. In his first year the student chooses three options from a list of honours courses, one of which must be a language (another language, history, philosophy are the common choices for the other two). These optional subjects must be continued in the second year, and two of them in the third year. Normally the third is continued in the fourth year, but may be replaced by an advanced course in Middle English. The student is thus required to continue two subjects outside the department at the honours level for at least three years, and another for two. This gives him a relatively close acquaintance with two or three other disciplines. In its English courses, in Professor Woodhouse's words, English Language and Literature "throws its first emphasis on the study of texts and its second emphasis on the application of historical method," and students are given a load of courses in major authors and works (such as Shakespeare and Chaucer) which, beginning in first year, steadily increases in number and complexity until the senior year, when at least six courses (such as "Victorian Poetry," "The Modern Novel," "Nineteenth-Century Thought") must be taken and eight may be chosen. In addition, there is training (in first year) in bibliography and research techniques and in the senior year work in practical criticism.

Like English Language and Literature, the other fifteen honours courses put a certain emphasis on options selected from within approved groups, though in some courses the freedom of choice is quite restricted, and, in a few like Classics, only the one-hour pass option is selected by the student.

Classics. English, Greek, and Latin are required at entrance, and stipulated English courses are carried on for two years. The student studies Greek and Latin, Greek and Roman History, and appropriate courses in Fine Art for four years. The depth of the course may be gauged from the fact that in his senior year the student is studying Pindar, Theocritus, Lucan, and Petronius, among others. *Latin (English or Italian Option)* and *Latin (French or Greek Option)* are two mutations from the basic Classics course, both to a degree tailored to meet the needs of the Ontario high school system since both qualify graduates for Type A certificates issued by the Ontario College of Education.

Islamic Studies. This course has no special entrance requirements and students who have B standing in the first year of the General Course and have studied Arabic are permitted to enter into second year. The course includes an extensive list of options from two groups, one linguistic, the other cultural, and 40 hours of Islamic studies in four years. These studies include Arabic, Turkish, and Persian linguistics and literature and history. A dissertation is required in fourth year.

Ancient Near Eastern Studies. Entrance to this course is the same as to the previous one. Options are rather more restricted, and are taken entirely in languages, and the amount of specialization is even greater than in the other similar course. A total of 47 hours is taken in Hebrew, Aramaic, Akkadian, and the appropriate histories in four years. No dissertation is required, but there is considerable research work, especially in connection with the five linguistics courses in the senior year.

Modern Languages and Literatures. This course admits students with the special qualifications mentioned already. A student who has taken Slavics in his first year may enter into the second year of that course from this. In general this course concentrates on the literatures of the various languages available (French, German, Italian, Spanish, Slavics), but there is emphasis on oral work and phonetics. The student may, if he qualifies, spend his third year abroad at a university in either or both of the two foreign countries whose language and literature are chosen as honour subjects in third and fourth years. In the first two years of this course, the student may elect options in history or philosophy. In the senior years no options are available.

Modern History. Students are admitted from a first year, Social and Philosophical Studies, common to a related group of honours subjects, or from the General Course with B standing. The choice of options is broad but the number of options available decreases until in fourth year only one is available, from a large list that includes languages, philosophy, and fine art. The 24 hours of history in the three years of the course includes the student's choice from among British, Canadian, Western, Russian, and Asian; and in the final year the student chooses, after consultation, from among an extensive list of detailed courses that includes, for example, "The Age of Sir John A. Macdonald," "The English Reformation from Cranmer to Whitgift," "The American Revolution," and "The History of the Soviet Union 1917–56." *Modern History (English Option)* substitutes basic honours English courses such as Chaucer, Shakespeare, Old English, Victorian Poetry for some of the history and qualifies a student for admission to the Type A course in English and History at O.C.E. *Modern History and Modern Languages* follows the course outline of *Modern Languages* for the first two years, but substitutes honours courses in history for some of the intensive work in literature of the final years of the other course. The student is still required to continue two modern languages in his senior years.

Philosophy. Students are admitted into the second year from Social and Philosophical Studies. Only one option may be taken from among economics, psychology, or sociology. Students do 23 hours of philosophy in the final three years of this course, covering the important texts systematically and methodically from early Greek thought through Joad and positivism and pragmatism, and investigating logic, aesthetics, and ethics. *Philosophy (English or History Option)* is a variant in which the options in the social sciences are replaced by basic honours courses in either English or history and the programme in philosophy is not diminished very much.

Slavic Studies. This is a course which may be entered either through the General Course with B standing, through the common first year in

Social and Philosophical Studies, or through one of the variants of Modern Languages. It wholly lacks a first year. But in the final three years, students take required Russian history courses, one other honours option from among philosophy, political science and economics, and at least 25 hours of Slavics. Courses so far available include Russian, Polish, Serbo-Croatian, and Ukrainian languages and a broad range in Russian literature and culture.

Fine Art. Options available throughout include the languages, history, and philosophy, and philosophy is required in each of the last two years. The study of painting, sculpture, and architecture, in critical and historical courses, in lectures and studio both, could involve a maximum of 43 hours in four years. The course is extremely flexible, and the proportion of practical to critical work can vary greatly to suit the student's needs, so that as many as 15 hours or as few as 4 hours may be taken in the studio. Courses range from Etruscan archaeology to twentieth-century architecture.

Music. The emphasis on technique in this honours course is still greater than in the previous one. Entrance requirements include proof of vocal or instrumental proficiency by certificate or demonstration. And while the amount of time given to practical work is severely limited in the course, in most cases students pursue their practical studies independently together with their course work. The number of options available accounts for the restricted time given to music itself. History is required in the first two years, philosophy and English in the second and third years, and English and fine art in the final two years. In addition, one other language must be chosen. Of the 27 hours of music courses, approximately half are courses in the materials of music and the problems of technique, and the others are historical.

East Asiatic Studies. This is one of the newer honours courses at Toronto, but, unlike Slavics, its students specialize for four years. In fact, 8 hours of East Asiatic studies are taken in first year, together with options in Islamic studies, history, and philosophy. English is required in the first two years, but, in the final two, because of the nature of the course, the student can take all of his courses in his speciality. If he does, he can take as many as 34 hours of East Asiatic studies in these final two years. The large list of courses includes both Japanese and Chinese literature, language, culture, philosophy, and art.

After this survey, obviously certain generalizations can be made about the Toronto honours system. In the first place, the curriculum is in no case inhibiting. There is always provision for flexibility, though the degree of flexibility may vary from *Classics* at one end of the scale, with virtually no outside options, to *Fine Art*, with an extensive, carefully chosen list of attractive options in related subjects. Second, though the core of each course is laid down by the individual department or departments, the student can "tailor" the course to suit himself in most cases, sometimes, as in Fine Art, altering the emphasis to be placed on technique or practical work, or, as in *English Language and Literature*, choosing certain "depth" courses such as advanced Old or advanced Middle English, in the area of his speciality. Third, though many departments restrict the options available to certain kinds, as in *Philosophy*, the system is sufficiently flexible that the student may pursue substantially the same basic curriculum while enrolled in another related course, but with totally different options, in this case in *Philosophy (History or English Option)*. Fourth, in almost every course, it is possible, and in some inevitable, that the student should pursue more than one subject or discipline towards his degree. In *English Language and Literature*, for example, provision is made for an interested student to take honours Latin courses for four years to support his English work. In the various courses grouped under *Modern Languages and Literatures*, students are required to follow two languages through to a degree. In *East Asiatic Studies*, a student may do both Chinese and Japanese. In each of the various combinations of history with literatures, *at least* two subjects of specialization must be chosen. Fifth and finally, the degree of relationship between the courses is fortunately so extensive that little wastage can occur through a student's poor choice of a speciality initially. Transfer is easily possible between courses with related subject-matter; and, in addition, the common first year, *Social and Philosophical Studies*, utilized by several departments in the humanities and others in the social sciences, permits a certain amount of experiment and allows a broad base for later specialization (while still maintaining honours standards) for those departments that prefer this.

That the honours courses in the humanities at Toronto do not permit study of mathematics or natural sciences, is, of course, regrettable. But their omission is explicable in terms of the amount of specialization required in some areas, as in *East Asiatic Studies*, and desired by the individual department, as in *Classics*. On the other hand, a large number of honours (as well as pass) options in the social sciences are available in almost all courses, and in some courses, like *Philosophy*, at least one of these is compulsory.

III

Though the honours courses elsewhere in Canada fall generally into the three categories described before, there is considerable variation among them both in courses offered and in the standards that are maintained. There is no great uniformity regionally either, as the institutions seem to respond to similar conditions in somewhat different ways.

For example, in the Maritimes, *St. Mary's University* in Halifax offers honours work in only three departments, English, Philosophy, and History. This restriction of honours courses is intelligible, since, with a student body of about 600, St. Mary's is the smallest institution in Canada offering honours degrees. St. Mary's admits from junior matriculation with a general average of 60 per cent, and honours work proper is restricted to junior and senior years. Students intending honours make application in registering for sophomore year, and are thus effectively guided by their honours department for three of their four years. In essence, the distinction between honours and pass consists in quantity of courses (24 instead of 22), passing a comprehensive examination in all the work of the honours field, quality of performance (65 per cent for entrance, 70 per cent while in course) and a more intimate liaison between student and department.

At *Dalhousie* in Halifax, on the other hand, while entrance requirements are the same, the opportunities for honours work are much greater. Honours degrees may be obtained in the humanities in Classics, English Language and Literature, French, German, History, Modern Languages (including Spanish and Russian), and Philosophy. The emphasis is similarly on number of courses, though the number required for honours at Dalhousie is only 22. Standards in course are lower, only 65 per cent being required, but for first class honours, 80 per cent is needed. A comprehensive examination is prescribed here too, and, in addition, each humanities department prescribes certain courses "that will provide a suitable foundation for the Honours Course" for the freshman and sophomore years, since at Dalhousie, as at St. Mary's, honours work is a matter of concentration in the final two years of the course.

At *New Brunswick*, where junior matriculation is also the level from which students enter, honours work is distinguished from both B.A. general work and B.A. major work. General degrees resemble the Toronto general degree without concentration, but in each case at U.N.B., the student must be in attendance for four years, not three as at Toronto for its general course B.A. At U.N.B., only students who have attained 70 per cent in sophomore year are eligible for honours work, which is, here too, confined to junior and senior years. Standards in course are "higher" than at Dalhousie, for at least 70 per cent in the honours courses of the two years, with no less than 65 per cent in the work of either year, is the minimum requirement for the degree. The structure of the courses resembles the Toronto system, for U.N.B. distinguishes between single and joint honours. In English, French, German, History, and Philosophy, honours may be taken singly or jointly, while Greek and Latin must be taken jointly. There is no comprehensive examination, but not only are additional courses in the honours subjects required for the degree, one or two extra "related" (optional) subjects must be added to the student's load.

At *Acadia*, on the other hand, no such elaborate apparatus as this for distinguishing honours students from others exists. Students qualify for honours degrees by doing "additional work of high quality in the Junior and Senior years." According to the Department of English, the honours "prescription is designed principally to prepare a student for graduate study," but it is also intended for the student who wishes a fuller undergraduate education. For this student, a fifth year of honours work after the ordinary four is suggested as an alternative road to a degree. In the English Department, whose honours programme is the fullest, a comprehensive examination, one competent research paper, and ten full courses given by the department demarcate the honours zone.

At *Mount Allison*, the distinction between pass and honours is in part quantitative, one additional course being required in each of the honours years (senior and junior). A thesis is stipulated, but no comprehensive examination. But concentration is much heavier than elsewhere in this region, and, as in English where only six electives are permitted in honours years, 75 per cent of the work of these years is in the honours subjects. English provides the backbone for the humanities honours programme, since degrees are granted in English, English and Greek, English and History, English and Latin, and English and Philosophy, in addition to those in French, History, Latin, Philosophy, Classics, and Philosophy and Greek.

At *Memorial University*, where students are admitted from Grade XI, honours in humanities are offered only in English, Classics, Languages, and History. Of a total enrolment of over 2,000, about 1½ per cent are in honours in the humanities. The course outline resembles that elsewhere in the Maritimes in that honours work is restricted to the final two years. But a larger list of required options, which includes options in the sciences and mathematics, is provided and a basic framework of required humanities courses, to which are super-added the courses taken in the student's honours subject. Eight courses in the "Major" are required and four in a "Minor." There is no research project or comprehensive.

In Quebec, at *McGill*, the distinction between general and honours degrees is "rather by quality than by quantity," although the calendar implies that the honours courses could be regarded as in some cases "providing pre-professional training." Emphasis is also placed on intimate working relationships with the staff and on tutorials, group or individual, rather than classes or lectures. Students are admitted with senior matriculation and must, in the first, pre-honours year make at least second-class standing in the proposed honours degree subjects. Degrees are available in English, French, German, History, Latin, Philosophy and Classics singly, and in most of these in "Joint Honours." For example, joint honours is available, in subjects in combination with English, in English and French, English and German, English and Greek, English and History, English and Latin, and English and Philosophy. For full honours, for example in English, students take a total of ten courses in the honours subject, in English including four stipulated period courses from the Renaissance forward and Chaucer and Shakespeare. In some subjects (of which, peculiarly enough, English is not one) like Philosophy there is a comprehensive examination in fourth year, which, in the case of Philosophy, presumes "a knowledge of the major classical works in each of these fields, some of which may not be dealt with in any lecture course or seminar." But this comprehensive examination is not in addition to, but rather replaces the separate examinations in the courses of that year.

At *Bishop's*, where only four students were in 1963 taking honours in the humanities, students are admitted to first year with Quebec Grade XI or McGill Junior Matriculation. Honours work is confined to junior and senior years and a 70 per cent average must be maintained to stay in course, as was earlier pointed out. Honours degrees are available in Classics, English, Modern Languages (French and German), History, Latin and Philosophy, and a variety of combinations, for example, English and French and Latin and French. In some cases, combination honours degrees are offered in which an honours subject (history) is combined with another type of arts subject (economics).

In Ontario, most universities approach even closer to the Toronto honours system, though there is no exact duplicate anywhere. Virtually every university or college of any size offers honours courses, though two of the newer and smaller institutions, *Laurentian University* of Sudbury and Port Arthur's *Lakehead College* still do not. The limiting factor here may be the university library.

York University, in Toronto, as was earlier mentioned, has the most interesting scheme for honours degrees. Like most Ontario universities, it accepts senior matriculants with 60 per cent average on the nine papers of Grade XIII. But, unlike Toronto, while it offers them a three year "ordinary programme" towards a general B.A., it has divided its honours work into "general" and "specialized." Both the honours systems lead in four years to the degree of Bachelor of Arts with Honours, but, whereas the "specialized" degree resembles the Toronto system of specialization and degrees are granted in English, French, History, Philosophy, though not in any combinations of subjects as yet, the general honours programme is intended to, in the third year, acquaint the student with an alien culture "such as that of the Soviet Union, China or Islam," and in the fourth year with "selected contemporary problems." Time will be the deciding factor at York, since students do not begin "honours" work until third year in either programme, taking first two years of a liberal arts programme which includes languages, social and natural sciences and mathematics, but not necessarily English, and two courses designated Humanities I and II, "The Roots of Western Culture" and "Modern European Civilization." Provision is made for a thesis in some departments.

Royal Military College at Kingston, though its special function and interest necessarily shape the curriculum, offers a very full basic honours programme in the humanities. Admission requirements resemble Toronto's, except that mathematics and two sciences are compulsory, and officer cadets take two preliminary years, as at York, the first one prescribed and the second dictated by the student's choice of an Arts, Science, or Engineering degree course in his junior and senior years. In the humanities, honours work is available in English, French, and History, and no student with less than 66 per cent in his honours field and 60 per cent over-all is permitted to take honours. Options are limited as at Toronto; for example, in English, options are selected from French, philosophy, history, geography, and politics. In the end, the distinction between honours and general is partly quantitative, since students in honours take two more courses than the others.

At Waterloo, both Waterloo University College (of Waterloo Lutheran University) and the University of Waterloo offer honours work. *Waterloo University College* has a variable entrance requirement, which permits graduates of Grade XIII with 60 per cent in either nine or eight papers to be admitted to the Faculty of Arts, and, on occasion, others with an average no lower than 55 per cent. Some candidates are admitted with an average of 60 per cent in seven or eight papers but they must make up their deficiency in first year. Honours work here consists of three years after a general first year in which the student must obtain suitable standing. Honours is at present available in Classics; English Language and Literature; a series of combinations with English—English and French, English and German, English and History, English and Latin, and English and Philosophy; three combinations with French—French and German, French and Latin, and French and Spanish; History; Philosophy; History and Philosophy; and two combinations with Philosophy derived from Toronto's honours Philosophy—Philosophy and Psychology, and Philosophy and Sociology. Some departments have introduced comprehensive examinations. At the *University of Waterloo* the Toronto admission standards apply, but there is still reliance on a common first year. Honours courses offered resemble those at the other Waterloo institution, with the addition of English and Spanish, French and Russian, German and Russian, Philosophy and Literature and, an interesting course, Philosophy and Mathematics. Comparison between Toronto's English Language and Literature and Waterloo's Honours English is interesting. In the three honours years, students read a total of 33½ hours in English as against a minimum of 27 calendar hours at Toronto. Options (no distinction is made between pass and honours) are restricted to six in these three years, plus an aesthetics course and a course in "classical civilization" which is a condensation of Toronto's annual Greek and Latin Literature requirement in the third year. There are examinations on summer reading in the third and fourth years, and a comprehensive examination and senior honours essay before graduation. Courses are based on the Toronto curriculum, and progress is roughly chronological, with the divisions between courses chronological as well, rather than, as at Toronto sometimes, generic. For example, Toronto's 4k, "Nineteenth-Century Thought," and 4j, "Victorian Poetry," together with the second term of 3i, "The Novel," produce here two courses in "The Early Victorians" and "The Later Victorians."

At the *University of Western Ontario*, admission requirements are as Toronto's but honours work is still restricted to three years after a common first year. The Department of Education accepts an honours degree from U.W.O. as qualification for a Type B certificate, though in a few cases for Type A. Honours degrees are available in Comparative Literature (French, German, Russian, English), English Language and

Literature, and the five ordinary combinations with English, French, French and Latin, German, German and History, History, History and Philosophy, Latin with Greek, Music, Philosophy, Philosophy and German, Philosophy and Psychology, and Philosophy and Sociology. Compared to Toronto's system, the principal distinction would seem to be a lower order of flexibility, attendant perhaps on a smaller staff. So, for example, in the English Language and Literature course, two schemes of options are prescribed, one confining the student entirely to literatures and languages. Provision is made for some departments to require a comprehensive examination.

At *Assumption University of Windsor*, admission to the preliminary year is either from Grade XII or from Grade XIII with nine papers. Honours work, four years beyond Grade XIII, is restricted to the three years following on a common first year, and most departments have instituted a comprehensive examination in the graduating year. Though only 54 of 371 students (14.3 per cent) chose honours work in 1963, a certain range of honours degree courses is available. Besides English Language and Literature, there are the following combinations with English: English and French, English and History, English and Philosophy (either language or philosophy option), English and Spanish. French and Spanish, History (economics or philosophy option), Philosophy (science option), and Philosophy and Psychology are also available. Peculiarly, no Classics courses or options of any kind are offered; and the restriction in the size of the honours programme undoubtedly fosters the student apathy towards honours.

At *McMaster University* in Hamilton, admission requirements resemble Toronto's, but the common first year, found here as elsewhere in Ontario, is the most concentrated such year available, being divided into humanities, social sciences, and natural sciences curricula. Students are required to take six hours of work in areas outside their area of special interest, however, and these are provided for in the first year curriculum. But the tendency is for humanities departments to insist that students make certain choices only, even within the already restricted first year Humanities I curriculum. In fact, however, within years two and three, there is little effective distinction made between the "pass" and "honours" student. In English, for example, both take 30 units of work in the second year, while the honours student takes one more unit (31) in third year, from the same list of English courses in part. The pass student has more freedom with his electives, since the honours student is restricted to options from the languages, history, and philosophy, and, in third year, 6 units "basic elective." But since the pass degree here is, like Toronto's general degree, the reward of a three year course, the real distinction would seem again to be largely quantitative. In fourth year in Honours English students take 29 "units" of required English and only 3 of "senior division electives." The result in English of the failure to discriminate between pass and honour classes earlier and the intense concentration in fourth year is in part the breakdown of chronology, as difficult honours courses have to be held over to fourth year, and the student then takes together "Chaucer," "Twentieth-Century Poetry," and "English Literature of the Renaissance." Honours degrees are offered at McMaster in Classics; English; the five ordinary combinations with English as well as English and Russian; Fine Arts; Fine Arts and French; four combinations with French; History; German and Russian; History and Philosophy or Politics or Religion; Latin and Greek; Philosophy; and Philosophy and Religion. Though the range of courses is considerably restricted by comparison with Toronto's, some of the combinations here are unique to McMaster in Canada.

Carleton University in Ottawa admits either to a qualifying university year from Grade XII with at least 70 per cent or to first year with 60 per cent in Grade XIII, though exceptions are made to the latter requirement to benefit students "with a reasonable chance of success." Honours may be pursued from the first year if the student enters with 75 per cent from senior matriculation or has obtained B average standing in the qualifying year. Otherwise students with B standing in their honours subject enter from the first general year. The requirement for the honours degree is in part quantitative at Carleton, too, as honours candidates take 20 courses in four years instead of the 15 required of pass students. But there is flexibility even here and students are permitted, if "of exceptional ability," to complete an honours degree in three years (as they would a pass degree) by taking one course in each of the summers. As at McMaster, some courses in the honours subject are taken in common with pass students, but, unlike McMaster, even in second and third years, certain courses are restricted to honours candidates. Here, as at McMaster, fourth year provides for the most effective concentration, and, at Carleton in his final year, the student, in English for example, is encouraged to undertake independent study in a field of concentration of his choice and to present a graduating essay on his topic, on which he is examined orally. In English and some other subjects there is a comprehensive examination based on an approved list of texts. Honours are only available in Classics, English, French, German, and Philosophy at present, though programmes of combined honours may be created for the individual student.

In western Canada, the situation varies from province to province but each of the major institutions offers honours degrees. At *Manitoba*, where students are now accepted with junior matriculation (beginning in 1964, senior matriculation is to be required), honours work does not begin until the third year. An honours degree here requires three years of honours work, so that an honours degree takes five years, as against four for a general degree. To enter honours, a student must have averaged 60 per cent in second year, and at least 67 per cent in his honours subjects. To continue in honours, a student must pass each examination with at least 50 per cent and maintain a 60 per cent average. In effect, then, honours is in part a quantitative distinction here too, since in the end an honours graduate takes 25 courses in five years while the pass student takes only 20 in four years. Unfortunately, probably because of the extra year required for the degree, the temptation to enter honours seems rather slight, and in 1963 only 93 students were enrolled for honours in humanities out of a total Arts registration of 2,693. There is a full range of honours courses available, both in single subjects and in combinations of subjects. For example, History, English, French, German, Icelandic, Philosophy may be studied alone or in combination. Latin and Greek may only be taken in combinations, as Latin with English, French, German, Philosophy, History, or Political Science. There is a system of options available which declines until, in the fourth and fifth years, only one is permitted; i.e., in the final year 80 per cent of the student's work is done in his honours subject.

At *Saskatchewan*, which also admits from junior matriculation at present, the distinction between the Ordinary degree and the Honours "degree" is again partly quantitative. For the Ordinary course, three years and 15 classes are required, while the Honours course takes four years and 20 classes. In the humanities, the student enters the common humanities first year (Type A of the five types of Ordinary degree courses), and towards its end after consultation with the honours department he intends to work in, an Ordinary second year is planned for him. He is not admitted to Honours, however, until he has taken 10 Ordinary courses and achieved an average of 70 per cent in them, usually at the end of the second year. If the student completes the requirements for Honours, he is awarded both a Bachelor of Arts (in third year) and an Honours Certificate (at the end of the fourth). Honours work can be taken in Greek, Latin, English, French, German, History, and Philosophy. A comprehensive examination is normally given in the final year. There are no provisions for combinations of honours subjects.

At *Alberta,* entrance is normally from Grade XII into a common first year programme, directed, however, for the individual student by his choice of future subject of concentration or honours department. Here, too, the honours degree takes one year longer than the general degree. Some departments now permit specially qualified students to enter directly into honours work in the first year, and these departments provide a first year honours programme. Failure in this special first year programme does not penalize the student, who is permitted to continue to the completion of his three-year degree in the appropriate pass pattern. For promotion from year to year in the honours courses, an average of at least 65 per cent is required. Honours work is available in a small number of departments, but within these departments there is considerable flexibility in constructing degree courses, and a number of combinations of subjects is available. Classics may be taken alone or together with Ancient History and Archaeology, Latin can be taken with either French or English. Degrees are also available in History, Philosophy, Philosophy and Greek, and a variety of modern language subjects, including Slavonic and Soviet Studies, Moderns with either Latin or English, and the Romance Languages and German. Some departments specify comprehensive examinations, with Philosophy requiring two, of which one may take the form of a thesis.

At both the University of Victoria and the University of British Columbia admission is from junior matriculation. At *Victoria,* where only a limited number of honours courses is offered, there are two routes to an Honours B.A., either in four years for Single or Combined Honours or in five for Double Honours. Honours begins here in third year, and since both normal honours and the general course take four years, the distinction is again made in terms of work load. For Single or Combined Honours, 51 units are required in the last three years; for Double Honours, 66 units must be taken in the final four years. To enter honours, a student must have at least second class standing in his second year and in his special subjects, and for graduation he is sometimes required to present an essay, which normally counts from 3 to 6 units. Some departments also stipulate a general examination. Honours degrees are offered in English, French, German, Greek, Latin, History, Philosophy, and Spanish. There are also two interesting intradepartmental courses available in International Studies and Renaissance Studies. At the *University of British Columbia,* whereas a General B.A. requires 60 units, a Single or Combined Honours degree requires 66 and a Double Honours degree 81 units. The length of time required for these degrees is the same as at Victoria, and honours work begins in third year here too. Standards for admission to honours are the same, but the graduating essay is a regular, not an extraordinary, part of the curriculum. The general examination, which may be oral, is at the discretion of the departments concerned. Degrees are offered in Music, Asian Studies, Greek, Latin, Classics, English, Fine Arts, French, German, History, International Studies, Italian, Philosophy, Renaissance Studies, International Studies, Slavonic Studies, Romance Studies, Spanish, and Theatre.

3. GRADUATE STUDIES

THE EXPANSION of graduate work in the humanities is indicated by the student enrolment shown in Table I. Other institutions which provided no detailed break-down of enrolment by subject would add considerably to the list: of 744 graduate students at British Columbia, for example, 117 were in the humanities, and Ph.D.'s are offered in Classics and English, and will shortly be offered in history. So far, however, the number of Ph.D. students in the humanities is very limited, and only two degrees had been granted by 1963. Assumption University of Windsor reported 15 M.A. students in English, history, and philosophy; Waterloo, 9 M.A. students in the humanities, Bishop's 4, and Sherbrooke, which is just starting a graduate programme, 18 full-time and 39 part-time students in French, English, Latin, and history.

Some comparisons can be made with the report for 1946, which gave no indication of subject, but totals proceeding to higher degrees. At that time, the totals for Toronto, McGill, McMaster, Western Ontario, Dalhousie, Manitoba, and British Columbia were 192, 75, 9, 15, 11, 20, and 20, as against 435, 159, 76, 83, 34, 82, and 117. (In each case the figures for Toronto are lowered by the peculiarities of the Toronto system, whereby many pre-M.A. students, and many post-M.A. students not officially accepted yet as Ph.D. candidates, are not included in the count. The number of Toronto students pursuing graduate degrees in English, for instance—at varying distances—would be closer to 200. The 1946 report suggested for that year a total graduate number of 328 rather than 192. A similar adjustment would be necessary now.)

By comparison with 1946, not only is there a large increase in the number of graduate students, but also in the number of institutions prepared to offer the Ph.D. in subjects in the humanities. In English, for example, Ph.D.'s are offered by no fewer than eight universities, and in history by almost as many. Moreover, graduate instruction is now formally organized in practically all major institutions. The Director of Graduate Studies at British Columbia became Dean in 1949, New Brunswick appointed its first Dean of Graduate Studies in 1950, Alberta in 1957, Manitoba in 1949. In many cases the elevation of graduate studies from something to be handled by a committee (a common pattern until after 1946) to a fully fledged school or faculty with its own adminis-

TABLE I

Students Proceeding to Higher Degrees in the Humanities, 1962–3

Subject	Alberta	Carleton	Dalhousie	McGill	McMaster	Manitoba†	Memorial	Montreal*	Mt. St. Vincent†	Sask.	Toronto	U.N.B.	U.W.O.
Classics	2	—	1	2	6	4	—	—	—	—	13	1	—
English	20	2	22	33	19	24	11	62	12	5	137	12	24
French	2	2	2	18	—	6	—	58	—	1	R.L.	R.L.	10
German	13 Mod.	—	1	9	6	14	—	—	—	1	11	3	2
Romance Languages	} Lang.	—	—	1	14	—	—	142	—	—	see above	see above	3
Slavics	—	—	—	—	—	8	—	—	—	—	15	—	—
Near East. and Islamic	—	—	—	19	—	4	—	—	—	—	17	—	—
History	—	9	5	42	20	20	9	22	—	2	94	7	35
Philosophy	—	—	3	15	11	4	—	—	—	1	77	3	9
Music	—	—	—	—	—	—	—	—	—	—	5	—	—
Fine Art	—	—	—	—	—	—	—	—	—	—	8	—	—
Canadian Studies	—	4	—	—	—	—	—	—	—	—	—	—	—
Divinity	—	—	—	20	—	—	—	30	—	—	—	—	—
Linguistics	—	—	—	—	—	—	—	—	—	—	—	—	—

*Includes part-time graduate students proceeding to M.A., Ph.D., or *doctoral*.
†All students proceeding to M.A.

trative officers was brought about mainly by the expansion of graduate work in the sciences, and does not necessarily reflect anything like a full development of graduate facilities in the humanities. In 1946 the editors of the survey noted that for the most part, outside Toronto and McGill, "graduate instruction is by means of reading courses devised to suit the student's interests and needs or the capacities of the department" (p. 127). This is by no means the case now, but the provisions made in 1962-3 for graduate work at Manitoba, for example, can be taken as still typical of many outside the very large universities. In Classics, 6 advanced honour courses from the undergraduate prescription are available to graduate students, and 4 exclusively graduate courses. In English, 6 honour courses "are available for credit in the pre-M.A. course," and 2 graduate courses "designed by the student's adviser" and related to his thesis topic, or, if English is a minor graduate subject, "arranged in consultation" with his major department. French offers a similar arrangement. German offers 7 formal graduate courses, as does history; philosophy offers 8, Near Eastern language and literature 3. The seven courses in German are all offered by the same instructor. Of the courses in history, 4 are listed as "for major or ancillary credit," the others "for ancillary credit only." A recent decision to expand graduate work by offering the Ph.D. in English, French, and history gives rise to some misgivings. Staff of professorial rank number 12 in English, 9 in French, and 7 in history, and not all of these, to judge by the bibliography of publications, are productive scholars. Some reinforcement would be supplied by the affiliated colleges, but the resources in staff are still very slender for a Ph.D. programme.

Alberta offers the Ph.D. in English, "certain fields" of history, in Romance, Germanic, and Slavonic languages, and in philosophy, the M.A. also in Classics and linguistics. Classics offer 16 graduate courses, English 22, history 12, French 24, German 21, Spanish 5, Slavics 8, philosophy 16, comparative literature 3 (as part of modern languages), and linguistics 10 (both special and language courses). Staff at the professorial level (1962-3, Edmonton only) are for English 23, Modern Languages 16, philosophy 7, history 13, and Classics 4.

British Columbia has added to its Ph.D. offerings, which now include philosophy and Romance languages, as well as Classics and English, with history to be added very soon. M.A.'s are offered in practically all departments, including International Studies. The fields for Ph.D. work in many departments are limited and defined, and the research project and course requirements of each candidate are specified and annually reviewed by a special committee. For the M.A., since British Columbia has a three-year course for the B.A., a total of 18 units of course work is required, of which the M.A. thesis may replace either 3 or 6 units. Supplemental examinations may be allowed in graduate courses for students who have failed to obtain the necessary second-class standing. Admission to graduate work calls for first-class standing in at least two courses in the chosen field in the third and fourth year of undergraduate work, and second-class in all others. English offers 18 graduate courses, French 22, German 6, Greek 8, history 6, Italian 3, Latin 6, philosophy 7, Spanish 5. Instructors of professorial rank number 32 in English, 6 in Classics, 6 in German, 11 in history, 5 in philosophy, 16 in Romance studies, 7 in Slavonic studies. Here again the staff resources seem slender in some departments for a full Ph.D. programme.

Saskatchewan offers the M.A. in Classics, English, French, German, history, and philosophy. English offers 9 graduate courses; in other departments the main emphasis seems to be on the thesis. The university is embarking on a Ph.D. programme in English and history. The calendar makes the following stipulations: "The University accepts candidates for the Ph.D. degree only when it is satisfied that the Departments concerned are in a position to give the course and that the candidate is qualified to undertake the work." "Application . . . shall be made on behalf of the student by the Head of the Department in which he plans to do his work. The application shall summarize briefly . . . [among other things] special facilities, staff experience, etc., which should justify acceptance of the particular investigation as a suitable one for a Ph.D. candidate." An examiner from outside the University is provided for. (External readers of theses are also used by U.N.B. and Memorial, and are being considered by Alberta.)

In the Maritime Provinces, only the University of New Brunswick offers graduate work beyond the M.A. in the humanities; it has a few students working towards the Ph.D. in English, mainly in the Elizabethan period, in which the library is well enough equipped, especially with microfilm, to get the student well started on his research before going abroad to finish. Graduate work to the M.A. is offered in a few other departments, sometimes, as in philosophy, in restricted fields (in this case, to work in the twentieth century, and mainly from the journals, since the library is not adequate for other periods). Seven graduate courses are offered in English, four in history; philosophy conducts two seminars for its graduate students, as well as some shared by honours and graduate students. Philosophy and English are relatively flourishing, but the language departments, both modern and ancient, are faced with students inadequately prepared in secondary school, and find it necessary to devote their efforts to establishing proper undergraduate courses. Classics in particular suffers, being understaffed, and has found it impossible to maintain a full programme of honour courses.

Dalhousie offers the M.A. in Classics, English, French, German, history, and philosophy; Acadia in Classics, English, French, history; Mount Allison in Classics, English, history, and philosophy (with plans for other departments); Mount St. Vincent in English and history; Memorial in English and history, the emphasis in history being on "original contributions to the knowledge of Newfoundland history."

In central Canada, Laval carries on advanced studies towards the *doctorat* in Classics, French, German, Spanish, history, and philosophy, with a special Centre Espagnol for Hispanic studies which through the Presses Universitaires publishes a review and also doctoral theses. The University of Ottawa offers work to the *doctorat* in French, Canadian literature, Classics, Slavic studies, and philosophy, and offers special facilities for studies in medieval Latin. The University of Montreal offers the *doctorat* in philosophy and history, and in its special Institute of Slavic Studies. (It is worth noting that the 142 graduate students reported at Montreal in Slavics is the highest number for any single discipline in the humanities in Canada, approached only by the figures for English at Toronto.) Its Institute of Medieval Studies has a library of 30,000 volumes, supplemented by rich collections of microfilm, and attracts a large number of research students. The Institute of Linguistics also has a special library, and a centre for lexicography. Sherbrooke offers a three-year course after the *Baccalauréat* to the M.A. degree in French, English, Latin, and history, two of the years being spent in course work, the third on the thesis. Bishop's University gives the M.A. in English, history, and theology, with a major subject supported by two third or fourth year undergraduate courses in cognate subjects as minors, followed by a thesis and oral examination.

Carleton, Assumption, and the University of Waterloo are all developing graduate work, offering the M.A. in English, French, and history; in English, philosophy, and history; and in history and German, respectively. Both Carleton and Assumption list 13 graduate courses in English; Carleton offers 4 graduate courses in French and 3 in history; Assumption 8 in philosophy and 4 in history; Waterloo 5 half-courses in history and 6 courses in German.

The University of Western Ontario offers the M.A. in Classics, English, German, history, philosophy, and Romance languages and literatures. In Hebrew it offers 9 graduate courses, but since there is no undergraduate honour course, there is presumably no M.A. in the subject. Ph.D. work is at present limited to English, history, and philosophy. In English (1962–3), 15 instructors offer 11 courses (more will probably be offered before this description is published); in history, 10 offer 9 courses; in philosophy, 9 offer 14. In 1962 Romance graduate courses were confined to French only.

McMaster offers the M.A. in Classics, English, German, history, philosophy, Romance languages, and Russian, and the Ph.D. in history. For the size of the staff, offerings in graduate courses are extensive: 4 members of the Classics department offer 12 courses, 5 in philosophy 12 courses. In English, 11 offer 16 courses, in German 4 offer 7, in Romance languages 5 offer 10, and in Russian 3 offer 7. In history 9 offer 13 formal courses and also reading courses. It is, I think, a sign of careful planning that the department offering the Ph.D. has a high proportion of staff to courses; the normal procedure in graduate instruction is for the instructor to offer first a course in the area in which he did his own doctoral research, then to offer an alternative within roughly the same area as his own research develops or broadens. In time he will perhaps cultivate an entirely new interest, but will take some years to bring this to the point of offering a course. If the need for offering a full range of graduate courses with a small department leads the instructor to give courses in areas to which he has not been able to devote several years of research, the courses can be satisfactory only as make-up for undergraduate deficiencies or for an M.A. considered primarily as an extension and continuation of undergraduate instruction.

McGill offers the Ph.D. in English, French, history, and Islamic studies (through the Institute of Islamic Studies). In Classics, German, and philosophy it offers the M.A. A staff of 3 in Classics offer 9 courses, 4 in German 9, 10 in philosophy 11 courses and special seminars. Seventeen in English offer 19 half-courses (mostly of one hour a week, and some also open to honours undergraduates), 9 in the Institute of Islamic Studies offer 41 courses, including elementary courses in the languages. In history, 8 instructors offer direction of research in 15 fields.

Queen's, according to its calendar, offers the Ph.D. in history and philosophy, and "under certain circumstances" in German. In English, French, Classics, and Spanish it offers only the M.A., although it has in the recent past conferred at least one Ph.D. in English. In philosophy, the Ph.D. may be taken only in specified areas: the seventeenth and eighteenth centuries, Greek philosophy, contemporary English and American philosophy, particularly epistemology, the philosophy of mind, and ethics. Six members of staff offer 16 courses, including one in the philosophy of language. In history, 9 staff members offer 11 courses.

For the doctorate, students must not only qualify in graduate courses, but must choose for special studies two of the following: later medieval history, eighteenth-century French history, history of the British Empire, Russian history, twentieth-century British history, history of the United States from 1815 to 1865, Canadian history to 1867, Canadian history since 1867.

In English, 11 staff members offer 17 courses, of which only 5 were to be given in 1963–4. In French, 7 instructors offer courses in Old French, French-Canadian literature, contemporary French literature, and an unspecified "special period" of literature. Candidates for the M.A. are required to do two courses and a thesis. In German, 4 instructors offer 6 courses: linguistics; medieval literature; baroque literature and literature of the Enlightenment; the German Romantics; Goethe; and a "special programme." Five members of the Classics department offer 4 Greek courses (drama, epic, Plato, and post-Aristotelian philosophy), 2 Latin courses (satires and epics) and ancient history. Spanish, like French, requires two courses and a thesis for the M.A. Five staff members are listed, but the 3 courses named in the calendar, "Old Spanish," "Drama of the Sigla de Oro," and "Trends in the Modern Novel," are given by 2 of them.

Toronto, as might be expected from its size and from the size of its graduate school, has the most comprehensive offering. The Ph.D. is given in Classics (24 instructors, 57 courses), in English (34 instructors, 62 courses), in Germanic language and literature (10 instructors, 17 courses), in history (20 instructors, 36 courses), in Near Eastern and Islamic studies (11 instructors, 60 courses—of which about 50 are in language and literature: Akkadian, Aramaic, Coptic, Egyptian, Arabic, Ethiopian, Persian, Turkish, Urdu, Hebrew, Hellenistic Greek, related philology—the rest in history and archaeology). For the Ph.D. in philosophy, 26 instructors offer 45 courses; in Romance languages and literature, 34 offer 65 courses (in French, Italian, Spanish, Provençal, Catalan, and Italian dialects); in Slavics, 6 offer 16 courses and special reading courses. The M.A. is offered in East Asian studies (3 instructors, 4 courses), in Fine Art (5 instructors, 7 courses). The Mus.M. is offered in musicology, music education, and composition (8 instructors, 24 courses).

In 1963–4, Toronto established a new graduate degree of Master of Philosophy, which certain departments will offer. The new degree will undoubtedly gain its chief acceptance by departments in the humanities and social sciences; it is not likely to be offered in the sciences, since it is designed to overcome problems which seldom arise with the Ph.D. in science. The considerations which led to the establishment of the Phil.M. were mainly the following:

1. The demand for future university staff is not likely to be met, or met in time, by production of Ph.D. graduates in the humanities, since the average time for completion of the degree is some five years after the honours B.A. Many students complete all the requirements except the thesis, accept an appointment, and find it difficult to finish their degree.

2. If a sufficient number of completed Ph.D.'s cannot be produced to meet the demand, it is highly desirable that something representing more than the M.A., but capable of being completed in fewer years than the Ph.D., should be available as a qualification for academic posts.

3. It must be recognized that some university teachers are not, and will not be, primarily productive scholars. Many in the past, after completing the research for the Ph.D. thesis, have found their main interest in teaching rather than research, and have still been highly valuable members of faculty. For such students, training in research techniques can be satisfactory at a level short of the full Ph.D. thesis.

In essence, the Phil.M. is the Ph.D. without the thesis. It calls for two years of residence instead of the three for the Ph.D., but its requirements in course work, general examinations, and standards of performance in these, are the same as for the Ph.D. A major essay or research paper, based on independent research, on a subject approved by the Phil.M. committee, must be submitted, formally appraised by an appointed reader, and defended at an oral examination. A representative of the Phil.M. committee will occupy the chair at the oral examination, and report on it to the Council of the School of Graduate Studies. A bound copy of the research paper will be deposited in the University library. These regulations suggest that the research paper will be treated more formally than an M.A. thesis, since they embody much of the procedure now attached to the Ph.D. thesis. The time limit on the new degree is rather stringent. For the Ph.D., the student is allowed seven years from his first acceptance as a Ph.D. candidate, which means at least eight years from the B.A., and often nine. For the Phil.M. he is allowed one academic year after completion of residence requirements, with a possible single extension of one year.

The chief differences between the programmes for the two degrees, apart from the thesis, are in departmental requirements. In English, for example, the Ph.D. candidate is required to do a minor subject outside the department. This is usually related to his thesis subject, and is commonly in history, philosophy, or another literature. In place of this, the Phil.M. student does a further graduate course in English. Seven courses are required in each case. A student who had completed the Phil.M. and then decided to take the Ph.D. would be required to do the further year of residence, to make up the minor, to show first-class standing in a course in the field of his research, and to do a Ph.D. thesis with its attendant oral examination. Students working towards the Ph.D. who fail to meet any of its requirements will not be allowed to transfer to the Phil.M.; the intention is firm to keep the standard as high for the new degree as for the Ph.D.

The requirements for graduate degrees at the various universities which offer them are, on paper at least, generally pretty uniform across Canada, except perhaps at Memorial University and the University of New Brunswick, where there is more tendency to approach the English pattern of graduate work by placing all or nearly all the emphasis on the thesis rather than on course work, general examinations, and the like. Very few institutions or departments have abandoned the M.A. thesis, although some allow an M.A. to be earned simply through graduate courses. Nearly all institutions now place a time limit on degrees, usually of five or six years for the Ph.D., from three to five for the M.A.

The most notable changes since 1946, as has been noted, are the increase in the number of graduate students, and the increase in the number of institutions offering graduate work, and especially work to the Ph.D. level. So far these two tendencies have not been closely correlated, as the statistics show. There has been a very large growth in enrolment at Toronto, a fairly spectacular one at Montreal, less spectacular ones elsewhere. McMaster, Western Ontario, and Manitoba, and in some departments Alberta, have developed in numbers to a point where they seem likely soon to match some of the older graduate schools, but applicants for the Ph.D. degree are still very scarce, and are likely to remain so for some time. The university launching a Ph.D. programme in the humanities is facing a very formidable task. It is very easy to offer a Ph.D., but it is not easy to get good students to take it until it has established its quality in the academic market, which is essentially a continental one. The prestige of an institution's Ph.D. is gained in a number of ways. It is perhaps gained first by the quality of undergraduates produced by the institution—this has certainly been true in the cases of Harvard, Yale, Princeton, and Toronto. The undergraduate training earns respect for the graduate training. The interesting report by the Mount Allison Faculty Association, *The Idea of Excellence at*

Mount Allison (May 1962), recognizes this clearly, and proposes strengthening at the undergraduate level. It suggests that a policy already put into effect by the Chemistry Department, of bringing students back to do research at the University for the summer of their third year, could be imitated by the departments in the humanities as a way of encouraging and training undergraduates to carry on independent study. "Such work with the best undergraduates," it points out, "may prove more rewarding to the faculty member interested in research than work with less-than-best graduate students." Secondly, the degree earns prestige through the quality of the staff and of their publications by which they mainly become known. When a department head encounters an applicant with an unfamiliar Ph.D. the first question to enter his mind is "Whom has he worked under?" The quality of the scholars who have directed the student is of fundamental importance. Thirdly, the degree gains prestige from its holders. Once a degree is established, it can afford to be held by a small proportion of duds or pedestrian sloggers, but in its early stages it can afford only the best. Publications, and good publications, by holders of the degree are its final guarantee. The young degree, then, needs to attract the very best sort of student; but the best sort of student has his choice of the best institutions and degrees. In two successive years at Toronto, for example, the student who was at the top of the class in honours English was offered graduate fellowships by eight distinguished American universities. Without wishing to be rude, I would say that it is very unlikely that a top student offered a Ph.D. opportunity at Harvard, Yale, Princeton, Chicago, or California will be tempted by one from, let us say, the University of the Yukon. It would be highly unrealistic to ignore this fact, or its implications. It would also be highly unrealistic to think that the reputation of, say, a Yukon Ph.D. can be built on students not good enough to get offers elsewhere. The large number of low-value Ph.D.'s produced by minor institutions in the United States is sufficient evidence.

To some extent, no doubt, the pressure to offer Ph.D.'s has come from administrations which cannot see why a Ph.D. cannot be given as simply and readily in the humanities as in science. To some extent, also, it has been felt necessary, in order to attract good staff, to be able to offer the chance of teaching graduate courses. As some of the figures already cited show, a number of institutions already have more graduate courses than students—a good scholar will be attracted by the thought of a graduate seminar of good and responsive students; he will not be retained by being allowed to offer a course no one is there to take, or by a seminar of second-class students. A fully developed undergraduate honours course would offer him more of a chance to teach his special subject to a lively group, as the Mount Allison report suggests.

I am by no means suggesting that there should not have been an expansion of Ph.D. work, or that there should be no further expansion. I think it is not only inevitable, but salutary, that more graduate schools in the humanities should develop in Canada. What I am concerned with is that they should be good graduate schools, capable of earning continental, even international, respect. Anything less will lower the prestige of all Canadian degrees. And I am concerned with what seems to me the relatively casual way in which graduate work is in some cases being allowed to expand. I have watched certain universities develop their resources in science. They decide that they must start by strengthening the departments—say, physics and chemistry. To do this, they must first get a really good man, at whatever it will cost, and then give him a free hand for four or five years to make appointments, build up equipment, and plan programmes. As a result, we read, for example, in a recent copy of *The Listener*, of a physicist who leaves the University of London, where he has been for seventeen years, to go to western Canada, where he at once is given more equipment for research than he had had in his seventeen years at London. As a first-class man, he will attract others, perhaps some of his former colleagues and students, and in a few years will have built a strong, active, and well-equipped department, capable of training first-class Ph.D. students.

This is the way in which every university in Canada builds a good department in science, and prepares to offer graduate work in science. But this is not the way they prepare to offer graduate work in the humanities. Yet a good department in the humanities is just as hard to build, and to preserve, as one in the sciences, and first-class men are just as rare, and just as heavily competed for. And they have to be competed for, in salary, in status, and in equipment and in opportunities to pursue their own research, in the same way as the scientists. This is the first thing that ought to be realized by universities ambitious to establish a good Ph.D. in the humanities.

Another danger inherent in the establishment of a second-class Ph.D. is that it will devalue the M.A. One encounters the argument that the M.A. is already devalued, and that this makes a Ph.D. necessary. It is undoubtedly true that many American universities have made their M.A. a consolation prize for rejected Ph.D. candidates, but it has never been necessary, nor indeed habitual, for Canada to follow American educational practices *in toto*, and an equally valid argument could be offered for making the Canadian M.A. as stringent a degree as the University of London one, or as the Oxford B.Litt. In actual fact, at a number of Canadian universities, the M.A. represents a very valuable and often very thorough year of graduate training. I can think of two M.A. theses in English that have been published in book form, and I know of several others that ought to have been. If the M.A. is allowed to become merely another year of continued undergraduate work, it might well deserve to become merely a terminal course for those unfit for research. But it can just as readily be made a thorough training in techniques of scholarship, completed by a solid, if limited, application of these techniques in the thesis. In this form, it could equip the Canadian graduate student to proceed to a Ph.D. more thoroughly trained, and less dependent on direction and supervision, than most of his fellows on the continent.

What the future developments in graduate work will be I am of course unable to foresee. The pattern will depend partly upon what aid is available for graduate students, as well as upon what efforts are made to plan the schools of graduate study. The bold scheme set in effect by the Province of Ontario might, one hopes, be imitated elsewhere. It provides fellowships of $1,500 for virtually every graduate student of reasonable promise, with a further $500 for continued graduate work in the summer. These fellowships are tenable at any university in the Province, and are specifically intended to meet the coming demand for academic staff in the Province. A proportion of the fellowships have been made available to students from outside Ontario, and students who have already spent a year in residence as graduate students are considered for purposes of application as residents. It is impossible at present to isolate the results of this scheme, after only a year of operation, but it cannot fail to attract into graduate work, and ultimately into academic teaching, a considerable number of very good students who would normally have been deterred by the risky gamble of the competition for too few and too inadequate fellowships. I believe the Province of Quebec deserves credit for being the first to offer this sort of direct assistance on a large scale. It is obviously desirable that other provinces should follow suit. A very large proportion of students in the humanities need a year abroad to complete the research for their thesis, and this calls for a comparatively generous fellowship. If each province undertook to support its own graduate students through all the years of required residence, fellowships like the Canada Council pre-doctoral fellowships could be reserved for study outside Canada. Even for this purpose alone, their number is already inadequate. The present allocation of funds for them allows for about eighty fellowships, which must provide for all the humanities and the social sciences. This year some thirty-five candidates in English alone were admitted at Toronto to their final year of residence; and this is before the effects of the Province of Ontario Fellowships have really begun to be felt at this level. The amount that Ontario is committing annually to graduate fellowships is extremely generous by comparison with the total amount applied by the Canada Council to all purposes; if the Government of Canada is to play a comparable part in supporting graduate work and preparing future academic staff, its present contribution must be at least doubled.

The universities themselves, often with the help of gifts and endowments, have considerably increased the number and value of their own fellowships, although in many institutions the number open to students in the humanities is extremely limited. At the University of New Brunswick, for example, out of nineteen fellowships available, two are for the "Study of Historical Relations of New Brunswick and the State of Maine and the United States of America," all the rest are for science, economics, business administration, or law. This is a general pattern; at Toronto, apart from open fellowships (many of them established by the University itself), only a small handful of fellowships are available to students in the humanities, as compared with business administration and the sciences. Those provided by industry are all in science and applied science. Fellowships and scholarships given by industrial interests are seldom made open to the humanities. The imbalance already created by the generous support given science students through the National Research Council is thus aggravated by private support. Only a public support on the same scale as that of the National Research Council can redress the balance.

One further development in graduate work in recent years must be noted. This is the growth of institutions or centres designed to cut across departmental and disciplinary divisions. Some I have already mentioned in this chapter. Carleton has for some years had an Institute of Canadian Studies, which not only offers interdisciplinary studies at the graduate level, but also undertakes the publication of important texts and documents, and has sponsored a number of lecture series. Toronto has established centres of Medieval Studies, Linguistics, and Russian and East European Studies. The first of these is the most interesting, since it brings together the special resources of the Pontifical Institute of Mediaeval Studies, of the department of history, and of several literature departments. It is too soon to say what effect such centres will have, but there seems more promise in such interdisciplinary studies at the graduate level than at the undergraduate.

4. UNIVERSITY FACULTY

THE ONE FACT which dominates this whole survey of the humanities in Canada, the accelerating expansion of institutions in size and numbers, naturally dominates a survey of the present and future situation in regard to faculty. In 1947 the editors deplored the large proportion of scholars who emigrated to the United States, and the conditions that induced them to do so. If the editors had had a record of the number of new appointments to staffs of Canadian universities for the fifteen years from 1931 to 1946, they would have recognized how few Canadian scholars had any chance whatsoever of staying in Canada in academic employment. Many whose memory goes back to those years will have personal knowledge of scholars who wished to stay in Canada, despite adverse conditions for scholarship, but could find no appointment, and of others, determined to stay in Canada, who simply abandoned a career in scholarship for one in business or other affairs. All this is now changed. The expansion of opportunity is sufficiently indicated by the fact that since 1946 something like eighty Ph.D.'s in English graduated from Toronto have found places in Canadian departments. Other disciplines like history, philosophy, and modern languages have had similar success. Moreover, the large gap between Canadian and American academic salaries has come close to disappearing, as also has the gap between institutions within Canada. In 1946, salaries for full professors averaged from Toronto's $6,200 down to below $3,000 in several of the smaller institutions (a full table is given in the 1947 report, p. 174). By 1963, minimum salaries at Toronto were $13,000 for professor, $9,500 for associate professor, $7,500 for assistant professor, and $6,000 for lecturer, and the median salary for full-time teachers in 48 institutions was $8,685. Apart from the Maritimes, salaries in major universities across Canada have tended to equal or approach closely to the Toronto minimum, and in the lower grades of appointment sometimes better it. The result of this levelling is clearly seen in recent appointments; it has been possible for Canadian universities to compete in the American market, particularly for good junior staff, and for universities in western Canada, for example, to compete on something like even terms with their eastern rivals. And since, for much of the last fifteen years, Canadian salaries were rising at a much faster rate than British or European, and no comparable expansion of universities was taking place on the other side of the Atlantic, Canadian institutions were in a good position to attract young British and European graduates. Canadian faculties have consequently retained the cosmopolitan quality which is one of their greatest sources of strength. At the same time, the increased availability of fellowships for study abroad allowed more and more Canadian students to take part of their training abroad, and it is important, in surveying university calendars, to remember that a large proportion of staff shown as holding only Canadian degrees will in fact, in many areas of scholarship, have spent at least a year of graduate training or research outside Canada. The avoidance of parochial inbreeding in the academic world is of the highest importance.

The present state of faculty is, on the whole, vastly better than in 1946, and to visit universities across Canada is to be struck by the quality, particularly of the new young scholars, in most institutions, by the activity in research, and the energetic confidence in their work. It is when one looks to the future, and even the immediate future, that one is assailed with fears and misgivings. One sees everywhere conflicting pressures. To a university administrator with a limited budget, there is an obvious conflict between increasing salaries and increasing staff, and it is a somewhat ominous sign that hours of teaching are generally much the same as in 1946: a large number of places I visited reported loads of from ten to thirteen hours a week, often accompanied by heavy burdens of marking and correction of exercises and themes. In view of the coming flood of students, it has been estimated that by 1970 Canada will require additional staff in numbers equal to the present staff; this doubling of staff is presumably calculated on a basis which would retain roughly the present teaching load. If such vast numbers of new staff are not available, the alternatives of over-loading or of diluting with inferior staff are equally terrifying.

Another disquieting fact is that expansion of the student body brings to some departments a disproportionate increase in the least scholarly part of their discipline. It is customary to prescribe for students in professional courses, and in the social sciences, first- and sometimes second-year courses in the humanities, especially in English or another modern language, partly as a limited approach towards a liberal education, partly as an acquisition of a possibly useful skill. This throws an enormous burden on the department concerned, and introduces factors over which the head of the department has no control yet which interfere with the planning and structure of a good department. Sections of freshmen English, for example, may become so numerous that they necessitate what is virtually a separate staff, for whom no opportunity of doing senior work can be provided. It then becomes more and more difficult to recruit staff, since no good young scholar, interested in scholarship, is satisfied to teach freshmen and only freshmen, particularly if they are not interested in the subject for its own sake. At one of the Canadian universities already suffering from this pressure, junior members of the department of English teach ten hours a week and mark during the year between 350 and 400 essays. The problem is capable of some solution where a large graduate school is developed, as at Toronto, since graduate students can be employed as teaching fellows to teach a single section; this has the double merit of supporting the graduate student and saving the permanent staff, although it perhaps creates other problems pedagogically. Several universities have tried to lighten the load on instructors by employing markers for essays, often former women students who have married and welcome part-time work. No one that I have spoken with felt that this was a satisfactory solution. If a regular corps of experienced and conscientious markers could be built up, whose duties would include interviews with the students to discuss their work, it could no doubt develop into an adequate system. At present it is a rather bad alternative to avoid a worse. What one fears most is that as this problem becomes accentuated with growing numbers, good staff will become increasingly particular about what sort of teaching it will undertake, and there will be a steady decline in quality and training in the staff willing to carry on the routine and drudgery of the department. If, as seems likely, it becomes necessary to give permanent status in the department to what are inevitably willing hacks, their increasing numbers will tend to bring us back to the conditions deplored by the 1946 survey. One does meet, to be sure, a few academics who are good scholars and born teachers and who take a special interest in the problems of the non-Arts freshman, and if we could find an adequate supply of them, our troubles would disappear; but in my experience they are the rarest of academic commodities.

A related problem which affects large departments and particularly those with a strong element of the "service" course is the tendency which seems to have become part of tradition in many Canadian universities for senior members of the department to establish a kind of proprietorship in senior courses. It seems natural, no doubt, that the senior expert in a given field should conduct the course in it, and in the days when departments were small, no one had the ambition to deprive him of the task. But as departments grow, there are likely to be one or two bright junior members whose special area of study is the same as that of seniors. It is seldom feasible, and perhaps never advisable, to multiply senior courses until each man has his own little territory. But nothing is much more frustrating to a first-rate young scholar than to know that he has to wait for a retirement to lecture to advanced students in the subject he is expert in. One cannot, I think, reasonably expect a tiring senior scholar to give up an advanced course he is fond of to accept a group of freshmen, but it should be possible to lighten his load and at the same time give the junior a chance by turning part of the course into a tutorial, say, in charge of the junior, or by splitting the course to allow the junior some time with advanced students. It would, I think, be a generally good thing if the right of property in courses could be abandoned.

Apart from this special problem, which does not affect all departments or all institutions, there remains the general problem of where we are to get the large numbers of properly trained scholars we shall need in the next few years. The expansion in the United States, and the rapid creation of new universities in England, may make recruitment from abroad more difficult. We must count on training more of our own future staff. A number of steps have in fact been taken already towards this end. The Canada Council has been putting major emphasis on pre-doctoral fellowships to assist graduate students to complete the doctorate, and in 1963 the Government of the Province of Ontario established a large number of graduate fellowships. The Woodrow Wilson Fellowships in the United States, which are directly designed to produce college and university teachers, have been greatly increased in number and very generously extended to Canada. A new type of Woodrow Wilson Fellowship has been introduced to aid a proportion of the Fellows in their final Ph.D. year.

These measures have gone a long way towards ensuring support for the large majority of graduate students. But two problems at least remain. One is the slowness of the process by which Ph.D.'s in the humanities are produced. It seems possible that the provision of adequate fellowships will speed up the process in many cases; in the past, the student who had finished his formal residence and all other requirements except the thesis was very strongly tempted to accept an instructorship, and to finish his thesis as best he could. Too often the pressure of teaching new courses, and the impossibility of extended leave, meant that completion of the degree was deferred year after year. In those institutions where promotion was dependent on finishing the Ph.D. the student was placed in an almost impossible position by conflicting pressures. Graduate schools have set time limits, with a tendency towards increased rigour, from the date of acceptance of a candidate to the last possible date for submission of the thesis. There is little disposition, however, to devaluate the degree by demanding less, and the nature of research in the humanities does not encourage very limited thesis subjects. The provision of ample fellowships for a final year devoted entirely to completion of the thesis would undoubtedly remove the temptation in the great majority of cases, and increase the rate of production of finished Ph.D.'s. The number of Canada Council pre-doctoral fellowships is obviously quite inadequate for this purpose, and since the Government of Ontario Fellowships are tenable only at Ontario universities, they cannot, invaluable as their help is, meet the common need of a final year abroad. The eighty or so Canada Council pre-doctoral fellowships are spread out, of course, not only over all the disciplines of the humanities and social sciences as well, but over all the stages after the M.A., so that the number available for the final year of students in the humanities is extremely small. One can add to these the very few Queen Elizabeth II Fellowships, which will in future be reserved for advanced graduate students; but the total in relation to the need implied in doubling present staff is pitifully inadequate.

A second problem which has so far received very little attention is that of recruiting graduate students. A good deal has been said about expanding existing graduate schools, and about starting Ph.D. pro-grammes in more and more universities, as if there were a vast pool of potential Ph.D.'s lined up waiting for room in a graduate school. This seems to me a highly optimistic and erroneous assumption. The raw material for the graduate school must come from the undergraduate, and good graduate training must be built on a reasonably solid and specialized undergraduate course. To get a large increase in the number of Ph.D.'s in, say, history or English, we must have a large increase in the number of first-class or very high second-class honour graduates in those subjects. The numbers of students now enrolled in honour courses in the humanities are, generally speaking, the numbers from whom we can expect to select our Ph.D.'s of the next four to seven years. Of the total, not more than a third can be expected to be graduate material, and this third will certainly not be enough for our needs. A vigorous policy of recruiting at the undergraduate level is needed.

One recent development at Toronto is designed to increase the pro-duction of university staff, namely the creation of a new degree, the Master of Philosophy, or M.Phil. The requirements for this degree, described in the preceding chapter, are intended to obviate the problems created by unfinished Ph.D.'s. Course requirements, and general examinations, will be closely similar to those for the Ph.D., but residence requirements will be a year less (two years after the honour B.A. instead of three), and instead of the Ph.D. thesis a more limited piece of research or study will be required. The assumptions underlying the establishment of this degree are open to debate, and were indeed strenuously debated at Toronto. It can, I think, be said that if the supply of Ph.D.'s is bound to prove inadequate to the demand over the next ten years, and this seems highly probable, then it is useful to have a degree which represents a longer and more rigorous training than the M.A., and which in some respects (perhaps all respects except research) is quite comparable with the Ph.D. The new degree is not to be available to failures from the Ph.D. course. Time alone will justify or fail to justify the new degree: time will show whether good students have been deterred from a Ph.D. course by the length and ardour of its requirements, and whether they will be induced into an academic career by the M.Phil., and time will show whether the M.Phil. will be accepted by institutions as a satisfactory qualification for full appointments.

As more and more universities undertake graduate work at advanced levels, the problem of staff increases. A good graduate school in the humanities demands a carefully planned balance in the staff. There has been a good deal of talk about a sort of division of labour among universities, of each cultivating a special area. It is indeed almost inevitable that a university should be stronger in some departments than in others, and in some areas of discipline, but it is highly doubtful how far this should be planned. It should certainly not be planned without a very full awareness of what strength involves. It is almost impossible to isolate an area in the humanities; it is possible to isolate technical problems, perhaps, but it is not possible to build a school restricted to isolated problems. At most points, the disciplines touch each other: the student working in eighteenth-century English literature needs to know something of English history of the period, and the philosophy, and probably of French literature. The strength of the staff of a graduate school lies in having as complete a collection of experts as possible, so that the student can be advised, and supervised, at all necessary points. The planning of staff, then, involves not only the balancing of a single department, but of a whole structure. Granted that the structure will be stronger at some points than others, but it must be as strong as possible at all. The problem, in short, is closely similar to that of building a library collection. It is very difficult, if not impossible, for a graduate student to be trained adequately by a staff member who has not himself done research in the same area; staff must be chosen with a careful intention of covering main areas and types of research in the closely linked disciplines.

Planning of staff appointments is closely related, in state-supported universities, to budget arrangements. As competition for scholars increases, it expresses itself not only in competitive salary or rank, but also in attempts to make an attractive offer earlier than one's rivals. Fifteen years ago, the normal time for settling academic appointments for the following autumn was in April, or March at the earliest. Now negotiations are often started in October or November, and completed by the New Year. It is not uncommon for some appointments to be arranged more than a year ahead. Where the university is dependent on an annual and uncertain budget, it is placed at a serious disadvantage, and some provincial governments are now offering something like an assured minimum budget over a limited number of years. The administrative procedures by which appointments are made have also in some universities been too inflexible and too slow in operation to allow a firm offer to be made at the right time to a good potential appointment. This can be particularly disastrous in seeking young scholars, who cannot afford to ignore a bird in hand, however attractive a bird the bush might eventually contain. Every university administration needs now to know fairly precisely what binding commitments it can make for at least the year after next.

5. THE UNIVERSITY LIBRARIES

TO TRAVEL across Canada visiting universities and their libraries with a clear memory of what such a journey had to offer in 1946 must give rise, in any but the most atrabilious temperament, to a measure of gratification. At that time, as the authors of the first edition of this survey pointed out, the inadequacy of the library collections was aggravated by the general inadequacy of the provision for housing them. In their notes on sixteen libraries, they record two as having "excellent new quarters" and a "building reasonably modern and adequate"; the other fourteen range from "beautiful building, badly planned" to "complete inadequacy in space." It is, I think, safe to say that physical conditions of the sort general in 1946 are now exceptional. Thanks to a more enlightened policy of public support, to the $50,000,000 Canada Council fund to assist such building, and in some cases also to generous private benefactions, new and better library buildings are to be found in almost every university in Canada. A few institutions, in fact, are planning their second large new building to house graduate and research libraries.

The collections themselves have also undergone a growth that must offer some sense of encouragement. Even if one remembers, as indeed one must, the limited significance of rough counts of holdings, the varied methods by which the counts are likely to be arrived at, the ignoring of quality in a merely quantitative approach, the ignoring of duplicates, of distinctions between primary and secondary material, of distribution of material by period, and so on, one can still accept a degree of rough correlation between the sheer size of a library and its probable usefulness for study and research. With all these *caveats* in mind, it is still worth noting the growth of holdings since the survey of 1946. In Table II, the counts as provided by the librarians are, unless otherwise indicated, by volumes. The counts are generally for roughly the end of 1962, and consequently in many cases are now well out of date. In an attempt to avoid one area of uncertainty, that of definition of subject, I asked each librarian for counts by Library of Congress classifications which Dr. Ranz, then librarian of the University of British Columbia, kindly prepared for me. Where an institution used another system of classification (this is rarer now than in 1946), I asked for as close an approximation as possible to the LC categories. These categories are:

English, PE, PR-PS; German, PF 3001-5999, PT 1-4897; French, PC 2001-3761, PQ 1-3999; Italian, PC 1001-1977, PQ 4001-5999; Spanish, PC 4001-4977, PQ 6001-8929; other modern languages, PB, PC 1-986, 3801-3975, 5001-5498, PD, PF 1-558, PG-PH, PQ 9000-9999, PT 5001-9999; Latin, PA 2001-2915, 6001-9595; Greek, PA 227-1179, 3051-5665; Near Eastern Languages, PJ-PK; Far Eastern Languages, PL 1-4961; Comparative Literature, PN; Comparative Philology, P; Philosophy, B-BJ; Theology and History of Religion, BL-BX; Music and Fine Arts, M-N; History, C-F.

As I have suggested, charts of holdings are of limited value: different libraries use different methods, of highly varying accuracy, in arriving at estimates; they vary in what they include in the count, and undoubtedly some are torn between the wish to make their holdings as impressive as possible for the prestige of their institution and the contrary wish to make them as unimpressive as possible to call attention to their needs. Nevertheless, counts give some notion of the sort of balance present in a collection, of relative holdings in different disciplines, and of the breadth, if not the depth, of the library's coverage. It would, of course, be vastly more useful if standard methods could be established in all institutions for arriving at estimates.

One thing the figures show pretty clearly and unequivocally is the accelerated rate of acquisition, and of expenditure on acquisition, in the major libraries. Since the report for 1946, total holdings have increased at Toronto from 430,000 to nearly 2,000,000 (in 1962–3, in fact, the two million mark was passed), at McGill from 422,000 to 782,000, at Queen's from 208,000 to 460,000, at Western Ontario from 169,000 to 300,000. Even more spectacular are the increases at British Columbia from 160,000 to nearly 500,000, at Ottawa from 138,000 to over 300,000, at Saskatchewan from 91,000 to over 237,000, at New Brunswick from 30,000 to 116,000, at the University of Montreal from 100,000 to over 300,000, and at Bishop's from 20,000 to nearly 50,000. Many of the new institutions, like Carleton with its 100,000, Calgary with its 60,000, Sir George Williams and Waterloo with over 50,000 each, and Memorial with over 70,000, St. Mary's with 60,000, have holdings which in 1946 would have put them into the top half of a list of institutions. The middle point of 45 institutions ranked in 1946 by holdings was occupied by Ontario Agricultural College with 43,495 volumes; the median in the present listing comes at 70,000 volumes. In 1946, only four Canadian universities showed more than 200,000 volumes; in 1962 ten do.

It will be apparent, moreover, from the valuable report of Dr. Edwin E. Williams (*Resources of Canadian University Libraries for Research*

TABLE II

LIBRARY HOLDINGS IN THE HUMANITIES ACCORDING TO LIBRARY OF CONGRESS CATEGORIES, 1962

Institution	Total Holdings	Holdings in Humanities	English	German	French	Italian	Spanish	Other Modern Languages	Latin	Greek	Near Eastern	Far Eastern	Comparative Literature	Comparative Philology	Philosophy	Theology and History of Religion	Music and Fine Art	History
Acadia	119,000	29,120	10,135	805	1,185	75	175	375	500	500	70	20	920	70	2,450	—	1,900	9,940
Alberta	288,338	64,060	13,140	3,892	3,892	405	1,035	5,713 (mainly Slavic)	968	968	67	85	2,407	383	4,747	2,812	5,197	18,314
Alberta, Calgary	60,000	18,389	4,650	750	1,116	27	31	260	290	422	62	38	839	142	2,254	1,004	1,328	5,227
Assumption	99,980	—	7,725	275	2,739	206	1,439	1,899	447	230	39	17	1,320	96	5,944	3,900	1,033	7,200
Bishop's	49,000	n.r.	3,000	300	1,100	100	150	25	500	750	100	—	200	100	1,200	7,000	450	6,200
U.B.C.	493,517 (Williams)	239,000	41,150	6,200	14,000	1,650	3,900	7,200 (6,000 Slavic)	2,250	2,550	500	950	9,000	1,350	10,400	8,500	17,450	53,350
Carleton	100,341	41,600	7,626	1,060	2,932	67	676	735	488	495	17	35	—	600	2,999	1,713	991	7,501
Dalhousie	125,000		20,000	2,000	4,500	500	500	2,000 (Russian)	[4,500				—		[7,000		n.r.	n.r.
Lakehead	30,000		4,000	—	[2,000				[800		38				1,200 (incl. Psych.)		250	3,400
Laurentian	37,749	—	2,789	122	4,439	113	90	6	42	203	16	—	355	21	854	424	297	3,482
Huntington	3,082	n.r.	965		[252				n.r.	n.r.	n.r.	n.r.	n.r.	n.r.	2,025	624	n.r.	n.r.
Sudbury	4,462	n.r.	45	343	30				n.r.	n.r.	n.r.	n.r.	n.r.	n.r.	777	1,830		n.r.
Laval	529,205	89,933	3,383	659	26,510	469	360	1,203	3,000	2,093	310	242	800	231	7,654	13,780	8,000	21,313
McGill	782,000	209,486	35,452	9,250	16,981	2,680	6,000	4,380	3,875	6,600	880	625	4,040	2,023	12,000	7,000	18,150	79,575
McMaster	161,100	73,360	16,350	2,790	5,100	190	1,000	1,000	1,200	1,300	200	90	1,100	220	6,220	19,540	5,240	16,820
Manitoba	230,494 (Williams)	112,087 (incl. 27,588 bound periodicals)	27,426	5,085	5,943	233	317	9,876 (Icelandic); 7,984 (Slavic)	1,545	2,314	40	61	2,333	850	8,029	3,606	12,269	23,238
Memorial	70,000 (titles)		4,780	390	930	30	360	165	230	280	20	60	—	—	1,300	790	1,390	3,750
Mennonite, Winnipeg	10,500		570	250	n.r.										300	5,000	270	450
Montreal	313,240 (Williams)	65,000	4,580	674	16,951	400	910	849	1,269	1,186	155	83	1,521	179	13,239	10,301	5,255	21,362
Mt. Allison	n.r.	n.r.	15,570	1,240	[3,200	100	583	420	1,180	960	200	85	2,400	100	2,300	7,500	5,700	13,200
U.N.B.	116,000	n.r.	12,598	1,331	3,141	—	—	581	750	909	40	16	833	104	3,285	1,825	2,100	10,650
Ottawa	305,625 (Williams)	n.r.	—	—	—	—	—	—	—	—	—	—	—	—	—	—	—	—

Institution	Total Holdings	Holdings in Humanities (titles)	English	German	French	Italian	Spanish	Other Modern Languages	Latin	Greek	Near Eastern	Far Eastern	Comparative Literature	Comparative Philology	Philosophy	Theology and History of Religion	Music and Fine Art	History
Queen's	460,000	n.r.	21,800	3,575	6,150	900	2,225	950	1,850	1,825	325	82	2,700	275	7,450	11,400	5,774	28,000
R.M.C.	86,000	n.r.	45	343	30	—	n.r.	n.r.	n.r.	n.r.	n.r.	—	761	935	—	552	659	12,500
Saskatchewan	237,000	74,424	16,607	3,145	5,646	279	133	3,321	966	1,104	181	63	2,528	327	3,775	3,941	4,602	23,183
Regina	45,000	13,400	4,000	400	1,000	50	50	400	200	300	—	—	500	500	1,300	700	—	4,000
St. Dunstan's, P.E.I.	20,000	n.r.	2,000	40	200	60	30	—	350	200			75		100	1,500	350	2,500
Sacré Coeur	15,000	n.r.	1,000	—	3,000	—	—	—	[2,000	252			—		1,000	2,000	1,000	3,000
St. Francis Xavier	n.r.	n.r.	3,976	152	725	—	—	—	231				2,006 (incl. lit.)	583	1,665	3,784	1,381	5,395
St. Mary's, N.S.	60,000	—	2,300	96	527	68	36	118	234	115	5		538	24	1,528	2,558	188	5,055
Sherbrooke	6,545 (Arts)	—	846	32	2,478	7	71	73	279	201			457	23	182	506	210	1,172
Sir George Williams	51,416	19,698	8,034	321	1,654	49	220	89	275	355	9		—	4	997	760	2,009	6,695
Toronto	1,892,804	40,536	31,104	8,282	18,667	6,642	8,285	7,927	3,972	4,613	4,019	3,316	3,894	825	7,695	14,427	15,374	48,536
St. Michael's (Toronto)	96,113	95,152	10,400	5,000	7,400	—	—	—	[10,000	—						35,000		25,000 (rough)
Trinity (Toronto)	66,500	n.r.	4,647	955	1,600	158	84	96	626	1,110	113	5	1,320	96	5,944	3,900	1,033	7,200
Victoria (Toronto)	131,000 (79,587 titles)	n.r.	10,360	2,550	2,450	404	—	—	[2,658		223		—	917	2,880	—	287	7,085
Victoria, B.C.	103,091	40,536	20,130	1,786	2,471	—	353	385 (Russian)	590	599			—	—	1,887	—	—	12,335
Waterloo	54,000	30,000	6,100	1,000	2,100	75	800	1,000	360	425	[35	[10	700	100	1,550	725	300	5,000
Waterloo Lutheran	50,000	n.r.	4,950	1,400	1,700	55	1,000	350	600	450	175	60		75	2,700	9,700	1,050	4,900
U.W. Ont.	300,000	n.r.	17,304	946	1,524	544	545	1,400	800	610	288		2,460	600	5,020	8,850	4,570	33,475
Christ the King	7,353	n.r.	1,076	16	954	244	6	29	73	69	2	15	251	33	399	704	16	1,605
Huron	36,000	n.r.	5,794	172	1,930	95	—	84	300	286	114		618	33	3,362	13,362	504	5,485
York	23,260	n.r.	4,920	142	1,147	105	170	887	88	174	38	34	570	26	1,590	733	584	5,026

NOTE: Square brackets have been used to indicate entries which cover several categories.

in the Humanities and Social Sciences, Ottawa, 1962) that the greatest part of this growth has been in recent years; it is very significant that for some of the major libraries his 1961 figures are by 1962 far out of date. Some indication can be given by taking a few examples of expenditures for books. Dr. Williams shows for the University of Alberta expenditures for books in 1931 of $12,000, in 1956 of $42,700, and in 1961 of $183,700. In 1962 the expenditure was about $215,000 for books, $44,000 in periodical subscriptions, and a supplementary budget of $50,000 had been asked for. For 1963 it was planned to ask for $250,000 for books, and $100,000 capital development fund to allow for the purchase of expensive items. The budget for periodical subscriptions was to go up to $55,000. At the same time, the University of Alberta at Calgary had raised its total library expenditures from $43,000 in 1961 to well over $100,000 in 1962. The University of Toronto spent, again according to the Williams report, $51,500 for books in 1931, $131,128 in 1956, and $327,127 in 1961. By 1962 its total budget was about $1,250,000, of which about half, or over $600,000, was spent on books. How far this rapid recent acceleration of expenditure can go is uncertain, but it is evident that in a number of the major universities there is a recognition of the need for a radically new scale of appropriations for library expenditure. For many years, in reports to the Humanities Research Council, I tried to preach the doctrine that the contents of a library, the collection it housed, was of more importance than the building, and even more difficult and expensive to acquire. It seems evident that a library building without a proper library in it is as useless as a building to house a cyclotron without the cyclotron. No institution would dream of putting up a building for a cyclotron without planning at the same time sufficient capital to provide the cyclotron. It would not think it enough to provide out of the annual budget each year $100,000 worth or so of cyclotron parts.

I am aware of the limits of my analogy; it is perfectly true that a collection of library parts, even of odd bits, can function to some extent, while a cyclotron is complete or nothing. But it is also much truer than many suppose that a proper library is a complete and complex whole, in which all the parts balance and co-ordinate with one another, and that this balance and co-ordination cannot be achieved by random supply of spare parts. In advocating that the contents of a library building should be treated as a single major item of capital expenditure, I had and have several considerations in mind. One of these is of course the recognition of the scale of expenditure necessary to establish an adequate collection; a more important one is that the spending of a large capital sum would call for careful and adequate planning. It is quite possible now for an institution, with annual grants of $100,000, to spend in ten years $1,000,000 on books, without, I think, the sort of careful survey of needs that would inevitably accompany the spending of $1,000,000 as a single capital grant.

For many years, the sole problem facing academics in their libraries was how to get money for books; the problem of the librarians was where to put the few annual acquisitions. The small annual funds were generally allotted to departments by a combination of representation by population and straight haggling, and ordering of books was usually determined by the aggressive interests of a few scholars who knew what they wanted and got their orders in first before the fund was exhausted. In practice, this system, if system it can be called, was not entirely valueless. It meant that every purchase was carefully thought about, and that every book added to the library took its place in a rational scheme. It was under this system, for example, that the Italian and Spanish holdings at Toronto were so admirably enlarged by the late Professors Shaw and Buchanan. Granted a succession of zealous and aggressive scholars of varied interests, this system would in time create a good library by a sort of random accretion of specialities. But short of a century or two, it will not produce a properly balanced library. For it is not enough, and this again I have argued in earlier reports, to build up a collection in, say, a period of English literature, without at the same time building at least an adequate collection in the history, philosophy, and other literatures of the same period. And since the history of the humanities is continuous, a next step must be to ensure at least an adequate collection in the same areas of the preceding period. The subjects of the humanities cannot properly be studied in any kind of isolation; subject must be related to subject and period to period, and a proper library must provide for this necessary related cross-reference. This is why some sort of general planning is essential. If it seemed fifteen years ago that all our libraries needed was more money, it now appears that they need more money and also more planning, and the more money they get, the more absolutely necessary this planning becomes. We need large libraries, but a large library is not necessarily a good library.

It is obvious that as grants increase, and purchases multiply, the problem of planning becomes more difficult. Nearly every university librarian I have talked with has been very much concerned with it; it is only in the smaller libraries that ordering of books by the faculty members still seems at all satisfactory. The basic problem is that systematic ordering takes time, and systematic ordering on a large scale takes a great deal of time, which few faculty members have to spare. The right kind of planned ordering, which would look beyond the boundaries of a discipline to achieving a proper balance and a well co-ordinated collection, calls for a great deal of time spent by a carefully constituted committee or Library Council. In many institutions there is no such body. I would suggest that the task of building a library collection is too vital to be left to chance, and too heavy a responsibility to be left to the hypothetical spare time of a faculty member.

Several possibilities suggest themselves. One is that certain members of the faculty should be relieved of part of their teaching duties to allow them time to devote to surveying the holdings of the library and planning purchases to fill gaps and strengthen holdings in their own discipline. Part of their time could be spent in meetings with colleagues and with library staff to discuss problems of balance and of gaps in other disciplines. This scheme has what seems to me the disadvantage of leaving control of the growth of the library too exclusively in the hands of the academic staff, and thus tending to aggravate a tendency which already, I think, has gone too far, to separate academic from library staff. A generation ago, university librarians were usually academics themselves, running the library on something like an amateur basis, not always with a high degree of efficiency, but with precisely the same conception of the library's function and status as their academic fellows. As libraries expanded, the shortcomings of the amateur became more serious, and the older generation have been replaced almost universally by professionally trained librarians. These have in the main been preoccupied with the problems of organization, often faced with changing systems of cataloguing, with moves to new buildings, and of course with the technical tasks of rapid expansion. I suggest no disparagement whatsoever in saying that their point of view as professionals has tended to be different from that of the academic amateur. This has in many institutions brought about a degree of separation, if not opposition, of library and academic staff, and a tendency on the part of the academic staff to think of librarians as the mechanics who keep the machine working but have no conception of its proper function. I think the sooner this attitude can be dispensed with the better. It can only be dispensed with by bringing the librarian completely into the academic community, and entrusting him with academic tasks.

This means, to start with, a sound policy of staff provision for the library. As long as a librarian is given only barely enough staff to carry on the routine duties of running the library machine, his preoccupations are almost certain to be restricted to the mechanics of librarianship, particularly if inadequate salaries give him a floating population of staff which is perpetually in a state of being trained in mechanical duties. If it is true that academics cannot build up a sound library collection in their spare time, this is also true of librarians. The many librarians I have talked with have convinced me that great advantages could be gained by providing more generously for their staffs, and by including in their staffs members with academic training on a par with that of the academics. The ideal is perhaps suggested by the staff of the British Museum Library, which can offer expert advice to any academic. Some start has been made in the right direction at some institutions, and there are probably more examples that I am aware of. At Saskatchewan, for example, a full-time bibliographer has been added to the staff of the university library to co-operate with the department of English in building up their eighteenth-century collection. At Toronto, on the recommendation of a special Dean's committee which studied the problem of building up the Slavic holdings, the library took over the responsibility for book selection, and brought in a bibliographer with full academic training in the field to do a survey, make a report, and take charge of acquisitions. The Toronto library has also started to build up a series of bibliographies of holdings and desiderata in various areas. In all these activities, the library takes at least some of the initiative, and carries much of the academic responsibility, in co-operation with the academic staff. The shift of a reasonably important share of responsibility for acquisitions to a properly trained library staff seems to me highly advisable. It means a corresponding shift of funds from departments to the library's general fund, which is also very necessary; the general fund allows the purchase of items or collections beyond the financial range of a department, when these are of importance to more than one department, and it allows funds to be applied to special areas according to a broad view of the needs of the library as a total collection. The policy in Toronto, and perhaps elsewhere, is to enlarge the general fund by limiting the expansion of the departmental funds, not by cutting them. Since every department benefits from the general fund, and can indeed recommend purchases from it, everyone is satisfied. What seems to me most important, however, is the co-operation in academic responsibility thus established. A further step has been taken at Toronto by having members of the library staff give lectures in bibliography in various academic departments.

All that I have said about the importance of establishing sound methods of acquisition, and of the need for a balanced, well co-ordinated collection, implies, and is meant to imply, that there is no such collection in Canada. On the inadequacy of every university library in Canada I am totally and impassionedly in agreement with Dr. Williams, President Bissell, and nearly every one else who has taken a close look at the libraries. As Dr. Williams has rightly insisted, the specialized collection must be built on a sound general collection: "the peaks will be relatively isolated and perhaps rarely visited unless they rise from a fairly high plateau rather than from sea-level" (p. 54). The more advanced the work undertaken in the humanities at an institution, the higher the plateau needs to be, the less isolated the peaks. Ideally, to continue the same metaphor, the real research library must exhibit chains of connected peaks rising from a high plateau. A narrow special collection will be of little use for research in a library that provides no context for it. Dr. Williams cites as an example the Icelandic collection at Manitoba, which would gain immensely in significance as part of a much broader collection for Scandinavian studies. It would be reasonable to suppose again that this collection should be suitably buttressed by a soundly built general holding in Germanic philology and history. Another example, and no doubt many could be gathered, is the Kipling collection at Dalhousie. This too is a lofty but slender peak rising abruptly from a very flat and low plain. If it formed the core of a reasonably massive collection of Kipling's contemporaries, of Anglo-Indian writings, of English short stories, or of anything to provide a context, a system of comparisons and relations, it could develop into a useful centre for research. One can agree with Dr. Williams that some building on strength is desirable, while recognizing that there are two ways of building on strength, both I think equally important. One way is adding directly to the special collection, making the peak higher, or turning a high part of the plateau into a peak. The other is at the same time to try to extend the peak into part of a range. This again calls for careful planning of acquisitions and distribution of funds. A point may readily be reached with a special collection where additions become very expensive, and a small extra completeness will cost more than a relatively large filling in of context. My own disposition here would be to fill gaps in the special collection with microfilm or Xerox, and to spend money more heavily on deficiencies in the context. At any rate, there must be a fuller recognition of the importance of the context.

The Williams report, excellent as it is, has perhaps the effect through its sampling method of throwing chief emphasis on deficiencies in secondary material. The view of research which seems to underlie it is that the scholar's chief problem is to become acquainted, not simply with the best that has been thought and said on his subject, but with everything, down to the most obscure periodical article. One can agree that a scholar must get a command of the secondary material, partly as a piece of his training, partly as a stimulus to his own ideas, and partly to guarantee his own originality. But the essential part of his own research is surely concerned with primary materials. The foundation of all research in the humanities must always be the text, and the research student must learn how far he can trust editors by an appeal from them to the text. From my own rapid survey of libraries in Canadian institutions, I would judge the deficiency of primary materials to be at least as serious as of secondary. In many areas, it is more serious, because less effort is being made to overcome it. We all recognize that the state of the libraries must dictate areas of research in the humanities; this is the meaning of the talk of "peaks." It would be ultimately very damaging if the state of the libraries also dictated the kinds of research. If our graduate schools are to turn out students properly trained in the literary disciplines, for example, these students must have acquired and had some practice in the elements of textual scholarship. In English literature, if I may cite what is most familiar to me, the nineteenth century offers an almost virgin area for their practice. It would still be relatively easy and inexpensive to build up collections of successive editions of most major and all minor authors of the period; if first editions are rare they could be filmed, and subsequent editions bought. First editions of all the later works of Tennyson and Browning can still be bought easily and cheaply; it is shocking to see how few of these are to be found in many libraries. Nor does there seem to be much tendency to collect as complete sets of successive editions revised by the author as could still be easily acquired. These would allow major tasks of editing to be carried on in Canada, and stimulate an important branch of humanistic research. I was not able, on my survey, to study in detail the lists of acquisitions at many libraries, but I studied a few with a view to this problem. At some institutions which were spending on a scale, for Canada, relatively lavish, an overwhelming proportion of the money was being spent on books published in the last five or ten years—that is, purely on secondary material. I realize that the problem is not a simple one, that the secondary material of today will become the primary material of the next century or the one after, and that the silliest and most ephemeral work of criticism may become in the future an important document in the history of taste or the history of ideas, but in the necessary scheme of priorities our libraries are faced with, it seems to me more profitable, in spite of Dr. Williams, to buy a few original editions of an author rather than a recent ephemeral book about him. There is a special urgency about the matter, since prices of primary materials are rising so rapidly; a fairly substantial collection of nineteenth-century works could still be acquired at a reasonable cost, however.

Periodicals create, indeed, a special and vexatious problem. As more libraries, stimulated by the motives described by Dr. Williams, feel bound to subscribe to more and more journals, the guaranteed library subscriptions multiply, the chance of failure or the cost of subsidy diminishes, and the pressure of scholars and of institutions for prestige leads to the founding of new journals. One sometimes has a nightmare vision of all the universities and colleges in the world turning out newly spawned periodicals by Malthus' law, and the libraries expiring from the sheer glut. Some notion of the magnitude of the problem is provided by the observation that a new institution like the University of Alberta at Calgary was already, by January 1962, subscribing to 956 journals (in all disciplines), and trying to acquire back files. Of the first 63 journals on their list, over a quarter had back files of more than fifty volumes to be sought. At a library like Toronto's, the number of journals subscribed to becomes astronomical. Most of the smaller institutions have found it necessary to limit their periodical commitments; where the budget is mainly distributed to departments, each department is faced with the decision of how much of its budget it wishes to spend on periodicals, and which periodicals it finds most essential.

One of the most important developments since 1946 is in the use of microfilm, microcard, and Xerox reproductions. In 1946 only fifteen institutions reported owning any microfilm, and only a dozen had more than one projector or reader. Now many of the larger universities subscribe to the STC series, and a number are making extensive film collections of newspapers and periodicals. Mount Allison and Calgary are collecting files of the London *Times* and of the New York *Times*, Mount Allison and Saskatchewan are getting films of the *Quarterly Review*, Saskatchewan of the *Edinburgh Review*, Calgary of a collection of early Canadian newspapers, and so. The University of New Brunswick makes extensive use of microfilm, especially of the STC collection, for research. A related development is in staff research, especially large projects, where microfilm or Xerox allows the collection and collation of bodies of rare material. The Burney project at McGill works extensively with microfilm, and the J. S. Mill editors at Toronto use Xerox largely for collation of editions. Attitudes towards these mechanical aids vary considerably among academics, from almost complete distrust to almost complete confidence. The danger at the moment is perhaps in the latter. If complete reliance on microfilm leads to the conviction that it is a fully adequate substitute for the printed original, some types of scholarship for which reproductions are unsuitable will tend to disappear, as will the habit of final appeal always to the printed text itself, or even more importantly to the manuscript. Microfilm has been and will be an invaluable supplement to Canadian libraries, but one hopes it will not become a substitute. The department of English at Toronto has adopted what seems a useful practice; if it orders a book of special importance, it gives instructions that if the copy is not obtained, a microfilm copy is to be ordered, but further search for an original is to continue.

The problem of securing out-of-print works is a very pressing one, and is bound to become more so as competition increases. Here again careful planning seems necessary. The usual slow process, of receiving a bookseller's catalogue, having a faculty member or members go through it making selections and returning it to the order department of the library, results in probably no more than one book in ten being received. As Dr. Williams has pointed out (p. 57), "the largest and wealthiest of the American libraries can sometimes persuade dealers to send proof-sheets of their catalogues by air-mail." Dealers will also hold items or collections for wealthy customers. What he suggests is an Office of Canadian Library Resources in the National Library to act as purchasing agent for Canadian universities in the world's second-hand market. One sees a good many practical difficulties in the working of such an agency, but these should not be insoluble, and it is hard to conceive of a good alternative. This or any other scheme depends first of all on the preparation by each library, after a systematic survey, of a list of desiderata. And this brings us back to the familiar starting-place, of planning and the provision of staff for planning. On a rough estimate, I would say that practically every library I visited needed half again as much staff, and that each one particularly needed better salaries to attract staff with the right kind of training, academic as well as professional, to do the necessary planning.

It all comes down eventually to a question of financial support. The authors of the 1947 report had hoped for some recognition by the national government of the national importance of the problems. Since they published their recommendations, a Union Catalogue of university library holdings in Canada has been undertaken, and is well advanced, a National Library has been established, and although its proper building will not be ready for another three years, it has, under Dr. Kaye Lamb, contributed a great deal towards the compilation of national bibliographies, surveys of manuscript holdings, and so on. The founding of the Canada Council has also, particularly through the capital grants for buildings, represented an important contribution from a national body to university libraries. But there has been little disposition at the national level to recognize the vital importance of building collections if not equal to those elsewhere in the world, at least fit to be compared with them; or that this is a task demanding resources of the same order as those provided for buildings. The Canada Council has indeed made a few grants for special purposes to library collections, but in amounts that can only be considered tokens. The calls on the Council for other purposes, equally necessary, are already so far beyond its power to answer that it is unreasonable to expect it, without vastly increased funds, to play any important part in creating adequate libraries, but a clear recognition in its policy that the contents of a library building are as much a national concern as the building, and call for expenditure on a parallel scale, might have assisted—might even now assist—in establishing a national policy.

SPECIAL COLLECTIONS
(as reported by the Librarians)

ACADIA UNIVERSITY

The Eric Dennis Collection of Canadiana covers practically all fields of Canadian life, with a high proportion of works on Canadian history. It does not include Canadian literature (see John Logan Collection below). A catalogue was published in 1938.

The Thomas Chandler Haliburton Collection contains all the published works of Haliburton (many in first as well as later editions) plus material about the writer.

The John Daniel Logan Collection of Canadian Literature is made up of creative Canadian material and Canadian literary criticism.

The William Inglis Morse Library is a special collection covering many fields, including a number of books in humanities, especially in history. It is a gift of the late Dr. William Inglis Morse.

In addition to the special collections already mentioned, the Acadia University Library has a Maritime Baptist Historical Collection. For the most part, this collection contains works that would be classed in the BL-BX Section of the Library of Congress classification system; but it does contain a number of works by Silas Tertius Rand dealing with the Micmac language, such as his *Dictionary of the Micmac Language* and his *Legends of the Micmacs*.

UNIVERSITY OF ALBERTA

We have two endowment funds for the purchase of materials that are in the humanistic field, but it would perhaps be incorrect to consider them separate collections.

I refer first to our Colonel Woods fund for Canadian–United States relations. At an earlier time books bought from this fund were housed together in our Reference Reading Room. We have now transferred this collection to the main stacks and dispersed it according to the classification of each book. Initially, the selection policy for this material had a politico-historical orientation, but of recent years many literary titles have been purchased. The subject is now construed as Canadian–American civilization.

The other fund is the R. R. Gonsett Trust Fund. This fund was established in memory of a Canadian scientist of Ukrainian origin. The selection policy is exclusively works in, by, and about Ukrainians. However, there have been occasional indiscretions when a Russian volume was purchased. A partial effect of this fund is seen by the fact that our Slavic collection is second in size only to our English.

The library is also a repository for photostats of the Dove Cottage MSS., and has a collection of MSS. of the German dramatist, Georg Keyser.

UNIVERSITY OF ALBERTA, CALGARY

Because the library was originally a Normal School library, it is fortunate in having a large number of old education texts including many elementary readers. This material is shelved in a closed area.

In the summer of 1960, following the move to the new location, the library received about 500 volumes from the Rutherford Library and numerous runs of journals. The books were mostly Canadiana and were duplicates of the A. C. Rutherford Collection.

In May the Alumni Association of the University of Alberta presented a gift of $5,000 for the purchase of books in international relations. The fund will be administered by the Area Studies Committee.

BISHOP'S UNIVERSITY

In this library, we keep books of special Canadian interest in a "Canadiana" section. There are about 5,000 volumes in this section; this may qualify as a special collection in your meaning. Such of these books as fall into the humanities have been included in the rough estimate given [Table II]. We have also about 1,000 items pertaining to the local history of the Eastern Townships of Quebec. One of the projects which we hope to undertake when we can hire more staff is the cataloguing and classification of this material in a special collection. At present it is largely unprocessed.

UNIVERSITY OF BRITISH COLUMBIA

The figure of 239,000 volumes [Table II] does not include the following important blocks of material:

(a) General periodicals, most of which are of literary interest—18,000.

(b) Howay-Reid Collection (Canadian history and literature)—12,000 volumes.

(c) The Reference Collection—18,000 volumes of which perhaps 12,000 would be of humanities interest.

(d) University of British Columbia theses.

Nor does it include the following collections, which are uncatalogued but organized and available for use.

(e) Fairly important holdings of micro-reproductions.

(f) Rich holdings of government publications.

(g) The University Archives (i.e. material relating to the University of British Columbia).

(h) The P'u-pan Collection (Chinese history, literature, philosophy, etc.) —50,000 volumes.

(i) The Institute of Pacific Relations Collection (history, economics, political science, and sociology relating to Asia and the Pacific area)—5,000 volumes.

(j) The Murray Collection (Canadian history and literature).

(k) The Donaldson Collection on Burns.

The Howay-Reid and Murray Collections in Canadian history and literature and the P'u-pan Collection of Chinese materials comprise very strong holdings in their respective field of study. The Salmond Collection on Mary, Queen of Scots, and the Donaldson Collection on Burns cover intensively their more restricted fields. The general collections contain strong holdings of French-Canadian and Slavonic materials.

DALHOUSIE UNIVERSITY

Kipling Collection. The Kipling Collection of Dalhousie consists of biographies, newspapers, periodicals, first editions, bibliographies, and manuscripts. We believe we have one of the most complete collections of Kipling in the world. James McG. Stewart's *Bibliography of Kipling*, published by Dalhousie, indicates the scope of our holdings, as well as being the definitive bibliography of Kipling to date. The collection is being used by scholars both on and off campus. At present, we have two M.A. students at work on theses on Kipling.

Morse Collection. A collection of documents, letters, rare books, rare bindings, early Canadiana, maps and paintings dealing mainly with the history of Nova Scotia. We have published a catalogue of this collection. There is a small but steady demand for the material by scholars.

McGILL UNIVERSITY

Manuscripts. Good only for the fur trade period 1790–1810. A catalogue was published in February 1963.

Redpath Tracts. A collection of 1,300 volumes of bound pamphlets from 1561 to 1900, nearly all in English constitutional history. Partly listed, chronologically, in *A catalogue of books . . . together with a collection of historical, ecclesiastical and political tracts from 1624, etc.* (privately printed, Cambridge, 1884) and *Catalogue of a collection of historical tracts 1561–1800 . . .* annotated by Stuart J. Reid (privately printed, London, 1901).

Ribbeck Pamphlets. The eight or nine thousand pamphlets on Greek and Roman literature and history collected by Otto Ribbeck the German classical scholar. Mostly 19th century.

Islamic Institute. The library has about 23,250 volumes on the Islamic countries, a great percentage being in Arabic.

Blackader Library of Architecture. Strong only in French architecture of the seventeenth and eighteenth centuries and in its collection of Vitruvius and the early printed books of architecture.

Stearn Marionette Collection. A collection of books and pamphlets on the puppet theatre together with a collection of ancient and modern puppets. There is a typed catalogue, *The Rosalynde Stearn Marionette Collection* (Montreal, 1961).

Lande Blake Collection. A collection of all the facsimile reproductions of Blake's colour printing, of all books about Blake, of Blake's engravings, and of all books illustrated by Blake.

Hume-Rousseau Collection. All editions of Hume and all books on Hume, together with most of the early editions of Rousseau. The original letters of Hume and Rousseau to the Comtesse de Boufflers at the time of the famous quarrel are here. Several books from Hume's library are included in the collection.

William Colgate Printing Collection. About 4,000 items on the history and techniques of hand-printing before the nineteenth century, with examples of the work of the small modern private presses. It contains such rarities as the 1683 edition of Moxon, the Fell type-specimen of 1695, the Bodoni "Manuale typografico" of 1818, and the first Vatican type-specimen of 1828. A catalogue is in preparation.

Napoleon Collection. About 5,000 volumes and about 1,500 contemporary prints on the Emperor and his time. A catalogue of the prints is near completion.

Stephen Leacock Collection. All the editions of Leacock's writing together with many of his MSS.

Rilke Collection. All the first editions of Rilke and all important subsequent ones, together with all commentaries.

Osler Library. A collection on the history of science, including Medicine. A printed catalogue was published by the Oxford University Press in 1929 and is now out of print but in course of being reprinted.

Australian history and literature. The only large collection of Australian history and literature known to be in Canada is at McGill. The numerical size of the collection is not accurately known as much has not yet been catalogued.

MOUNT ST. VINCENT COLLEGE

While we feel that we are one of the growing, smaller libraries in Canada, we do not feel that our collections at present contain actual resources for scholarly research on the graduate level—except, perhaps, in the field of English literature in which we are building up resources to support our programme of studies leading to the Master's degree in English literature.

Our special collection is predominantly in the field of English literature and more specifically in the prose and poetry of the eighteenth and nineteenth centuries—though even in this field, it is representative of the actual works by these authors rather than of works about them. (We have complete editions—some de luxe, some first editions, some limited with special illustrations by artists of the time.) In this collection, we have also a group of 69 fore-edge paintings, dating perhaps from 1767–1850 but in most instances unrelated to the texts of the books on which they are executed. We have autographed sets or various titles of late nineteenth- and early twentieth-century English authors—and a number of autographed works of the private presses of Great Britain.

Our second growing interest is in the field of Catholic theology and philosophy—including in the former, scripture and liturgy, Mariology and Christology, church history and the Church Fathers etc. but mostly in English. Our philosophy collection is strongest in Thomistic or scholastic philosophy; we are interested also in the history of philosophic systems and modern philosophy—but again, with our undergraduate students' needs in mind . . . total holdings about 10,000 volumes.

Our Nova Scotiana collection is extremely small—perhaps less than 1,000 volumes—but it does have items which are hard to acquire at the present time—some relating to the Indian in Nova Scotia.

UNIVERSITY OF NEW BRUNSWICK

A great stimulus to the Library was the gift by Lord Beaverbrook in 1950 of more than 14,000 fine volumes to be housed in the new wing of the library built by him. This distinguished collection covers most fields, with particular strengths in history, biography, and memoirs, and first and rare editions.

Another gift was the Rufus Hathaway Collection of Canadian Literature which came to us in 1933 on the death of the well-known bibliophile. Containing more than 2,000 volumes of poetry, fiction, essays, biography, and criticism, and a manuscript collection, it is strong in first, special, and autographed editions of Bliss Carman, Charles G. D. Roberts, Theodore Goodridge Roberts, Duncan Campbell Scott, Archibald Lampman, William Wilfred Campbell, and many other Canadians as well as Sir Gilbert Parker and Goldwin Smith. The deposit of the Hathaway Collection in the city and university which made so distinguished a contribution to Canadian literature in the nineteenth and early twentieth centuries has been important. Its presence undoubtedly had much to do with the founding and flourishing of the poetry magazine, *The Fiddlehead*, which has now an international reputation with contributors and readers. In the Graduate School more than twenty Master's theses in English have been completed using the resources of the collection and more are under way. Current publications in Canadian literature are added to the collection each year and we have a continuing programme of searching for and buying Canadian works of the past.

In the past seven years, we have begun to lay the foundation for graduate and faculty research in English literature of the sixteenth and seventeenth centuries. We have concentrated on this period because it is one in which relatively few books were published, so that completeness is attainable as they become available in microfilm and microcard form. We are acquiring on microfilm all English books published between 1475 and 1640, as listed in Pollard and Redgraves' *Short Title Catalogue*. When this project is completed we plan to subscribe to the continuation of the series, which will bring us all English books published up until 1700. We have the microcard publications of the Hakluyt Society; we receive the Malone Society reprints; we are receiving the volumes of the Victoria County History of England. We are members of the Bibliographic Society. In addition to our significant Shakespearean collection we have *Hakluyt's Voyages, Purchas' Pilgrimes*, the *Stationers' Register*, and many other major and minor works indispensable for literary research in the period. To date, three Master's theses have been completed using some of the above-mentioned material, and a doctoral thesis is in progress.

For the study of Middle English language and literature we have bought on microcards the publications of the Chaucer Society and of the Early English Text Society. We have obtained in microfilm form, Migne's *Patrologiae Cursus Completus* (Greek and Latin series), useful for the religious background to medieval studies and for research in pre-Renaissance English, as well as, of course, for research in late Latin.

Historical research at the University has been based largely on our Archives Collection of books, pamphlets, newspapers, and manuscripts relating to New Brunswick and the Maritime Provinces. Our very extensive files of New Brunswick newspapers covering the period from the end of the eighteeenth century to the present are an invaluable source. Our growing microfilm files contain, besides many of these newspapers, the indispensable Colonial Office despatches of eighteenth- and nineteenth-century New Brunswick, and a long run for nineteenth-century Nova Scotia. Available here, or in the nearby Legislative Library, are the legislative journals, bills, reports, and accounts from the foundation of the Province. Among the collections of historical manuscripts deposited with us, some in perpetuity and others pending the possible establishment of a Provincial Archives in this capital are: the Winslow papers and the papers of Chief Justice Saunders, both dating from Loyalist days; papers of three nineteenth-century colonial governors—Lieut.-Governor Manneers-Sutton (photostats), Lieut.-Governor Sir Arthur Hamilton Gordon (Stanmore Papers, originals), and Lieut.-Governor Sir Edmund Walker Head (photostats); the letterbooks and scrapbooks of the Canadian Governor-General, the Marquis of Lorne; the large collection of the papers of the Canadian prime minister, R. B. Bennett; the papers of the New Brunswick-born British Prime Minister, Andrew Bonar Law; a collection of letters from the Duke of Kent, 1791–1803; collections of papers of other distinguished New Brunswickers, including Sir Douglas Hazen, Hon. Peter Mitchell, and Sir Leonard Tilley. Several of these collections were secured through the good offices of our Chancellor, Lord Beaverbrook.

QUEEN'S UNIVERSITY

The following is a brief statement regarding special collections.

Archives. The Archives department contains a research collection of original letters, MSS., typescripts, photostats, transcripts, microfilm and other archival material. Included are personal papers of more than thirty men who have been prominent in the public life of Canada. (See *Political Papers in the Douglas Library Archives, 1961.*) There are also early records of Queen's University and the Synod of the Presbyterian Church (1815–1900). Records of early settlement in Kingston and vicinity are found in land deeds, letters patent, marriage registers, militia rolls, family papers, and account books. There is a large collection of business, legal, and municipal records of Kingston, scrapbooks, newspaper clippings, early broadsides, playbills and other ephemera. The Shortt-Haydon collection of historical maps, prints, portraits, and other illustrations is kept in the Archives department.

A Note on the Manuscript Collection in the Douglas Library (1943) provides a guide to resources which had been accumulated up to that time. Since then, the collection has greatly expanded. Preliminary inventories have been prepared for the major manuscript groups; a new guide to the collection is in course of preparation.

Canadiana. The Edith and Lorne Pierce Collection of Canadiana contains *c.* 6,300 volumes, of which 1,300 are French-Canadian imprints. It includes also an impressive collection of Canadian literary MSS., typescripts, a.l.s. and other records. (See *A Catalogue of Canadian Manuscripts Collected by Lorne Pierce and Presented to Queen's University Library*, Toronto: Ryerson Press, 1946, 164 pp. The collection now contains more than twice the number of items listed in this catalogue, including the private papers of the late Dr. Lorne Pierce.)

John Buchan Library. This collection comprises the working library of John Buchan, Lord Tweedsmuir, including 35 bound manuscripts of his major works, first and later editions of all his publications, scrapbooks, and correspondence. The book collection contains *c.* 5,000 volumes, almost entirely in the humanities and social sciences. (See *A Checklist of Books by and about John Buchan in the Douglas Library, Queen's University*, Boston: G. K. Hall & Company, 1961, 74 pp.)

Minor collections. Other special collections include the *Bible Collection* (*c.* 600 volumes); *G. H. Clarke Collection* (chiefly English *belles lettres*); *James Roy Collection* (English and Scottish Literature); *Elizabeth Gray Collection* (private press and limited editions); the *Howard Murray Collection* (early printed books and first editions); the rare book collection (incunabula and early imprints).

International law. The law library contains a large and expanding collection in international law, one of the few major collections in this field in Canada.

Government Documents. Queen's has long been a depository for all federal government publications, and regularly receives selected publications of the provincial governments, the United Kingdom, United Nations, United States, and other foreign countries. An application is pending for Queen's library to become a full depository for all United Nations Publications.

During the past ten years we have expanded departmental libraries in the Fine Arts (Agnes Etherington Art Centre) and the social sciences (Dunning Hall). Library facilities for theology, medicine, and the pure and applied sciences have also been enlarged. The law library (capacity, 80,000 volumes) was opened in 1960.

ROYAL MILITARY COLLEGE OF CANADA

Our principal special collection is that devoted to Military Studies (8,252 titles, 11,262 volumes). "Military" in this context means, in effect, "navy, army, air force," and in this collection we have concentrated "military" material from all sections of the L.C. classification. "MS a," for example, contains *general* books devoted to the problems of British and Imperial defence, separate sections dealing with the general history of each of the British Armed Services, biographies of British service leaders, Army and Navy lists, comprehensive regimental histories, and the like. Books on British military history, 1792–1815, are classed in MS 10 (Napoleonic Wars). In fact each chronological division in the Collection will contain a section devoted to British military history. This is a cumbersome arrangement from certain points of view, but it suits our particular purposes very well indeed. The whole Military Studies Collection is shelved on the second floor of the library and it has its own section devoted to periodicals, and its own author-subject catalogue.

I should also mention our 12,000 volume collection of Military History, Art, and Science in German. This contains a very large number of important sets of research materials relating to war, to individual wars, and to military history of Europe in general. It is also rich in biographical material, and there is a special section of some 3,500 volumes devoted to the Nazi period. At the moment the collection is being re-catalogued. It was originally catalogued in Ottawa according to the Dewey decimal system. The work was badly done, however, hence our present effort. We expect to transfer some 2,500 volumes to our Military Studies Collection during the current year.

Saint Mary's University

We have what we call the Jesuit Community Library, about 4,000 volumes, mostly theology and philosophy. Any student requesting a book from this library can always obtain it, unless one of the Fathers is using it.

A Rare Book Collection, about 3,000 volumes, is waiting to be catalogued. There are about 4,000 bound volumes of periodicals.

University of Saskatchewan, Regina

We have made a start on French-Canadian materials, and hope to have assembled something worthwhile in this area a few years hence.

Sir George Williams University

Our collection is for the most part general in nature with the exception that we do possess a modest collection of Canadiana of better than 3,000 volumes. These are made up chiefly of historical, bibliographical, and literary works in the English language. Imprint dates are predominantly nineteenth and early twentieth century. A bibliography of this collection was published in mimeographed form in 1945 with a supplement in 1946.

University of Toronto

This survey is presented by means of excerpts from *Resources of Canadian University Libraries for Research in the Humanities and Social Sciences,* the report of a survey for the National Conference of Canadian Universities and Colleges, by Edwin E. Williams, Counselor to the Director on the Collections, Harvard University Library.

Philosophy. A relatively strong collection.

On the basis of our holdings of files in Mr. Williams' sample list of periodicals, Toronto is in the lead, especially when the holdings of the Pontifical Institute of Mediaeval Studies (part of the University of St. Michael's College) are included.

Particularly strong in the history of philosophy. Good in ancient philosophy. Strong in mediaeval Arabic philosophy. Pontifical Institute has an outstanding collection of mediaeval philosophy (particularly its microfilms of mediaeval manuscripts).

Good collections on Nietzsche, Schopenhauer, and Spinoza. Victoria University has an excellent Erasmus collection.

Religion. The University of Toronto, including the Pontifical Institute, has the strongest resources in Canada. Special Wesley collection at Victoria University.

History in General, Historiography, and Auxiliary Sciences. Toronto's over-all strength makes its collection more nearly adequate than those of any other Canadian library. Toronto has some strength on the history of medicine, notably the Banting collection.

Ancient History. Toronto's holdings are considerably stronger than those of any other Canadian library for ancient Greek and Roman history, and Toronto is the only library in the country with significant research collections on the ancient Near East.

Mediaeval History. The outstanding collections in mediaeval history are housed at Toronto (including those of the Pontifical Institute). Toronto is relatively strong in mediaeval English history, particularly in sources and in constitutional and legal history. It is relatively weak in early printed works and in local publications.

British History. Toronto's collection on British history is Canada's strongest. Toronto is relatively strong in nineteenth-century material but is weak in pamphlets, periodicals of secondary importance, newspapers and local history. Toronto's holdings are described as adequate for introductory research toward the Ph.D., but the student must normally supplement them by working in other libraries.

French History. Toronto has at least twice as much material on French history as any other library in the country but its collection, which is strongest for the period of the Enlightenment, is described as adequate for no more than a beginning in work beyond the M.A.

German History. Toronto's holdings in German history are perhaps three times as extensive as those of any other Canadian library, but since their total is in the order of 5,000 volumes (less than half Toronto's total for French history and less than one-fourth of its British history collection), this does not indicate particular strength. The modern period has been emphasized. A major item is the *Verhandlungen* of the Reichstag for 1867–1909. The collection is described as adequate to support graduate study in limited areas only to the M.A. level.

History of Eastern Europe including the Slavic Nations. Toronto ranks behind U.B.C. in this field. It is building systematically and recently borrowed an expert from Columbia University to survey its Slavic collections which are stronger in literary than in historical publications. Ukrainian, Serbo-Croatian, and Russian history are represented by better collections than the other areas. A Slavic specialist has been added to the Library staff with responsibility for acquisition work and, in collaboration with the faculty, for selection.

Other Modern European History. For the Scandinavian countries, the Low Countries, Switzerland, Italy, Spain, and Portugal or general modern European history, Toronto has the best collection. There are plans at Toronto for strengthening the research materials for Renaissance history.

The Commonwealth Nations and Others of Africa, Southern Asia and the Pacific. Toronto is in second place behind U.B.C. but collections in Canada in this field are surprisingly weak.

Near Eastern History. Toronto possesses the only considerable research collection on the ancient Near East. A separate Department of Islamic Studies has now been established and a beginning is being made in building up resources for research in the modern period.

Far Eastern History. Toronto has just begun collecting in the Japanese field. Its Chinese collection is unusually rich in archaeological material. Toronto is well on the way toward developing library resources capable of supporting research to the Ph.D. level.

American History. Largest collection is at Toronto.

Canadian History (excluded from the Williams survey). A good collection in Canadian history for both the early and the later period.

Music. Research in music is a new field for Canadian universities. Toronto now has a collection capable of supporting advanced research in some areas with definitive editions of the major composers, good bibliographical tools, and micro-reproductions of source material. Ethno-musicology is a field of special interest.

Fine Arts. Research in the fine arts is at an early stage of development. The classical field is Toronto's strongest point and, in medieval art, there is a notable collection of photographs of French and English illuminated manuscripts of the twelfth and thirteenth centuries. Resources for this period are supplemented by those of the Pontifical Institute. There is also valuable research material on Chinese art. Victoria University is building up a Blake collection.

General Linguistics and Comparative Literature. Research strength in the broad fields of general linguistics and comparative literature depends, in large measure, on resources in individual languages and literatures. There can be little doubt that Toronto is in first place.

Classical Languages and Literatures. Toronto stands alone. Its monographic collections are at least twice as extensive as those of any other university library and the quality of its serial files is indicated by the fact that its holdings are complete or nearly complete for nine of the ten journals on Williams' sample list. There is a particularly good Petronius collection and Victoria University has a small collection of Greek papyri. Weaknesses exist in Roman law, numismatics and other auxiliary sciences and in pratistics. The Pontifical Institute supplements Toronto's holdings for Latin and medieval Christian authors but is not strong in Greek.

Italian Language and Literature. In Italian, Toronto's lead over the next strongest Canadian collection, both in serial files and monographs, is enormous; no other library has one-fifth as much. There is strength in the historical background and development of the Italian language and in local languages of Italy. In literature, the outstanding feature is a collection of some 500 sixteenth- and seventeenth-century plays. Holdings in the mediaeval period are also strong and are supplemented by those of the Pontifical Institute. Contemporary literature appears to be the weakest field.

A catalogue has been published: Beatrice Corrigan, *Catalogue of Italian Plays 1500–1700, in the Library of the University of Toronto* (University of Toronto Press, 1961).

French Language and Literature. Toronto is ranked first in over-all strength. Relatively strong areas in the Toronto collection include Old French language and literature, Old Provençal, sixteenth-century literature, nineteenth-century prose fiction except for minor authors and the twentieth-century novel up to 1950. The Rare Book Room contains an interesting collection of some 275 Noëls. The collection has been strengthened by the Will library particularly in the period of the religious wars (1540–1630) and in seventeenth- and eighteenth-century theatre.

Spanish Language and Literature. Toronto's lead over other universities in Spanish is not quite so striking as in Italian but it clearly has the only genuine research collection in Canada for Spanish. In the linguistic field it is strong in historical studies, medieval texts, and lexicographical works. There are weaknesses in toponomastics and dialect studies but these are being remedied. In literature, the Golden Age is best represented, particularly the comedies, of which there are over 700. Spanish periodicals and literary works of the nineteenth century, as well as Spanish American materials of both the colonial period and the nineteenth century, are also among the strong points but contemporary literature on both sides of the Atlantic has been neglected to some extent.

A catalogue has been published: J. A. Molinaro, J. H. Parker, and Evelyn Rugg, *A Bibliography of Comedias Sueltas in the University of Toronto Library* (University of Toronto Press, 1959).

Catalan seems to be represented only at Toronto which is stronger in literary than in linguistic materials; it is anticipated that the collection will be systematically improved. In Portuguese, however, interest seems to be minimal, even at Toronto.

English Language and Literature. Toronto has Canada's best research collection for English language and literature as a whole and for most subdivisions of the field. Its holdings of periodical files on Williams' sample list are less extensive than those of U.B.C.

Toronto does not have a great collection of original editions but it is receiving the *Short-Title Catalogue* microfilms and other major series of micro-reproductions. There is noteworthy strength in Anglo-Irish literature from the 1880's to the present (particularly W. B. Yeats) including a 3,000 volume collection in the Rare Books Room.

Holdings on Milton are good, and Victoria University has an outstanding Coleridge collection which includes books from Coleridge's own library and manuscripts. There are more than 400 first or trial editions of Tennyson, and the collection of the Dickens Fellowship at Toronto is on permanent loan. In general, Toronto's collection is stronger in literature than in language and the chief weakness that was noted is in scholarly foreign-language works prior to 1920.

American Literature. No Canadian university can be described as having a strong collection for research in American literature. Toronto has more material than the others except for the contemporary period.

Canadian Literature (excluded from the Williams survey). Good collection of Canadian literature in English. Strong collection of Canadian literature in French, especially for the period from 1920 to date.

German Language and Literature. Toronto is the only Canadian library that is supporting research in German beyond the M.A. Its collection of monographs in the subject is at least as large as any other in the country and its lead in serial publications is substantial. Early nineteenth-century periodicals and novels of World War II are well represented but naturalism and expressionism have been neglected. Most of the graduate students, it is reported, prefer to work on recent or contemporary authors.

Slavic Languages and Literatures. Toronto is actively building a research collection. The country's best Ukrainian collection appears to be at Toronto, which is probably also in the lead for Russian literature particularly nineteenth-century classics and émigré periodicals. There is some strength in Polish but Toronto's collection for Slavic linguistics is inferior to British Columbia's. Toronto's Slavic material has recently been surveyed and responsibility for development of the collection has been assigned to a member of the library staff.

Near Eastern Languages and Literatures. Toronto has one of the two significant Canadian research collections. Toronto has a long-established and excellent collection on the ancient languages and literatures of the area, with particular strength in Akkadian, Aramaic (including Syriac), Egyptian, and classical Hebrew. Coptic, Egyptian, Sumerian, Hellenistic Greek, and pre-Islamic Arabic are also covered. Toronto is now beginning to enter the field of research in the modern Near East.

Far Eastern Languages and Literatures. Toronto has one of the two Canadian research collections in this field. It is not yet a fully adequate collection for advanced research in literature, which is less well represented than art and archaeology. Toronto's strength in literature is chiefly in the period of the literary revolution from 1915 to 1940. Relatively little has been done in Japanese literature as yet.

Other Languages and Literatures. No Canadian university has yet developed a research collection for Sanskrit and Indian studies but the Asian programme at Toronto is now beginning to enter this field.

To these descriptions supplied by the University of Toronto Librarian may be appended the following special report.

TORONTO: EAST ASIATIC LIBRARY

The East Asiatic Library has some 70,000 volumes of texts in Chinese and Japanese, a special collection of works in Sanskrit and minor collections in Tibetan and other languages of East Asia. It covers all fields of the humanities and social sciences, with emphasis on language and literature, history, philosophy, religion, and fine arts. It also has a substantial collection of current journals in Chinese and Japanese, some of them with complete sets of back numbers.

The Chinese collection constitutes the main body of the Library. It is particularly strong in classics, having all the representative editions of Confucian, Taoist, and other texts by classical authors. Its strength in ancient civilization was further consolidated by a recent addition of books on art and archaeology formerly kept at the Royal Ontario Museum. The culture of later periods has in no sense been neglected; all major authors, from the Tang Dynasty to the Literary Revolution in our century, are represented in standard editions. Another feature of the Chinese collection is its resources in local history and geography; some of the books are primary sources rarely accessible elsewhere.

The Japanese collection, begun two years ago, is less extensive. It has, however, all the major works of Japanese literature in modern standard editions. It is also strong in reference works; it has most of the important dictionaries and encyclopaedias published since the last war. Its history section is expanding, with emphasis on ancient and medieval periods.

With an honours course in Sanskrit due to start in 1964, a collection of works in classical Indian studies is now being built. Acquisitions of approximately 60 journals and 90 series of texts in Sanskrit, Pali, and Prakrit is under negotiation. The present plan aims at a research collection of some 10,000 volumes in this field.   (Professor UEDA)

TORONTO: ST. MICHAEL'S COLLEGE

The richest areas in respect to special collections are of course the holdings of the Pontifical Institute of Mediaeval Studies—especially its microfilm manuscripts, the rather rich and out-of-the-way collection of journals of theology at St. Basil's Seminary, and the growing materials of the Ecumenical Centre.

TORONTO: VICTORIA UNIVERSITY

Special collections:

Alumni Collection (chiefly literature and biography)	1,477	volumes
Addison (Sociology)	315	"
Canadiana	2,472	"
Erasmiana	278	"
Hunter (English—chiefly Shakespeare)	147	"
Jackman Collection on Transportation	1,846	"
Hymnology	671	"
Maclean Collection on North American Indians	622	"
Robins Folklore Collection	250	"
Tennyson Collection (uncatalogued)	562	"
Coleridge Collection (books)	200	"
Treasure Room Collection (chiefly English and Art)	411	"
Warner Collection of local American History	98	"
Wesleyana Collection	252	"
Rièse Collection of contemporary French literature (uncatalogued)	1,500	"

UNIVERSITY OF WESTERN ONTARIO

The library maintains a regional collection of material, manuscript and printed, bearing on the history and development of the fourteen counties of southwestern Ontario. In connection with this operation the library brings out two small publications: *Western Ontario Historical Notes* and *Western Ontario History Nuggets.*

This library is primarily a library of Canadian material and an attempt is made to acquire all Canadian publications of University presses, journals of societies and government documents. Since we have been fortunate in some gifts, the collections in Canadian material not only are moving forward on a broad front, but have great depth.

After Canadian material the next best collections are those dealing with the United States. Thanks to the acquisition policy of Professor Fred Landon, our United States material is probably exceeded in Canada only by that of the University of Toronto, and perhaps not even by that institution.

When we leave Canada and the United States, the U.W.O. Library is not as rich as it might be. The most notable collection of material outside the continent probably is to be found in our holdings of Australian material. The Williams Report on the resources of Canadian university libraries suggested that Western Ontario appears to be stronger than Queen's and McMaster, for Australia and New Zealand.

The history department has endeavoured to build up material bearing on the Renaissance, nineteenth-century England, and the French Revolution. Consequently, thanks to an aggressive buying policy, this library will be fairly well equipped in these fields within the next year or two. New photographic processes have enabled the library to acquire material which hitherto has been completely unobtainable. The new acquisitions have been added to a good foundation of nineteenth-century British periodicals and some fairly important French Revolution material which came with the Professor Mason estate some years ago.

South Africa has been the subject of some collecting during recent years and the Department of Geography has recommended many important works in African geography. At the same time the Department of Politics has recommended some good current material on politics in Africa. If the recommendations continue as they have been coming in, the University will be fairly well equipped for students of the current African scene.

UNIVERSITY OF WESTERN ONTARIO: HURON COLLEGE

The library is adequate for all normal undergraduate purposes; it is open to, and used by, students and faculty of the University; it is the main theological collection for clergy and other interested persons in the region.

In one field only do we have the basis for anything worthy to be dignified as "a special collection." The Spenser collection of Dr. J. G. McManaway, director of the Folger Shakespeare Library, was bought for us. This consists of the usual modern texts and studies, four large compendia of offprints of learned articles, many eighteenth-century items—Warton, Hughes, Upton, Church, Jortin; and the only copy in Canada of Natalis Comes' *Mythologia.* To this we have added George Sandys' *Ovid* (1640), Harington's *Ariosto* (1634), and the first collected edition of Spenser (1611). It is very difficult to develop this collection without a capital grant: the College is not expanding, and the library budget is no more than adequate for current needs.

THE SIGNIFICANT GROWTH in scholarly research and publication made so evident by a comparison of the present bibliography with that of 1946 is due to a number of causes. It marks obviously a change in attitude or in emphasis on the part of institutions and staff, a change from viewing research and publication as a useful but not essential adjunct to the function of teaching to viewing it as an integral part of the university teacher's task. The publications listed in 1946 are evidence that this attitude has always been held by some scholars, but the survey of 1946 makes it equally clear that they were in a minority, and that they often received little encouragement from their institutions or their colleagues. The significant change is one of degree, but it is a large one. In part it derives from the general academic situation. Up to 1946, the universities of Canada had been comparatively static for fifteen years; very few staff appointments were being made, the student bodies remained at much the same level, few new departments were created. Promotions were slow, openings were few, and there was little movement of staff from one institution to another.

The rapid expansion since then has brought a totally new situation. Above all, the academic market has become fluid, with new institutions springing up, new departments being created, old departments doubling and tripling in size; there is a constant flow of academic staff from institution to institution, and from country to country. Promotion can now be, and often is, very rapid. The obvious way to become known, and to compete most successfully in this exciting market-place, is by publication, or at least by the promise of publication. And for the institution, the obvious way to attract the lively and ambitious staff member is to offer encouragement for his research, to offer inducements in aids to research, and to acquiesce in the importance he attaches to it. And in those institutions which are increasingly offering graduate degrees, research becomes an essential condition for the supervision of student research. Consequently, one now meets the perfectly valid argument put forward by administrators planning to extend graduate work that it is necessary, in trying to attract the best scholars, to be able to offer the inducement of a graduate course. Graduate teaching and opportunities for research thus become important "fringe benefits."

Most universities now provide for leave for research, but arrangements vary widely. The old notion of a "sabbatical" year to be spent resting from the labours of the six previous years seems to be generally abandoned; leave is now given for the prosecution of a specific project. The name of the old sabbatical carried with it also a suggestion of a natural right to leave, obscurely related to the Lord's Day; the usual attitude now is that the institution has a duty to encourage good research by providing for leave, rather than that the scholar has a right to demand it. Useful pressure has been brought to bear on the universities by donors of fellowships, who often inquire what support the candidate will receive from his own institution. The larger the institution, of course, the easier it becomes, in some respects at least, to permit leaves. A large department can rearrange teaching assignments readily, and can indeed plan to carry on with one or two members on leave every year—this system is in effect in some departments at Toronto, which, by reason of its size and, to be sure, the genuine interest of its administration in research, makes very generous provision for leave. At small institutions with small departments and small budgets, the problem is very difficult; even if money can be found, finding a satisfactory *locum tenens* for the instructor on leave is increasingly unlikely, and the teaching loads on the remaining staff are often already too heavy to be increased. If small institutions are to hold their own in the competitive market for staff, the problem of provision of leave for research is one of the most urgent they will have to face. Most young instructors and lecturers, particularly the energetic ones, make leave and other facilities for research their first inquiry.

Most research projects in the humanities of any considerable size are likely to necessitate, or could certainly be facilitated by, two years of leave, one at the early stage when a large library is needed for the collection without interruption of the mass of primary material, the collation of editions, and so on, and another at the final stage of writing, which calls for a relatively long period free from distraction, and again with full library resources for final checking and for the filling of gaps which become apparent only at this stage. The period in between leaves can be profitably spent in organizing and mulling over the material, in supplementing it with microfilm or, where possible, from the local library, and in trial drafts. What this suggests is that leaves need to be systematically related to the research project. At Toronto, and doubtless at other large universities, this is in large measure the practice; if the research is important and the scholar competent, leave may be granted at five-year intervals, which seems a reasonable time between the main stages. The scholar has the choice between a whole year's leave at half salary, which gives him roughly sixteen months to work, or a half year's leave on full salary, which gives him about nine months. I believe I am right in saying that no other university in Canada follows the Toronto pattern; the others tend either to give leave at longer intervals or with lesser proportions of salary; in particular, I believe the half-year leave is unique. Many institutions supply relatively generous aid in other directions, in grants for summer travel and research, in grants for travel to learned conferences, for microfilm, for stenographic aid, and so on. The universities of western Canada have made special efforts to offset their distance from the large libraries by grants for travel, and also encourage attendance at conferences by widespread grants. Memorial University in Newfoundland adopts a similar policy. The smaller the university, or the more remote it is from the large centres, the more important it becomes to encourage and assist *liaison* with other scholars, and to break down the isolation which the report of 1946 found one of the serious handicaps to the Canadian scholar. And this is, of course, a form of support which is more feasible for the small institution than for the large, and offers only financial, not administrative problems. Opportunities to meet other scholars, and to join in reading and discussing papers, are of fundamental importance in the communal life of Canadian scholarship. Grants for travel and research, when combined with a four-month period of freedom, are also highly useful to the individual scholar. But a four-month period for research and writing is more satisfactory for the production of learned articles than for the writing of learned books, and for major works of scholarship the writer must have longer periods of freedom.

In the 1947 report, Professor Kirkconnell suggested (pp. 172–3) that teaching loads in Canadian universities were not heavy enough to interfere with scholarship. As is customary, he defined teaching load simply in terms of hours per week in class. This seems to me far too elementary a view of the problem. Three hours a week may represent a freshman course with an enrolment of forty or fifty students and a large amount of term work to be marked, as in a language subject, or it may represent a small advanced honour course with two or three students; or a graduate course with one—or with twenty. There is no simple equivalent by hours for the highly varied loads of preparation and marking. Nor do teaching hours take into account hours spent in interviewing students, and particularly the time given to supervision of graduate students. There is little doubt in my mind, after interviewing members of staff across Canada, that the growth of the student body, and above all the expansion of graduate work, have seriously increased the load without any technical increase in teaching hours. Most academics now find it increasingly difficult to carry on much major research or to do much major writing during the session; a good many can produce an article or two, or some reviews, but important work has to wait for summer or for extended leaves. The discontinuity of effort this entails is very wasteful. It also goes far to explain the inordinate length of time so many of the young members of staff need to finish their doctoral theses. It may well prove impossible, in view of the anticipated enrolment and the increasing difficulty in getting staff, to achieve much real reduction in teaching load, but it should be clearly understood that present loads in most institutions seriously hamper research and diminish scholarly production. As competition for staff increases, the best candidates tend more and more to make inquiries into teaching conditions during the session, and into the chances of continuing writing and research throughout the year.

Assistance in the form of fellowships for research was in 1946 so meagre as to warrant the conclusion that "Canadian scholarship in the humanities has never experienced the stimulus of subsidised research" (p. 189), the most notable aid recorded being from four to six Guggenheim Fellowships distributed over all disciplines. Very few of these, naturally, came to scholars in the humanities. Soon after the publication of the 1947 report, the Humanities Research Council was able, through grants for limited periods from the Carnegie Corporation and Rockefeller Foundations, to offer a few pre-doctoral fellowships. By 1951, the financial position of the Council made it possible to grant 19 scholars aid in research, but the value of the grants had to be limited to $300 or less. Seventeen pre-doctoral fellowships of from $500 to $1500 were also awarded in 1949–51. In the next two years, 14 post-doctoral grants of $400 or less, and 13 pre-doctoral fellowships were awarded. As the amounts for post-doctoral research suggest, these served to assist travel and summer research. In the meantime, the Nuffield Foundation, beginning with 1949, had offered Dominion Travelling Fellowships in the humanities and social sciences, which made possible a full year's post-doctoral research in England. One or two of these a year went to scholars in the humanities, and the restriction on Guggenheim Fellowships, which limited Canadians to study in the United States, meant that for some years the Nuffield Fellowships were virtually the only aids to a full year's research in Britain. Valuable as they were in themselves, they perhaps performed the further service of pointing up the need for such aid on a much larger scale. In 1954 the Carnegie Corporation of New York made a grant to the Humanities Research Council of Canada of $15,000 a year for five years to be applied to this purpose. This enabled the Council to make 8 grants a year of $2000 or $2500, tenable for a year's research during leave of absence, with no restrictions on place of tenure. Under this scheme scholars went variously to English, European, and American centres of research as their work demanded. At the same time, the Council's funds permitted an expansion of the number of grants for summer research to 20 a year, and an increase of grant to as much as $700 for scholars going to Europe. Pre-doctoral fellowships were increased to 12 or 13 full-time (whole year) and 17 or 18 part-time awards, $1200–$1500 for the former, and up to $700 for the latter.

It would be less than fair to the Humanities Research Council of Canada (and to its sister body, the Social Science Research Council of Canada) and to the Carnegie Corporation and the Rockefeller Foundation to underestimate the importance of their work in this period. Not only did it make possible the provision of some $290,000 in grants (partly contributed by Canadian private donors) over a space of five years, but it developed a full scheme and machinery for the administration of grants, establishing of categories, setting conditions of award, and so on.

With the establishment of the Canada Council, and with the income from its capital grant of $50,000,000 applicable to fellowships, a large-scale expansion was possible. It was natural that the Canada Council should enlist the experience of the two Research Councils in planning and administering the new scheme, and from 1957 until the end of 1963 specially selected committees of the Research Councils acted as selection boards to recommend awards to the Canada Council. For each category of fellowship a separate committee was set up, made up of mature scholars representative of different disciplines and of the large Canadian academic community. These committees were not drawn solely from the Council membership, but were usually chaired by a present or past member. Personnel of each committee was changed annually. The expenses of the committees were met by the Canada Council, but members received no honorarium for their services. The extent of members' contribution to the cause of scholarship is indicated by the record: in the five-year period from 1958 to 1963, they examined the full dossiers of 2,993 applicants, making 989 awards. As one who has served on these committees, I can testify to the seriousness and willingness with which they undertook a task which they recognized as of vital importance to Canadian scholarship, and to the disinterested integrity I invariably encountered in the judgment of applicants. The evidence of their success, and the sufficient reward of their labours, can be seen in the great growth of research activity and publication recorded in the bibliography of research.

The main attention of the Canada Council, as a result of the huge expansion of universities, has been given to the problem of future staff. This concern is reflected in the apportionment of funds to the various categories of grant. This apportionment has been made always by the Canada Council, not by the Research Councils or on their advice. It will be noted that fellowships for a full year's post-doctoral research number only 15 at present (for the humanities and social sciences), which is little if any improvement on the 8 for the humanities alone offered by the Humanities Research Council in 1954. Pressure to provide pre-doctoral fellowships is of course bound to increase, and the need to support future university staff through to the Ph.D. is desperate. Given the inelasticity of the Canada Council funds, each need competes with the others, and I foresee a grave danger that the impressive achievement of the past fifteen years will be impossible to match, let alone surpass, over the next fifteen years unless much greater provision can be made to encourage research and scholarly production beyond the Ph.D. thesis. The thesis ought to be the beginning of a career of scholarship; if support and encouragement stop with the thesis, for many it will necessarily be the end.

Another great encouragement to scholarship has undoubtedly been the possibility of publication; it takes a rare kind of dedication indeed to pen away laboriously at pages no readers will ever see. The editors of the 1947 survey noted the frequency in Canada of learned scholars who published little or nothing of their learning. Of the two editors of that survey, one was inclined to blame sheer laziness for the dearth of publication (p. 173); the other called attention rather to the difficulty of publication (p. 191). A rapid and rough check of books listed in the 1947 bibliography turns up some interesting evidence of conditions up to that time. Of 261 books by Canadian scholars, almost exactly half were published in Canada. But of this half, 32 were obviously school texts, and others look suspiciously like school texts. Of 48 genuine research works published in English-speaking Canada, half were published by the University of Toronto Press. An almost equal number, 46, were published in Quebec. Of the rest of the 261, the largest group, 55, were published in the United States, mostly by university presses. A good many of these undoubtedly represent Ph.D. theses. Another 34 were published in Europe, by far the greatest number being French doctoral theses. The final group of 46 were published in England, or jointly in England and the United States. French-speaking scholars had, then, rather more success in being published in Canada than abroad; English-speaking ones, apart from school texts, had twice as much chance abroad as at home. Since the 261 works were produced by 131 out of the 746 academics asked for bibliographies, it seems probable that at least some of the silent 600 were defeated by the impossibility of finding a publisher, and that there existed in 1947, in the words of an editor of the survey, "a massive backlog of unpublished Canadian research material in the humanities."

The present situation is a much happier one, and again credit must be given first of all, chronologically at least, to the Humanities Research Council, to the American foundations which gave it support, and to the Canada Council which in due time continued and enlarged that support. As a result of the 1947 survey, a Committee on Aid to Publication was formed by the Humanities Research Council. Until it acquired funds sufficient for subsidy, its activities were confined to providing expert readers for manuscripts and making their reports available to possible publishers. The University of Toronto Press co-operated by publishing, without collateral subsidy, as many of the works recommended to it by the Council as possible. This may seem a very limited service to start with, but its importance was by no means negligible. The prestige of Canadian scholarship naturally depends on its ability to meet an international standard, to compete on even terms of quality with works produced anywhere in the world. Since the readers chosen for manuscripts by the Committee were drawn from the whole international academic community, the manuscripts were subjected to judgment by that international standard. If a manuscript failed in some respects to meet it, the reports of the readers, which were often made available (anonymously) to the author, usually offered valuable advice towards revision. Where the reports were favourable, they gave confidence, not only to the author but also to his publisher, that his work could be a credit to both in the world of international scholarship.

By 1948 and 1949 it was possible to add to recommendation of manuscripts small grants as subsidies—five works received a little over $1500. These grants were payable to the author upon publication. In 1950–1, seven authors received $2300, in 1951–3 six received $3600, in 1953–6 nine received $3800. By the end of 1959, 42 books had been published with Council aid on the recommendation of the Committee. The Canada Council early recognized the importance of this phase of the Research Council's activities, and provided special annual grants for the purpose. As the number of manuscripts submitted and approved has increased, the Canada Council has correspondingly increased the grant, until it reached $20,000 a year. Some indication of the increased scholarly activity in the humanities, and of the importance of the scheme for aid to publication, is given by the volume of business done by the Committee. Manuscripts submitted annually rose from 24 in 1958–9 to 45 in 1962–3. Since close to half of the works tend to be approved by the readers, it is clear that $20,000 is already an insufficient sum for adequate subsidy, and is likely to become rapidly even less sufficient. The normal maximum subsidy is now $1500.

How far and in what way the subsidies encourage publishers to produce scholarly works they would not otherwise have produced is a question in the economics of publishing that I am not competent to deal with. It is obvious that at present costs, $1500 cannot represent a very large proportion of what it takes to produce an attractive edition of a scholarly work of any size. But the subsidy, though paid to the author himself immediately after publication, is usually by arrangement handed over to the publisher. It thus serves to provide a quick, if small, return of investment, and has somewhat the effect of adding $5 a copy to his receipts from the first 300 library copies he sells. Or alternatively it allows him to offer the whole edition at a somewhat lower price, giving it a chance at a wider market. The present subsidies are obviously not large enough to attract those commercial publishers who feel no other inducement, such as prestige, to enter the realms of scholarship, and I feel that this is a good thing. More money is needed for subsidy, first of all to increase the number of grants, secondly perhaps to increase their size, but without presuming to guess what limit there should be on individual grants, I favour a limit. For scholarly publication entails a special kind of responsibility for the publisher. It demands a fully trained editorial staff, familiar with the problems of scholarly editing, and with scholarly criteria, and able to establish a consistent and complete system of editorial procedure. Such a staff can be found in old established commercial firms in Britain, but the nature of Canadian commercial publishing has not generally favoured or encouraged the creation of one. And the inducement to build one cannot come from subsidy. It seems likely that as Canadian publishing matures, it may wish to play a major part in scholarly publishing in the humanities as it is now tending to in the social sciences. It will then be induced to compete in quality of editorial work for the sake of its own reputation. Meanwhile the greatest part of our humanistic studies published in Canada are produced by the university presses, and particularly by the University of Toronto Press, whose contribution to the expansion of research and publication is indeed an impressive one.

The Press exists, as its Director has affirmed (*Press Notes from the University of Toronto Press*, vol. VI, no. 3), "primarily to insure the efficient communication by scholars of the results of their academic research." In view of this primarily academic aim, it is interesting to note that in 1963 the Press published 92 new books, considerably more than any other publisher in Canada. It is indeed now one of the largest and most active of members in the Association of American University Presses, "vying for leadership with such famous imprints as Harvard, California, Chicago, and Yale." What this growth means to the Canadian scholar is made evident by an analysis of publication figures. From 1947 to 1963, works by scholars in the humanities teaching in Canadian institutions have been published by the Press in the following numbers: 31 in English literature, 10 in Classics, 10 in Romance languages, 2 in German, 7 in Slavics, 3 in Near East language and literature, 3 in Far East, 8 in Art and Archaeology, 4 in Music, 65 in History, 11 in Philosophy, and 4 in Bibliography, a total of 157. Of these, 76, or almost exactly half, were by scholars outside of Toronto—from all parts of Canada. (These figures do not of course include the many works in the humanities by authors who are not "Canadian" also published by the Press.) Of the 157, only 28 were published before 1952–53; the real expansion has taken place since. Only 8 of the 157 have been texts (including a dictionary for Anglo-Saxon poetry and selections in Classical Arabic). Eleven of the titles have been published jointly, mostly with publishers in the United Kingdom. This pattern of reciprocal arrangements on appropriate titles by Canadian and by English authors for joint simultaneous publication in Canada and Britain is a developing one; it has several advantages for the scholar, chief of which are more rapid access to reviews, and wider facilities for publicity and distribution.

At the same time as the Press has expanded its production, it has expanded its arrangements for its own publicity and distribution. Following a sales arrangement with the University of Chicago Press in 1954 a sales manager was appointed; later the Press set up its own United States warehouse. Every publication of the Press is fully catalogued in the American *Books in Print* and fully reported in the quarterly *Scholarly Books in America*. The first is a service enjoyed by no other publisher outside the United States. It has sales agents throughout the world and its books are represented at international book fairs. As a result of these successes, the works of Canadian scholars are now exported all over the world, and more than half of the sales are foreign ones. A significant and typical example is the sale to Japan of more than 200 sets of the first volumes of the *Collected Works of John Stuart Mill*.

Some part of the publication in the humanities has been fostered through the establishing of series. The first of these was the University of Toronto Department of English Studies and Texts, begun in 1942, and now about to publish its thirteenth item. The series was followed in 1949 by Near and Middle East, and the Romance series, in 1952 by a series of *Phoenix* supplementary volumes in Classics, and in 1956 by *Canadian Slavonic Papers*. At the beginning, the Toronto Department of English helped to subsidize its series, but under the present arrangements of the Press all costs have been assumed by the Publications Fund of the Press, with the sole exception of grants in aid of particular works from the Humanities Research Council of Canada. No author of any work is ever called upon for a personal subsidy; in recent years also a standard royalty has normally been paid to the author on all copies sold, whether his work was subsidized or not. This in itself is a welcome achievement; scholars of my generation can remember the heavy financial penalty publication often used to entail for the individual scholar—I remember the head of a department at a very distinguished American university telling me that it took him ten years to pay off the debts created by his first book. When one considers that the Press also subsidizes ten journals, five of them in the humanities (*Canadian Historical Review, University of Toronto Quarterly, Phoenix, Canadian Journal of Linguistics*, and *Canadian Journal of Theology*), its performance, and the service it renders to Canadian scholarship, become astounding.

And it is very important to remember that the Press accomplishes all this with no subsidy from the University of Toronto's general funds. This is so remarkable, and so seldom realized, that I feel it only fair to quote the Director's words in full (again from *Press Notes*, vol. VI, no. 3):

It is indeed worth noting, however, that the moneys placed at the disposal of scholarly publishing through this account are furnished *wholly by the Press itself*, having been earned through its other publishing and technical printing operations. During the past six years alone, the Press will have made available to the University in this way more than half a million dollars for the purpose of underwriting the net budgeted deficits of books and journals of scholarly worth which otherwise would have had to go unpublished. It is worthy of note, too, that among the sixty university presses in North America which have qualified for membership in the Association of American University Presses, only the Press at this particular institution has been able to shoulder thus far the whole of the net costs of the University's research publishing programme, while at the same time remaining entirely independent of University endowments or subsidies, direct or indirect. All salary, maintenance, and other operating costs of all the University of Toronto Press departments, as well as all costs of financing the very extensive expansion of buildings and equipment which the Press has undertaken during the past seven or eight years, have been assumed by the Press independently, and do not represent a charge on other University funds. Thus instead of being subsidized, the Press is a provider of subsidies. I should add that every senior official of the Press, in every department, takes immense satisfaction from the use thus being made of the net income derived from his daily efforts.

This unique achievement carries with it a number of implications for the Canadian scholar. It means, of course, that his works, given an attractive format and a suitable introduction to world markets, can obviously in general hold their own with similar books published abroad. There is little doubt that the success of the Press is due, not only to brilliant management, but to a supply of a reasonable number of scholarly manuscripts capable of commanding some international notice. It is also due to an emphasis on design, on attractive typography and format, and on meticulous editing. Twenty years ago, Canadian books were, and looked like, country cousins; now they can stand comparison in any company. The revolution in style, accompanied by positive methods of marketing, have given the Canadian scholar's book at least an even chance in international competition.

Secondly, the policy of the Press means that it can, in effect, pay attention only to the scholarly quality and importance of a work, and, where these are not in doubt, virtually ignore the size of the market it might reach. The Advisory Committee on Publications, which approves works for subsidized publication by the Press, is a senior academic body, concerned only with the scholarly merits of the work, as reported on by expert appraisers. There is, of course, a limit to the number of scholarly works that could be published at a loss, set by the actual resources of the Press, but the limit operates only at the scholarly level, not at the level of possible sales. The scholar is competing with his fellows for a place in the schedule of publishing primarily as a scholar, and judged by the criteria of scholarship. This is an entirely healthy competition, and has undoubtedly contributed to the maturing of Canadian scholarship.

The officials of the University of Toronto Press would be the first to agree that their own expansion has been accompanied by, and in part caused by, the expansion and maturing of scholarship which it itself was fostering, and that the development of the activities of the Press is part of the total development of activities in research and scholarly authorship. This development and maturing have, in turn, made possible projects for which, a generation ago, scholarly resources were not available. Such a project as the *Dictionary of Canadian Biography*, for example, could not, I think, have been undertaken successfully a generation ago, even had its endowment been then available. It calls for a high degree of developed historical scholarship, and an accumulation of historical bibliography, which were not then in existence. To some extent, the enlargement of resources made by technological developments has allowed the planning of large projects; collation of the John Stuart Mill editions with the help of Xerox, and the lavish use of microfilm for the Fanny Burney project at McGill are examples. But the growth of the university press is an obvious prerequisite for projects that are to involve years of planning and production of multiple volumes, and very heavy capital investments. It is no exaggeration to say that the *DCB* and the *Collected Works of John Stuart Mill* mark the real coming of age of Canadian scholarly publishing.

The uniqueness of the University of Toronto Press in its achievement, uniqueness not only in relation to the rest of Canada, but to the rest of the continent, with its sixty university presses, naturally raises the question of whether its success can be duplicated elsewhere. If not, what can we expect from other university presses? Les Presses de l'Université Laval, for example, were playing an important part in academic publishing in 1947, and have continued to do so, as the bibliography of publications demonstrates. They have not in the past had a complete organization of editorial staff and promotional staff, but are in process of setting them up, as is the McGill University Press. Most other university presses in Canada are imprints only. Toronto and Laval have been developing a measure of co-operation; they have published some titles jointly, and have also arranged joint publication of some works in English and French—Laval, for example, is to do a French edition of the *DCB*, and articles prepared for the *Dictionary* in either language are edited in either Quebec or Toronto and then translated for the other edition. This sort of co-operation should be valuable for both presses, and should lead to a rapid development of the editorial and production staff at Laval. This I take to be the most important first step in creating a great press.

It seems to me inevitable that any university with serious intentions of establishing a university press should face the necessity of relatively heavy subsidization particularly during its first ten or fifteen years. A Press obviously cannot hope to do much in the way of self-support until it has a back-list to support it. And its back-list must establish itself by quality, by quality of scholarship, of editorial preparation, and of physical production. If it is to gain respect—and a market—the Press's first books must be fit to stand comparison and competition. Competent readers, a competent advisory board, competent editorial staff, and competent production staff are, then, the first requisites. The sensible way to start marketing is probably to reach an arrangement at first with another press. If Canadian scholarship and scholarly production continue to expand, as one hopes they will, and as they assuredly will if given proper support, there will be increasing need, and indeed opportunity, for more university Presses in Canada. The service they render will depend largely on the care with which they are planned and developed, and the financial support they are given by their universities.

Two further forms of aid to scholarship deserve mention. One is the formation of national societies, and the establishing of annual conferences for them. In 1946, the editors of the survey recommended "that under the auspices of the Humanities Research Council associations might be formed" in English, Modern Languages, Philosophy, Classics, and Orientals (p. 194). In 1950–1, the Council sponsored, and indeed organized, the formation of the Humanities Association of Canada, a national body with local branches across Canada, "designed to appeal to everyone, amateur or professional, who had an interest in one or more of the different humane studies." The Council provided funds for the first years, and has continued limited support, particularly through grants to members to attend the annual conference. Since that time, national associations of university teachers of Classics, English, French, German, and Slavics have been formed, as well as a Canadian Historical Association, a Canadian Catholic Historical Association, a Canadian Linguistic Association, and a Canadian Philosophical Association. All of these associations have a two-or-three day annual meeting; many of them continue through the year with meetings of local branches. Many of them publish journals or bulletins, which serve the double purpose of publishing scholarly contributions and keeping members *au courant* with developments in their discipline across Canada. The effect of the journals in particular has often been quite profound in creating a sense of national community. Studies in philosophy in English-speaking Canada, for example, tend to follow a pattern which is unlike that of either British or American studies, and until Canadian philosophers established their own journal, *Dialogue*, in September 1962, their contributions either found difficulty in being published, or their characteristic note was swamped or assimilated in foreign journals. In view of the strength of philosophy as a scholarly subject in Canada, it is clear that the preservation of its particular identity is valuable. In other subjects, the situation is rather different, but it is still of importance to the morale of Canadian scholars, and to their sense of community, that their own journals should help establish their reputation. Much had already been done, of course, by the *Dalhousie Review*, *Queen's Quarterly*, and the *University of Toronto Quarterly* in certain areas, chiefly English and history, as frequent citations in international bibliographies make clear. It is a matter for some pride, for example, that a recent British collection of essays on Tennyson reprinted a quarter of its text from *UTQ*. But the quarterlies were, and still are, limited in the number of articles acceptable from any one discipline, and limited in the degree of specialization suitable to their purpose. For many subjects of research, and for many whole scholarly disciplines, the quarterlies could grant no access.

The second of the further aids is the series of visits by senior scholars, carried out from time to time under the auspices of the Humanities Research Council. The first was, of course, the origin of the historic report of 1946–7. In 1957 the Council asked five scholars to prepare a progress report, and Professors Daniells, Berry, Priestley, Lebel, and Rothney visited institutions in their respective areas of Canada. Three years later the same visitors made a further tour and report. On every tour most of the time was devoted to interviews with scholars, discussing their research and plans for research, and there is ample evidence that in many quarters the visits were found stimulating and encouraging. My own impression was that it is often easier for a young scholar to discuss his work and his problems with a visitor than with his immediate colleagues, and that an elder colleague can often offer suggestions on publication, on grants, sometimes on methods of research. Moreover, I am sure that the visits helped emphasize the value and importance of research.

APPENDICES

BIBLIOGRAPHY OF WORKS
ON EDUCATION

ROBIN S. HARRIS

A Bibliography of Higher Education, edited by R. S. Harris and A. Tremblay (University of Toronto Press; Presses de l'Université Laval, 1960) provides a reasonably complete list of references to all aspects of Canadian higher education up to the end of 1958. Some 4,000 items are listed chronologically in sections: see particularly the sections devoted to Canadian Culture, The Faculty of Arts and Science, Faculté des Arts: Enseignement secondaire classique, The Humanities (with subsections devoted to Archaeology, Art-Music-Drama, Classics, English, French, History, Modern Languages other than English and French, Philosophy, Religious Knowledge), Graduate Studies and Research. A Supplement to *A Bibliography of Higher Education in Canada*, covering the five-year period, 1959–1963, and with additional items for the earlier period, is currently being compiled by R. S. Harris and Jean-Marie Joly and is scheduled to be published in 1965 by the same publishers.

What follows is a list of items of particular significance for the humanities bearing on individual institutions, the general Canadian cultural and educational scene, the role of the humanities, and graduate studies and research. With the exception of the references to individual institutions, items are restricted to those published since January 1, 1950.

INSTITUTIONAL HISTORIES

ACADIA: R. S. Longley, *Acadia University 1838–1938*. Kentville: Kentville Publishing Co., 1938.

ALBERTA: J. Macdonald, *The History of the University of Alberta*. Edmonton: University of Alberta, 1958; P. E. Weston, "A University for Calgary," *Alberta Historical Review*, XI (1962), 1–11.

BISHOP'S: D. C. Masters, *Bishop's University: The First Hundred Years*. Toronto: Clarke, Irwin, 1950.

BRITISH COLUMBIA: H. T. Logan, *Tuum Est: A History of the University of British Columbia*. Vancouver: University of British Columbia, 1958.

CARLETON: E. A. Corbett, *Henry Marshall Tory: Beloved Canadian*. Toronto: Ryerson, 1954.

DALHOUSIE: D. C. Harvey, *An Introduction to the History of Dalhousie University*. Halifax: McCurdy Printing Co., 1938; F. W. Vroom,

A Chronicle of King's College 1789–1939. Halifax: Imperial Publishing Co., 1941.

LAVAL: H. Provost, *Historique de la Faculté des Arts à l'Université Laval.* Quebec: Enseignement secondaire, 1952; M. Lebel, "La Faculté des Lettres de Laval," *Revue de l'Université Laval*, VI (1952), 449–64.

LOYOLA: T. P. Slattery, *Loyola and Montreal: A History.* Montreal: Palm Publishers, 1962.

McGILL: H. MacLennan, ed., *McGill: The Story of a University.* Toronto: Thomas Nelson, 1960.

MANITOBA: W. L. Morton, *One University: A History of the University of Manitoba, 1877–1952.* Toronto: McClelland & Stewart, 1957.

MONTRÉAL: Université de Montréal, *Mémoire à la Commission Royale d'Enquête sur les Problèmes constitutionnels.* Montréal: Université de Montréal, 1954.

NEW BRUNSWICK: A. G. Bailey, ed., *The University of New Brunswick Memorial Volume.* Fredericton: University of New Brunswick, 1950.

OTTAWA: J.-L. Bergevin, *L'Université d'Ottawa . . . 1848–1928.* Ottawa: University of Ottawa, 1929.

QUEEN'S: D. D. Calvin, *Queen's University at Kingston, 1841–1941.* Kingston: Queen's University, 1941.

ST. FRANCIS XAVIER: A. Laidlaw, *The Campus and the Community.* Montreal: Harvest House, 1961.

SASKATCHEWAN: C. King, *The First Fifty.* Toronto: McClelland & Stewart, 1959; A. Morton, *Saskatchewan: The Making of a University.* Toronto: University of Toronto Press, 1959.

SHERBROOKE: *Une revue succincte des débuts de l'Université de Sherbrooke.* Université de Sherbrooke, 1958.

SIR GEORGE WILLIAMS: H. C. Cross, *One Hundred Years of Service with Youth: The Story of the Montreal Y.M.C.A.* Montreal: Y.M.C.A. 1951.

TORONTO: W. S. Wallace, *A History of the University of Toronto.* Toronto: University of Toronto Press, 1927; C. T. Bissell, ed., *University College: A Portrait, 1853–1953.* Toronto: University of Toronto Press. 1953; C. B. Sissons, *A History of Victoria University.* Toronto: University of Toronto Press, 1952; T. A. Reed, ed., *A History of the University of Trinity College, Toronto.* Toronto: University of Toronto Press, 1952.

WESTERN: J. J. Talman and R. D. Talman, *Western—1878–1953.* London: University of Western Ontario, 1953; J. J. Talman, *Huron College.* London: Huron College, 1963.

YORK: M. G. Ross, *The New University.* Toronto: University of Toronto Press, 1961.

Historical information on institutions not listed above can normally be found in the annual calendar. The *Report of the Royal Commission on Education in New Brunswick* (J. Deutsch, Chairman, Fredericton, 1962) contains interesting material on the New Brunswick institutions.

GENERAL

ANGERS, P. *Problèmes de culture au Canada français*. Montréal: Beauchemin, 1960.

BISSELL, C. T., ed. *Canada's Crisis in Higher Education*. Toronto: University of Toronto Press, 1957.

Commission Royale d'Enquête sur les Problèmes constitutionnels. *Rapport* . . . (4 vols.) and *Annexes*. Québec, 1956.

DESJARDINS, G. *Les Ecoles du Québec, l'enseignement primaire, l'enseignement spécialisé, les collèges classiques, l'enseignement universitaire, 1635–1950*. Montréal: Bellarmin, 1950.

DUNTON, D., and D. PATTERSON, eds. *Canadian Universities in a New Age*. Ottawa: National Conference of Canadian Universities and Colleges, 1962.

FALARDEAU, J.-C. *Essais sur le Québec contemporain*. Québec: Presses de l'Université Laval, 1954.

———— *Roots and Values in Canadian Lives*. Toronto: University of Toronto Press, 1961.

FRÈRE UNTEL (pseud.). *Les Insolences du Frère Untel*. Montréal: Editions de l'Homme, 1960.

HARRIS, R. S. "Higher Education in Canada," *Dalhousie Review*, XLII (1963), 423–36.

LATREILLE, A., éd. *Le Canada Français aujourd'hui et demain*. Paris: A. Fayard, 1961.

LEBEL, MAURICE. *Le Conseil Canadien de Recherches sur les Humanités*. Québec, Les Presses de l'Université Laval, 1954 (2e édition, 1956).

———— *L'Université au XXᵉ siècle*. Québec, Imprimerie Franciscaine Missionnaire, 1958 (2e édition, 1961).

———— *Humanisme et Technique, Science et Recherche*. Québec, Imprimerie Franciscaine Missionnaire, 1959.

———— *Trois Cultures et Sagesse*. Québec, Imprimerie Franciscaine Missionnaire, 1960.

———— *Le Mirage des Etats-Unis et de la Russie dans l'enseignement supérieur au Canada*. Québec, Imprimerie Franciscaine Missionnaire, 1961.

LORTIE, L., and A. PLOUFFE, éds. *The Roots of the Present: Studies Presented to Section I of the Royal Society of Canada*. Toronto: University of Toronto Press, 1960.

LUSSIER, I. *Roman Catholic Education and French Canada*. Toronto: Gage, 1960.

PARK, J., ed. *The Culture of Contemporary Canada*. Ithaca: Cornell University Press, 1957.

PHILLIPS, C. E. *The Development of Education in Canada*. Toronto: Gage, 1957.

ROSS, M., ed. *The Arts in Canada: A Stock-taking in Mid-Century*. Toronto: Macmillan, 1958.

Royal Commission on National Development in the Arts, Letters and Sciences. *Report of* . . . and *Royal Commission Studies*. Ottawa: King's Printer, 1951.

STANLEY, G., and G. SYLVESTRE, eds. *Canadian Universities Today*. Toronto: University of Toronto Press, 1961.

TREMBLAY, A. *Les Collèges et les écoles publiques: conflit ou coordina-tion?* Québec: Presses de l'Université Laval, 1954.

VACHON, L.-A. *Unité de l'Université.* Québec: Presses de l'Université Laval, 1962.

WADE, M., ed. *Canadian Dualism: Studies of French-English Relations.* Toronto: University of Toronto Press; Québec: Presses de l'Université Laval, 1960.

THE HUMANITIES

BISSELL, C. T. "American Studies in Canadian Universities," *Queen's Quarterly,* LXVI (1959), 384–87.

———— "The Humanities and the Crisis," *Canadian Bar Journal,* I (1958), 28–35.

———— "The University and the Intellectual," *Queen's Quarterly,* LXVII (1961), 1–14.

FARNHAM, W. D. "The Study of American History in Canadian Universi-ties," Canadian Historical Association, *Annual Report* (1958), 63–76.

FRYE, N. *By Liberal Things.* Toronto: Clarke, Irwin, 1959.

———— "Humanities in a New World," in M. Ross, ed., *University of Toronto Installation Lectures* (Toronto: University of Toronto Press, 1958), 9–23.

———— "The Study of English in Canada," *Dalhousie Review,* XXXVIII (1958), 1–7.

GILMOUR, G. P. "The Plight of the Individual," *Dalhousie Review,* XXXVIII (1958), 313–23.

IRVING, J. A. *Philosophy in Canada: A Symposium.* Toronto: University of Toronto Press, 1952.

KIRKCONNELL, W. "The Humanities," in J. Katz, ed., *Canadian Education Today* (Toronto: McGraw-Hill, 1956), 200–10.

———— "The Place of Slavic Studies in Canada," *Slavistica,* XXXI (1957).

LÉVESQUE, G.-H. "Humanisme et sciences sociales," *Revue Dominicaine,* LVIII (1952), 212–23.

MACMILLAN, E. *Music in Canada.* Toronto: University of Toronto Press, 1955.

PACEY, D. "The Humanist Tradition," in A. G. Bailey, ed., *The University of New Brunswick Memorial Volume* (Fredericton, 1950), 57–68.

PIRLOT, P. "L'Allergie culturelle: sciences—humanités," *Revue de l'Uni-sité Laval,* XV (1960), 299–315.

PRESTON, R. A. "The Humanities in the Cadet Colleges," *RMC Review,* XXXIII (1952), 86–95.

RICOUR, P. *Les Humanités greco-latines: idole ou vrai dieu.* Montréal: Chanteclair, 1953.

SALTER, F. M. "And God Said, Let there be Light," Royal Society of Canada, *Transactions,* 3rd series, LII (1958), s. 2, 69–75.

VANIER, P., éd. *Mélange sur les humanités.* Québec: Presses de l'Université Laval, 1954.

WALLACE, M. W. "The Humanities," in *Royal Commission Studies* (Ottawa, 1951), 99–110.

WHALLEY, G. "The Humanities and Science: Two Cultures or One?" *Queen's Quarterly*, LXVIII (1961), 237–48.

WOODHOUSE, A. S. P. "The Humanities: Sixty Years," *Queen's Quarterly*, LX (1954), 538–50.

—— "The Nature and Function of the Humanities," Royal Society of Canada, *Transactions*, XLVI (1952), s. 2, 1–17.

GRADUATE STUDIES AND RESEARCH

DUMONT, F. et Y. MARTIN, éds. *Situation de la recherche sur le Canada français*. Québec: Presses de l'Université Laval, 1962.

HALPENNY, F. G., and PRIESTLEY, F. E. L. *The Thesis and the Book* (pamphlet; in English and French). Toronto: University of Toronto Press, 1962.

HARMAN, E., ed. *The University as Publisher*. Toronto: University of Toronto Press, 1961.

HENEL, H. "Humanistic Scholarship," *Queen's Quarterly*, LVII (1950), 93–100.

LEBEL, M. "Humanisme et technique, science et recherche," *Revue de l'Université Laval*, XIII (1958), 226–42.

MACLURE, M. "Literary Scholarship," in J. Park, ed., *The Culture of Contemporary Canada* (Toronto: Ryerson, 1957), 221–24.

SMITH, M. B. "Status and Scholarship in the Humanities," *Dalhousie Review*, XXXIX (1959), 370–77.

WILES, ROY MCKEEN. *Scholarly Reporting in the Humanities*. 3rd ed., Toronto: University of Toronto Press, 1961.

WILLIAMS, E. E. *Resources of Canadian University Libraries for Research in the Humanities and Social Sciences*. Ottawa: N.C.C.U.C., 1962.

For Contrast and Comparison

BERELSON, B. *Graduate Education in the United States*. New York: McGraw-Hill, 1960.

PRICE, A. G. *The Humanities in Australia: A Survey with Special Reference to the Universities*. Sydney: Angus & Robertson, 1959.

THOMPSON, W. P.: *Graduate Education in the Sciences in Canadian Universities*. Toronto: University of Toronto Press, 1963.

BIBLIOGRAPHY OF SCHOLARLY PUBLICATIONS

REFERENCES IN THE FOLLOWING BIBLIOGRAPHIES have been checked where possible. It has sometimes been necessary, from pressure of space, to give only a select list from an author's extensive publications—where this is done, it is indicated. Many authors made their own selection. Abbreviations follow the standard practice of *PMLA*. For journals not in the *PMLA* list, a simple, and I hope obvious, system has been followed: *Journal* is regularly represented by *J*, *Review* by *R*, *Quarterly* by *Q*, *Bulletin* by *Bull*, and so on. For each author (A) lists book works; (B) articles; (C) reviews; (D) work in progress.

Unlike its predecessor in the 1947 *Humanities in Canada*, which was organized solely by institution, this one is organized by subject as well. It seemed useful to bring together the publications in a single subject; even in the comparatively limited bibliography of 1947 it was difficult to see readily what, for example, Canadian scholars had contributed to classical scholarship. Within each subject, institutions are arranged alphabetically, and within institutions the scholars. The bibliographies vary in the terminal date of their listings, the laggards sometimes unjustly getting the fullest and latest entries. Bibliographies are those supplied to us by individual scholars in response to a request sent to their institution.

Some movements of staff will have taken place since this bibliography was prepared; it has seemed simplest to enter location as of 1962–3.

AUR: Aberdeen University Review
AC: Action Catholique
AN: Action Nationale
AU: Action Universitaire
AHR: American Historical Review
AJA: American Journal of Archaeology
AJP: American Journal of Philology
AJSL: American Journal of Semitic Languages and Literatures
AJT: American Journal of Theology
ASEER: American Slavic and East European Review
AA: Art and Archaeology
ACUTE: Association of Canadian University Teachers of English
BC: Book Collector

BA: Books Abroad
BASOR: Bulletin of the American Schools of Oriental Research
BNYPL: Bulletin of the New York Public Library
CF: Canada Français
CAUT Bull: Canadian Association of University Teachers Bulletin
CEA Critic: Canadian Education Association Critic
Can For: Canadian Forum
CHA Rep: Canadian Historical Association Report
CHR: Canadian Historical Review
CJEPS: Canadian Journal of Economics and Political Science
CJRT: Canadian Journal of Religious Thought

CJT: *Canadian Journal of Theology*
Can L: *Canadian Literature*
CMJ: *Canadian Music Journal*
CSP: *Canadian Slavonic Papers*
CH: *Church History*
CJ: *Classical Journal*
CP: *Classical Philology*
CQ: *Classical Quarterly*
CW: *Classical Weekly*
CE: *College English*
C'weal: *Commonweal*
Comp Lit: *Comparative Literature*
DR: *Dalhousie Review*
Dub R: *Dublin Review*
Enc Br: *Encyclopaedia Britannica*
Enc Can: *Encyclopaedia Canadiana*
EHR: *English Historical Review*
ELH: *English Literary History*
Eng St: *English Studies* (Amsterdam)
ESC: *Enseignement Secondaire au Canada*
EIC: *Essays in Criticism*
E & S: *Essays and Studies*
FR: *French Review*
FS: *French Studies*
GL&L: *German Life and Letters*
HJAS: *Harvard Journal of Asiatic Studies*
HSS: *Harvard Slavic Studies*
HSCP: *Harvard Studies in Classical Philology*
HAHR: *Hispanic American Historical Review*
HR: *Hispanic Review*
HAC Bull: *Bulletin of the Humanities Association of Canada*
HLQ: *Huntington Library Quarterly*
Int J: *International Journal*
JAAC: *Journal of Aesthetics and Art Criticism*
JAOS: *Journal of the American Oriental Society*
JAS: *Journal of Asian Studies*
JBL: *Journal of Biblical Literature*
JCLA: *Journal of the Canadian Linguistic Association*
JCEA: *Journal of Central European Affairs*

JEGP: *Journal of English and Germanic Philology*
JHI: *Journal of the History of Ideas*
JNES: *Journal of Near Eastern Studies*
JP: *Journal of Philosophy*
JPPR: *Journal of Philosophy and Phenomenological Research*
JR: *Journal of Religion*
JRS: *Journal of Roman Studies*
JRAS: *Journal of the Royal Asiatic Society*
JRSA: *Journal of the Royal Society of Arts*
KR: *Kenyon Review*
LTP: *Laval Théologique et Philosophique*
MAR: *Manitoba Arts Review*
MRS: *Mediaeval and Renaissance Studies*
MS: *Mediaeval Studies*
MH: *Medievalia et Humanistica*
MFS: *Modern Fiction Studies*
MLN: *Modern Language Notes*
MLQ: *Modern Language Quarterly*
MLR: *Modern Language Review*
MP: *Modern Philology*
MDU: *Monatshefte für Deutschen Unterricht*
NEQ: *New England Quarterly*
N&Q: *Notes and Queries*
OH: *Ontario History*
PNCFLT: *Pacific Northwest Conference of Foreign Language Teachers, Proceedings*
PQ: *Philological Quarterly*
PhQ: *Philosophical Quarterly*
PhR: *Philosophical Review*
PACPA: *Proceedings of the American Catholic Philosophical Association*
PMLA: *Publications of the Modern Language Association of America*
QJS: *Quarterly Journal of Speech*
QQ: *Queen's Quarterly*
Ren: *Renaissance*
RN: *Renaissance News*
REL: *Review of English Literature*

RES: *Review of English Studies*
RM: *Review of Metaphysics*
RA: *Revue d'Assyriologie*
RTC: *Revue Trimestrielle Canadienne*
RUL: *Revue de l'Université Laval*
RUO: *Revue de l'Université d'Ottawa*
RP: *Romance Philology*
RR: *Romanic Review*
ROMB: *Royal Ontario Museum Division of Art and Archaeology Bulletin*
Sask H: *Saskatchewan History*
SR: *Sewanee Review*
SB: *Shakespeare Bulletin*
SQ: *Shakespeare Quarterly*
ShS: *Shakespeare Studies*
SEEJ: *Slavic and East European Journal*
SEES: *Slavic and East European Studies*

SlR: *Slavic Review*
SEER: *Slavonic and East European Review*
SAQ: *South Atlantic Quarterly*
SEL: *Studies in English*
SP: *Studies in Philology*
SRen: *Studies in the Renaissance*
TLS: *Times Literary Supplement*
TAPA: *Transactions of the American Philological Association*
TASJ: *Transactions of the Asiatic Society of Japan*
TRSC: *Transactions of the Royal Society of Canada*
UTQ: *University of Toronto Quarterly*
WatR: *Waterloo Review*
WHR: *Western Humanist Review*
YR: *Yale Review*
ZRP: *Zeitschrift für Romanische Philologie*

CLASSICAL AND MEDIEVAL STUDIES

Classics

ACADIA UNIVERSITY

NEATBY, L. H.: (A) *In Quest of the North-West Passage* (Toronto, 1958), 194 pp.; *The Link between the Oceans* (Toronto, 1960), viii + 139 pp. (B) "Joe and Hannah," *Beaver*, outfit 290 (1959), 16–21; "Arctic Journals," *QQ*, 66 (1960), 575–88; "McClure and the Passage," *Beaver*, outfit 291 (1960), 33–41; "The Greely Ordeal," *Beaver*, outfit 292 (1961), 4–11. (C) *Beaver, DR, QQ*. (D) "The Conquest of the Last Frontier" (in hands of publisher); two contributions to the *Dictionary of Canadian Biography*.

UNIVERSITY OF ALBERTA

WINSPEAR, A. D.: (A) (with Lenore Eweke) *Augustus and Roman Reconstruction* (Madison, Wis., 1933), 301 pp.; (with Tom Silverberg) *Who was Socrates?* (New York, 1939), 96 pp. (2nd ed., 1960); *The Genesis of Plato's Thought* (New York, 1940), 390 pp. (2nd ed., 1956; 3rd ed., paperback, 1961); *Selections from Lucretius in English Verse*, Wisconsin Anthology, 1952; *The Roman Poet of Science* (New York, 1956), 299 pp. (2nd ed., London, 1960; 3rd ed., paperback, 1963); *Lucretius and Scientific Thought* (Montreal, 1963), viii + 156 pp. (B) Chapters on Greek and Latin literature in *Barnes' Intellectual and Cultural History of Western Europe*; "Lucretius' Sense of Humor" in *Thought from the Learned Societies* (Toronto, 1961). (D) The Emergence of the Christian Church (in an early stage).

CLASSICAL AND MEDIEVAL STUDIES

ASSUMPTION UNIVERSITY OF WINDSOR

FANTAZZI, CHARLES: (D) Study of the pastoral in the Greek and Roman traditions (as unpublished dissertation, ready within the year; further adaptations will make it ready for publication).

BISHOP'S UNIVERSITY

PRESTON, ANTHONY W.: (D) A biography of Lucius Cary, Lord Falkland (fifteen chapters written).

VALLILLEE, GERALD R.: (A) *Handbook for Teachers of Grade XI Latin* (Quebec, 1962). (B) "The Nausicaa Episode," *Phoenix*, 9 (1955), 175–9. (C) *Delta*. (D) Plautus and the Dramatic Tradition (bibliography complete).

UNIVERSITY OF BRITISH COLUMBIA

ELIOT, C. W. J.: (A) *Coastal Demes of Attika* (Toronto, 1962), viii + 181 pp. (B) "New Evidence for the Speed of the Roman Imperial Post," *Phoenix*, 9 (1955), 76–80; (with J. E. Jones and L. H. Sackett) "Τὸ Δέμα: A Survey of the Aigaleos-Parues Wall," *Annual Br School Athens*, 52 (1957), 152–92; (with Malcolm F. McGregor) "Kleisthenes: Eponymous Archon 525/4 B.C.," *Phoenix*, 14 (1960), 27–35. (C) *Classical World, Hesperia, Phoenix*. (D) Several articles concerned with Greek archaeology and history (all at the stage of second or third draft).

GRANT, W. LEONARD: (B) "The Shorter Latin Poems of George Buchanan," *CJ*, 40 (1945), 331–48; "Cicero and the Tractatus Coislinianus," *AJP*, 69 (1948), 80–6; "Hebrew, Aramaic, and the Greek of the Gospels," *Greece and Rome*, 20 (1951), 115–22; "Elegiac Themes in Horace's *Odes*," in Mary White, ed., *Studies in Honour of Gilbert Norwood* (Toronto, 1952), 194–202; "Two Eclogues of Giano Anisio," *PQ*, 33 (1954), 10–19; "Ut Universo Orbi Prodessent," *Phoenix*, 8 (1954), 64–70; "European Vernacular Works in Latin Translation, *S Ren*, 1 (1954), 120–56; "Christoforo Landino and Richard of Segbrok," *PQ*, 34 (1955), 74–6; "A Note on Petrarch's *Africa*, I, 4–6," *PQ*, 34 (1955), 76–81; "Early Neo-Latin Pastoral," *Phoenix*, 9 (1955), 19–26; "New Forms of Neo-Latin Pastoral," *S Ren*, 4 (1957), 71–100; "Later Neo-Latin Pastoral: Part I," *SP*, 53 (1956), 429–51, and Part II, *SP*, 54 (1957), 481–97; "A Classical Theme in Neo-Latin," *Latomus*, 9 (1957), 690–706; "Neo-Latin *lusus pastoralis* in Italy," *MH*, 11 (1957), 94–8; "An Eclogue of Giovanni Pontano," *PQ*, 36 (1957), 76–83; "An Eclogue of Giovanni Quatrario," *S Ren*, 5 (1958), 7–14; "Neo-Latin Verse-Translations of the Bible," *Harvard Theol R*, 52 (1959), 205–11; "Neo-Latin Materials at St. Louis," *Manuscripta*, 3 (1959), 3–18; "A Neo-Latin 'Heraldic' Eclogue," *Manuscripta*, 4 (1960), 149–63; "Neo-Latin Biblical Pastorals," *SP*, 58 (1961), 25–43; "Neo-Latin Devotional Pastorals," *SP*, 58 (1961), 597–615; "Naldo Naldi and Cod. Urb. lat. 1198,"*Manuscripta*, 6 (1962), 64–75. (D) Book on Neo-Latin pastoral (now completed); critical edition of Naldo Naldi's minor Latin poems (completed); critical edition of Naldo Naldi's Latin epic *Volaterrais* (all MSS. now collated); "The Biography of Naldo Naldi" (accepted and scheduled for Oct., 1963, issue of *SP*); "The Major Poems of Naldo Naldi" (scheduled for Oct., 1962, issue of *Manuscripta*); "The Minor Poems of Naldo Naldi: Part One" (scheduled for Feb., 1963, issue of *Manuscripta*); "The Minor Poems of Naldo Naldi: Part Two" (accepted by *Manuscripta*, no date set).

MCGREGOR, MALCOLM F.: (A) (with B. D. Merritt and H. T. Wade-Gery) *The Athenian Tribute Lists* (Princeton, 1949–53). (B) Various articles on Greek history and epigraphy. (C) *AJP, CP, Classical World, Phoenix*. (D) One paper in press—*Phoenix*; two papers in preparation (both drafted and under revision); three reviews.

RIDDEHOUGH, GEOFFREY B.: (A) *The Prophet's Man* (Toronto, 1926), 12 pp. (B) "Joseph of Exeter: The Cambridge Manuscript," *Speculum*, 24 (1949), 389–96; "Man-into-Beast Changes in Ovid," *Phoenix*, 8 (1959), 201–9. (C) *DR, JEGP, Phoenix, QQ*.

CARLETON UNIVERSITY

HODGE, A. TREVOR: (A) *The Woodwork of Greek Roofs* (Cambridge, 1960), xv + 149 pp. (B) "A Roof at Delphi," *Annual Br School at Athens* (1954). (C) *Amer J Arch, Classical World*. (D) (with Richard Tomlinson, University of Birmingham) article on unfinished surfaces on the Temple of Nemesis at Rhamnous (now in first draft); general work in Sicilian and Western Greek building technique.

SWALLOW, ELLENOR: (B) "Anna Soror," *CW*, 44 (1951), 145–50; "Dido's Pyre," *CW*, 45 (1951), 65–8; "The Strategic Fifth *Aeneid*," *CW*, 46 (1953), 177–9. (C) *Classical Bull, CW*. (D) Elementary Greek grammar and syntax (for university use; near completion); "Children in Classical Literature," a chapter for a collection of essays (accepted for publication); a study of the treatment of "failure" in classical antiquity (likely to need several years of work still).

UNIVERSITÉ LAVAL

LEBEL, MAURICE: (A) *Natural Law in the Greek Period* (South Bend, Indiana, 1949), 242 pp.; (contributor to) *Thèses des gradués canadiens dans les Humanités, 1921–1946* (Ottawa, 1951), xxviii + 194 pp.; *Pourquoi apprend-on le Grec?* (Québec, 1952), 32 pp.; *Explications de textes anglais et français* (Québec, 1953), 232 pp.; *Le Conseil canadien de Recherche sur les Humanités* (Québec, 1954, 1956), 42 pp.; *Lettres de Grèce* (Québec, 1955), 34 pp.; *L'Explication des textes littéraires* (Québec, 1957), xxiii + 342 pp.; *Images de la Turquie* (Québec, 1957), 65 pp.; *Recherches sur les images dans la poésie de Sophocle* (Athènes, 1957, 1961), 159 pp.; *Quelques considérations sur le rôle de l'Université au XXᵉ siècle* (Québec, 1957, 1961), 30 pp.; *Humanisme et Technique, Science et Recherche* (Québec, 1959), 19 pp.; *La langue parlée* (Québec, 1960), 31 pp.; *Le mirage des Etats-Unis et de la Russie dans l'Enseignement supérieur au Canada* (Québec, 1961), 32 pp.; *Propos inédits et interdits sur l'éducation* (Québec, 1963), 49 pp. (B) "Etat présent des travaux sur Sophocle," *TRSC*, 43 (1949), 57–68; "Actualité d'Eschyle," *RUL*, 7 (1952), 105–19; "Les mythes grecs dans la tragédie française contemporaine," *RUL*, 8 (1954), 663–70; "Entretien national sur l'Humanisme," *Culture*, 16 (1955), 3–27; "Alfred de Vigny et l'antiquité grecque," *TRSC*, 50 (1956), 57–67; "Etat présent des travaux sur Sophocle," *RUL*, 14 (1959), 116–30; "Denys d'Halicarnasse et le Traité de l'arrangement des mots," *TRSC*, 54 (1960), 43–52; "Trois Cultures et Sagesse," *RUL*, 15 (1960), 239–53; "Le mythe de Prométhée dans la littérature ancienne et dans la littérature contemporaine," *RUL*, 16 (1961), 36–48; "La Tradition du Nouveau," *RUL*, 17 (1962), 224–48. (C) *Bull de l'Association Guillaume Budé, CJ, Culture, ESC, HAC Bull, L'Instruction Publique, Phoenix, RUL, TRSC.* (D) Traduction française, la première du genre, de *An Apologie for Poetry* (1595) par Sir Philip Sidney (travail terminé, avec introduction, notes et commentaires); traduction française du *Traité de l'arrangement des mots* par Denys d'Halicarnasse (travail terminé, reste à finir l'introduction, à recenser les meilleurs manuscrits du texte grec et à préparer une édition critique); essais d'histoire et de littérature grecques (ouvrage presque terminé).

LECHEVALIER, JEAN: (B) "Sur la manière de donner une indication de date en latin et en français," *ESC*, 37 (1957), 32–3; "En marge du concours intercollégial de version latin," *ESC*, 37 (1958), 62–4; "Etude d'une phrase de Tite-Live comportant un double liaison," *ESC*, 38 (1959), 41–2; supplément à l'article précédent, *ESC*, 38 (1959), 39; "Pourquoi et comment scander des vers latins," *ESC*, 41 (1962), 15–21. (C) *ESC*.

MCGILL UNIVERSITY

GARSTANG, J. B.: (A) *The Story of Jericho* (London, 1948), xv + 200 pp. + 19 plates, 24 figures, 2 maps. (B) "The Tragedy of Turnus," *Phoenix*, 4 (1950), 47–58; "The Crime of Helen and the Concept of *fatum* in the *Aeneid*," *CJ*, 57 (1962), 337–45; "*Deos Latio*: Western Asia Minor and the Gods of Aeneas," *Vergilius*, 8 (1962), 18–26. (D) A study of Vergil's technique of "integration," with special reference to the route of the Trojans from Troy to Latium, and a note on *hybris* in *Aeneid* 9, 176–755 (both nearing completion).

GORDON, C. D.: (A) *The Age of Attila* (Ann Arbor, Mich., 1960), xxi + 228 pp. (C) *Phoenix*. (D) A modern version of Gavin Douglas's *Aeneid* (in hands of publisher for examination).

SCHACHTER, A.: (B) "Horse Coins from Tanaga," *Numismatic Chronicle*, sixth series, 18 (1958), 43–6; "A Note on the Reorganization of the Thespian Museia," *Numismatic Chronicle*, seventh series, 1 (1961), 67–70; "Inscriptions from Boeotia: A Note," *Annual Br School of Athens*, 56 (1961), 176–8.

WOLOCH, G. MICHAEL: (B) "Athenian Trainers in the Aeginetan Odes of Pindar and Bacchylides," *Classical World*, 56 (1963), 102–4. (C) *Classical World*. (D) Prosopography of Eastern Roman Empire (beginning).

MCMASTER UNIVERSITY

McKAY, ALEXANDER GORDON: (A) *Athens and Macedon: A Study of Relations from the Sixth to the Mid-Fifth Century B.C.* (doctoral dissertation, Princeton University, 1950), 222 pp. (microfilm), resumé, *Dissertation Abstracts*, 15 (1955), 564; *Naples and Campania, Texts and Illustrations* (Vergilian Society of America, 1962), x + 265 pp.; *Ancient Rome, the City and the Monuments: Ancient Latium and Etruria* (Vergilian Society of America, 1962), 76 pp. (B) "Herodotus and Alexander I of Macedon,"

TAPA, 80 (1949), 428–9; "A Survey of Recent Work on Aeschylus," *CW*, 48 (1955), 145–50, 153–9; "The Greeks at Cumae," *Vergilian Digest*, 3 (1957), 5–11; "Latin Studies in Canada," *Romanitas*, 5 (1962), 323–31. (C) *AJP, CJ, Classical News and Views, Classical World* (associate editor, regular column "In the Journals"), *Phoenix, Romanitas, Vergilius, Wat R* (Associate Editor), *Yearbook of General and Comp Lit.* (D) Masters of Campanian Painting: The Mural Art of Herculaneum, Pompeii, and Stabiae (nearing completion); Ancient Latium and Etruria: The Cities and the Monuments (texts and illustrations) (completed MS.); Pliny's Correspondence: A Selection in Translation (nearing completion); (with D. M. Shepherd) Roman Lyric Poetry: A Textbook for Colleges and Universities (nearing completion); The Greek and Roman Cities of Sicily (texts and illustrations) (MS. completed).

TRACY, HERMAN LLOYD: (A) (with D. Breslove and A. G. Hooper) *A Latin Reader for Canadian Schools* (Toronto, 1959), xxiv + 157 pp. (B) "Plato as Satirist," *CJ*, 33 (1937), 153–62; "An Intellectual Factor in Aesthetic Pleasure," *Ph R*, 50 (1941), 498–508; "Notes on Plutarch's Biographical Method," *CJ*, 37 (1942), 213–21; "Aristotle on Aesthetic Pleasure," *CP*, 41 (1946), 43–6; "*Aeneid* IV: Tragedy or Melodrama?," *CJ*, 41 (1946), 199–202; "Horace's *Ars Poetica*: A Systematic Argument," *Greece and Rome*, 17 (1948), 104–15; "The Pattern of Vergil's *Aeneid* I–VI," *Phoenix*, 4 (1950), 1–8; "Thought-sequence in the Ode," *Phoenix*, 5 (1951), 108–18; "Dramatic Art in Aeschylus' *Agamemnon*," *CJ*, 47 (1952), 215–18; "Hades in Montage," *Phoenix*, 8 (1954), 136–41; "Double Tableaux in Greek Tragedy," *CJ*, 53 (1958), 338–45. (C) *CJ, Phoenix, QQ.* (D) Articles on "*Fata Deum* and the Action of the *Aeneid*" and "The Lyric Poets' Repertoire," both prepared for oral delivery (being revised, nearly ready for publication).

UNIVERSITY OF MANITOBA

BERRY, EDMUND G.: (A) *Emerson's Plutarch* (Cambridge, Mass., 1961), ix + 337 pp. (B) "Hamlet and Suetonius," *Phoenix*, 2 (1947–8), 73–81; "The *De Liberis Educandis* of Pseudo-Plutarch," *HSCP*, 63 (1958), 387–99; "Notes on Montaigne's Plutarch," in *Studies in Honor of Ullman* (*Classical Bull*, 1960), 133–5. (C) *CJ, Phoenix, QQ.*

EAGLE, EDWIN D.: (B) "Cataline and the *Concordia Ordinum*," *Phoenix*, 3 (1949), 15–30; "*In Principio Verbum*," *CJ*, 50 (1955), 225–332.

MORRIS, K. DON: (B) "Horror and Sensationalism in the Works of Seneca and Lucan," *Kentucky FLQ*, 8 (1961), 15–21. (D) "The Classicist: A Modern Schizophrenic" (to be published in *Classical Outlook*, spring, 1963); "Lucan: The Slighted Poet" (to be published in *CJ*, fall, 1963); "Notes on Lucan's Concept of Duality" (ready for final revision).

MEMORIAL UNIVERSITY OF NEWFOUNDLAND

REARDON, B. P.: (D) Lucian: Selected Pieces (a translation with introduction, accepted for publication by Library of Liberal Arts, New York); Lucian: A Writer in His Age (general book on Lucian and second century A.D., to be finished by summer, 1963).

MOUNT ALLISON UNIVERSITY

CRAKE, J. E. A.: (B) "The Annals of the Pontifex Maximus," *CP*, 35 (1940), 375–86; "Roman Politics from 215 to 209 B.C.," *Phoenix*, 17 (1963), 123–30.   (C) *Phoenix*.

UNIVERSITY OF NEW BRUNSWICK

CATTLEY, R. E. D.: (B) "Art of Punning," *Atlantic Advocate*, 51 (1961), 77–81.   (C) *Atlantic Advocate, Classical News and Views, Phoenix*.   (D) Introduction for *The Mummer's Play of St. George* (to be published by University of New Brunswick Press); article on The Classical Travellers' Guild—the aims, and an account of the cruise, July, 1962.

MILHAM, MARY ELLA: (A) *A Glossarial Index to De Re Coquinaria of Apicius* (Madison, Wis., 1952), iv + 211 pp.; (co-author) *College English I* and (sole author) *College English II* (Madison, Wis., 1952), approx. 150 pp. each.   (B) "Some Late Latin Peculiarities of *piper*," *RP*, 7 (1954), 346–7; "Decalogue for General Classics," *CJ*, 53 (1957), 106–7; "Aspects of Non-technical Vocabulary in Apicius," *AJP*, 80 (1959), 67–75; "An Inventory of the Double Accusative in Apicius," *CP*, 54 (1959), 40–2; "*Alb*-roots Derivatives in Apicius," *TAPA*, 91 (1960), 142–5; "Case and Prepositional Usage in Apicius," *Glotta*, 34 (1960/61), 276–302.   (D) Apicius, *De Re Coquinaria*, a new critical edition (to be submitted to Teubner Press at Leipzig by April 1, 1963); "Vat. Urb. lat. 1146 as Chief MS. of Apicius" (will be completed by May, 1963, and will be offered to *CQ* or *Philologus*); "Toward a Stemma of Apicius" (should be ready by Dec., 1963, for publication in *Italia Mediaevale e Umanistica*).

SMITH, LEONARD CAMPBELL: (B) "The Chronology of Books XVIII–XX of Diodorus Siculus," *AJP*, 82 (1961), 283–90; "Demochares of Leuconoe and the Dates of His Exile," *Historia*, 11 (1962), 114–18.   (C) *AJP, Historia, JRS, J Hellenic S*.   (D) "Date of Re-founding of League of Corinth by Demetrius Poliorcetes" (complete except for final revision, few additional notes); "The Water-Nymph Coventina and Her Cult in Britain and Spain" (awaiting more material through Inter-Library Loan); "Possible Sighting of a Super-Nova from Greece in 303/2 B.C." (ready for publication, subject to final check).

QUEEN'S UNIVERSITY

REESOR, MARGARET E.: (B) "The Stoic Categories," *AJP*, 78 (1957), 63–82; "The Meaning of Anaxagoras," *CP*, 55 (1960), 1–8; "Stoicism" for the *Enc Amer*.   (C) *AJP, CP*.   (D) "The Master Argument of Diodorus Cronus" (article, almost completed).

UNIVERSITY OF SASKATCHEWAN

LEDDY, J. F.: (A) *The Humanities in an Age of Science* (Charlottetown, P.E.I., 1961), 39 pp.   (B) "Tradition and Change in Quintilian," *Phoenix*, 7 (1953), 47–56; "Toynbee and the History of Rome," *Phoenix*, 11 (1957), 139–52.   (C) *HAC Bull, Phoenix, QQ*.   (D) An English translation of Thomas Willis's *Cerebri Anatome*, about 65,000 words in length, for the tercentenary edition by McGill University Press early in 1964 (nearing completion).

UNIVERSITY OF TORONTO—UNIVERSITY COLLEGE

GOOLD, G. P.: (A) (with Maurice Pope) *The Cretan Linear A Script* (Cape Town, 1955); (introduction to) Richard Bentley, *Epistola ad Joannem Millium* (Toronto, 1962), 154 pp.   (B) "De Fonte Codicum Manilianorum," *Rheinisches Museum für Philologie*, 97 (1954), 359–72; "Observationes in Codicem Matritensem M. 31," *Rheinisches Museum für Philologie*, 99 (1956), 9–17; "A Lost Manuscript of Lucretius," *Acta Classica*, 1 (1958), 21–30; "A New Text of Catullus," *Phoenix*, 12 (1958), 93–116; "Adversaria Maniliana," *Phoenix*, 13 (1959), 93–112; "First Thoughts on the Dyscolus," *Phoenix*, 13 (1959), 139–60; "Homer and the Alphabet," *TAPA*, 91 (1960), 272–91; "A Greek Professorial Circle at Rome," *TAPA*, 92 (1961), 168–92. (C) *Phoenix.*   (D) "Richard Bentley: A Tercentenary Commemoration," to appear in *HSCP*, 1963 (completed); critical notes on the text of Ovid's amatory poems (completed); a biography of Richard Bentley (recently begun).

HEICHELHEIM, F. M.: (A) *Die Auswärtige Bevölkerung im Ptolemäerreich* (Leipzig, 1925), viii + 109 pp.; *Wirtschaftliche Schwankungen der Zeit von Alexander bis Augustus* (Jena, 1930), iv + 142 pp.; *Wirtschaftsgeschichte des Altertums vom Paläolithikum bis zur Völkerwanderung der Germanen, Slawen und Araber* (2 vols., Leiden, 1939), xiv + 1239 pp.; (editor with E. N. Adler and I. G. Tait) *The Adler Papyri* (the Greek texts) (Oxford, 1939), viii + 118 pp. + 16 plates; *Sylloge Nummorum Graecorum vol. IV, Fitzwilliam Museum: Leake and General Collections*, Parts 1–5 (London, 1940–58), 72 plates; (with Elemer Balogh) *Political Refugees in Ancient Greece, from the Period of the Tyrants to Alexander the Great* (Johannesburg, 1943), xvi + 134 pp.; *Byzantinische Seiden* (*Byzantine Silks, Soieries byzantines*) (Basel, 1949, 1953), 25 pp. (in German, English, and French); (trans.) Luigi Einaudi, *Greatness and Decline of Planned Economy in the Hellenistic World* (Berne, 1950), 18 pp.; (trans. with J. Stephens) *An Ancient Economic History from the Paleolithic Age to the Migration of the Germanic, Slavic, and Arabic Nations* (Rev. and complete English ed., vol. I, Leiden, 1958), xii + 542 pp.; (with A. Grohmann) *Die Arabischen Papyri aus der Giessener Universitäts-Bibliothek* (Giessen, 1960), xii + 94 pp. + 12 plates; (with C. A. Yeo) *A History of the Roman People* (Englewood Cliffs, N.J., and London, 1962), xv + 480 pp.; *A Chronological Table of Hellenistic History* (Oslo, 1962), 20 pp.   (B) "Zum Verfassungsdiagramm von Kyrene," *Klio*, 21 (1927), 175–82; "Die Ausbreitung der Münzgeldwirtschaft und der Wirtschaftsstil im archaischen Griechenland," *Schmollers Jahrbuch*, 55 (1931), 229–54; "Zu Pap. Bad. 37. Ein Beitrag zur römischen Geldgeschichte unter Trajan," *Klio*, 25 (1932), 124–31; "Zum Ablauf der Währungskrise des römischen Imperiums im dritten Jahrhundert n. Chr.," *Klio*, 26 (1933), 96–113; "Griechische Staatskunde von 1902–1932 (1934)," *Bursians Jahresberichte über die Fortschritte der klassischen Altertumswissenschaft*, Supplement 250 (1935), 145–289; "Roman Syria," in T. Frank, *Economic Survey of Ancient Rome*, IV, 2 (1938), 181–258; "The Cairo Genizah," *Jewish Outlook*, July 1948, 6; "Ugarit and Elijah," *Jewish Outlook*, Aug. 1948, 4; "The Cross Hill Excavation," *Archaeological Newsletter*, 12 (May 17, 1949), 94 f.; "Modern Forgeries in the Mildenhall Treasure?" *Symbolae Osloenses*, 27 (1949), 141–2; "Ezra's Palestine and

Periclean Athens," *Zeitschrift für Religions- und Geistesgeschichte*, 3 (1951), 251–3; "A Forgotten Consul Suffectus?" *Epigraphica*, 2 (1951), 61–3; "The Earliest Musical Notations of Mankind and the Invention of our Alphabet," *Epigraphica*, 3 (1952), 111–15; "Roman Coins from Iceland," *Antiquity*, 26 (1952), 43–5; (with C. H. Roberts and E. G. Turner) *Catalogue of Greek and Latin Papyri in the John Rylands Library, Manchester*, 4 (Manchester, 1952), 19–66; "Autonomous Price Trends in Egypt from Alexander the Great to Heraclius I," *Museum Helveticum*, 10 (1953), 192; "The Bacchylides Paian in Toronto," *Symbolae Osloenses*, 30 (1953), 77–81; "The Wilbour Papyrus," *Historia*, 2 (1953), 129–35; "New Evidence on the Ebro Treaty," *Historia*, 3 (1954), 211–19; "On Ancient Price Trends from the Early First Millennium B.C. to Heraclius I," *Finanzarchiv*, 15 (1955), 498–511; "The Toronto Epitome of a Sicilian Historian," *Symbolae Osloenses*, 31 (1955), 88–95; "Römische Sozial- und Wirtschaftsgeschichte," in F. Valjavec, ed., *Historia Mundi*, 4 (Berne and Munich, 1956), 397–488; "Effects of Classical Antiquity on the Land," in W. L. Thomas, Jr., ed., *Man's Role in Changing the Face of the Earth* (Chicago, 1956), 165–82; "Man's Role in Changing the Face of the Earth in Classical Antiquity," *Kyklos*, 9 (1956), 318–55; "The Historical Date for the Final Memnon Myth," *Rheinisches Museum für Philologie*, C (1957), 259–63; "Pap. Oxy. 2088: A Fragment from Cato's *Origines*?" *Aegyptus*, 37 (1957), 250–8; "A New Aeschylus Fragment?" *Symbolae Osloenses*, 34 (1958), 15–18; (with L. H. Neatby) "The Early Roman Currency in the Light of Recent Research," *Acta Antiqua*, 8 (1960), 51–85.   (C) Pauly-Wissowa, *Realenzyklopädie der klassischen Altertumswissenschaft* (numerous articles about Celtic gods, ancient economic history, etc.), *Encyclopaedia of the Social Sciences, Oxford Classical Dictionary, Der Kleine Pauly*.

NORWOOD, FRANCES: (B) "Hero and Leander," *Phoenix*, 4 (1950), 9–20; "Cognate Accusative Relative Clauses in Greek," *AJP*, 73 (1952), 281–8; "The Tripartite Eschatology of *Aeneid* 6," *CP*, 49 (1954), 15–26; "The Magic Pilgrimage of Apuleius," *Phoenix*, 10 (1956), 1–12.   (C) *CP, Phoenix*.   (D) Review for *Phoenix* (in press); review for *CP* (to be submitted in January, 1963); article on the *relegatio* of Ovid (completed); critical study of Apuleius (a projected book on a subject on which the author has already given a public lecture and several graduate courses, and published an article).

RIST, J. M.: (B) "The Order of the Later Dialogues of Plato," *Phoenix*, 14 (1960), 207–21; "Plotinus on Matter and Evil," *Phronesis*, 6 (1961), 154–66; "The *Parmenides* Again," *Phoenix*, 16 (1962), 1–14; "The Indefinite Dyad and Intelligible Matter in Plotinus," *CQ*, 12 (1962), 99–107. (C) *CQ, Classical World, MS, Phronesis, Phoenix*.   (D) Eros and Psyche: Studies in Plato, Plotinus, and Origen (to be published, fall, 1964); articles, mostly on Plotinus, for *Phoenix, TAPA, Arch für die Gesch der Philos, MS, Dialogue, Phronesis* (submitted); "In Search of the Divine Denis," in W. S. McCullough, ed., The Seed of Wisdom (to be published, spring, 1964).

RUDD, W. J. N.: (B) "The Poet's Defence," *CQ*, 5 (1955), 142–56; "The Names in Horace's Satires," *CQ*, 10 (1960), 161–78; "Patterns in Horatian Lyric," *AJP*, 81 (1960), 373–92; "Horace's Encounter with the Bore,"

Phoenix, 15 (1961), 79–96; "Horace, *Satires* 1.6," *Phoenix*, 15 (1961), 196–212. (C) *AJP, CQ, Phoenix.* (D) A book on the *Satires* of Horace (nearing completion).

THOMPSON, D. F. S.: (A) (ed., with H. C. Porter) *Erasmus and Cambridge: The Cambridge Letters of Erasmus* (Toronto, 1963), x + 233 pp. (B) "The Latin Epigram in Scotland: The Sixteenth Century," *Phoenix*, 11 (1957), 63–78; "Aspects of Unity in Catullus 64," *CJ*, 57 (1961), 49–57. (C) *Phoenix.* (D) A book on the poet Catullus (MS. not yet completed); an article on some non-literary uses of paper in ancient Rome (MS. with *Phoenix*).

WALLACE, W. P.: (A) (with Mary Wallace) *Asklepiades of Samos* (Oxford Univ. Press, 1941), xv + 107 pp.; *The Euboian League and its Coinage* (New York, 1956), xi + 180 pp. + 16 plates.   (B) "An Eretrian Proxeny Decree of the Early Fifth Century," *Hesperia*, 5 (1936), 273–84; "The Egyptian Expedition and the Chronology of the Decade 460–450 B.C.," *TAPA*, 67 (1936), 252–60; (with Mary Wallace) "Catalogue of Greek and Roman Coins at the University of Colorado," *U of Colorado St*, 25 (1938), 237–78; supplement to above, *U of Colorado St*, C1 (1941), 159–62; "Meleager and the 'Soros,' " *TAPA*, 70 (1939), 191–202; "The Demes of Eretria," *Hesperia*, 16 (1947), 115–46; "Greek Coins and Greek History," *Phoenix*, 1 (1947), 30–5, reprinted in *Can Numismatic J* (1959), 330–6; "The Public Seal of Athens," *Phoenix*, 3 (1949), 70–3; "Some Eretrian Mint Magistrates," *Phoenix*, 4 (1950), 21–6; "The Spartan Invasion of Attica in 431 B.C.," in Mary White, ed., *Studies in Honour of Gilbert Norwood* (Toronto, 1952), 80–4; "Kleomenes, Marathon, the Helots, and Arkadia," *J Hellenic St*, 74 (1954), 32–5; "Impurities in Euboean Monetary Silver," Amer. Numismatic Society, *Museum Notes*, 6 (1955), 35–67; "The Coinage of the Euboian League," *Archaeology*, 8 (1955), 264–7; "Loans to Karystos about 370 B.C.," *Phoenix*, 16 (1962), 15–28. (C) *Phoenix.* (D) "The Coinage and History of Karystos," to be one of the "Numismatic Notes and Monographs" of the Amer. Numismatic Society (begun); "The Early Coinages of Athens and Euboia" and "The Meeting-point of the Histiaian and Macedonian Tetrobols" (completed articles for the *Numismatic Chronicle*); articles on prosopography of Korystos, the sixth-century laws of Eretria, Thucydides, and the Histiaian Tetrobols (in hand).

WOODBURY, LEONARD: (B) "The Epilogue of Pindar's *Second Pythian*," *TAPA*, 76 (1945), 11–30; "Pindar, *Isthmian* 4.19 F.," *TAPA*, 78 (1947), 368–75; "The Seal of Theognis," in Mary White, ed., *Studies in Honour of Gilbert Norwood* (Toronto, 1952), 20–41; "Simonides on *Arete*," *TAPA*, 84 (1953), 135–63; "The Tongue and the Whetstone: Pindar, *Ol.* 6.82–3," *TAPA*, 86 (1955), 31–9; "Parmenides on Names," *HSCP*, 63 (1958), 145–60; "Apollodorus, Xenophanes, and the Foundation of Massilia," *Phoenix*, 15 (1961), 134–55. (C) *CP, HSCP, Phoenix, TAPA.* (D) Studies in the history of early Greek thought—work on Protagoras of Abdera is most advanced.

UNIVERSITY OF TORONTO—VICTORIA COLLEGE

McLEOD, WALLACE E.: (A) *The Family of Richard Vanderburgh of Richmond Hill (1797–1869)* (privately printed, 1962) ii + 32 pp.   (B) "An

Unpublished Egyptian Composite Bow in the Brooklyn Museum," *Amer J Arch*, 62 (1958), 397–401; "Egyptian Composite Bows in New York," *Amer J Arch*, 66 (1962), 13–19; "Boudoron, an Athenian Fort on Salamis," *Hesperia*, 29 (1960), 316–23; "Oral Bards at Delphi," *TAPA*, 92 (1961), 317–25. (C) *Amer J Arch, Hesperia, TAPA, Phoenix, J Soc Archer-Antiquaries*. (D) "Kiveri and Thermisi" (completed, for *Hesperia*); "Inscribed Pottery of the Middle Helladic Period at Lerna" (preliminary catalogue completed, commentary complete in outline).

MONTMOLLIN, D. DE: (A) *La Poétique d'Aristote; Texte primitif et additions ultérieures* (Neuchâtel, 1951), 375 pp. (C) *Phoenix*. (D) Edition of Aristotle's *Poetics* (not yet ready for publication); several articles on Homer's text and the Homeric question; an article on "Platon et la méthode d'Hippocrate" (partly completed).

UNIVERSITY OF TORONTO—TRINITY COLLEGE

CONACHER, D. J.: (B) "Some Euripidean Techniques in the Dramatic Treatment of Myth," *UTQ*, 22 (1952), 55–71; "Orestes as Existentialist Hero," *PQ*, 33 (1954), 404–17; "Theme and Techniques in the *Philoctetes* and *Oedipus* of André Gide," *UTQ*, 24 (1955), 121–35; "Theme, Plot, and Technique in the *Heracles* of Euripides," *Phoenix*, 9 (1955), 139–52; "Religious and Ethical Attitudes in Euripides' *Suppliants*," *TAPA*, 87 (1956), 8–26; "The Paradox of Euripides' *Ion*," *TAPA*, 90 (1959), 20–39; "Euripides' *Hecuba*," *AJP*, 82 (1961), 1–26; "Freedom and Necessity in Greek Tragedy," *QQ*, 67 (1961), 514–29; "A Problem in Euripides' *Hippolytus*," *TAPA*, 92 (1961), 37–44. (C) *Phoenix, TAPA, Can For*. (D) A literary-critical study of Euripidean drama (about three-quarters finished).

DALZELL, ALEXANDER: (B) "Public Recitation at Rome," *Hermathena*, 86 (1955), 20–8; "Maecenas and the Poets," *Phoenix*, 10 (1956), 151–62; "Some Recent Work on the Text of Lucretius," *Phoenix*, 14 (1960), 96–105. (C) *Phoenix*. (D) A study of Roman literary patronage.

GRUBE, GEORGE M. A.: (A) *Plato's Thought* (London, 1935), 320 pp. (paper back, Boston, 1958); *The Drama of Euripides* (London, 1941, 1961), 456 pp.; (trans. with introduction and commentary) *Aristotle on Poetry and Style* (*Poetics* and *Rhetoric*) (New York, 1958), 110 pp.; (trans., with introduction and notes) *Longinus on Great Writing* (*On the Sublime*) (New York, 1957), 66 pp.; (trans., with introduction, commentary, and appendices) *A Greek Critic: Demetrius on Style* (Toronto, 1961), viii + 172 pp.; (B) "The Authenticity of the *Hippias Major*," *CQ*, 20 (1926), 134–48; "Two Notes on the *Hippias Major*," *Classical R*, 40 (1926), 188–9; "Plato's Theory of Beauty," *Monist* (1927), 269–88; "Marriage Laws in Plato's *Republic*," *CQ*, 21 (1927), 95–9; "The God of Plato," *CJRT*, 6 (1929), 165–72; "The Language and Logic of the *Hippias Major*," *CP*, 24 (1929), 369–75; "The Sense of Taste in *Timaeus* 65b–66c," *CP*, 25 (1930), 72–5; "Note on *Phaedo* 104d, 1–3," *CP*, 26 (1931), 197–9; "The *Cleitophon* of Plato," *CP*, 26 (1931), 302–8; "The Composition of the World-Soul in the *Timaeus*," *CP*, 27 (1932), 80–2; "The Structural Unity of the *Protagoras*," *CQ*, 27 (1933), 203–7; "Dionysus in the *Bacchae*," *TAPA*, 66 (1935), 37–54; "Platonist or Aristotelian," *Phoenix*, 2 (1947–8), 15–28; "Why

Study the Classics in This Busy World?" *UTQ*, 19 (1949), 81–92; "Dionysius of Halicarnassus on Thucydides," *Phoenix*, 4 (1950), 95–110; "Antisthenes was No Logician," *TAPA*, 81 (1950), 16–27; "Thrasymachus, Theophrastus, and Dionysius of Halicarnassus," *AJP*, 73 (1952), 251–67; "The Gods of Homer," *Phoenix*, 5 (1951), 62–75 (also in Mary White, ed., *Studies in Honour of Gilbert Norwood*, Toronto, 1952); "Three Greek Critics," *UTQ*, 21 (1952), 345–61; "Theophrastus as a Literary Critic," *TAPA*, 83 (1952), 172–83; "Greek Medicine and the Greek Genius," *Phoenix*, 8 (1954), 123–35; "Rhetoric and Literary Criticism," *Quarterly J Speech* (1956), 339–44; "Dionysius of Halicarnassus: A Greek Literary Critic," *TRSC*, 50 (1956), 9–19; "Notes on the περὶ ὕψους," *AJP*, 78 (1957), 355–74; "A Note on Aristotle's Definition of Tragedy," *Phoenix*, 8 (1958), 26–30; "Theodorus of Gadara," *AJP*, 80 (1959), 337–65; "Educational, Rhetorical, and Literary Theory in Cicero," *Phoenix*, 16 (1962), 234–57.   (C) *AJP*, *Phoenix*.   (D) Marcus Aurelius' Meditations (now in press); Ancient Literary Theory and Criticism (to be completed by summer, 1963).

PHILIP, J. A.: (B) "The Biographical Tradition—Pythagoras," *TAPA*, 90 (1959), 185–94; "Mimesis in the *Sophistes* of Plato," *TAPA*, 92 (1961), 453–68; "The Fragments of the Presocratic Philosophers," *Phoenix*, 10 (1956), 116–23; "Parmenides' Theory of Knowledge," *Phoenix*, 12 (1958), 63–6.   (C) *Phoenix*, *TAPA*.   (D) Pythagoras—a monograph.

WHITE, MARY E.: (A) (ed.) *Studies in Honour of Gilbert Norwood* (Toronto, 1952), xvii + 278 pp.   (B) "The Greek and Roman Contribution," chapter 1 in *The Heritage of Western Culture* (Toronto, 1952), 1–25; "The Duration of the Samian Tyranny," *J Hellenic St*, 74 (1954), 36–43; "Greek Tyranny," *Phoenix*, 9 (1955), 1–18; "The Dates of the Orthagorids," *Phoenix*, 12 (1958), 2–14; "Greek Colonization," *J Economic Hist*, 21 (1961), 443–54.   (C) *Phoenix* (editor); *J Int Aff*.   (D) "Some Agiad Dates: Pausanias and His Sons" (completed for *Historia*); a study of the Peisistratid tyranny in Athens (maps, plans, illustrations all prepared, writing more than half done).

UNIVERSITY OF TORONTO—ST. MICHAEL'S COLLEGE

FISHWICK, D.: (A) (co-author) *The Foundations of the West* (Toronto, 1963).   (B) "The Imperial Cult in Roman Britain," *Phoenix*, 15 (1961), 159–73, 213–29.   (C) *Phoenix*.   (D) "The Talpioth Ossuaries Again" (submitted); "Notes on the ROTAS-SATOR Square" (submitted); "The Imperial Cult in Africa" and "The Imperial Cult in Roman Germany" (in preparation).

LEE, M. OWEN: (A) (associate editor) *The New Saint Basil Hymnal* (Cincinnati, 1958).   (B) "Orpheus and Eurydice: Some Modern Versions," *CJ*, 56 (1961), 307–13; "Orpheus and Eurydice: Blueprint for Opera," *CMJ*, 6 (1962), 23–36.   (D) Articles on Virgil, Catullus, and Plautus (ready for publication).

UNIVERSITY OF VICTORIA

SMITH, PETER L.: (D) Research on aspects of Latin lyric poetry and on Euripidean imagery (both embryonic).

UNIVERSITY OF WESTERN ONTARIO

GERBER, DOUGLAS E.: (B) "Pindar, *Pythian* 2.56," *TAPA*, 91 (1960), 100–8; "Pindar, *Nemean* 7.31," *AJP*, 84 (1963), 182–8; "What Time Can Do (Pindar, *Nemean* 1.46–7)," *TAPA*, 93 (1962), 30–6. (C) *AJP*, *Phoenix, TAPA*. (D) A book on the Greek Lyric poets (to be completed in late 1964).

RAYMOND, A. E.: (A) *The Literary Structure of Ritual Passages in Sophocles* (Chicago, 1949), 121 pp. (on microfilm). (B) "What was Anchises' Ghost to Dido?" *Phoenix*, 6 (1952), 66–8. (C) *Phoenix.*

Medieval Studies

PONTIFICAL INSTITUTE OF MEDIAEVAL STUDIES

BOYLE, L. E.: (B) "The *Oculus Sacerdotis* and Some Other Works of William of Pagula," *Trans Royal Hist Soc*, 5 (1955), 81–110; "The Constitution *Cum ex eo* of Boniface VIII: Education of Parochial Clergy," *MS*, 24 (1962), 263–302. (C) *MS, Traditio.* (D) Edition of the *Oculus Sacerdotis* by William of Pagula.

ESCHMANN, I. T.: (A) *On Kingship* (Toronto, 1949), 119 pp. (B) "Bonum Commune melius est quam Bonum Unius, eine Studie über den Wertvorrang des Personalen bei Thomas von Aquin," *MS*, 6 (1944), 62–120; "A Catalogue of St. Thomas's Works," in Etienne Gilson, *The Christian Philosophy of St. Thomas Aquinas* (New York, 1956), 381–437. (C) *MS.*

FLAHIFF, G. B.: (B) "The Use of Prohibitions by Clerics against Ecclesiastical Courts in England," *MS*, 3 (1941), 101–16; "The Writ of Prohibition to Court Christian in the Thirteenth Century," *MS*, 6 (1944), 261–313, and 7 (1945), 229–90; "*Deus Non Vult*: A Critic of the Third Crusade," *MS*, 9 (1947), 162–88. (C) *MS.*

GILSON, ETIENNE: (A) *Le Thomisme* (5th ed., Paris, 1945), 552 pp.; *Jean Duns Scot* (Paris, 1952), 700 pp.; *L'Esprit de la Philosophie Médiévale* (2nd ed., Paris, 1948), 446 pp.; *History of Christian Philosophy in the Middle Ages* (New York, 1955), 829 pp.; *Elements of Christian Philosophy* (New York, 1960), 357 pp.; *Being and Some Philosophers* (2nd ed., Toronto, 1952), 235 pp.; *The Philosopher and Theology* (trans. by Cécile Gilson; New York, 1962), 236 pp.; (with Thomas Langan) *Modern Philosophy: Descartes to Kant* (New York, 1963), xvii + 570 pp. (B) "Autour de Pomponazzi: Problématique de l'âme en Italie au début du XVIᵉ siècle," *Arch d'Hist Doctrinale et Littéraire du Moyen-âge*, 28 (1961), 163–274. (C) *Arch d'Hist Doctrinale et Littéraire du Moyen-âge, MS.*

HARING, NICHOLAS: (A) *Die Theologie der Erfurter Augustiner—Eremiten Bartholomäus Arnoldi von Usingen* (Limburg, 1939), 299 pp. (B) "The Commentary of Gilbert, Bishop of Poitiers, on Boethius' *Contra Eutychen et Nestorium*," *Arch d'Hist Doctrinale et Litteraire du Moyen-âge*, 21 (1954), 241–357; "A Christmas Sermon by Gilbert of Poitiers," *MS*, 23 (1961), 126–35; "The Porretans and the Greek Fathers," *MS*, 24 (1962), 181–209; "The *Liber de diversitate naturae et personae* by Hugh of Honau," *Arch d'Hist Doctrinale et Litteraire du Moyen-âge*, 24 (1962), 103–216. (C) *Arch d'Hist Doctrinale et Litteraire, MS.* (D) The works of Clarembald, Archdeacon of Arras.

MCLAUGHLIN, TERENCE PATRICK: (A) *Le très ancien droit monastique de l'occident* (Paris, 1935), xxii + 273 pp.; (ed.) *Summa Parisiensis on the Decretum Gratiani* (Toronto, 1952), xxxiii + 272 pp.; (ed.) *The Church and the Reconstruction of the Modern World: The Social Encyclicals of Pope Pius XI* (New York, n.d.), 433 pp.   (B) "The Teaching of the Canonists on Usury," *MS*, 1 (1939), 81–147, and 2 (1940), 1–22; "The Extravagantes in the Summa of Simon of Bisignano," *MS*, 20 (1958), 167–76.   (C) *MS*.

MAURER, ARMAND A.: (A) (trans., with introduction and notes) *On Being and Essence by St. Thomas Aquinas* (Toronto, 1948), 63 pp.; (trans., with introduction and notes) *The Division and Methods of the Sciences* (from St. Thomas Aquinas's Commentary on the *De Trinitate* of Boethius) (Toronto, 1958), xxxvi + 96 pp.; *Medieval Philosophy*, vol. II of Etienne Gilson, ed., *A History of Philosophy* (New York, 1962), xxiv + 435 pp. (B) "*Esse* and *Essentia* in the Metaphysics of Siger of Brabant," *MS*, 8 (1946), 68–86; "Form and Essence in the Philosophy of St. Thomas," *MS*, 13 (1951), 165–76; "Henry of Harclay's Question on the Univocity of Being," *MS*, 16 (1954), 1–18; "St. Thomas and the Analogy of Genus," *New Scholasticism*, 29 (1955), 127–44; "Adam of Buckfield, Sententia super Secundum Metaphysicae," in J. R. O'Donnell, ed., *Nine Mediaeval Thinkers* (Toronto, 1955), 99–144; "The State of Historical Research in Siger of Brabant," *Speculum*, 31 (1956), 49–56; "Ockham's Conception of the Unity of Science," *MS*, 20 (1958), 98–112.   (C) *MS, Mod Schoolman, New Scholasticism*.   (D) The section on nineteenth- and twentieth-century American and English philosophies in vol. IV of Etienne Gilson, ed., *A History of Philosophy* (about half finished).

MUCKLE, J. T.: (A) *Algazel: Metaphysics* (Toronto, 1933), 247 pp.; *The Story of Abelard's Adversities* (Toronto, 1954), 70 pp.   (B) "Utrum Theologia sit Scientia: A Quodlibet Question of Robert Holcot," *MS*, 20 (1958), 127–53.

O'DONNELL, J. R.: (A) (ed.) *Nine Mediaeval Thinkers* (Toronto, 1955), 382 pp.   (B) "The Exigit Ordo of Nicholas of Autrecourt," *MS*, 1 (1939), 179–280; "The Syncategoremata of William of Sherwood," *MS*, 3 (1941), 46–93; "The Philosophy of Nicholas of Autrecourt and His Appraisal of Aristotle," *MS*, 4 (1942), 97–125; "The Meaning of 'Silva' in the Commentary on the *Timaeus* of Plato by Chalcidius," *MS*, 7 (1945), 1–20; "Tractatus Magistri Guillelmi Alvernensis *De Bono et Malo*," *MS*, 8 (1946), 245–99, and 18 (1956), 218–71; "The Doctrine of Being in the Philosophy of William of Auvergne," *PACPA* (1946), 220–5; "Themistius' Paraphrasis of the Posterior Analytics in Gerard of Cremona's Translation," *MS*, 20 (1958), 239–315; "A Fifteenth-Century Book of Hours–Missal," *MS*, 21 (1959), 296–303; "A Manuscript of the *de Consolatione Philosophiae* of Boethius in the Royal Ontario Museum," *Bull Div Art and Archaeology*, 24 (1956), 10–13; "Coluccio Salutati on the Poet-Teacher," *MS*, 22 (1960), 240–56; "Bernard Silvester's Commentary on the Aeneid," *MS*, 24 (1962); (trans., with introduction) "The Paraclesis of Desiderius Erasmus: An Exhortation to the Study of Christian Philosophy," in *The Wisdom of Catholicism* (New York, 1949), 519–31; (trans., with introduction and notes) "Letter of Francis Petrarch to Denis of Borgo-San Sepolcro," in *The Wisdom of Catholicism* (New York, 1949), 444–53; (trans., with introduction and notes) "Prosper of Aquitaine on Grace and Free Will," in *The*

Fathers of the Church, 7 (New York, 1949), 333–418. (C) *Latomus, Mod Schoolman, New Scholasticism, Phoenix, Speculum.* (D) Edition of Thomas of York.

OWENS, JOSEPH: (A) *The Doctrine of Being in the Aristotelian Metaphysics* (Toronto, 1951, 1957, 1961), xi + 461 pp.; *St. Thomas and the Future of Metaphysics* (Milwaukee, 1957), 97 pp.; *A History of Ancient Western Philosophy* (New York, 1959), 434 pp.; *An Elementary Christian Metaphysics* (Milwaukee, 1963), xvi + 384 pp. (B) "An Aristotelian Text Related to the Distinction of Being and Essence," *PACPA*, 21 (1946), 165–72; "Up to What Point is God Included in the Metaphysics of Duns Scotus?" *MS*, 10 (1948), 163–77; "Report of a Recent Thesis Defended at the Pontifical Institute of Mediaeval Studies," *MS*, 11 (1949), 239–45; "The Reality of the Aristotelian Separate Movers," *RM*, 3 (1950), 319–37, reprinted in J. Collins, ed., *Readings in Ancient and Mediaeval Philosophy* (Westminster, 1960), 75–81; "Theodicy, Natural Theology, and Metaphysics," *Mod Schoolman*, 28 (1951), 126–37; "Comments on Mr. Anderson's Theses," *RM*, 5 (1952), 467–9; "The Conclusion of the Prima Via," *Mod Schoolman*, 30 (1952–53), 33–53, 109–21, 203–15; "The Special Characteristics of the Scotistic Proof that God Exists," *Analecta Gregoriana*, 67 (1954), 311–27; "A Note on the Approach to Thomistic Metaphysics," *New Scholasticism*, 28 (1954), 454–76; "The Causal Proposition—Principle or Conclusion?" *Mod Schoolman*, 32 (1955), 159–71, 257–70, 323–39; "The Intelligibility of Being," *Gregorianum*, 36 (1955), 169–93; "Our Knowledge of Nature," *PACPA*, 29 (1955), 63–86; "The Number of Terms in the Suarezian Discussion of Essence and Being," *Mod Schoolman*, 34 (1957), 147–91; "Common Nature: A Point of Comparison between Thomistic and Scotistic Metaphysics," *MS*, 19 (1957), 1–14; "The Accidental and Essential Character of Being in the Doctrine of St. Thomas Aquinas," *MS*, 20 (1958), 1–40; "The Interpretation of the Heraclitean Fragments," in C. J. O'Neil, ed., *An Etienne Gilson Tribute* (Milwaukee, 1959), 148–68; "Thomistic Common Nature and Platonic Idea," *MS*, 21 (1959), 211–23; "Aristotle on Categories," *RM*, 14 (1960), 73–90; "Diversity and Community of Being in St. Thomas Aquinas," *MS*, 22 (1960), 257–302; "St. Thomas and Elucidation," *New Scholasticism*, 35 (1961), 421–44; "Unity and Essence in St. Thomas Aquinas," *MS*, 23 (1961), 240–59; "Aquinas on Infinite Regress," *Mind*, N.S., 71 (1962), 244–6. (C) *MS.* (D) Seven articles accepted for publication in near future; contributions of interrogations to Philosophical Interrogations to be published in 1963; complete revision of *The Doctrine of Being in the Aristotelian Metaphysics*, for its fourth printing in 1963; two major articles (completed but for final revision).

PEGIS, A. C.: (A) *St. Thomas and the Problem of the Soul in the Thirteenth Century* (Toronto, 1934), 213 pp.; (ed.) *Essays in Modern Scholasticism* (Westminster, 1944); (ed.) *The Basic Writings of St. Thomas Aquinas* (2 vols., New York, 1945), 1097 and 1179 pp.; *Christian Philosophy and Intellectual Freedom* (Milwaukee, 1960), 89 pp. (B) "St. Thomas and the Origin of the Idea of Creation," in *Philosophy and the Modern Mind* (Michigan, 1961); "Thomism as a Philosophy," in *Saint Thomas Aquinas and Philosophy* (Connecticut, 1961), 15–30. (D) History of Greek philosophy in Etienne Gilson, ed., *History of Philosophy*, I.

PHELAN, Rt. Rev. Mgr. GERALD B.: (A) *Feeling Experience and its*

Modalities (Louvain and London, 1925), 292 pp.; *Jacques Maritain* (New York, 1937), 57 pp.; *St. Thomas and Analogy* (Milwaukee, 1948), 56 pp.; *Some Illustrations of St. Thomas' Development of the Wisdom of St. Augustine* (Chicago, 1946); *The Wisdom of St. Anselm* (Latrobe, 1961), 62 pp.; (trans.) *On the Governance of Rulers* (De regimine principum) (Toronto, 1935), 143 pp.   (B) "Cardinal Mercier, an Appreciation," *DR*, 6 (1926), 9–17; "The Frontiers of Psychology and the Philosophy of Religion," *PACPA*, 2 (1926), 79–94; "Psychology and Ethics," *PACPA*, 4 (1928), 45–61; "The Lateran Treaty," *DR*, 9 (1930), 427–38; "Progress in Philosophy," "Presidential Address," *PACPA*, 7 (1931), 27–40; "The Sequence of Courses in Philosophy in Catholic Colleges," *National Cath Educ Ass Bull*, 29 (1932), 102–8; "The Concept of Beauty in St. Thomas Aquinas," in *Aspects of the New Scholastic Philosophy* (New York, 1932), 121–45; "The Teaching of Philosophy in Non-Catholic Universities in Canada," *L'Academie Canadienne Saint-Thomas d'Aquin*, 3 (1932) (in *AC* (1934) 85–115); *Catholic Education*, Pamphlet 7, and *Social Reconstruction, I–V*, Pamphlets 10–14 (Toronto: St. Michael's College, 1933). "An Unedited Text of Robert Grosseteste on the Subject Matter of Theology," in *Hommage à M. le Professeur Maurice de Wulf* (Louvain, 1934), 172–9; "St. Thomas' Theory of Education," *RUO*, 4 (1934), 24–8; "Aestheticism and the Liturgy," *Liturgical Arts*, 4 (1935), 87–90; "The Freedom of the Artist," *Liturgical Arts*, 5 (1936), 125–9; "The Philosophy of Education," *Proc Archdiocesan Convention of the Confraternity of Christian Doctrine* (Toronto, 1937), 30–3; "Sanctification of the Intellect," in *The Press in the Service of Faith and Religion* (Milwaukee, 1939), 30–40; "Verum Sequitur Esse Rerum," *MS*, 1 (1939), 11–22; "Person and Liberty," *PACPA*, 16 (1940), 53–69; "Theology in the Curriculum of Catholic Colleges and Universities," in *Man and Modern Secularism* (New York, 1940), 128–42; "St. Thomas and the Modern Mind," *Mod Schoolman*, 20 (1942), 37–47; "Justice and Friendship," *Thomist*, 5 (1943), 153–70; "A Note on the Formal Object of Metaphysics," in A. C. Pegis, ed., *Essays in Modern Scholasticism* (Westminster, 1944), 47–51; "Group Relations as a Philosophical and Theological Problem," *J Religious Thought* (spring-summer, 1945), 137–52; "Philosophy and the History of Ideas," *TRSC*, 40 (1946), 21–9; "The Existentialism of St. Thomas," *PACPA*, 21 (1946), 25–40; "How Can Scholarship Contribute to the Relief of International Tensions: Use of the Material Scholarship Supplies," in Lyman Bryson, Louis Finkelstein, and R. M. MacIver, eds., *Learning and World Peace* (New York, 1948), 116–21; "Artistic Liberty and Moral Responsibility," *St. Mary's Chimes*, 61 (1952), 75–81; "Being and the Metaphysicians," in *From an Abundant Spring* (P. J. Kennedy and Sons, 1952), 423–47; "The Origins and Historical Evolution of the Universities," in *The Mission of the University* (Fribourg, Switzerland, 1953), 29–46; "Humanism and Education," *Eng Cath Educ Ass Ontario* (1953), 10–15; "The Prevalent Conception of Democracy," in Malcolm Ross, ed., *Our Sense of Identity, a Book of Canadian Essays* (Toronto, 1954), 280–7; "Education and Culture," *Eng Cath Educ Ass Ontario* (1954); "Law and Morality," in J. A. McWilliams, ed., *Progress in Philosophy* (Milwaukee, 1955), 177–97; "The Being of Creatures," *PACPA*, 31 (1957), 118–25; "The Problem of Communication between Catholic and Non-Catholic Educators and Philosophers," *PACPA*, 31 (1957), 193–200; "Being, Order, and Knowledge," Cardinal Spellman–Aquinas Medalist's Address, *PACPA*, 33 (1959), 12–20; "The Pontifical Institute of Mediaeval Studies at Toronto," *Dub R* (1959), 1–14; "Philosophy and Theology—a Contrast," presidential address for 1960, *TRSC*, s. 2, 55 (1961), 97–102.   (C) *C'weal, MS, Mod Schoolman, New Scholasticism, PACPA, PhR, TRSC*.

RAFTIS, J. A.: (A) *The Estates of Ramsey Abbey* (Toronto, 1957), 341 pp.   (B) "Rent and Capital at St. Ives," *MS*, 20 (1958), 79–92; "Marc Bloch's Comparative Method and the Rural History of Mediaeval England," *MS*, 24 (1962), 349–68; "Christopher Dawson: Pioneer Historian of Unity," *Basilian Teacher*, 6 (1961), 9–22; "The Christian Mission in the Industrial Order," *Basilian Teacher*, 6 (1961), 117–24; "Western Monasticism and Economic Reorganization," *Comp St in Society and Hist*, 3 (1961), 452–69.   (D) Tenure and Mobility: Studies in the Social History of the Mediaeval English Village.

RYAN, J. J.: (A) *Saint Peter Damiani and His Canonical Sources* (Toronto, 1956), 213 pp.   (B) "Cardinal Humbert de S. Romana Ecclesia," *MS*, 20 (1958), 206–38; "Letter of an Anonymous French Reformer to a Byzantine Official in South Italy: De simoniaca heresi (Ms. Vat. lat. 3830)," *MS*, 15 (1953), 233–42.

SHEEHAN, M. M.: (A) *The Will in Medieval England* (Toronto, 1963). (B) "A List of Thirteenth-Century Wills," *Genealogists' Mag*, 13 (1961), 259–65; "The Church and Secular History," *Basilian Teacher*, 6 (1961), 23–5.

SHOOK, L. K.: (trans.) Etienne Gilson, *The Christian Philosophy of St. Thomas Aquinas* (New York, 1956), 502 pp.   (B) "The Burial Mound in *Guthlac A*," *MP*, 58 (1960), 1–10; "The Prologue of the Old-English *Guthlac A*," *MS*, 23 (1961), 294–305.   (C) *MS, MP*.   (D) The Old English Guthlac materials.

SYNAN, EDWARD A.: (B) "The Universal and Supposition in a *Logica* Attributed to Richard of Campsall," in J. R. O'Donnell, ed., *Nine Mediaeval Thinkers* (Toronto, 1955), 183–232; "The Universal in an Anti-Ockhamist Text," in C. J. O'Neil, ed., *An Etienne Gilson Tribute* (Milwaukee, 1959); "Richard of Campsall's First Question on the Prior Analytics," *MS*, 23 (1961), 305–23; "The Covenant of Husband and Wife," in John M. Oesterreicher, ed., *The Bridge* (New York, 1961–2), 4, 119–70; (with M. Raffaella de Sion) "Bahya Ibn Pakuda, Tutor of Hearts," in *The Bridge*, 4, 252–73; "Abraham Heschel and Prayer," in *The Bridge*, 1, 256–65.   (C) *MS, Speculum*.   (D) Study of the relationships between popes and the Jews during the Middle Ages (in preliminary stages of investigation).

ENGLISH STUDIES

ACADIA UNIVERSITY

JEWITT, A. R.: (B) "Charles Kingsley: An Appreciation," *DR*, 4 (1924–5), 193–202; "Early Halifax Theatres," *DR*, 5 (1925–6), 444–59.   (D) A work on Halifax theatre in the eighteenth century; studies in the thirteenth-century text of *Ancrene Wisse*.

116   THE HUMANITIES IN CANADA

KIRKCONNELL, WATSON: *Kapuskasing, An Historical Sketch*, Queen's University, Dept. of History, Bulletin No. 38 (Kingston, 1921), 15 pp.; *Victoria County Centennial History* (Lindsay, 1921), 261 pp.; *European Elegies, One Hundred Poems Chosen and Translated from European Literatures in Fifty Languages* (Ottawa, 1928), 166 pp.; *The European Heritage, A Synopsis of European Cultural Achievement* (London, 1930), 184 pp.; *The North American Book of Icelandic Verse* (New York, 1930), 228 pp.; *The Tide of Life* (Ottawa, 1930), 80 pp.; *The Magyar Muse, An Anthology of Hungarian Poetry 1400–1932, Edited and Translated, Together with Specimens from Ostiak and Vogul, Foreword by Francis Herczeg of the Hungarian Academy* (Winnipeg: Kanadai Magyar Ujsag, 1933), 228 pp.; *The Eternal Quest* (Winnipeg: Columbia Press, 1934), 136 pp.; *A Golden Treasury of Polish Lyrics, Selected, Englished and Annotated by Watson Kirkconnell, with a Foreword by Roman Dyboski, Professor in the University of Krakow* (Winnipeg: Polish Press, 1936), 109 pp.; *Canadian Overtones, An Anthology of Canadian Poetry Written Originally in Icelandic, Swedish, Norwegian, Hungarian, Italian, Greek and Ukrainian, and Now Translated and Edited with Biographical, Historical, Critical and Bibliographical Notes* (Winnipeg: Columbia Press, 1935), 104 pp.; *The Death of King Buda, A Hungarian Epic Poem by János Arany, Rendered into English Verse by Watson Kirkconnell, in Collaboration with Lulu Putnik Payerle, with a Foreword by Géza Voinovich, Secretary-General of the Hungarian Academy and Notes by Professor Arpád Berczik of the University of Budapest* (Cleveland: Benjamin Franklin Bibliophile Society, 1936), 159 pp.; *The Flying Bull, and Other Tales* (Toronto, 1940), 189 pp.; *The Quebec Tradition, An Anthology of French- Canadian Prose and Verse, Selected by Séraphin Marion and Translated into English by Watson Kirkconnell*, Collection Humanitas, Faculty of Letters, University of Montreal (Montreal, 1946), 245 pp.; (with A. S. P. Woodhouse) *The Humanities in Canada* (Ottawa, 1947), 287 pp.; (with Paul Crath) *Prince Ihor's Raid against the Polovtsi* (Saskatoon: Peter Mohyla Institute, 1947), 18 pp.; *A Little Treasury of Hungarian Verse* (Washington: American Hungarian Federation, 1947), 55 pp.; *Icelandic History in Icelandic Vocabulary* (Winnipeg: Columbia Press, 1948), 12 pp.; *Common English Loan Words in East European Languages* (Winnipeg: Ukrainian Free Academy of Sciences, 1952), 20 pp.; *Canadian Toponymy and the Cultural Stratification of Canada* (Winnipeg: Ukrainian Free Academy of Sciences, 1954), 16 pp.; *The Place of Slavic Studies in Canada* (Winnipeg: Ukrainian Free Academy of Sciences, 1958), 16 pp.; (trans., with an introductory essay by William J. Rose and notes by H. B. Segel) *Pan Tadeusz or The Last Foray in Lithuania, by Adam Mickiewicz* (Toronto, 1962), xx + 388 pp.; (trans., with C. H. Andrusyshen) *The Ukrainian Poets, 1189–1962* (Toronto, 1963), xxx + 500 pp.; (trans., with C. H. Andrusyshen) *The Poetical Works of Taras Shevchenko* (Toronto, 1964), lii + 564 pp.   (B) (selected) "Fort Henry, 1812–1914," *QQ*, 28 (1921), 1–9; "The Greek Epigram," *QQ*, 32 (1925), 225–44; "Epilogue to 'Dramatis Personae,' " *MLN*, 41 (1926), 213–19; "Linguistic Laconicism," *AJP*, 48 (1927), 34–7; "The Bunyan Tercentenary," *DR*, 8 (1928), 200–6; translations from Neruda, Heyduk, Zeyer, Vrchlicky, Machar, Brezina, Novak, Vajansky, and Hviezdoslav in Clarence A. Manning, ed., *An Anthology of Czechoslovak Verse* (New York, 1929), 72 pp.; "The Genius of Slavonic Poetry: A Comparative Study," *DR*, 9 (1930), 500–6; "A Magyar Miscellany," *SEER*, 9 (1931), 713–24; 14 (1938), 277–87; 21 (1943), 175–9; 23 (1945), 25–34; "La poésie française au Canada," *Journal des Poètes*, 2 (Bruxelles, 1932), 36–40; "Petoefi Jelentoe-sége az Uj-Világ Szempontjábol," inaugural address as honorary member of the Petoefi Society of Hungary, *A Petoefi Társaság Koezloenye* (Budapest) (Nov., 1932), 72–80; "Icelandic-Canadian Poetry," *DR*, 14 (1934), 331–44; "Ukrainian Poetry in Canada," *SEER*, 13 (1934), 139–46; "A Polish Miscellany," *SEER*, 14 (1935), 1–10; "Canada's Leading Poet: Stephan G. Stephansson," *UTQ*, 5 (1936), 266–77; "Hungary's Linguistic Isolation," *Hungarian Q* (Budapest) 1 (1936), 92–100; "Icelandic Poetry Today," *Life and Letters Today*, 15 (1936), 42–9; "Manitoba Symphony," in Rupert Lodge, ed., *Manitoba Essays* (Toronto, 1937), 432 pp.; "The New Roman Empire," *DR*, 17 (1937), 33–46; "The Poetry of Ady," *Hungarian Q*, 2 (1937), 501–14; "Recent Polish Poetry," *Life and Letters Today*, 17 (1937), 40–6; "The Rhaetoromanic Tradition," *TRSC*, s. 2 (1937), 25–31; "Letters in Canada: New Canadian Letters" (annually), *UTQ* (1937–63); "Loan-words in Latin," *MAR*, 1 (1940), 17–20; "Quintessence of Hungary," *Hungarian Q*, 3 (1938), 494–504; "A Skald in Canada," *TRSC*, s. 2 (1939), 107–21; "Endre Ady, Selected Verse," *SEER*, American Series, 3 (1944), 106–7; "Forefathers' Eve, Part III, Act I, scenes 7–9" and "To My Russian Friends," in *Poems by Adam Mickiewicz*, translated from the Polish by various hands and edited by George Rapall Noyes (New York: Polish Institute of Arts and Sciences, 1944), 298–335 and 367–8; "The Humanities in Our Time," *Canadian School Journal* (1945), 140–5, 172, also in *CF*, 33 (1945); "Some Latin Analogues of Milton," *TRSC*, s. 2 (1946), 173–89; article on "Ukrainian Literature," in *Columbia Dictionary of Modern European Literature* (New York, 1947), 829–31; "Greek History in Greek Vocabulary," *TRSC*, s. 2 (1947), 79–98; "Avitus' Epic on the Fall," *LTP* (1947), 222–42; "The Blanket of the Dark," *Baltic R* (Stockholm) (1947); "John MacLean's 'Gloomy Forest,'" *DR* (1948), 158–62; "Six Sixteenth Century Forerunners of Milton's 'Samson Agonistes,'" *TRSC*, s. 2 (1949) 73–85; "Education," in G. W. Brown, ed., *Canada* (Toronto, 1950), 436–56; "Metaphysics and Human Freedom," *Acadia Bull* (Nov., 1951); "Spanish-American Poetry," *Proc Shevchenko Scientific Society* (New York-Paris) 1 (1952); "Stephan G. Stephansson and North America," *Icelandic Canadian*, 12 (1953); "Einstein's Influence on Philosophy," *Symposium, Einstein Memorial Meeting* (Halifax, 1955); "Canadian Scholars," *Acadia Bull* (April, 1955); "The Tapestry of Hungarian Poetry," in *World Literature* (Pittsburgh, 1956), 134–53; "Thoughts on Education," in R. C. Chalmers and John A. Irving, eds., *Challenge and Response* (Toronto, 1959); "Religion and Philosophy: An English-Canadian Point of View," in Mason Wade, ed., *Canadian Dualism* (Toronto and Québec, 1960), 41–55; "A Scotch-Canadian Discovers Poland," in Victor Turek, ed., *The Polish Past in Canada* (Toronto, 1960), 57–70; "Homesickness in Several Minor Keys," *TRSC*, s. 2 (1961), 57–62). (C) *DR, CHR, LTP, QQ, RUO, SEER, TRSC, UTQ*. (D) The Invincible Samson: The Theme of Samson Agonistes in World Literature, with Translations of the Major Analogues (book, in hands of publisher); A Slice of Canada: Memoirs (book, completed but undergoing chronic revision); The Hungarian Poets (book, completed).

WANAMAKER, M. G.: (B) "Canadian English: Whence? Whither?" *J. Educ. N.S.*, 9 (1959), 22–6.

RHODENIZER, VERNON BLAIR: (A) *A Handbook of Canadian Literature* (1930), 299 pp.; *Canada for Man, and Other Poems* (1958), 16 pp. (B) Article on Canadian literature in *Lincoln Library of Essential Information* (1929), 222–4; introduction to *At the Sign of the Hand and Pen: Nova Scotian Authors* (1949), 43 pp.; introduction to *Canadian Poetry in English* (1954), xxiii–xxxvi; critical articles as editor of the *Can Poetry Mag* from 1957 to 1961; "The Contemporary Scene in Canadian Poetry," *Can Author and Bookman* (spring, 1958), 10–12.   (C) *Can Author and Bookman, Can Poetry Mag.*   (D) Canadian literature in English (three sections in press).

UNIVERSITY OF ALBERTA

BALDWIN, R. G.: (B) "Grading Freshman Essays," *College Composition and Communication*, 11 (1960), 110–15; "Phineas Fletcher: His Modern Readers and His Renaissance Ideas," *PQ*, 40 (1961), 462–75; "Pattern in the Novels of Edward McCourt," *QQ*, 68 (1961–2), 574–87; "The Yeoman's Canons: A Conjecture," *JEGP*, 61 (1962), 232–43; "Dubious Claims for the Anatomy in *The Purple Island*," *N&Q*, NS, 9 (1962), 377–8.   (C) *DR, QQ.*

CHAPIN, DONALD F.: (D) (co-editor, with F. Bessai) English Poetry of the Later Middle Ages: An Anthology (preparation advanced).

ELDER, A. T.: (B) "Irony and Humour in the *Rambler*," *UTQ*, 30 (1960–1), 57–71; "A Johnson Borrowing from Addison?" *N&Q*, NS, 8 (1961), 53–4.   (D) "Recurring Settings and Themes in the Western Novels of Robert J. C. Stead" (accepted by *Can L*); an article on the structure of Johnson's essays in the *Idler* (begun).

FORREST, JAMES F.: (B) "Dryden, Hobbes, Thomas Goodwin and the Nimble Spaniel," *N&Q*, NS, 9 (1962), 381–2; "Bunyan's Ignorance and the Flatterer: A Study in the Literary Art of Damnation," *SP*, 60 (1963), 12–22; "Mercy with Her Mirror," *PQ*, 42 (1963), 121–6.   (C) *CJT, Secondary School Teachers of Alberta Mag.*   (D) "Shakespeare on the Screen," *SSTA Mag* (in press); "Some Spiritual Symbols in Puritan Literature," *CJT* (in press); book on Bunyan and the Puritan ethos (begun).

GODFREY, D. R.: (B) "The Player's Speech in *Hamlet*: A New Approach," *Neophil*, 34 (1950), 162–9; "The Essence of Aldous Huxley," *Eng St*, 32 (1951), 97–106.   (C) *Eng St, Neophil.*   (D) "Imagination and Truth: Some Romantic Contradictions," *Eng St* (to appear in 1963); "The 'Impact of the Unseen' in the Novels of E. M. Forster" (first draft completed).

JONES, J. T.: (B) " 'What's that *ducdame*?' (*AYLI*, II. v. 60)," *MLN*, 62 (1947), 563–4; "Tactics in Scott's Novels," *Can Army J*, 4 (1950), 59–65; "The Military Lessons of Scott's *Old Mortality*," *RMC Can R* (1959), 177–81; "Shakespeare's Pronunciation of 'Glendower'," *Eng St* 43 (1962), 248–52.   (D) Certain pronunciations in English verse historically considered.

KREISEL, HENRY: (B) "Joseph Conrad and the Dilemma of the Uprooted Man," *Tam R*, No. 7 (spring, 1958), 78–85.   (C) *Can For, DR, Prism,*

QQ, Tam R, UTQ. (D) "Pattern and Design in Conrad's *Lord Jim*" (nearly complete); "Virginia Woolf: The Isolated Personality" (about half done).

MACINTYRE, JEAN: (D) "*King Lear*, III. vi. 7" (ready for publication); "A New Source for Spenser's Marinell" (ready for publication); "Colin Clout and Spenser's Theory of the Poet" (ready for publication); a study of the structure of *The Faerie Queene* (begun).

MCMASTER, R. D.: (B) "Dickens and the Horrific," *DR*, 38 (1958–9), 18–28; "Birds of Prey: A Study of *Our Mutual Friend*," *DR*, 40 (1960–1), 372–81; "*Little Dorrit*: Experience and Design," *QQ*, 67 (1960–1), 530–8; "The Unexplained Interior: A Study of E. W. Mandel's *Fuseli Poems*," *DR*, 40 (1960–1), 392–6; "Man into Beast in Dickensian Caricature," *UTQ*, 31 (1961–2), 354–61. (C) *Alphabet, DR, QQ, UTQ.* (D) "The Symbolism in *Sartor Resartus* and Carlyle's Criticism of Civilization" (nearly ready for publication); "The Political and Intellectual Background of William Morris' *News from Nowhere*" (begun); "Death to Resurrection in *Little Dorrit* and *A Tale of Two Cities*" (about to begin).

MANDEL, E. W.: (B) "Toward a Theory of Cultural Revolution: The Criticism of Northrop Frye," *Can L*, No. 1 (summer, 1959), 58–67; "Kanadische Literatur in Englischer Sprache" (trans. by A. Arnold), *Neue Zürcher Zeitung* (8 Januar 1961), Blatt 6, 67–8; "Contemporary Canadian Poetry: The Angry Poets," *English Teacher*, 1 (1961), 96–107; "C. P. Snow's Fantasy of Politics," *QQ*, 69 (1962–3), 24–37; "Lapwing You Are. Lapwing He: A Note on Icarus in Myth and Poetry," *Alphabet*, No. 4 (June, 1962), 59–62; "Anarchy and Organization," *QQ*, 70 (1963–4), 131–41. (C) *Alphabet, Can For, Can L, DR, Fiddlehead, QQ, Tam R.* (D) An article on Martha Ostenso's *Wild Geese* (planned); a book on patterns in Canadian literature (planned); a book on the poetry of Christopher Smart (partly written).

ROSE, EDWARD J.: (B) "Hopkins and Romanticism: Self, Grace, and Poetic Theory in 'As Kingfishers Catch Fire,' " *ACUTE Report* (1961), 9–18. (C) *ACUTE Report, Bucknell R, Can For, DR, English Teacher, Fiddlehead, QQ.* (D) "The Structure of Blake's Jerusalem," *Bucknell R* (to appear in 1963); "The Wit and Wisdom of Thoreau's 'Higher Laws,' " *QQ* (to appear in 1963); " 'A World with Full and Fair Proportions': The Aesthetics and The Politics of Vision," in *Western Thoreau Centenary: Selected Papers* (in press); proposed articles on Blake, Emerson, Melville, Henry Miller, Thoreau (some of them completed).

UNIVERSITY OF ALBERTA, CALGARY

ADAM, I.: (B) "Restoration through Feeling in George Eliot's Fiction: A New Look at Hetty Sorrel," *Victorian Newsletter*, No. 22 (fall, 1962), 9–12. (D) "Character as Destiny in George Eliot's Fiction" (being revised for publication); a book on George Eliot (in planning stages).

ALEXANDER, JEAN: (B) "Parallel Tendencies in English and Spanish Tragedy in the Renaissance," in *Studies in Comparative Literature* (Baton Rouge, 1962), 84–101; "Poe's 'For Annie' and Mallarmé's *Nuit d'Idumée*," *MLN*, 77 (1962), 534–6. (D) An article on Quevedo's imagery (in research stage).

BROOKS, J. B.: (B) "Middleton's Stepfather and the Captain of *The Phoenix*," *N&Q*, NS, 8 (1961), 382–4. (D) An edition of Middleton's *The Phoenix* (about one-third completed).

GUY, E.: (C) *DR*. (D) "Keats's Use of 'Luxury,'" *Keats-Shelley J* (in press).

MAGEE, WILLIAM H.: (B): "Trends in the Recent English-Canadian Novel," *Culture*, 10 (1949), 29–42; "Local Colour in Canadian Fiction," *UTQ*, 28 (1958–9), 176–89; "Language Study in Alaska," *ACLS Newsletter*, 12 (1961), 25–6; ["Linguistics in Alaska"], *Language*, 37 (1961), 314–16. (D) Canada in Fiction (nearing completion).

SCARGILL, MATTHEW HARRY: (A) (trans., with Margaret Schlauch) *Three Icelandic Sagas* (Princeton, 1950), iv + 150 pp.; *Notes on the Development of the Principal Sounds of Indo-European through Proto-Germanic and West Germanic into Old English* (Toronto, 1951), 42 pp.; *An English Handbook*, with an introduction by H. B. Allen (Toronto, 1954), xvi + 182 pp.; (with others), *The Beginning Dictionary* (Toronto, 1962). (B) "'All Passion Spent': A Revaluation of *Jane Eyre*," *UTQ*, 19 (1949– 50), 120–5; "Gold Beyond Measure: A Plea for Old English Poetry," *JEGP*, 52 (1953), 289–93; "Sources of Canadian English," *JEGP*, 56 (1957), 610–14; over a dozen others. (C) *JCLA*, *JEGP*, *J Speech and Hearing Disorders*, *UTQ*. (D) Intermediate Dictionary of Canadian English (ready in 1963); Senior Dictionary of Canadian English (to be ready in 1965); Historical Dictionary of Canadianisms (to be ready in 1967).

TENER, ROBERT H.: (B) "Richard Holt Hutton," *TLS* (Apr. 24, 1959), 241; "Bagehot and Tennyson," *TLS* (Aug. 21, 1959), 483; "Swinburne as Reviewer," *TLS* (Dec. 25, 1959), 755; "The *Spectator* Records, 1874– 1897," *Victorian Newsletter*, No. 17 (spring, 1960), 33–6; "R. H. Hutton's 'Essays Theological and Literary': A Bibliographical Note," *N&Q*, NS, 7 (1960), 185–7; "Clough, Hutton, and University Hall," *N&Q*, NS, 7 (1960), 456–7; "Bagehot, Jeffrey, and Renan," *TLS* (Aug. 11, 1961), 515; "More Articles by R. H. Hutton," *BNYPL*, 66 (1962), 58–62. (C) *N&Q*, *TLS*. (D) A biography of Richard Holt Hutton (about two-fifths complete).

ASSUMPTION UNIVERSITY OF WINDSOR

CROWLEY, C. P.: (A) (ed.) *Modern Catholic Prose and Poetry*, in two volumes. (B) "The Structural Pattern of Charles Williams' 'Descent into Hell,'" *Papers Michigan Academy of Science, Arts and Letters*, 39 (1953), 421–8; "The Grail Poetry of Charles Williams," *UTQ*, 25 (1955–6), 484–93; "Intuition of Tyrone Guthrie," *Cath Theatre*, 14 (1955); "I Liked Your Play, Father: It was a Scream," *Cath Theatre*, 15 (1956); "Culture on the Campus," *Alumni Times Quarterly Publication of Assumption University of Windsor*, 1 (1956); "The Theological Universe of Graham Greene," *Basilian Teacher* (1962).

LEMIRE, EUGENE D.: (A) *The Unpublished Lectures of William Morris* (dissertation on microfilm). (B) (with Sara Leopold) "What is a Graduate Program?" *Graduate Comment* (spring, 1959). (D) "Morris's Reply to Whistler" (accepted by *J William Morris Soc*); "Tennyson's Weeper in

Context" (ready for publication); "The Utopias of Butler, Bellamy and Morris" (proceeding).

MCNAMARA, EUGENE: (A) *Discovery* (Windsor, 1962). (B) "Prospects of the Catholic Novel," *America* (Aug. 19, 1957); "The Lost Innocence of Childhood," *Critic* (April-May, 1959); "William Styron's *Long March*: Absurdity and Authority," *WHR*, 15 (1961), 267–72; "The Post-Modern American Novel," *Blackfriars Mag* (April, 1962) and *QQ*, 69 (1962–3), 265–75. (C) *America, Amer Book Collector, Critic, Evidence, St. Jude Mag.*

SULLIVAN, JOHN F.: (A) (co-author) *The College Research Paper* (Dubuque, Iowa, 1958). (C) *C'weal.* (D) Ph.D. Dissertation, Shakespeare and the Concept of Authority; Poetry in English, 1900–1930 (text commissioned by Edward Arnold and Macmillan of Canada, due Jan., 1963).

BISHOP'S UNIVERSITY

GRAY, JAMES: (B) "[James] Beattie and the Johnson Circle," *QQ*, 58 (1951–2), 519–32; "Dr. Johnson and the King of Ashbourne," *UTQ*, 23 (1953–4), 242–52; "Boswell's Brother Confessor: William Johnson Temple," *Tennessee St in Lit*, 4 (1959); "Dr. Johnson and the 'Intellectual Gladiators,'" *DR*, 40 (1960–1), 350–9. (C) *DR, EIC, PMLA, QQ, Tennessee St in Lit, UTQ.* (D) "Dr. Johnson as Boswell's Moral Tutor" (ready for publication); The Religious Views of Samuel Johnson (to be completed by end of 1963); (with Jean Hagstrum) an edition of the sermons of Dr. Johnson, for the Yale edition of the Works of Johnson.

UNIVERSITY OF BRITISH COLUMBIA

AKRIGG, G. P. V.: (A) *Jacobean Pageant or The Court of King James I* (Cambridge, Mass., 1962), xii + 431 pp. (B) "The Curious Marginalia of Charles, Second Lord Stanhope," in J. C. McManaway, G. E. Dawson, and E. E. Willoughby, eds., *Joseph Quincy Adams Memorial Studies* (Washington, 1948), 785–801; "The Renaissance Reconsidered," in N. Ausubel, ed., *The Making of Modern Europe* (New York, 1951), 2, 73–80; "England in 1609," *HLQ*, 14 (1950–1), 75–94; "The Arrangement of the Tragedies in the First Folio," *SQ*, 7 (1956), 443–5; "Shakespeare's Living Sources," *QQ*, 65 (1958–9), 239–50. (C) *QQ, SQ.* (D) A study of Shakespeare and the court of Elizabeth and James (in first stages).

BEACH, D. M.: (B) "A Domineering Pedant o'er the Boy: Love and Rhetoric in Euphuistic Fiction," *ACUTE Report* (1961), 19–28. (D) A book on the development of Elizabethan prose narrative (begun).

BERNER, ROBERT L.: (B) "The Required Past: *World Enough and Time*," *MFS*, 6 (1960), 55–64. (D) A volume on Wallace Stevens for Barnes and Noble's American Authors and Critics series (to be published in early 1964).

CLUBB, ROGER L.: (B) "The Paradox of Ben Jonson's 'A Fit of Rime against Rime,'" *JCLA*, 5 (1961). (C) *Comp. Lit, JCLA, Modern Drama.* (D) Book on Ben Jonson's non-dramatic poetry (partly written).

DANIELLS, ROY: (A) (ed.) Thomas Traherne's *A Serious and Pathetical Contemplation* (Toronto, 1941), 127 pp.; *Milton, Mannerism and Baroque*

(Toronto, 1963), x + 229 pp.   (B) "T. S. Eliot and His Relation to T. E. Hulme," *UTQ*, 2 (1932–3), 380–96; "Baroque Form in English Literature," *UTQ*, 14 (1944–5), 393–408; "Earle Birney et Robert Finch," *Gants du Ciel*, No 11 (printemps, 1946), 83–96; "English Baroque and Deliberate Obscurity," *JAAC*, 5 (1946–7), 115–21; "Humour in *Paradise Lost*," *DR*, 33 (1953–4), 159–66; "Poetry and the Novel," in Julian Park, ed., *The Culture of Contemporary Canada* (Toronto and Ithaca, 1957), 1–80; "Emily Carr," in R. L. McDougall, ed., *Our Living Tradition*, Fourth Series (Toronto, 1962), 119–34; "The Long-enduring Spring," *Can L*, No. 12 (spring, 1962), 6–14.

FREDEMAN, WILLIAM E.: (B) "Earle Birney: Poet," *BC Lib Q*, 23 (1959–60), 8–15; "D. G. Rossetti's 'Early Italian Poets,'" *BC*, 10 (1961), 193–8; "Pre-Raphaelites in Caricature: 'The Choice of Paris: an Idyll' by Florence Claxton," *Burlington Mag*, 102 (1960), 523–9.   (D) Pre-Raphaelitism: A Biblio-Critical Study (ready for publication); an anthology of critical articles on Pre-Raphaelites (ready for publication); "Rossetti's Impromptu Portraits of Tennyson Reading *Maud*," (to appear in *Burlington Mag*); bibliographical article on current Morris research (to appear in No. 3 of *J William Morris Soc*).

FRIEDSON, ANTHONY M.: (A) *Books* (London, 1958), 160 pp.   (C) *Can L.*   (D) The Novels of Joyce Cary (ready for publication).

GOSE, ELLIOTT: (B) "The Strange Irregular Rhythm: An Analysis of *The Good Soldier*," *PMLA*, 72 (1957), 494–509; "Coleridge and the Luminous Gloom: An Analysis of the 'Symbolical Language' in 'The Rime of the Ancient Mariner,'" *PMLA*, 75 (1960), 238–44; "'Cruel Devourer of the World's Light': *The Secret Agent*," *NCF*, 15 (1960–1), 39–51.   (C) *Can. L, Nineteenth Century Fiction, PMLA.*   (D) "Psychic Evolution: Darwinism and Initiation in *Tess of the d'Urbervilles*" (to appear in *NCF* in 1963); The Romantic Novel in Nineteenth Century England (in planning stages).

HOPWOOD, V. G.: (B) "Dream, Magic, and Poetry," *JAAC*, 10 (1951), 152–9; "The Interpretation of Dream and Poetry," *UTQ*, 21 (1951–2), 128–39; "Centenary of an Explorer: David Thompson's 'Narrative' Re-considered," *QQ*, 64 (1957–8), 41–9; "New Light on David Thompson," *Beaver* (summer, 1957), 26–31; "More Light on David Thompson," *Beaver* (autumn, 1957), 58.   (C) *Can L.*   (D) An edition of David Thompson's *Travels*, with a biographical introduction (almost completed); a chapter on explorers' journals as literature, to appear in C. F. Klinck, *et al.*, eds., Literary History of Canada (begun).

INGRAM, REGINALD W.: (A) *Music and Poetry: Elizabethan Poetry* (New York, 1961).   (B) "Music in the Plays of Marston," *Music and Letters*, 37 (1956); "The Use of Music in English Miracle Plays," *Anglia*, 75 (1957), 55–76; "Operatic Tendencies in Stuart Drama," *Music Q*, 44 (1957).   (D) Music and Drama: Their Relationship in England, I, The Beginnings to 1642 (begun).

JORDAN, ROBERT M: (B) "The Narrator in Chaucer's *Troilus*," *ELH*, 25 (1958), 237–57; "The Limits of Illusion: Faulkner, Fielding, and Chaucer," *Criticism*, 2 (1960), 278–305; "Chaucer's Sense of Illusion: Roadside Drama Reconsidered," *ELH*, 29 (1962), 19–33.   (C) *Criticism, ELH, PMLA.*

(D) "The Non-dramatic Disunity of the Merchant's Tale," *PMLA* (to appear in 1963); book on Chaucer and mediaeval aesthetics (half completed).

MERIVALE, PATRICIA: (D) The Pan Motif in Modern English Literature (first draft completed).

MILLER, CRAIG WILLIAM: (D) The Unity of Coleridge's Thought (based on Ph.D. dissertation, A Study of the Key Words in Coleridge's Prose Writing, tentatively accepted for publication by University of Washington Press); "Coleridge's Concept of Nature" (ready for publication).

PINKUS, PHILIP: (B) "Swift and the Ancients-Moderns Controversy," *UTQ*, 29 (1959–60), 46–58; "*A Tale of a Tub* and the Rosy Cross," *JEGP*, 59 (1960), 669–79; "Satire and St. George," *QQ*, 70 (1963–4), 30–49. (D) A History of Grub Street (to be completed in 1963); Eighteenth-Century Satire (begun).

QUARTERMAIN, PETER A.: (C) *ETC: A Review of General Semantics.* (D) Language, Literature, and Science (textbook to be completed early in 1964); an historical study of the American attitude toward the past, provisionally entitled The Continuity of Consciousness (begun).

ROBBINS, WILLIAM: (A) *The Ethical Idealism of Matthew Arnold* (London and Toronto, 1959), xii + 259 pp.; *Humanistic Values in English Literature* (Toronto, 1960), 57 pp.; (ed. with E. Morrison), *As a Man Thinks . . . Essays British, American and Canadian* (3rd ed., Toronto, 1962). (B) "Some Modern Guides to Faith," *UTQ*, 14 (1944–5), 375–92; "Matthew Arnold and Ireland," *UTQ*, 17 (1947–8), 52–67; "*Hamlet* as Allegory," *UTQ*, 21 (1951–2), 217–23; "English as an Integrating Study," *J Educ. Faculty and College of Educ.: Vancouver and Victoria*, No. 1 (March, 1957), 39–49. (C) *UTQ*. (D) The Brothers Newman—An Essay in Comparative Biography (in early stages).

ROSS, IAN: (B) The Form and Matter of *The Cherrie and the Slae*," *Texas St in Eng*, 37 (1958), 79–91; "Verse Translation at the Court of King James VI of Scotland," *Texas St in Lit and Lang*, 4 (1962), 252–67. (D) A Life of Henry Home, Lord Kames (1696–1782) (Ph.D. dissertation being revised for publication); "Boswell in Search of a Father? Or a Subject?" (completed); "A Blue-Stocking over the Border" (begun); "Thomas Reid and the Rise of the Common-Sense Philosophy" (planning stages).

SPAULDING, JOHN GORDON. (B) "Elementalism: The Effect of an Implicit Postulate of Identity on I. A. Richards' Theory of Poetic Value," in T. C. Pollock and J. G. Spaulding, eds., *A Theory of Meaning Analyzed* (Chicago, 1942), and also in M. Kendig, ed., *Papers from the Second American Congress on General Semantics* (Chicago, 1943), 438–47. (D) "The Preacher's Assistant: Sermon Bibliography 1660–1783" (half completed).

STEPHENS, D. G.: (B) "A Maritime Myth," *Can L*, No. 9 (summer, 1961), 38–48; "Protection of Mediocrity: The Royal Commission on Publications," *Can L*, No. 10 (autumn, 1961), 91–2. (C) *Can L*. (D) The Short Story in Transition (completed); articles on satire in Canadian literature and on the novel in Canada (in middle stages of preparation).

STEVENSON, WARREN: (B) "*Christabel*: A Re-interpretation," *Alphabet*, No. 4 (June, 1962), 18–35. (C) *Alphabet*, *QQ*. (D) "Shakespeare's Hand in *The Spanish Tragedy 1602*" (to appear in *SQ*).

TEDFORD, INGRID: (A) *Ibsen Bibliography, 1928–1957* (Oslo-Bergen, 1961), 80 pp.

CANADIAN SERVICES COLLEGE, ROYAL ROADS

KING, RALPH F. B.: (D) A series of articles (or a monograph) having to do with the History of the Conception of Genius in the Eighteenth Century (in preparation).

MCCAUGHEY, G. S.: (B) "The Canadian Services Colleges," *Professional Public Service*, 40 (1961), 11–15; "The Regular Officer Training Plan," *School Progress*, 31 (1962), 44–6. (C) *Victoria Daily Times*. (D) A book on textual problems involved in establishing the source of the folio version of *King Lear* (begun).

THORNE, WILLIAM BARRY: (D) "Folk Themes in *Much Ado*" (complete); The Influence of Folk-Drama upon Shakespeare (Ph.D. dissertation, half completed).

CARLETON UNIVERSITY

BEATTIE, MUNRO: (B) "Archibald Lampman," in C. T. Bissell, ed., *Our Living Tradition: Seven Canadians* (Toronto, 1957), 63–88; "Henry James, Novelist," *DR*, 39 (1959–60), 455–63. (C) *Can For, Ottawa Citizen, SAQ, UTQ.* (D) Chapter on poetry since 1920 for C. F. Klinck, *et al.*, eds., A Literary History of Canada (to be ready in 1963).

HANNA, MAUREEN: (D) Article on the influence of the liturgy on Passus XVIII of *Piers Plowman* (ready for publication).

HORNYANSKY, M. S.: (A) *The Golden Phoenix and Other French-Canadian Fairy Tales*, by M. Barbeau, retold by M. Hornyansky (Toronto, 1958), 144 pp. (B) "Darwinism in Literature," in H. H. J. Nesbitt, ed., *Darwin in Retrospect* (Toronto, 1960), 67–86. (C) *Tam R.*

JOHNSTON, GEORGE: (A) (trans., with notes and essay by P. Foote), *The Saga of Gisli* (Toronto, 1963), xiv + 146 pp. (B) "Carl Schaefer: Artist and Man," *QQ*, 61 (1954–5), 345–52; "Carl Schaefer," *Can Art*, 17 (1960), 66–71, 99; "On Translation—II," *Saga-Book*, 15, part 4 (1961), 394–402. (D) (translation, with Peter Foote) the *Faereyinga saga* (about half completed).

MCDOUGALL, ROBERT L.: (A) (ed.) *Our Living Tradition*, Second and Third Series (Toronto, 1959), xvi + 288 pp.; (ed.), *Our Living Tradition*, Fourth Series (Toronto, 1962), x + 158 pp. (C) *QQ*.

DALHOUSIE UNIVERSITY

BEVAN, ALLAN R.: (B) "James De Mille and Archibald MacMechan," *DR*, 35 (1955–6), 201–15; "Rockbound Revisited: A Reappraisal of Frank Parker Day's Novel," *DR*, 38 (1958–9), 336–47; "Poetry and Politics in Restoration England," *DR*, 39 (1959–60), 314–25. (C) *DR*. (D) Dryden as a Dramatic Artist (about two-thirds complete).

DAWSON, R. M.: (B) "The Structure of the Old English Gnomic Poems," *JEGP*, 61 (1962), 14–22. (C) *DR*. (D) An edition of the *Blickling Homilies* (very early stages).

FRASER, JOHN: (B) "The Novels of B. Traven," *Grad St of Eng* (fall, 1958), 7–17; "A Tribute to Dr. F. R. Leavis," *Western R*, 23 (1958–9),

139–47; "Descartes' *Discourse*: A Look at Its Rhetoric" (pseudonymous) *Grad St of Eng* (spring, 1959), 13–22; "Poetry and the Exacting Tape" (pseudonymous) *Grad St of Eng* (summer, 1959), 17–22.

MENDEL, SYDNEY: (B) "William Langland," *Books: J Nat Book League* (Dec., 1954), 302–3; "Hamletian Man," *Arizona Q*, 16 (1960), 223–36; "The Descent into Solitude," *Forum*, 3 (1961), 19–24. (D) Book on Hamletian figures in literature (about half complete).

PARKS, M. G.: (A) (ed., with an introduction by Lorne Pierce, illus. by C. W. Jefferys, parallel text by M. G. Parks) *Sam Slick in Pictures: The Best of the Humour of Thomas Chandler Haliburton* (Toronto, 1956), xx + 205; *Discoverers and Explorers in Canada, 1497–1763* (Toronto, 1956), 32 pp.; *Discoverers and Explorers in Canada, 1763–1911* (Toronto, 1957), 28 pp.; *The Rebellions of 1837 in Upper and Lower Canada* (Toronto, 1959), 35 pp.

SPROTT, S. E.: (A) *Milton's Art of Prosody* (Oxford, 1953), xii + 147 pp.; *The English Debate on Suicide from Donne to Hume* (LaSalle, Illinois, 1961), viii + 168 pp. (B) "The Legend of Jack Donne the Libertine," *UTQ*, 19 (1949–50), 335–53; "Cicero's Theory of Prose Style," *PQ*, 34 (1955), 1–17; "The Puritan Problem of Suicide," *DR*, 38 (1958–9), 222–33. (D) "Ralegh's *Sceptic* and the Elizabethan Translation of Sextus Empiricus" (to appear in *SP*); a study of the intellectual position of Christopher Marlowe (beginning).

WHITTIER, H. S.: (C) *DR*. (D) An analysis of Byron's *Don Juan* (about half complete).

UNIVERSITÉ LAVAL

MULLINS, STANLEY G.: (B) "La Révolte de Rimbaud," *RUL*, 4 (1949–50), 920–31; "Some Aspects of the Theatre in Seventeenth Century France," *Culture*, 11 (1950), 242–61; "Une Introduction à la Culture au Canada," *Culture*, 19 (1958), 15–26; "Traditional Symbolism in Adele Wiseman's *The Sacrifice*," *Culture*, 19 (1958), 287–97; "The Poetry of Peter Miller," *Culture*, 21 (1960), 398–408; "Ralph Gustafson's Poetry," *Culture*, 22 (1961), 417–22; "The Didactic Novel in Post-War Canadian Fiction," *Culture*, 23 (1962), 137–53; "Some Remarks on Theme in Martha Ostenso's *Wild Geese*," *Culture*, 23 (1962), 359–62. (C) *Annuaire Statistique de la Province de Québec, Culture, HAC Bull, QQ, RUL*. (D) Trends in the Post-War Canadian Novel (begun).

MCGILL UNIVERSITY

BERLIN, NORMAND: (B) "*Patience*: A Study in Poetic Elaboration," *Studia Neophilologica*, 33 (1961), 80–5.

DUDEK, LOUIS: (A) *Literature and the Press: A History of Printing, Printed Media, and their Relation to Literature* (Toronto, 1960), 238 pp. (B) "Patterns of Recent Canadian Poetry," *Culture*, 19 (1958), 399–415; "The Transition in Canadian Poetry," *Culture*, 20 (1959), 282–95; "Two Canadian Poets: Ralph Gustafson and Eli Mandel," *Culture*, 22 (1961), 145–51; "The Two Traditions: Literature and the Ferment in Quebec," *Can L*, No. 12 (spring, 1962), 44–51; "Canada's Literature of Revolt," *Nation*, 195 (Oct. 27, 1962), 269–72. (C) *Can For, Can L, Culture, Delta*. (D) An anthology of twentieth-century poetry.

FINLAYSON, JOHN: (B) "The Source of 'Arthur,' an Early Fifteenth-Century Verse Chronicle," *N&Q*, NS, 7 (1960), 46–7; "Two Minor Sources for the Alliterative 'Morte Arthure,' " *N&Q*, NS, 9 (1962), 132–3. (D) One article and one review to appear in *Medium Ævum*; one article to appear in *MP*; one article to appear in *JEGP*; one book on Middle English literature (half completed); one edition of a Middle English text (begun and accepted for publication).

HEMLOW, JOYCE: (A) *The History of Fanny Burney* (Oxford, 1958), 528 pp. (B) "Fanny Burney: Playwright," *UTQ*, 19 (1949–50), 170–89; "Fanny Burney and the Courtesy Books," *PMLA*, 65 (1950), 732–61; "Dr. Johnson and Fanny Burney—Some Additions to the Record," *BNYPL*, 55 (1951), 55–65, reprinted in M. Wahba, ed., *Johnsonian Studies* (Cairo, 1962); "Dr. Johnson and the Young Burneys," in F. W. Hilles, ed., *New Light on Dr. Johnson* (New Haven, 1959), 319–39. (D) An edition of the Journals and Letters of Fanny Burney (Madame d'Arblay), 1791–1840; a printed catalogue of the Burney Papers; a biography of Susanna Elizabeth Burney.

HEUSER, ALAN: (A) *The Shaping Vision of Gerard Manley Hopkins* (London, 1958), viii + 128 pp. (C) *QQ*.

MASSEY, IRVING: (A) (trans., with introduction and notes), Alfred de Vigny's *Stello: A Session with Doctor Noir* (Montreal, 1963), xxiv + 191 pp. (B) "The Contribution of Neurology to the Scepticism of Alfred de Vigny," *J Hist Med*, 9 (1954), 329–48; "Form and Content in a Rimbaud Poem," *RR*, 48 (1957), 17–25; "Subject and Object in Romantic Fiction," *Symposium*, 11 (1957), 185–203; "Shelley's 'Music, When Soft Voices Die': Text and Meaning," *JEGP*, 59 (1960), 430–38. (C) *Comp Lit*. (D) A two-volume study of Mary Shelley's work as editor of P. B. Shelley's poems (vol. I ready for publication).

PUHVEL, MARTIN: (B) "New Light on an Old Custom," *Folklore*, 71 (1960), 106–8; "The Legend of the Church-building Troll in Northern Europe," *Folklore*, 72 (1961), 567–83; "The Folklore of the Seal in Northern Europe," *Folklore*, 74 (1963). (C) *Folklore*. (D) An Introduction to Estonian, a grammar-reader with glossary (almost complete).

ROBINSON, BRIAN: (B) "Lettres canadiennes-anglaises en 1960," *Archives des Lettres canadiennes* (University of Ottawa, 1961). (C) *Montreal Star*. (D) "Montreal as a Setting for Canadian Fiction."

WALKER, RALPH S.: (A) (ed., with introduction and glossary) John Knox's *History of the Reformation*, abbreviated (Edinburgh, 1940), 72 pp. (2nd ed., 1958); (ed., with introduction and notes) *James Beattie's London Diary, 1773* (Aberdeen, 1946), 145 pp.; (ed., with introduction and notes) *James Beattie's Day-Book, 1773–1798* (1948), 226 pp.; (ed., with introduction and notes) Ben Jonson's *Timber; or, Discoveries* (Syracuse, 1953), vi + 135 pp. (B) "Ben Jonson's Lyric Poetry," *Criterion*, 13 (1933–4), 430–48, reprinted in W. R. Kent, ed., *Seventeenth-Century English Poetry* (New York, 1962); "An Introduction to Gerard Manley Hopkins," *AUR*, 25 (1937–8), 232–43; "The Literary Society," *AUR*, 30 (1943–4), 42–51; "The Beattie Portrait [by Reynolds]," *AUR*, 30 (1943–4), 224–6; "William Duncan Taylor," *AUR*, 33 (1949–50), 129–37; "Literary Criticism in Jonson's Conversations with Drummond," *English*, 8 (1950–1), 222–7;

"Ben Jonson's *Discoveries*: A New Analysis," *E&S*, NS, 5 (1952), 32–51; "Charles Burney, Junior, and the Cambridge University Library," *Trans Camb Biblio Soc* (1962); "The Scottish Universities," *CEA Critic* (1953). (D) James Boswell's Correspondence with John Johnston of Grange (in proof); a selection from the papers of Thomas Twining, Dr. Burney, and others (in preparation).

MCMASTER UNIVERSITY

BRINK, A. W.: (B) "Ellwood's *Davideis*: A Newly Discovered Version?" *J Friends' Hist Soc*, 49 (1959); "Early Influences in the Development of Isaac Penington," *Friends' Q*, 13 (1959).

KEITH, W. J.: (B) "Yeats's Arthurian Black Tower," *MLN*, 75 (1960), 119–23; "Yeats's Double Dream," *MLN*, 76 (1961), 710–15. (C) *Can For*. (D) A critical study of Richard Jefferies (1848–87) (ready for publication); book on the creative use of background, with special reference to Wordsworth, Hardy, and Lawrence (in planning stages).

LEE, ALVIN A.: (B) "From Grendel to the Phoenix: A Critical Study of Old English Elegiac Poetry," University of Toronto Dissertation Abstract (1961); "Old Wine in New Bottles," *Alphabet*, No. 4 (June, 1962), 36–43; "A Turn to the Stage: Reaney's Dramatic Verse, Part I," *Can L*, No. 15 (winter, 1963), 40–51. (D) A critical study of Old English elegiac poetry (in planning stages).

MARTIN, MARY FORSTER: (B) " 'If You Know Not Me, You Know Nobodie,' and 'The Famous Historie of Sir Thomas Wyat,' " *Library*, series 4, 13 (1932–3), 272–81; "Books as Weapons in an Armoury," *School*, 34 (1945); "Common Faults in Freshman English?" *Bull Ont Sec Sch Teachers' Fed*, 30 (1950); "Why Teach Written English?" *Bull Ont Sec Sch Teachers' Fed*, 34 (1954); "A Murthering Practise," *DR*, 35 (1955–6), 225–30; "An Early Use of the Feminine Form of the Word *Heir*," *MLN*, 71 (1956), 270–71; "Stow's 'Annals' and 'The Famous Historie of Sir Thomas Wyat,' " *MLR*, 53 (1958), 75–7. (D) An anthology of verse of the British Commonwealth (planning stages).

MORTON, RICHARD: (A) (ed., with W. M. Peterson) John Gay's *Three Hours After Marriage* (Painesville, Ohio, 1961). (B) Articles on Restoration, Eighteenth-, and Nineteenth-Century drama, in G. Watson, ed., *Camb Bibliog Eng Lit*, V (1957); "Textual Problems in Restoration Broadsheet Prologues and Epilogues," *Library*, series 5, 12 (1957), 197–203; "The Educative Force of Irony," *Liberal Educ* (Dec., 1960); "Narrative Irony in Robert Burns's *Tam O'Shanter*," *MLQ*, 22 (1961), 12–20; "Notes on the Imagery of Dylan Thomas," *Eng St* 43 (1962), 155–64. (D) A life of Sir Aston Cokayne, with an edition of the printed poems, 1658 (to be completed in 1963).

SHRIVE, F. NORMAN: (B) (with D. J. Dooley) "The Voice of the Burdash," *Can For*, 37 (1957–8), 80–2; "Granville-Barker and Edwardian Theatre," *Wat R*, 1 (1959), 34–46; "Charles Mair: A Document on the Red River Rebellion," *CHR*, 40 (1959), 218–26; "What Happened to Pauline?" *Can L*, No. 13 (summer, 1962), 25–38. (C) *Can L, QQ*. (D) Charles Mair: Literary Nationalist (ready for publication).

WILES, R. M.: (A) *Scholarly Reporting in the Humanities* (Ottawa, 1951;

2nd ed., 1958; 3rd ed., Toronto, 1961); *Serial Publication in England before 1750* (Cambridge, 1957), xvi + 391 pp. (B) "In My Mind's Eye, Horatio," *UTQ*, 18 (1948–9), 57–67; "Eighteenth Century Newspapers: A Neglected Primary Source," *Microcosm*, 3 (1957), 1–2; "Dates in English Imprints, 1700–52," *Library*, series 5, 12 (1957), 190–3; "Freshest Advices, Foreign and Domestick," *DR*, 38 (1958–9), 8–17; "Further Additions and Corrections to G. A. Cranfield's *Handlist of English Provincial Newspapers and Periodicals 1700–1760*," *Trans Camb Biblio Soc*, 2 (1958), 385–9. (C) *DR, MP, PQ, RN*. (D) A book on the beginnings of provincial journalism in England (ready for publication); article on a hitherto unreported monthly magazine published in Leeds in 1734 (ready for publication); book on English provincial life, based on material in the provincial newspapers (in early stages).

UNIVERSITY OF MANITOBA

GOLD, JOSEPH: (B) "The Humanism of William Faulkner," *Humanist*, 20 (1960), 113–17; "Truth or Consequences: Faulkner's 'The Town,'" *Mississippi Q*, 13 (1960), 112–16; "The Morality of *Lolita*," *Bull Br Ass Amer St*, NS, 1 (1960), 50–4; "*The Sound and the Fury*," *Explicator*, 19 (1961), 29; "Delusion and Redemption in Faulkner's *A Fable*," *MFS*, 7 (1961), 145–56; "Exit Everybody: The Novels of Ivy Compton-Burnett," *DR*, 42 (1962–3), 227–38; "The 'Normality' of Snopesism: Universal Themes in Faulkner's *The Hamlet*," *Wisconsin St in Contemporary Lit*, 3 (1962), 25–34; "Two Romantics: Jim and Stein," *CEA Critic*, 24 (1962), 1, 11–12; "William Faulkner's 'One Compact Thing,'" *Twentieth-Century Literature*, 8 (1962–3), 3–9. (D) Book on William Faulkner (ready for publication); a work on a definition of literary surrealism, with studies of selected authors (begun).

HOWARTH, HERBERT: (A) *The Irish Writers 1880–1940: Literature under Parnell's Star* (London, 1958; New York, 1959), x + 318. (B) "The Dilemma of Steven Runciman," *WHR*, 11 (1957), 127–34; "Eliot, Beethoven, and J. W. N. Sullivan," *Comp Lit*, 9 (1957), 322–32; "T. S. Eliot's *Criterion*: The Editor and His Contributors," *Comp Lit*, 11 (1959), 97–110; "Eliot and Hofmannsthal," *SAQ*, 59 (1960), 500–9; "Shakespeare's Gentleness," *ShS*, No. 14. (1961), 90–97; "A Segment of Durrell's Quartet," *UTQ*, 32 (1962–3), 282–93; "Lawrence Durrell and Some Early Masters," *BA*, 37 (1963), 5–11. (C) *BA, Comp Lit, UTQ*. (D) Book on T. S. Eliot (soon to be published); "Shakespeare's Flattery in *Measure for Measure*" (to appear in *SQ*); "*The Independent Review* in 1903" (in preparation).

KRUUNER, MARTA R.: (D) The Nature and Function of the Artist in the World of Thomas Mann (ready for publication).

LANDON, CAROL: (B) "Wordsworth, Coleridge and the *Morning Post*: An Early Version of 'The Seven Sisters,'" *RES*, NS, 11 (1960), 392–402.

SAUNDERS, DORIS B.: (C) *MAR, MP, QQ, UTQ*. (D) Book on Samuel Johnson (in planning stages).

STOBIE, MARGARET: (A) *An Outline of Middle English Grammar* (Toronto, 1938), viii + 112 pp. (B) "The Influence of Morphology on Middle English Alliterative Poetry," *JEGP*, 39 (1940), 319–36; "Chaucer's Shipman and the Wine," *PMLA*, 64 (1949), 565–9; "Patmore's Theory and

Hopkins' Practice," *UTQ*, 19 (1949–50), 64–80; "Ernest Hemingway: Craftsman," *Can For*, 33 (1953–4), 179–82; "The Formative Years," in two parts, *Beaver*, 286 (summer, 1955; autumn, 1955), 3–8; 42–7. (C) *Can L, QQ, Tam R*.

SWAYZE, WALTER EUGENE: (B) "The Sir William Watson Collection," *Yale U Lib Gaz*, 27 (1952), 71–6; "Some Uncollected Authors, XII: Sir William Watson," *BC*, 6 (1957), 285–6, 402; "An Offence unto Charity: Personal Reflections on a National Attitude," *QQ*, 64 (1957–8), 326–37; "The Role of the Humanities in Technical Colleges and Professional Schools of Canadian Universities," *HAC Bull*, No. 26 (Jan., 1959), 4–10, 17; "Early Wordsworthian Biography," *BNYPL*, 64 (1960), 169–95. (C) *QQ*. (D) World Stranger: A Critical Biography of Sir William Watson (almost complete); editions of Watson's collected poems, selected poetry and prose, and correspondence (planning stages); "Walt Whitman's Religion" (almost complete); "Regionalism and Nationalism in Canadian Literature" (almost complete).

WARHAFT, SIDNEY: (A) (ed., with John Woodbury) *English Poems, 1250–1660* (Toronto, 1961), xvi + 227. (B) "Anti-Semitism in *The Merchant of Venice*," *MAR*, 10 (1956), No. 3, 3–15; "ReJoycing with the Haundt and the Gracestopper: A Parababel," *CE*, 18 (1956–7), 103; "The Anomaly of Bacon's Allegorizing," *Papers Michigan Acad of Science, Arts and Letters*, 43 (1957), 327–33; "Science against Man in Bacon," *Bucknell R*, 7 (1958), 158–73; "Hamlet's Solid Flesh Resolved," *ELH*, 28 (1961), 21–30. (C) *Can L, QQ, RN, Tam R*. (D) Two articles, on Bacon and on Beckett (ready for publication); book on *Hamlet* (in progress); an edition of essays on Bacon (in planning stages).

MEMORIAL UNIVERSITY OF NEWFOUNDLAND

HALPERT, HERBERT: (A) (annotated) John Harrington Cox, *Folk Songs Mainly from West Virginia* (New York, 1939); (annotated) John Harrington Cox, *Traditional Ballads Mainly from West Virginia* (New York, 1939); (annotated) Richard Chase, *The Jack Tales* (Cambridge, 1943); (annotated) Vance Randolph, *Who Blowed Up the Church House and Other Ozark Folk Tales* (New York, 1952); (annotated) Vance Randolph, *The Devil's Pretty Daughter and Other Ozark Folk Tales* (New York, 1955); (annotated) Vance Randolph, *The Talking Turtle and Other Ozark Folk Tales* (New York, 1957). (B) "Some Ballads and Folk Songs from New Jersey," *J Amer Folklore*, 52 (1939), 52–69; "Indiana Folktales," *Hoosier Folklore Bull*, 1 (1942), 3–34; "The Cante Fable in New Jersey,"*J Amer Folklore*, 55 (1942), 133–43; "Indiana Storyteller," *Hoosier Folklore Bull*, 1 (1942), 43–61; "Family Tales of a Kentuckian," *Hoosier Folklore Bull*, 1 (1942), 61–71; "A Group of Indiana Folksongs," *Hoosier Folklore Bull*, 3 (1944), 1–15; "The Folksinger Speaks," *Hoosier Folklore Bull*, 3 (1944), 29–35, 48–55; "Tales of a Mississippi Soldier," *Southern Folklore Q*, 8 (1944), 103–14; "Tall Tales and Other Yarns from Calgary, Alberta," *Calif Folklore Q*, 4 (1945), 29–49; "Montana Cowboy Folk Tales," *Calif Folklore Q*, 4 (1945), 244–54; "Tales Told by Soldiers," *Calif Folklore Q*, 4 (1945), 364–76; "Aggressive Humor on the East Branch," *NY Folklore Q*, 2 (1946), 85–97; "Proverbial Comparison from West Tennessee," *Tennessee Folklore*

Soc Bull, 17 (1951), 49–61; "Riddles from West Tennessee," *Tennessee Folklore Soc Bull*, 18 (1952), 29–42; "Place Names of Kentucky Waterways and Ponds, with a Note on Bottomless Pools," *Kentucky Folklore Record*, 7 (1961), 117–19.   (C) *J Amer Folklore, Western Folklore, Kentucky Folklore Record, Tennessee Folklore Soc Bull, Southern Folklore Q, Midwest Folklore*.   (D) Revision of MS of large collection of legends and folk tales from southern New Jersey (about half done).

MACDONALD, ALASTAIR A.: (B) "Class-consciousness and the Novels of E. M. Forster," *HAC Bull*, No. 30 (April, 1960), 9–10, 18–24, 34; "Lewis Grassic Gibbon and the Regional Whole," *DR*, 39 (1959–60), 503–10; "Class-consciousness in E. M. Forster," *U Kansas City R*, 27 (1960–1), 235–40; "The Poet Gray in Scotland," *RES*, NS, 13 (1962), 245–56; "Enthusiasm Resurgent," *DR*, 42 (1962–3), 352–63.   (C) *Evidence, QQ*. (D) A critical study of Thomas Gray (early stages).

ORSTEN, ELISABETH M.: (B) "St. Mildred of Minster and Her Monastery," *Amer Benedictine R* (1957), 18–40; "Light in Darkness," *Bridge*, 3 (1958–9), 325–39; "The Ambiguities in Langland's Rat Parliament," *MS*, 23 (1961), 216–39.

SEARY, E. R.: (A) *A Biographical and Bibliographical Record of South African Literature in English* (Grahamstown, 1938), iv + 66 pp.; (ed.) *South African Short Stories* (1947), 233 pp.; (with G. M. Story) *Reading English: A Handbook for Students* (Toronto, 1958; London, 1959), x + 116 pp. (second, revised ed., published as *The Study of English*, New York, 1962, xii + 114 pp.); *Toponymy of the Island of Newfoundland*, Check-list No. 1 (St. John's, 1959), xx + 69 pp.; *Toponymy of the Island of Newfoundland*, Check-list No. 2 (St. John's, 1960), xxvi + 153 pp.   (B) "Robert Southey and Ebenezer Elliott: Some New Southey Letters," *RES*, 15 (1939), 412–21; "A Sequel to *Don Juan*," *MLR*, 35 (1940), 526–9; "Corn-Law Rhymer," *TLS*, No. 2496 (Dec. 2, 1949), 794; "South African Literature in English," in *Chambers' Enc* (1950), 760–3; "South African Literature in English," and biographies of South African writers, in *Cassell's Enc of Lit* (1953), I, 514–15 and *passim*; "The Place of Linguistics in English Studies," *JCLA*, regular series, 1 (Oct., 1955), 9–13; "The French Element in Newfoundland Place Names," *Onomastica*, No. 16 (1958), 16; "The Anatomy of Newfoundland Place Names," *Names*, 6 (1958), 193–207. (C) *JCLA, QQ, Standpunte* (Cape Town).   (D) "Linguistic Variety in Newfoundland Place Names," *Can Geog J* (to appear soon); Toponymy of the Island of Newfoundland, Check-list No. 3 (almost complete); An Ethnolinguistic Survey of the Avalon Peninsula (ready for publication); a second Canadian edition of *Reading English*.

STORY, G. M.: (A) *A Newfoundland Dialect Dictionary: A Survey of the Problems* (St. John's, 1956), 15 pp.; (with E. R. Seary) *Reading English: A Handbook for Students* (Toronto, 1958; London, 1959), x + 116 pp. (second, revised ed., published as *The Study of English*, New York, 1962, xii + 114 pp.); (ed., with Helen Gardner) *The Sonnets of William Alabaster* (Oxford, 1959), liv + 65 pp.; *Education and Renaissance* (Halifax, 1962), 17 pp.   (B) "Research in the Language and Place-Names of Newfoundland," *JCLA*, 3 (1957), 47–55; (with W. F. Forbes) "Science and the Humanities: The Unity of Knowledge," *J Chem Educ*, 34 (1957), 594–7;

"Dialect and the Standard Language," *J Nfld Teachers' Ass*, 49 (1957), 16–20; "Newfoundland English Usage," in *Enc Can*, VII (1958), 321–2; "Newfoundland Dialect," in A. B. Perlin, ed., *The Story of Newfoundland* (St. John's, 1959), 68–70; "Heber the Magnificent: Portrait of a Bibliophile," *HAC Bull*, No. 12 (Jan., 1961), 5–15; "George Herbert's *Inventa Bellica*: A New Manuscript," *MP*, 59 (1961–2), 270–2; "Some Recent Theories of Textual Criticism," in *Thought from the Learned Societies of Canada 1961* (Toronto, 1962), 48–62. (C) *DR, MP, Newfoundland Record, QQ.* (D) A critical edition of some sermons by Lancelot Andrewes (almost complete); A Newfoundland Dialect Dictionary (an interim glossary to be ready in a year or two).

MOUNT ALLISON UNIVERSITY

COLLIE, M. J.: (B) "Value and the Teaching of Literature," *Universities Q*, 12 (1957–8), 181–8; "Social Security in Literary Criticism," *EIC*, 9 (1959), 151–8; "The Old Pose and the New Poetry," *DR*, 41 (1961–2), 451–65; "The Rhetoric of Accurate Speech: A Note on the Poetry of Wallace Stevens," *EIC*, 12 (1962), 54–66. (D) Jules Laforgue, for the Writers and Critics series (in press); entries on all twentieth-century French poets for the proposed Penguin Guide to European Literature (almost completed); book of essays on twentieth-century French poets (to be completed in 1963); an edition of Laforgue's *Derniers Vers* (ready for publication).

MORRIS, IVOR: (B) "Cordelia and Lear," *SQ*, 8 (1957), 141–58; "The Tragic Vision of Fulke Greville," *SHS*, 14 (1961), 66–75.

SIDNELL, M. J.: (B) "Manuscript Versions of Yeats's *The Countess Cathleen*," *Papers Biblio Soc Amer*, 56 (1962), 79–103. (D) "The Evolution of Yeats's *The Countess Cathleen*" (ready for publication); "The Staging of Shakespeare at Stratford, Ontario" to appear in *E&S*, 1964 (begun).

UNIVERSITY OF NEW BRUNSWICK

COGSWELL, FRED: (A) (trans.), Robert Henryson's *The Testament of Cresseid* (Toronto, 1957), 24 pp.; (ed.), *A Canadian Anthology: Poems from 'The Fiddlehead', 1945–1959* (Fredericton, 1961), 76 pp.; (ed.), *Five New Brunswick Poets* (Fredericton, 1962), 64 pp. (B) "Poetry in Canada —Magazines," *Trace*, No. 14 (Oct., 1955), 3–7; "The Way of the Sea—A Symbolic Epic," *DR*, 35 (1955–6), 374–81; "Moses Hardy Nickerson: A Study," *DR*, 38 (1958–9), 472–85; "Nineteenth Century Poetry in the Maritimes and Problems of Research," *Newsletter Biblio Soc Can*, 5 (1961), 5–19. (C) *Can For, Can L, DR, Fiddlehead, HAC Bull, QQ.* (D) "Literature in New Brunswick before 1920," to appear in The Arts in New Brunswick (in press); "Literature in the Maritimes, 1715–1820," "Literature in the Maritimes, 1820–1880," "Literature in Newfoundland, 1715–1880," all to appear in C. F. Klinck, *et al.*, eds., A Literary History of Canada (complete); a life of John Galt, Esq. (beginning).

GALLOWAY, DAVID ROBERTSON: (A) *Shakespeare: Seven Radio Talks as Heard on C.B.C. University of the Air* (Toronto, 1961), 95 pp. (B) "The Ramus Scene in Marlowe's 'The Massacre at Paris,'" *N&Q*, 198 (1953),

146–7; " 'Alcides and His Rage': A Note on the 'Merchant of Venice,' "
N&Q, NS, 3 (1956), 330–1; " 'I am dying, Egypt, dying': Folio Repetitions
and the Editors," *N&Q*, NS, 5 (1958), 330–5; "Fluellen," *N&Q*, NS, 6
(1959), 116.   (C) *DR, Fiddlehead, N&Q*.   (D) "The Drama: Historical
and Contemporary" (to appear in The Arts in New Brunswick); "The Literature of the Explorers" (to appear in C. F. Klinck, *et al.*, eds., A Literary
History of Canada); an edition, with introduction and notes, of Robert
Hayman's *Quodlibets* (in planning stages).

JOHNSTONE, JOHN KEITH: (A) *The Bloomsbury Group: A Study of E. M.
Forster, Lytton Strachey, Virginia Woolf, and their Circle* (London and
New York, 1954), x + 383 pp. and viii + 383 pp.   (C) *DR, Fiddlehead,
QQ*.

KINLOCH, A. MURRAY: (B) "A Note on 'Beowulf' L 1828 B," *MLR*, 51
(1956), 71.   (D) A selection of Middle English lyrics of courtly love
(begun); an Anglo-Saxon grammar (begun).

LANE, LAURIAT, JR.: (A) *Approaches to Walden* (San Francisco, 1961),
viii + 135 pp.; (ed.) Charles Dickens's *Great Expectations* (1961); (ed.,
with G. H. Ford) *The Dickens Critics* (Ithaca, 1961), x + 417 pp.
(B) *"Oliver Twist*: A Revision," *TLS* (July 20, 1951), 460; "The Literary
Archetype: Some Reconsiderations," *JAAC*, 13 (1954–5), 226–32; "Why
Huckleberry Finn is a Great World Novel," *CE*, 17 (1955–6), 1–5, reprinted in B. Marks, ed., *Mark Twain's 'Huckleberry Finn'* (1959); "The
Devil in Oliver Twist," *Dickensian*, 52 (1956), 132–6; "Dickens' Archetypal
Jew," *PMLA*, 73 (1958), 94–100; "Dickens and the Double," *Dickensian*,
55 (1959), 47–55; "On the Organic Structure of *Walden*," *CE*, 21 (1959–
60), 195–202; "Allegory and Character and *The Scarlet Letter*," *Emerson
Soc Q*, No. 25 (1961), 13–16.   (C) *DR, Fiddlehead, MLN*.   (D) Two
articles on Thoreau (begun); book on Thoreau (in planning stages).

LENNAM, T. N. S.: (B) "A Nightingale amongst the China," *DR*, 36
(1956–7), 402–5; "The Happy Hunting Ground," *UTQ*, 29 (1959–60),
386–97, reprinted in M. Magalaner, ed., *A James Joyce Miscellany*, Third
Series (Carbondale, Illinois, 1962), 158–74.   (D) Ph.D. dissertation, A
Study of the "Wit" Interludes, including an edition of *The Marriage of Wit
and Science* (anon., printed by Thomas Marshe, *c.* 1570), of *The Marriage
between Wit and Wisdom* (from BM Add Ms 26782), a biographical sketch
of Francis Merbury, an account of Sir Edward Dering's (1598–1644)
collection of playbooks.

PACEY, DESMOND: (A) *Frederick Philip Grove* (Toronto, 1945), x + 150
pp.; (ed., with introduction and notes) *A Book of Canadian Stories* (Toronto,
1947), 295 pp. (revised edition, 1962, xxxviii + 340 pp.); *Creative Writing
in Canada* (Toronto, 1952), x + 220 pp. (revised and enlarged edition,
1961, x + 314 pp.); (ed. with an introduction) *The Selected Poems of Sir
Charles G. D. Roberts* (Toronto, 1955), xxvi + 100 pp.; (ed. with an
introduction) *Selected Poems of Dorothy Livesay* (Toronto, 1957), xxii +
82 pp.; *Ten Canadian Poets: A Group of Biographical and Critical Essays*
(Toronto, 1958), x + 350 pp.; (ed. with an introduction) Mazo de la
Roche's *Delight* (Toronto, 1960), x + 174 pp.   (B) "Balzac and Thackeray," *MLR*, 36 (1941), 213–24; "Henry James and His French Contemporaries," *Amer Lit*, 13 (1941–2), 240–56; "Frederick Philip Grove," *MAR*,

3 (spring, 1943), 28–41; "The Humanities in Canada," *QQ*, 50 (1943–4), 354–60; "In Defence of Basic English," *QQ*, 51 (1944–5), 117–23; "Washington Irving and Charles Dickens," *Amer Lit*, 16 (1944–5), 332–9; "A Probable Addition to the Thackeray Canon," *PMLA*, 60 (1945), 607–11; "The Novel in Canada," *QQ*, 52 (1945), 322–31; "The State of Canadian Poetry," *Can Student*, 24 (1945–6), 53–4, 59; "The First Canadian Novel," *DR*, 26 (1946–7), 143–50; "Flaubert and His Victorian Critics," *UTQ*, 16 (1946–7), 74–84; "The Future of the Novel," *QQ*, 54 (1947), 74–83; "Virginia Woolf as a Literary Critic," *UTQ*, 17 (1947–8), 234–44; "The Poetry of Duncan Campbell Scott," *Can For*, 38 (1948–9), 107–9; "Literary Criticism in Canada," *UTQ*, 19 (1949–50), 113–9; "Leacock as a Satirist," *QQ*, 58 (1951), 208–19; "A Reading of Lampman's 'Heat,' " *Culture*, 14 (1953), 292–7; "Areas of Research in Canadian Literature," *UTQ*, 23 (1953–4), 58–63; "English-Canadian Poetry, 1944–1954," *Culture*, 15 (1954), 255–65; "The Innocent Eye: The Art of Ethel Wilson," *QQ*, 61 (1954–5), 42–52; "The Role of the Critic," *Can Author and Bookman*, 32 (1956–7), 24–6; "The Canadian Writer and His Public," in *Studia Varia: Royal Society of Canada Literary and Scientific Papers* (Toronto, 1957), pp. 10–20; "A Colonial Romantic: Major John Richardson, Soldier and Novelist," *Can L*, No. 2 (autumn, 1959), 20–31, and No. 3 (winter, 1960), 47–56; "The Young Writer and the Canadian Cultural Milieu," *QQ*, 69 (1962), 378–90.   (C) *Can For, Can L, Culture, Fiddlehead, QQ, UTQ*. (D) "Canadian Fiction: 1920–1940," to appear in C. F. Klinck, *et al.*, eds., *A Literary History of Canada* (complete); "Contemporary Writing in New Brunswick," to appear in The Arts in New Brunswick (completed).

UNIVERSITY OF OTTAWA

CAMPBELL, A. P.: (B) "The Medieval Mystery Cycle Liturgical in Impulse," *RUO*, 33 (1963), 23–37.   (C) *Spiritual Life*.   (D) Quido Faba's *Rota Nova* (almost complete).

McGUINTY, DALTON J.: (D) The Christian Tradition in English Literature, a volume of essays and a companion anthology (begun).

MARCOTTE, PAUL J.: (B) "Gerard Manley Hopkins: Poet without Glitter," *Inscape*, No. 1 (spring, 1959), 4–17; "Architecture no *Fine Art*," *Inscape*, No. 2 (summer, 1959), 9–18; "On the Popularity of Certain Modern Novels," *Inscape*, No. 2 (summer, 1959), 30–33; "Literature and Beauty," *Inscape*, No. 3 (winter, 1959), 17–24; "Poetry and the Creative Process," *RUO*, 30 (1960), 385–99.   (C) *Inscape, RUO*.   (D) Speculative Literary Criticism (about half complete); A Commentary on Aristotle's "Poetics" (almost complete); "Mr. Addison's Concept of Literary Taste" (completed); "Pluralism and the Chicago Neo-Aristotelians" (completed); "Pater's 'Renaissance': Its Preface and Conclusion" (almost complete).

QUEEN'S UNIVERSITY

ANGUS, WILLIAM: (A) *Play Directing in School and Community* (privately published, 1962).   (B) "Expressionism in the Theatre," *QJS*, 19 (1933), 477–92; "Poor Richard's Alphabet and His Pronunciation," *Speech Monographs*, 2 (Oct., 1935), 60–71; "The Turks' Characteristic Difficulties in Learning English Pronunciations," *QJS*, 23 (1937), 238–43; "An Appraisal of David Garrick, Based Mainly on Contemporary Sources," *QJS*, 25 (1939), 30–42; "Artistic Stage Lighting," *Curtain Call* (Toronto) (Oct., 1939); "Actors and Audiences in Eighteenth Century London" in D. C. Bryant, *et al.*, eds., *Studies in Speech and Drama in Honor of Alexander M. Drummond* (Ithaca 1944), 123–38; "Theatre Design: A Producer's Point of View," *J Roy Archit Inst Can* (Dec., 1952); "Theatre," in *Enc Can* (1958). (C) *QJS, QQ.* (D) "Theatre in Canada" (to appear in *Enc Grolier Soc* (New York); an edition, with introduction and notes, of *The Actor: A Treatise on the Art of Playing* (London, 1750), anon., but written by Dr. (calling himself "Sir") John Hill.

FERGUSON, W. CRAIG: (B) "The Compositors of *Henry IV, Part 2, Much Ado About Nothing, The Shoemakers' Holiday,* and *The First Part of the Contention,*" *SB*, 13 (1960), 19–29. (C) *SB.*

MATTHEWS, JOHN P.: (A) *Tradition in Exile: A Comparative Study of Social Influences on the Development of Australian and Canadian Poetry in the Nineteenth Century* (Toronto, 1962), x + 197 pp. (C) *QQ.* (D) A Comparison of Canadian and Australian poetry in the twentieth century (begun); "Tennyson's *Idylls of the King* as Victorian Epic" (in planning stages).

SPETTIGUE, DOUGLAS O.: (D) (with Hugo McPherson) "English-Canadian Fiction, 1940–1960," for C. F. Klinck, *et al.* eds., A Literary History of Canada (completed).

STEDMOND, J. M.: (B) "The Modern Critic: British, American, and Canadian," *CE*, 17 (1955–6), 427–33; "Another Possible Analogue for Swift's *Tale of a Tub,*" *MLN*, 72 (1957), 13–18; "Hardy's *Dynasts* and the 'Mythical Method,'" *English*, 12 (1958), 1–4; "Genre and *Tristram Shandy,*" *PQ*, 38 (1959), 37–51; "Style and *Tristram Shandy,*" *MLQ*, 20 (1959), 243–51; "Sterne as Plagiarist," *E&S*, 41 (1960), 308–12; "Satire and *Tristram Shandy,*" *SEL*, 1, No. 3 (summer, 1961), 53–63. (C) *Can For, CE, DR, QQ.* (D) A book-length study of Laurence Sterne's *Tristram Shandy* and its tradition (about two-thirds complete).

WHALLEY, GEORGE: (A) *Poetic Process* (London, 1953), xl + 256 pp.; *Coleridge and Sara Hutchinson and the Asra Poems* (London and Toronto, 1955), xxii + 188 pp.; (ed., with introduction by W. O. Raymond) *Selected Poems of George Herbert Clarke* (Toronto, 1954), xxvi + 54 pp.; (ed., with introduction by F. R. Scott) *Writing in Canada* (Toronto, 1956), xii + 147 pp.; *The Legend of John Hornby* (London and Toronto, 1962), xiv + 367 pp.; (ed. with introduction) *Community of Scholars* (Toronto, 1963). (B) "The Mariner and the Albatross," *UTQ*, 16 (1946–7), 381–98; "The Bristol Library Borrowings of Southey and Coleridge, 1793–8," *Library*, series 5, 4 (1949), 114–32; "Coleridge and Southey in Bristol, 1795," *RES*, NS, 1 (1950), 324–40; "The Dispersal of S. T. Coleridge's Books," *TLS*, No. 2491 (Oct. 28, 1949), 704; "Coleridge and John Murray," *Quarterly R*, 289 (1951), 253–66; "The Integrity of *Biographia Literaria,*" *E&S*, NS, 6 (1953), 87–101; "Preface to *Lyrical Ballads*: A Portent," *UTQ*, 25 (1955–6), 467–83; "In the Land of Feast or Famine: The Legend of John Hornby," *Cornhill Mag*, 169 (1956–8), 191–213, reprinted in *Tam R*, No. 5 (autumn, 1957), 3–26, and reprinted in part in W. Toye, ed., *A Book of Canada* (London and Toronto, 1962), 312–17; "The Fields of

Sleep," *RES*, 9 (1958), 49–53; "Coleridge's Debt to Charles Lamb," *E&S*, NS, 11 (1958), 68–85; "Scholarship and Criticism," *UTQ*, 29 (1959–60), 33–45; "The Humanities and Modern Science: Two Cultures or One?" *Proc NCCUC*, 36 (1960), 45–54, reprinted in *QQ*, 68 (1961), 237–48, and in *Current*, No. 19 (1961), 58–64; "Coleridge on the *Prometheus of Aeschylus*," *TRSC*, 3rd series, s. 2, 54 (1960), 13–24; "Portrait of a Bibliophile VII: Samuel Taylor Coleridge 1772–1834," *BC*, 10 (1961), 275–90; and contributions to K. Coburn, ed., *The Notebooks of S. T. Coleridge* (New York and London, 1957 and 1961), to G. Watson, ed., *Camb Bibliog Eng Lit*, V (1957), and to Allan Wade, *Bibliography of W. B. Yeats* (2nd ed., London, 1958); "Coleridge Unlabyrinthed," *UTQ*, 32 (1962–3), 325–45. (C) *BC, Landfall, Library, MLR, QQ, RES, UTQ.* (D) Marginalia of S. T. Coleridge, being vols. XVII, XVIII, and XIX of the *Collected Coleridge* (almost complete); Poetical Works of S. T. Coleridge, being vols. I and II of the *Collected Coleridge* (well advanced); A bibliography of S. T. Coleridge (about one-third complete); Shaping Spirit, a selection of Coleridge's writings (about one-third complete).

ROYAL MILITARY COLLEGE

AVIS, WALTER S.: (A) (with others) *The Beginning Dictionary*, in Dictionary of Canadian English series (Toronto, 1962). (B) "Speech Differences along the Ontario-United States Border," "Part 1, Vocabulary," *JCLA*, 1 (1954), 13–18, "Part 2, Grammar and Syntax," *JCLA*, 1 (1955), 14–19, "Part 3, Pronunciation," *JCLA*, 2 (1956), 41–59; "Crocus Bag: A Problem in Areal Linguistics," *Amer Speech*, 30 (1955), 5–16; "Canadian English Merits a Dictionary," *Culture*, 18 (1957), 245–56; "Pronunciation and Canadian Dictionaries," *Translators' J*, 3 (1959), 21–4; "The New England 'Short O': A Recessive Phoneme," *Language*, 37 (1961), 544–88. (C) *Amer Speech, College English, JCLA, Pub Amer Dialect Soc, Translators' J.* (D) Intermediate Dictionary (in press) and Senior Dictionary (in MS) both part of Dictionary of Canadian English series; Dictionary of Canadianisms—the fourth part (citations are being collected—editing to begin in summer, 1963); several other articles in various stages of development.

WATTERS, R. E.: (A) *Canadian Anthology* (Toronto, 1955); *British Columbia: A Centennial Anthology* (1958), reprinted as *British Columbia* (Toronto, 1961); *A Check List of Canadian Literature and Background Materials, 1628–1950* (Toronto, 1959) (reprinted 1960); *The Creative Reader: An Anthology of Fiction, Drama, and Poetry* (rev., enlarged ed., New York, 1962). (B) "Ethel Wilson, the Experienced Traveller," *BC Lib Q*, 21 (1958), 21–7; "A Special Tang: Stephen Leacock's Canadian Humour," *Can L*, 5 (1960), 21–32; "Original Relations: A Genographic Approach to the Literature of Canada and Australia," *Can Lit*, 7 (1961), 6–17; introduction to Frederick Philip Grove's *The Master of the Mill* (Toronto, 1961); "A Quest for National Identity: Canadian Literature vis-à-vis the Literatures of Great Britain and the United States," *Proc the Third Int Congress of Comp Lit* (The Hague, 1962), 224–41; "Canadian Literature," in *Collier's Enc* (1962). (C) *Amer Lit, PMLA, Can L, QQ.* (D) Revision of *Canadian Anthology* (almost finished); a check list of articles and monographs about Canadian authors and Canadian literature (typescript completed); "English Social Patterns in Australian Fiction," a paper given in December, 1962, to a conference in Washington (needs further substantiation, revision, etc.).

ST. FRANCIS XAVIER UNIVERSITY

BANNON, R. V.: (A) *Eastland Echoes* (Toronto, 1937). (B) "Antoine Gaulin (1674–1770), an Apostle of Early Acadia," *Can Cath Hist Ass Report* (1951), 49–61; numerous articles contributed to Dictionary of Canadian Biography and *Enc Can*.

EDWARDS, W. X.: (B) "The MacPherson-Tompkins Era of St. Francis Xavier University," *Can Cath Hist Ass Report* (1952), 49–65.

REED, J. K.: (B) "Channel of Grace: A Study of George Herbert's *The Temple*," *U Colorado St in Eng* (spring, 1963).

SMETANA, CYRIL L.: (B) "Aelfric and the Early Medieval Homiliary," *Traditio*, 15 (1959), 163–204; "Aelfric and the Homiliary of Haymo of Halberstadt," *Traditio*, 17 (1961), 457–69. (D) The orthodoxy of the O.E. body and soul poem (to be completed August, 1963); the influence of the Latin originals on Aelfric's prose style (in germinal state).

UNIVERSITY OF SASKATCHEWAN

CHAMBERS, ROBERT D.: (A) (ed., with Carlyle King) *A Book of Essays* (Toronto, 1963), viii + 152 pp. (B) "Addison at Work on the *Spectator*," *MP*, 56 (1958–9), 145–53.

CHERRY, DOUGLAS R.: (B) "Ruskin: Unacknowledged Legislator of the Social Sciences," in *Thought from the Learned Societies of Canada 1961* (Toronto, 1962), 79–90; "The Fabianism of Shaw," *QQ*, 69 (1962–3), 83–93; "Shaw's Novels," *DR*, 42 (1962–3), 459–71. (C) *DR, QQ*. (D) An article on the idea of liberty in Wordsworth's poems (in early stages).

HARGREAVES, H. A.: (B) "Swinburne's Greek Plays and God, 'The Supreme Evil,'" *MLN*, 76 (1961), 607–16; "Mrs. Behn's Warning of the Dutch Thames Plot," *N&Q*, NS, 9 (1962), 61–3; "A Case for Mister Behn," *N&Q*, NS, 9 (1962), 203–5. (D) "Music in the Plays of John Marston" (begun).

KING, CARLYLE: (A) (ed.) *Saskatchewan Harvest: A Golden Jubilee Selection of Song and Story* (Toronto, 1955), 224 pp.; (ed., with A. S. Morton) *Saskatchewan: The Making of a University* (Toronto, 1959), 120 pp.; *The First Fifty* (Toronto, 1959), 186 pp.; (ed.) *Three Stories by Joseph Conrad* (Toronto, 1961), 247 pp. (B) "Aldous Huxley's Way to God," *QQ*, 61 (1954), 80–100; "The Politics of George Orwell," *UTQ*, 26 (1956–7), 79–91; "GBS and Music," *QQ*, 63 (1956–7), 165–78; "Irwin Edman's Candle," *DR*, 37 (1957–8), 223–34; "Joyce Cary and the Creative Imagination," *Tam R*, No. 10 (winter, 1959), 39–51. (C) *Can For, DR, QQ, Tam R*. (D) An edition of Canadian poetry (in the press).

SMITH, J. PERCY: (B) "Criticism and *Christabel*," *UTQ*, 21 (1951–2), 14–26; "Superman versus Man: Bernard Shaw on Shakespeare," *YR*, NS, 42 (1952–3), 67–82; "A Shavian Tragedy: *The Doctor's Dilemma*," in B. H. Lehman, *et al.*, eds., *The Image of the Work: Essays in Criticism* (Berkeley and Los Angeles, 1955), 187–207; "G.B.S. on the Theatre,"

Tam R, No. 15 (spring, 1960), 73–86. (D) A book on the early life and thought of Bernard Shaw (almost complete).

TRACY, CLARENCE: (A) *The Artificial Bastard: A Biography of Richard Savage* (Toronto, 1953), xviii + 164 pp.; (ed.) *The Poetical Works of Richard Savage* (Cambridge, 1962), 277 pp. (B) "Browning's Heresies," *SP*, 33 (1936), 610–25; "Caliban upon Setebos," *SP*, 35 (1938), 487–99; "Bishop Blougram," *MLR*, 34 (1939), 422–5; "The American Scholar Today," *QQ*, 49 (1941), 143–8; "Johnson and the Art of Anecdote," *UTQ*, 15 (1945), 86–93; " 'Democritus, Arise!': A Study of Dr. Johnson's Humour," *YR*, NS, 39 (1949–50), 294–310; "Subsistence Education," *QQ*, 61 (1954–5), 230–39; "The Unity of *Gulliver's Travels*," *QQ*, 68 (1961–2), 597–609; bibliographies of Robert and Elizabeth Barrett Browning, in G. Watson, ed., *Camb Bibliog Eng Lit*, V (1957), 582–3, 586–9. (C) *QQ*. (D) An edition of Dr. Johnson's *Life of Savage*, for the Yale edition of the complete works of Johnson (completed in draft); an edition of Richard Graves's *Spiritual Quixote* (to appear in 1963); a bibliography of first editions of Richard Savage, to appear in *BC* (almost complete); a critical book on the art of biography (in planning stages).

SIR GEORGE WILLIAMS UNIVERSITY

COMPTON, NEIL: (B) "The Mass Media," in M. Oliver, ed., *Social Purpose for Canada* (Toronto, 1961), 59–87; "[Television in Canada:] Climate," *Can Art*, 19 (1962), 339–40. (C) *Christian Outlook, Northern R.* (D) A Shakespeare Handbook (to be ready in 1963); The Gentleman in Eighteenth-Century England (research completed).

FRANCIS, WYNNE: (B) "Montreal Poets of the Forties," *Can L*, No. 14 (autumn, 1962), 21–34.

LAMB, S. S.: (B) "The Novels of Amos Tutuola," *Universitas* (1955); "Aspects of Beckett," in *Thought from the Learned Societies of Canada 1961* (Toronto, 1962). (C) *Can Art*. (D) A book on seventeenth-century poetry (begun).

SOMMER, RICHARD J.: (B) "The *Odyssey* and Primitive Religion," in *Arbok for Universitetet i Bergen*, Humanistisk Serie, No. 2 (Bergen and Oslo, 1962), 44 pp. (D) (with G. Roppen) Strangers and Pilgrims: The Metaphor of the Journey in Literature (Oslo, 1963) (in proof).

UNIVERSITY OF TORONTO—UNIVERSITY COLLEGE

BENTLEY, GERALD EADES, JR.: (B) "Blake, Hayley, and Lady Hesketh," *RES*, NS, 7 (1956), 264–86; "The Date of Blake's *Vala or The Four Zoas*," *MLN*, 71 (1956), 487–91; "Thomas Butts, White Collar Maecenas,"*PMLA*, 71 (1956), 1052–66; "William Blake as a Private Publisher," *BNYPL*, 61 (1957), 539–60; "A. S. Mathew, Patron of Blake and Flaxman," *N&Q*, NS, 5 (1958), 168–78; "Blake's Engravings and His Friendship with Flaxman," *SB*, 12 (1959), 161–88; "The Promotion of Blake's *Grave* Designs," *UTQ*, 31 (1962), 339–53. (C) *MP, PQ*. (D) (ed.) William Blake's *Four Zoas* (to appear in 1963); (with M. K. Nurmi) A Blake Bibliography (to appear in 1963); Records of the Life of William Blake (at the press); The Autobiography of John Linnell (to be completed in 1963); The Writings of William Blake in Prose and Verse (just beginning).

BESSINGER, J. B., JR.: (A) *A Short Dictionary of Anglo-Saxon Poetry* (Toronto, 1960), xviii + 88 pp. (second revised printing, 1961). (B) *"Beowulf* and the Harp at Sutton Hoo," *UTQ*, 27 (1957–8), 148–68; "The Sutton Hoo Ship-Burial: A Chronological Bibliography, Part Two," *Speculum*, 33 (1958), 515–22; "The Oral Text of Pound's *Seafarer*," *QJS*, 62 (1961), 173–7; "Computer Techniques for an Old English Concordance," *Amer Documentation*, 12 (1961), 227–9; *"Maldon and the Olafsdrápa*: An Historical Caveat," *Comp Lit*, 14 (1962), 23–35. (C) *JEGP, Speculum, UTQ*. (D) A computer-concordance of the Old English poetic corpus (rather more than half completed).

BISSELL, C. T.: (A) (ed.) *Our Living Tradition: Seven Canadians* (Toronto, 1957), xi + 149 pp. (B) "A Study of *The Way of all Flesh*," in H. Davis, W. C. Devane, and R. C. Bald, eds., *Nineteenth-Century Studies*, (Ithaca, 1940), 277–303; "The Novels of George Bernard Shaw," *UTQ*, 17 (1947–8), 38–51; "Fiction," in Letters in Canada, *UTQ* (1947–57); "Literary Taste in Central Canada during the Late Nineteenth Century," *CHR*, 31 (1950), 237–51; "Social Analysis in the Novels of George Eliot," *ELH*, 18 (1951), 221–39, reprinted in Austin Wright, ed., *Victorian Literature: Modern Essays in Criticism* (New York, 1961), 154–71; "A Common Ancestry: Literature in Australia and Canada," *UTQ*, 25 (1955–6), 131–42; "The Novel," in Malcolm Ross, ed., *The Arts in Canada* (Toronto, 1958), 92–6; "Samuel Butler and Evolution," in Thomas W. M. Cameron, ed., *Evolution: Its Science and Doctrine* (Toronto, 1960), 189–98; introduction to Sara Jeanette Duncan's *The Imperialist* (Toronto, 1961); introduction to Ernest Buckler's *The Mountain and the Valley* (Toronto, 1961); "The Butlerian Inheritance of G. B. Shaw," *DR*, 41 (1961–2), 159–73.

CARROLL, JOHN: (D) Selected Letters of Samuel Richardson (almost complete).

ENDICOTT, N. J.: (B) "The Novel in England between the Wars," *UTQ*, 12 (1942–3), 18–31; "Sir Thomas Browne as 'Orphan,' with Some Account of his Stepfather, Sir Thomas Dutton," *UTQ*, 30 (1960–1), 180–210. (C) *CHR, UTQ*.

GREENE, ROBERT A.: (B) "Henry More and Robert Boyle on the Spirit of Nature," *JHI*, 23 (1962), 451–74. (D) (with H. MacCallum) an edition of Nathanael Culverwel's *Discourse of the Light of Nature* (1652) (about half complete).

HEYWORTH, P. L.: (B) "Christ Church and Chaucer," *Oxford Mag* (June 21, 1962); "Thomas Smith, Humfrey Wanley and the Cottonian Library," *TLS*, No. 3157 (Aug. 31, 1962), 660. (D) An edition of *Jack Upland, Friar Dow's Reply*, and *Upland's Rejoinder*, from BM Harley MS 6641 and Bodleian MS Digby 41; an edition of the letters of Humfrey Wanley.

KERPNECK, HARVEY: (B) "George Meredith, Sun-Worshipper, and Diana's Redworth," *Nineteenth-Century Fiction* (June, 1953), 77–83; "A Shorn *Shagpat*," *BC* (spring, 1962), 80–94; "Kings of Modern Thought," *MLQ* (Dec., 1963), 392–6. (D) "The Road to Rugby Chapel" (accepted by *UTQ*); "Arnold and Wordsworth" (paper); Symbolism in the Novels of George Meredith (thesis).

LEECH, CLIFFORD: (A) (ed.) W. Mildmay Fane's *Raguaillo d'Oceano*,

1640, and *Candy Restored*, 1641 (Louvain, 1938), viii + 184 pp.; *Shakespeare's Tragedies and Other Studies in Seventeenth Century Drama* (London and New York, 1950), 239 pp. (second impression, 1961, 232 pp.); *John Webster: A Critical Study* (London, 1951), vi + 122 pp.; *A School of Criticism* (Oxford, 1955), 19 pp.; *John Ford and the Drama of His Time* (London, 1957), 144 pp.; *The John Fletcher Plays* (London and Cambridge, Mass., 1962), x + 180 pp.; *William Shakespeare: The Chronicles* (London, 1962), 47 pp.; *Webster: The Duchess of Malfi*, Studies in English Literature (London, 1963), viii + 120 pp.; *O'Neill*, Writers and Critics (London, 1963), 62 pp. (B) "The 'Meaning' of *Measure for Measure*," *ShS*, 3 (1950), 66–73; "Restoration Tragedy: A Reconsideration," *Durham UJ*, NS, 11 (1950), 106–15; "Restoration Comedy: The Earlier Phase," *EIC*, 1 (1951), 165–84; "The Unity of *2 Henry IV*," *ShS*, 6 (1953), 16–24; "The Comedy of Charles Chaplin," *Camb J* (Oct., 1953); "The Theme of Ambition in *All's Well that Ends Well*," *ELH*, 21 (1954), 17–29; "Studies in *Hamlet*, 1901–1955," *ShS*, 9 (1956), 1–15; "Art and the Concept of Will," *Durham UJ*, NS, 17 (1955), 1–7; "Shakespeare's Use of a Five-Act Structure," *Die Neueren Sprachen* (1957), 249–63; "The Structure of the Last Plays," *ShS*, 11 (1958), 19–30; "Shakespeare's Prologues and Epilogues," in D. C. Allen, ed., *Studies in Honor of T. W. Baldwin* (Urbana, Ill., 1958), 150–64; "The Two-part Play: Marlowe and the Early Shakespeare," *Shakespeare Jahrbuch*, 94 (1958), 90–106; "Marlowe's *Edward II*: Power and Suffering," *Crit Q*, 1 (1959), 181–96; "The 'Capability' of Shakespeare," *SQ*, 11 (1960), 123–36; "DeQuincy as Literary Critic," *REL*, 2, No. 1 (Jan., 1961), 38–48; "Eugene O'Neill and His Plays," *Crit Q*, 3 (1961), 242–56, 339–53; "Congreve and the Century's End," in C. B. Woods and C. A. Zimansky, eds., *Studies in English Drama Presented to Baldwin Maxwell* [*PQ*, 41 (1962)] (Iowa City, 1962), 275–93; "Marlowe's Humor," in R. Hosley, ed., *Essays on Shakespeare and Elizabethan Drama in Honor of Hardin Craig* (Columbia, Mo., 1962), 69–81; general editor of the Revels Plays (London and Cambridge, Mass.). (C) *Crit Q, DUJ, Economist, E&S, Etudes Anglaises, MLN, MLR, N&Q, RES, SQ, ShS, Speculum*. (D) An edition of *The Two Gentlemen of Verona*, for the New Arden Shakespeare (almost complete); an anthology of critical essays on Shakespeare's tragedies (almost complete); book on Marlowe (begun).

LEYERLE, JOHN F.: (B) "The Two Voices of William Dunbar," *UTQ*, 31 (1961–2), 316–38. (C) *Medium Ævum, UTQ*. (D) (with R. A. Foakes) Early English Drama, a collection of plays, mysteries, moralities, and interludes to about 1550 (just begun).

MACGILLIVRAY, JAMES R.: (A) *Keats: A Bibliography and Reference Guide*, with an essay on Keats' reputation (Toronto, 1949), lxxxii + 210 pp. (B) "Fiction," in Letters in Canada, *UTQ* (1937–46). (C) *UTQ*. (D) A biographical and critical study of Wordsworth (proceeding).

MCPHERSON, HUGO: (B) "The Novels of Hugh MacLennan," *QQ*, 60 (1953–4), 186–98; "The Two Worlds of Morley Callaghan," *QQ*, 64 (1957–8), 350–65; "Hawthorne's Major Source for His Mythological Tales," *Amer Lit*, 30 (1958–9), 364–5; "Hawthorne's Mythology: A Mirror for Puritans," *UTQ*, 28 (1958–9), 267–78; introduction to Gabrielle Roy's *The Tin Flute* (Toronto, 1958); "Carson McCullers," *Tam R*, No. 11 (spring,

1959), 28–40; "The Garden and the Cage: The Achievement of Gabrielle Roy," *Can L*, No. 1 (summer, 1959), 46–57; introduction to Hugh Mac-Lennan's *Barometer Rising* (Toronto, 1959); introduction to Morley Callaghan's *More Joy in Heaven* (Toronto, 1960); "The Mask of Satire," *Can L*, No. 4 (spring, 1960), 18–30, reprinted in A. J. M. Smith, ed., *Masks of Fiction* (Toronto, 1961), 162–75. (C) *AL, Can Art, Can L, QQ, Tam R, UTQ.* (D) Hawthorne's Mythology: A Study in Imagination (almost complete); a critical study of Joseph Conrad's middle and late works (begun); "Fiction: 1940 to the Present," a chapter in Literary History of Canada (completed).

MORGAN, PETER F.: (B) "Taylor and Hessey: Aspects of their Conduct of the *London Magazine*," *KSJ*, 7 (1958), 61–8; "John Hamilton Reynolds and Thomas Hood," *KSJ*, 11 (1962), 83–95. (D) An edition of the letters of Thomas Hood (almost complete).

PETTIGREW, J. S.: (B) "Tennyson's 'Ulysses': A Reconciliation of Opposites," *Victorian Poetry*, 1, No. 1 (Jan., 1963), 27–45. (C) *Can For, QQ.* (D) Ph.D. thesis, Tennyson's Craftsmanship: A Study of His Development to 1842 (almost complete).

PRIESTLEY, F. E. L.: (A) Edition of William Godwin's *Enquiry concerning Political Justice*, 3 vols. (Toronto, 1946); (with H. Brown, D. Hawkins, and K. Deutsch) *Science and the Creative Spirit* (Toronto, 1958); (special ed.) *The Canadian Dictionary* (Toronto, 1962); (general ed.) *Collected Works of John Stuart Mill* (Toronto, 1963–). (B) "Canadian English," in E. Partridge, *British and American English* (London, 1951), 72–9; "Creative Scholarship," in M. Ross ed., *The Arts in Canada* (Toronto, 1958), 98–101; "Platonism in Godwin's *Political Justice*," *MLQ*, 4 (1943), 63–9; "Keats and Chaucer," *MLQ*, 5 (1944), 439–47; "Blougram's Apologetics," *UTQ*, 15 (1946), 139–47; "Newton and the Romantic Concept of Nature," *UTQ*, 17 (1948), 323–36; "Tennyson's *Idylls*," *UTQ*, 19 (1949), 35–49, reprinted in J. Kilham, ed., *Critical Essays on the Poetry of Tennyson* (London, 1960); "A Reading of *La Saisiaz*," *UTQ*, 25 (1955), 47–59; "Drama and the Social Historian," *TRSC*, 51 (1957), s. 2, 23–9; "Science and the Poet," *DR*, 38 (1958), 141–53; "Canadian English," in *Enc Can*, IV, 8–11. (C) *DR, JHI, MP, UTQ.* (D) "Control of Tone in Tennyson's *The Princess*," to appear in *TRSC* (1964); "The Ironic Pattern of Browning's *Paracelsus*," to appear in *UTQ* (1964); "Pope and the Great Chain of Being," to appear in 1964; Eighteenth-Century Newtonianism in England (50,000 words written, to be completed 1965); short volume of critical essays on Tennyson (to be completed 1964, first draft complete).

PRITCHARD, ALLAN D.: (B) "George Wither and the Somers Islands," *N&Q*, NS, 8 (1961), 428–30; "Wither's *Motto* and Browne's *Religio Medici*," *PQ*, 40 (1961), 302–7; "George Wither: The Poet as Prophet," *SP*, 59 (1962), 211–30; "From These Uncouth Shores: Seventeenth-Century Literature of Newfoundland," *Can L*, No. 14 (autumn, 1962), 5–20. (C) *DR.* (D) "Wither's Quarrel with the Stationers: An Anonymous Reply to *The Schollers Purgatory*" (to appear in *SB*); "A Manuscript of Wither's *Psalms*" (to appear in *HLQ*); one or two other articles on Wither (almost complete); a longer study of the life and work of George Wither (in early stages).

PROUDFOOT, G. R.: (D) An edition of *A Knack to Know a Knave*, 1594 (in press); a critical edition of *The Shakespeare 'Apocrypha'* (begun).

SIRLUCK, ERNEST: (A) *Complete Prose Works of John Milton*, II, *1643–1648* (London and New Haven, 1959), xii + 840 pp.   (B) "A Note on the Rhetoric of Spenser's 'Despair,' " *MP*, 47 (1949–50), 8–11; "Milton Revises *The Faerie Queene*," *MP*, 48 (1950–1), 90–6; "*The Faerie Queene*, Book II, and the *Nicomachean Ethics*," *MP*, 49 (1951–2), 73–100; "Certain Editorial Tendencies Exemplified: A New Edition of Milton's *An Apology*," *MP*, 50 (1952–3), 201–5; "Milton's Critical Use of Historical Sources: An Illustration," *MP*, 50 (1952–3), 226–31; "*Eikon Basilike, Eikon Alethine*, and *Eikonoklastes*," *MLN*, 69 (1954), 497–502; "Shakespeare and Jonson among the Pamphleteers of the First Civil War: Some Unreported Seventeenth-Century Allusions," *MP*, 53 (1955–6), 88–99; "Howells' *A Modern Instance*: Title and Theme," *MAR*, 10 (1956), 66–72; "*To Your Tents, O Israel*: A Lost Pamphlet," *HLQ*, 19 (1956), 301–5; "Milton," in *Amer Peoples Enc* (1958); "*Areopagitica* and a Forgotten Licensing Controversy," *RES*, NS, 11 (1960), 260–74; "Milton's Idle Right Hand," *JEGP*, 60 (1961), 749–85; "Milton's Political Thought: The First Cycle," *MP*, 61 (1964), 209–24.   (C) *Can For, CH, HLQ, Int J, JEGP, MLN, MP, RES, UTQ*.   (D) Seventeenth-Century Epic and Mock-Epic Poems: A Critical Anthology (early stages); Milton and the Law of Nature (half completed); joint editor of a series of anthologies of criticism on special subjects, to be published by University of Chicago Press in collaboration with University of Toronto Press (first group of four planned for 1964).

WATT, F. W.   (A) *Steinbeck* (Edinburgh and London, 1962), 117 pp.   (B) "The National Policy, the Workingman, and Proletarian Ideas in Victorian Canada," *CHR*, 40 (1959), 1–26; "The Theme of 'Canada's Century', 1896–1920," *DR*, 38 (1958–9), 154–66; "Morley Callaghan as Thinker," *DR*, 39 (1959–60), 305–13, reprinted in A. J. M. Smith, ed., *Masks of Fiction* (Toronto, 1961), 116–27; "Fiction," in Letters in Canada, *UTQ* (1960–); "Canada," in A. L. McLeod, ed., *The Commonwealth Pen: An Introduction to the Literature of the British Commonwealth* (Ithaca, 1961), 11–34.   (C) *Can L, UTQ*.

WOODHOUSE, A. S. P.: (A) (ed., with an introduction) *Puritanism and Liberty, Being the Army Debates from the Clarke Manuscripts (1647–9) with Supplementary Documents* (London, 1938), 100 + 506 pp. (2nd ed., London, 1950); (with Watson Kirkconnell) *The Humanities in Canada* (Ottawa, 1947), 287 pp.   (B) "Collins and the Creative Imagination: A Study in the Critical Background of his Odes," in M. W. Wallace, ed., *Studies in English by Members of University College, Toronto* (Toronto, 1931), 59–130; "Milton, Puritanism and Liberty," *UTQ*, 4 (1934–5), 483–513; "Puritanism and Democracy," *CJEPS*, 4 (1938), 1–21; "The Argument of Milton's *Comus*," *UTQ*, 11 (1941–2), 46–71; "Notes on Milton's Early Development," *UTQ*, 13 (1943–4), 66–101; "William John Alexander, Critic and Teacher," *UTQ*, 14 (1944–5), 8–32; "The Approach to Milton: A Note on Practical Criticism," *TRSC*, 3rd series, s. 2, 38 (1944), 201–13; "Charles Norris Cochrane," *Proc RSC* (1946), 83–7; "Notes on Milton's Views on the Creation: The Initial Phases," *PQ*, 28 (1949), 211–36; "*Samson Agonistes* and Milton's Experience," *TRSC*, 3rd series, s. 2, 43

(1949), 157–75; "Nature and Grace in *The Faerie Queene*," *ELH*, 16 (1949), 194–228; "Religion and Some Foundations of English Democracy," *PhR*, 61 (1952), 503–31; "Milton's Pastoral Monodies," in M. E. White, ed., *Studies in Honour of Gilbert Norwood* (Toronto, 1952), 261–78; "Pattern in *Paradise Lost*," *UTQ*, 22 (1952–3), 109–27; "Theme and Pattern in *Paradise Regained*," *UTQ*, 25 (1955–6), 167–82; "Tragic Effect in *Samson Agonistes*," *UTQ*, 28 (1958–9), 205–22.   (C) *AHR, ELH, JEGP, MLN, MLR, MP, PhR, RES, UTQ*.   (D) Volume I of the Variorum commentary on Milton's poetry, to be added to the Columbia edition of Milton (almost complete); Volume V of the Yale edition of Milton's prose (begun); Religion and English Poetry, Weil Foundation Lectures, 1962 (soon to be published).

UNIVERSITY OF TORONTO—VICTORIA COLLEGE

BUITENHUIS, PETER: (A) (ed., with an introduction) Henry James' *French Writers and American Women: Essays* (Brantford, Conn., 1960), 81 pp.   (B) "Aesthetics of the Skyscraper: The Views of Sullivan, James and Wright," *Amer Q*, 9 (1957), 316–24; "Henry James on Hawthorne," *NEQ*, 32 (1959), 207–25; "From Daisy Miller to Julia Bride: 'A Whole Passage of Intellectual History,'" *Amer Q*, 11 (1959), 136–46; "The Essentials of Life: 'The Open Boat' as Existentialist Fiction," *MFS*, 5 (1959–60), 243–50; "The Value of Mencken," *WHR*, 14 (1960), 19–28; "Comic Pastoral: Henry James's *The Europeans*," *UTQ*, 31 (1962–3), 152–63; "Henry James and Daudet," *HAC Bull*, 12, No. 2 (winter, 1962), 62–9. (C) *Amer Q, Can For, NY Times Book R*, Toronto *Globe and Mail, UTQ, YR*.   (D) Henry James: The Grasping Imagination: A Study of his American Fiction (almost complete).

COBURN, KATHLEEN: (A) (ed.) *The Philosophical Lectures of Samuel Taylor Coleridge* (London and New York, 1949), 480 pp.; (ed.) *Inquiring Spirit: A New Presentation of Coleridge from His Published and Unpublished Prose Writings* (London and New York, 1951), 454 pp.; (ed.) *The Letters of Sara Hutchinson from 1800 to 1835* (London and Toronto, 1954), xxxviii + 474 pp.; (ed.) *The Notebooks of Samuel Taylor Coleridge*, I, *1794–1804* (New York, 1957) [text] xlii + 546 pp. and [notes] xlvi + 615 pp.; *The Notebooks of Samuel Taylor Coleridge*, II, *1804–1808* (New York, 1961) [text] xx + 478 pp. and [notes] xxxiv + 548 pp.   (B) "S. T. Coleridge's Philosophical Lectures of 1818–19," *RES*, 10 (1934), 428–37; "Notes on Washington Allston from the Unpublished Notebooks of S. T. Coleridge," *Gaz des Beaux Arts*, series VI, 26 (1944), 249–52; "Coleridge and Wordsworth and 'the Supernatural,'" *UTQ*, 25 (1955–6), 121–30; "Poet into Public Servant," *TRSC*, 3rd series, s. 2, 54 (1960), 1–11.   (D) "Hazlitt on The Disinterested Imagination" (to appear in a collection of critical essays on Romantic writers, edited by H. N. Frye, J. E. Jordan, and J. V. Logan and tentatively entitled Poets and Prose-writers of the Romantic Movement: Essays on Blake and Others); The Notebooks of Samuel Taylor Coleridge, Vol. III; a volume on Coleridge for the Twentieth Century Views series.

Fox, DENTON: (B) "Dunbar's *The Golden Targe*," *ELH*, 26 (1959), 311–34; "The Chronology of William Dunbar," *PQ*, 39 (1960), 413–25; "Henryson's *Fables*," *ELH*, 29 (1962), 337–56.   (D) A complete edition of Robert Henryson's poems (to be published within two years).

FRYE, NORTHROP: (A) *Fearful Symmetry: A Study of William Blake* (Princeton, 1947), 462 pp. (reprinted in paperback, 1958, and with a new preface, 1962); (ed., with introduction and notes) John Milton's *Paradise Lost and Selected Poetry and Prose* (New York and Toronto, 1950), xxxviii + 601 pp.; (ed., with an introduction) Pelham Edgar's *Across My Path* (Toronto, 1952), xii + 167 pp.; (ed., with an introduction) *Selected Poetry and Prose of William Blake* (New York, 1953), xxx + 475 pp.; (ed., with an introduction) C. T. Currelly's *I Brought the Ages Home* (Toronto, 1956), x + 312 pp.; (ed., with an introduction) "Lexis and Melos," in *Sound and Poetry: English Institute Essays 1956* (New York, 1957), xxviii + 156 pp.; *Anatomy of Criticism: Four Essays* (Princeton, 1957), x + 383 pp. (reprinted, German translation published, Italian translation in preparation); (ed., with an introduction) E. J. Pratt, *Collected Poems* (2nd ed.; Toronto, 1958), xxviii + 395 pp.; (ed., with introduction and notes) Shakespeare's *The Tempest* (Baltimore, 1959), The Pelican Shakespeare, 112 pp.; *By Liberal Things*, Installation Address as Principal of Victoria College (Toronto, 1959), 23 pp.; (ed., with an introduction) Thomas McCulloch's *The Stepsure Letters* (Toronto, 1960), x + 160 pp.; (ed., with a preface) Peter F. Fisher's *The Valley of Vision: Blake as Prophet and Revolutionary* (Toronto, 1961), xii + 261 pp.; (ed., with introduction) *Design for Learning* (Toronto, 1962), x + 148 pp.; *The Well-Tempered Critic* (Bloomington, Ind., 1963), xii + 160 pp.; *T. S. Eliot* (Edinburgh and London, 1963), 106 pp.; *The Educated Imagination* (Toronto, 1963), 68 pp.; *Fables of Identity: Studies in Poetic Mythology* (New York, 1963), vi + 264 pp. (B) "Music in Poetry," *UTQ*, 11 (1941–2), 166–79; "The Anatomy in Prose Fiction," *MAR*, 3 (1942), 35–47; "The Nature of Satire," *UTQ*, 14 (1944–5), 75–89, reprinted in C. A. Allen and G. D. Stephens, eds., *Satire: Theory and Practice* (Belmont, Calif., 1962), 15–30; (trans. by G. Sylvestre), "La tradition narrative dans la poésie canadienne-anglais," *Gants du Ciel*, 11 (printemps, 1946), 19–30; "Yeats and the Language of Symbolism," *UTQ*, 17 (1947–8), 1–17; "The Eternal Tramp," *Here and Now*, 1, No. 1 (Dec., 1947), 8–11; "David Milne: Appreciation," *Here and Now*, 1, No. 2 (May, 1948), 47–8; "The Argument of Comedy," in D. A. Robertson, Jr., ed., *English Institute Essays 1948* (New York, 1949), 58–73, reprinted in L. Dean, ed., *Shakespeare: Modern Essays in Criticism* (New York, 1957), 79–89; "The Church: Its Relation to Society," in Rev. H. W. Vaughan, ed., *The Living Church* (Toronto, 1949), 152–72; "The Function of Criticism at the Present Time," *UTQ*, 19 (1949–50), 1–16, reprinted in Malcolm Ross, ed., *Our Sense of Identity: A Book of Canadian Essays* (Toronto, 1954), 247–65; "The Four Forms of Prose Fiction," *Hud R*, 2 (1949–50), 582–95, reprinted in F. Morgan, ed., *The Hudson Review Anthology* (New York, 1961), 336–50; "Levels of Meaning in Literature," *KR*, 12 (1950), 246–62; "Blake's Treatment of the Archetype," in A. S. Downer, ed., *English Institute Essays 1950* (New York, 1951), 170–96, reprinted in J. E. Grant, ed., *Discussions of William Blake* (Boston, 1961), 6–16; "The Archetypes of Literature," *KR*, 13 (1951), 92–110, reprinted in J. E. Miller, Jr., ed., *Myth and Method: Modern Theories of Fiction* (Lincoln, Neb., 1960), 144–62; "Poetry and Design in William Blake," *JAAC*, 10 (1951), 35–42, reprinted in J. E. Grant, ed., *Discussions of William Blake* (Boston, 1961), 44–9; "A Conspectus of Dramatic

Genres," *KR*, 13 (1951), 543–62; "The Analogy of Democracy," *Bias* (Feb., 1952), 2–6; "Three Meanings of Symbolism," *Yale French Studies*, No. 9 (1952), 11–19; "Comic Myth in Shakespeare," *TRSC*, 3rd series, s. 2, 46 (1952), 47–58; "Trends in Modern Culture," in R. C. Chalmers, ed., *The Heritage of Western Culture* (Toronto, 1952), 102–17; "Towards a Theory of Cultural History," *UTQ*, 22 (1952–3), 325–41; "Characterization in Shakespearean Comedy," *SQ*, 4 (1953), 271–7; "English Canadian Literature, 1929–1954," *BA* (summer, 1955), 270–4; "The Language of Poetry," *Explorations*, 4 (1955), 82–90, reprinted in E. Carpenter and M. McLuhan, eds., *Explorations in Communication* (Boston, 1960), 43–53; "Oswald Spengler," in *Architects of Modern Thought* (Toronto, 1955), 83–90; "La Poesia anglo-canadiense," *SUR*, 240 (1956), 30–9; "The Typology of *Paradise Regained*," *MP*, 53 (1955–6), 227–38; "Towards Defining an Age of Sensibility," *ELH*, 23 (1956), 144–52, reprinted in J. L. Clifford, ed., *Eighteenth Century English Literature: Modern Essays in Criticism* (New York, 1959), 311–18; "Quest and Cycle in *Finnegan's Wake*," *James Joyce R*, 1 (1957), 39–47; "The Realistic Oriole: A Study of Wallace Stevens," *Hud R*, 10 (1957–8), 353–70; "William Blake," in C. W. and L. H. Houtchens, eds., *The English Romantic Poets and Essayists: A Review of Research and Criticism* (New York, 1957), 1–31; "Notes for a Commentary on *Milton*," in V. de S. Pinto, ed., *The Divine Vision: Studies in the Poetry and Art of William Blake* (London, 1957), 97–137; "Preface to an Uncollected Anthology," in E. G. D. Murray, ed., *Studia Varia: Royal Society of Canada Literary and Scientific Papers* (Toronto, 1957), 21–36; "Blake after Two Centuries," *UTQ*, 27 (1957–8), 10–21, reprinted in M. H. Abrams, ed., *English Romantic Poets: Modern Essays in Criticism* (New York, 1960), 55–67; "Blake's Introduction to Experience," *HLQ*, 21 (1957–8), 57–67; "Nature and Homer," *Texas Q*, 1 (1958), 192–204; "Poetry," in Malcolm Ross, ed., *The Arts in Canada* (Toronto, 1958), 84–90; "Culture and the National Will," published by Carleton U, Ottawa, for the Institute of Canadian Studies (n.p., n.d.); "Humanities in a New World," in *3 Lectures: University of Toronto Installation Lectures* (Toronto, 1958), 9–23, reprinted in Bloomfield and Robbins, eds., *Form and Idea* (New York, 1961), 162–81; "The Study of English in Canada," *DR*, 36 (1958–9), 1–7; "Sir James Frazer," in *Architects of Modern Thought*, 3rd and 4th series (Toronto, 1959), 22–32; "Religion and Modern Poetry," in R. C. Chalmers and J. A. Irving, eds., *Challenge and Response: Modern Ideas and Religion* (Toronto, 1959), 23–36; "Literature as Context," in W. P. Friederich, ed., *Comparative Literature*, 1 (Chapel Hill, N.C., 1959), 44–55, reprinted in C. A. Patrides, ed., *Milton's Lycidas: The Tradition and the Poem* (New York, 1961), 200–11; "George Gordon, Lord Byron," in G. B. Harrison (general ed.) *Major British Writers* (New York, 1959), II, 149–234; "Poetry," in Letters in Canada, *UTQ* (1950–9); "New Directions from Old," in H. A. Murray, ed., *Myth and Myth-Making* (New York, 1960), 115–31; "The Critical Discipline," G. Stanley and G. Sylvestre, eds., *Canadian Universities Today* (Toronto, 1961), 30–7, reprinted with some additions and alterations in F. K. Stewart, ed., *The Aims of Education* (Ottawa, 1961), 24–32; "The Structure of Imagery in *The Faerie Queene*," *UTQ*, 30 (1960–1), 109–27; "Myth, Fiction, and Displacement," *Daedalus*, 90 (1961), 587–605; "Academy without Walls," *Can Art*, 18

(1961), 296–8; "Recognition in *The Winter's Tale*," in R. Hosley, ed., *Essays on Shakespeare and Elizabethan Drama in Honor of Hardin Craig* (Columbia, Mo., 1962), 235–46; "Emily Dickinson," in Perry Miller (general ed.) *Major Writers of America* (New York, 1962), II, 3–46; "How True a Twain," in *The Riddle of Shakespeare's Sonnets* (New York, 1962), 25–53; "Shakespeare's Experimental Comedy," "The Tragedies of Nature and Fortune," and "Proposal of Toast," in B. W. Jackson, ed., *Stratford Papers on Shakespeare 1961* (Toronto, 1962), 2–14, 38–55, and 195–6; "The Imaginative and the Imaginary," *Amer J Psychiatry*, 119 (1962), 289–98; "The Road of Excess," in B. Slote, ed., *Myth and Symbol: Critical Approaches and Applications* (Lincoln, Neb., 1963), 3–20; "The Developing Imagination," in *Learning and Language in Literature* (Cambridge, Mass., 1963), 31–58. (C) *Hud R*. (D) Four lectures on Milton (to be published by U of T Press); the Bampton Lectures (to be published by Columbia U Press); an edition of a collection of essays on Blake for the Twentieth Century Views series; an essay on the theory of criticism to be contributed to a handbook published by the MLA; an essay on Blake to be contributed to a book on Romantic poets edited by James V. Logan; an essay to appear in a book of papers contributed to the Symposium on Creativity held at the U of Rochester in 1962; "The Drunken Boat: The Revolutionary Element in Romanticism" (to appear in the next volume of *English Institute Essays*); a paper on Yeats's *Vision* (to be contributed to a volume on Yeats in preparation for 1963); the concluding chapter to C. F. Klinck, *et al.*, eds., Literary History of Canada; "The Problem of Spiritual Authority in the Nineteenth Century" (a lecture to be published by Rice Institute, Texas); a lecture on the relation of critical theory to secondary school education, to be published by the NCTE.

GREENE, DONALD JOHNSON: (A) (ed., with G. Knox) *Treaty Trip: An Abridgement of Dr. Claude Lewis's Journal of an Expedition Made by Him and His Brother Sinclair Lewis to Northern Saskatchewan and Manitoba in 1924* (Minneapolis, 1959); *The Politics of Samuel Johnson* (New Haven, 1960), xx + 354 pp.; (with J. L. Clifford) *A Bibliography of Johnsonian Studies, 1950–1960* (a supplement to *Johnsonian Studies, 1887–1950*), M. Wahba, ed., *Johnsonian Studies* (Cairo and London, 1962), 263–350 (also issued separately). (B) "The Johnsonian Canon: A Neglected Attribution," *PMLA*, 65 (1950), 427–34; "Was Johnson Theatrical Critic of the *Gentleman's Magazine?*" *RES*, NS, 3 (1952), 158–61; " 'Logical Structure' in Eighteenth-Century Poetry," *PQ*, 31 (1952), 315–36; "Smart, Berkeley, the Scientists and the Poets," *JHI*, 14 (1953), 327–52; "With Sinclair Lewis in Darkest Saskatchewan: The Genesis of *Mantrap*," *Sask H*, 6 (1953), 47–52; "Jane Austen and the Peerage," *PMLA*, 68 (1953), 1017–31, reprinted in Ian Watt, ed., *Jane Austen*, Twentieth Century Views (New York, 1963); "Johnson's Contributions to the *Literary Magazine*," *RES*, NS, 7 (1956), 367–92; "Some Notes on Johnson and the *Gentleman's Magazine*," *PMLA*, 74 (1959), 75–84; "*The False Alarm* and *Taxation No Tyranny*: Some Further Observations," *SB*, 13 (1960), 223–31; "Recent Studies in the Restoration and Eighteenth Century," *SEL*, 1 (1961), 115–41; "Is There a 'Tory' Prose Style?" *BNYPL*, 66 (1962), 449–54; "Dr. Johnson's 'Late Conversion': A Reconsideration," in M. Wahba, ed., *Johnsonian Studies* (Cairo, 1962), 61–92; "Samuel Johnson and 'Natural Law,' " *J Brit Studies*,

2 (1962–3), 59–75.   (C) *Johnsonian Newsletter, J Br St, New Mexico Q, PMLA, PQ, RES.*   (D) A volume containing Johnson's political writings, apart from the Parliamentary debates, for the Yale edition of the Works of Samuel Johnson (almost complete); A List of the Writings Attributed to Samuel Johnson (almost complete); have accepted a commission to edit the eighteenth-century volume in a series of "period" anthologies to be published by Houghton Mifflin Co. (scheduled for 1964 or 1965).

HOENIGER, F. D.: (A) (ed.) Shakespeare's *Pericles*, The Arden Shakespeare (London and Cambridge, Mass., 1963), xci + 188 pp.   (B) "Symbolism and Pattern in Rilke's *Duino Elegies*," *GL&L*, NS, 3 (1949–50), 271–83; "The Meaning of *The Winter's Tale*," *UTQ*, 20 (1950–1), 11–26; "Prospero's Storm and Miracle," *SQ*, 7 (1956), 33–8; "A Wyatt Manuscript," *N&Q*, NS, 4 (1957), 103–4; "How Significant are Textual Parallels? A New Author for *Pericles?*" *SQ*, 11 (1960), 27–37; "Irony and Romance in *Cymbeline*," *SEL*, 2 (1962), 219–28.   (C) *Can For, DR, Erasmus, GL&L, N&Q, QQ, RN, SEL, SQ, UTQ.*   (D) A book on design in Shakespeare's romances, based on Ph.D. thesis (almost complete in rough draft); an article on two unpublished Dekker poems and the forger, J. P. Collier (almost complete).

KEE, KENNETH: (B) "Two Chaucerian Gardens," *MS*, 23 (1961), 154–62.   (D) An Anglo-Saxon prose reader in normalized Early West-Saxon orthography; studies in Chaucer's mirror imagery; studies on *The Battle of Maldon*, Raven Banners and *Beowulf*.

MACLEAN, KENNETH: (A) *John Locke and English Literature of the Eighteenth Century* (New Haven, 1936), 176 pp. (reprinted New York, 1962); *Agrarian Age: A Background for Wordsworth* (New Haven, 1950), xiv + 108 pp.   (B) "The Water Symbol in *The Prelude*," *UTQ*, 17 (1947–8), 372–89; "William Cowper," in *The Age of Johnson: Essays Presented to Chauncey Brewster Tinker* (New Haven, 1949), 257–67; "Imagination and Sympathy: Sterne and Adam Smith," *JHI*, 10 (1949), 399–410; "The Imagination in *Tristram Shandy*," *Explorations*, 3 (Aug., 1954), 59–64; "Window and Cross in Henry Adams' *Education*," *UTQ*, 28 (1958–9), 332–44; "Levels of Imagination in Wordsworth's *Prelude* (1805)," *PQ*, 38 (1959), 385–400.   (C) *Can For, J Hist Med, MP, PQ, QQ, RR, Tam R, UTQ.* (D) A study in concepts of imagination in eighteenth-century and Romantic literature (written in part).

MACLURE, MILLAR: (A) *The Paul's Cross Sermons, 1534–1642* (Toronto, 1958), viii + 261 pp.   (B) "A Mirror for Scholars," *UTQ*, 23 (1953–4), 143–54; "Shakespeare and the Lonely Dragon," *UTQ*, 24 (1954–5), 109–20; "William Faulkner, Soothsayer of the South," *QQ*, 63 (1956–7), 334–43; "Literary Scholarship," in J. Park, ed., *The Culture of Contemporary Canada* (Ithaca and Toronto, 1957), 222–41; "The Falling Man: Variations on a Theme in Modern Fiction," in R. C. Chalmers and J. A. Irving, eds., *Challenge and Response: Modern Ideas and Religion* (Toronto, 1959), 37–49; "Allegories of Innocence," *DR*, 40 (1960–1), 145–56; "Nature and Art in *The Faerie Queene*," *ELH*, 28 (1961), 1–20; "The Minor Translations of George Chapman," *MP*, 60 (1962–3), 172–82.   (C) *MP, QQ, RN, UTQ.*   (D) A critical study of George Chapman (first draft almost completed, part of introduction printed in *ACUTE Bull*, 1962).

MACPHERSON, JAY: (B) "The Air-born Helena," *Wat R*, 1 (1959), 48–54;

"A Country without a Mythology," *English Exchange*, 4, 3–21; "Narcissus: Some Uncertain Reflections," *Alphabet* (Sept., 1960), 41–57, and (July, 1961), 65–71. (D) Short article on Canadian autobiography for C. F. Klinck, *et al.*, eds., A Literary History of Canada.

ROBSON, JOHN M.: (A) (ed., with introduction) Edmund Burke's *An Appeal from the New to the Old Whigs* (Indianapolis, Ind., 1962), xxxvi + 131 pp. (B) "J. S. Mill's Theory of Poetry," *UTQ*, 29 (1959–60), 420–38; "Mill and Arnold: Liberty and Culture—Friends or Enemies?" *HAC Bull*, 12, No. 1 (Fall, 1961), 20–32. (C) *Can Art, DR, QQ, UTQ*. (D) Am Associate Editor for the University of Toronto Press edition of the *Collected Works of John Stuart Mill* (the *Principles of Political Economy* should be ready for publication before the end of 1964); a volume, Essays on Economics and Society, is virtually ready; The Ethics of John Stuart Mill (should be completed in 1964).

UNIVERSITY OF TORONTO—TRINITY COLLEGE

CHILD, P. A.: (B) "The Function of Tragedy," *QQ*, 32 (1924–5), 137–53; "The Noble Army of Martyrs in Huronia," *UTQ*, 5 (1935–6), 37–55; "Pierre Esprit Radisson and the Race of *Coureurs de Bois*," *UTQ*, 9 (1939–40), 407–27; "A Social Dynamic for Canada?" *UTQ*, 10 (1940–1), 255–68; introduction to Raymond Knister's *White Narcissus* (Toronto, 1962). (C) *CJRT, DR, QQ, UTQ*.

FALLE, GEORGE G.: (B) "Dryden: Professional Man of Letters," *UTQ*, 26 (1956–7), 443–55. (C) *Can For, CJT, CMJ, UTQ*. (D) A study of the poetry of John Dryden, 1685–1700 (in early stages).

KIRKWOOD, MOSSIE MAY: (A) *The Development of British Thought from 1820 to 1890; with Special Reference to German Influences* (Toronto, 1919), viii + 194 pp.; *Duty and Happiness in a Changed World* (Toronto, 1933), 207 pp.; *For College Women—and Men* (Toronto, 1938), x + 81 pp.; *Santayana: Saint of the Imagination* (Toronto, 1961), xii + 240 pp. (B) "The Thought of Aldous Huxley," *UTQ*, 6 (1936–7), 189–98; "Values in the Novel Today," *UTQ*, 12 (1942–3), 282–96; "The Teacher," in R. M. Saunders, ed., *Education for Tomorrow* (Toronto, 1946), 1–20; "A Philosophy Ancient and Modern," *UTQ*, 24 (1954–5), 146–55.

PARKER, R. B.: (B) "Alterations in the First Edition of Greene's *A Quip for an Upstart Courtier* (1592)," *HLQ*, 23 (1959–60) 181–6; "Middleton's Experiments with Comedy and Judgement," in J. R. Brown and B. Harris, eds., *The Jacobean Theatre* (London, 1961), 179–99; "Farce and Society: The Range of Kingsley Amis," *Wisconsin St in Contemporary Lit*, 2 (1961), 27–38; "Dramaturgy in Shakespeare and Brecht," *UTQ*, 32 (1962–3), 229–46. (C) *Can For, HLQ, N&Q, UTQ, Wisconsin St in Contemporary Lit*. (D) A critical edition of Robert Greene's *A Quip for an Upstart Courtier* (1592) (about half completed).

ROPER, GORDON: (A) (ed., with introduction) Nathaniel Hawthorne's *'The Scarlet Letter' and Selected Prose Works* (New York, 1949), xlvi + 432 pp. (B) "The Originality of Hawthorne's *The Scarlet Letter*," *DR*, 30 (1950–1), 63–79; "Melville's *Moby-Dick*, 1851–1951," *DR*, 31 (1951–2), 167–79; "Before *Moby-Dick*," *U Chicago Mag*, 48 (1955), 4–9; "Mark Twain and His Canadian Publishers," *Amer Book Collector*, 10 (1960), 13–29; introduction to Gabrielle Roy's *Where Nests the Water Hen*, trans.

by H. L. Binsse (Toronto, 1961); articles on "Sir Gilbert Parker" and "The Rev. Charles W. Gordon, Ralph Connor," in *Enc Br* (1961); "On Teaching *Moby-Dick*," *Emerson Soc Q*, 28 (1962), 2–4; (with M. Beebe and H. Hayford) "Criticism of Herman Melville: A Selected Checklist," *MFS*, 8 (1962–3), 312–46.   (C) *Can For, MP, QQ, UTQ*.   (D) An edition of Melville's *Typee*, as Volume I in *The Complete Works of Herman Melville* (ready for publication); "Canadian Fiction, 1880–1920," to appear in C. F. Klinck, *et al.*, eds., A Literary History of Canada (almost complete); (with Harrison Hayford) "Annotated Check List of the Works by and on Herman Melville, 1846–1960" (almost complete); a two-part article on Sara Jeannette Duncan (to appear in *Can L* late in 1963).

ROSS, MALCOLM MACKENZIE: (A) *Milton's Royalism* (Ithaca, 1943), xiv + 150 pp.; *Poetry and Dogma* (New Brunswick, N.J., 1954), xii + 256 pp.; (ed.) *Our Sense of Identity: A Book of Canadian Essays* (Toronto, 1954), xvi + 346 pp.; (ed.) *The Arts in Canada* (Toronto, 1958), vi + 176 pp.; (ed., with J. Stevens) *Man and His World* (Toronto, 1961), viii + 494 pp.   (B) "The Theatre and the Social Confusion," *UTQ*, 5 (1935–6), 197–215; "George Herbert and the Humanist Tradition," *UTQ*, 16 (1946–7), 169–82; "Milton and the Protestant Aesthetic: The Early Poems," *UTQ*, 17 (1947–8), 346–60; "History and Poetry," *Thought*, 26 (1951), 426–42; "Milton and Sir John Stradling," *HLQ*, 14 (1950–1), 129–46; "Fixed Stars and Living Motion in Poetry," *Thought*, 27 (1952), 381–99; "The Writer as Christian," *Faculty Papers* (National Council of the Protestant Episcopal Church) (New York, 1953), 17–30; "A Note on the Metaphysicals," *Hud R*, 6 (1953–4), 106–13; "American Pressures and Canadian Individuality: IV," *Centennial R*, 1 (1957), 379–85; "Goldwin Smith," in C. T. Bissell, ed., *Our Living Tradition: Seven Canadians* (Toronto, 1957), 29–47; general ed. of McClelland and Stewart's New Canadian Library.   (C) *Can For, Centennial R, Comp Lit, DR, Hud R, HLQ, QQ, Thought, UTQ*.   (D) A study of the interplay of the Catholic revival and the aesthetic movement in Victorian literary theory and practice (in progress).

UNIVERSITY OF TORONTO—ST. MICHAEL'S COLLEGE

DOOLEY, D. J.: (B) "The Satiric Novel in Canada Today," *QQ*, 64 (1957–8), 576–90; "Some Uses and Mutations of the Picaresque," *DR*, 37 (1957–8), 363–77; "The Limitations of George Orwell," *UTQ*, 28 (1958–9), 291–300; "Science as Cliché, Fable, and Faith," *Bull Atomic Scientists*, 15 (1959), 372–5; (with J. M. Beck) "Party Images in Canada," *QQ*, 67 (1960–1), 431–48.   (C) *DR, QQ*.   (D) A book-length critical study of Sinclair Lewis, accepted for publication (almost complete).

GERALDINE, SISTER M.: (D) "The Place of Erasmus' *Praise of Folly* in a Tradition of Learned Paradox" (to appear in *SP*); "Donne and the 'Mindes Indeavours' " (partly complete).

MCLUHAN, MARSHALL: (A) *The Mechanical Bride: Folklore of Industrial Man* (New York, 1951), viii + 157 pp.; (ed., with introduction) *Alfred Lord Tennyson, Selected Poetry* (New York, 1956), xxx + 394 pp.; (ed., with Edmund Carpenter) *Explorations in Communication* (Boston and Toronto, 1960), xii + 210 pp.; *The Gutenberg Galaxy: The Making of Typographic Man* (Toronto, 1962), vi + 294 pp.   (B) "G. K. Chesterton:

A Practical Mystic," *DR*, 17 (1936), 455–64; "Aesthetic Patterns in Keats's Odes," *UTQ*, 12 (1943), 167–79; "Education of Free Men," *St. Louis U St in Honour of St. Thomas Aquinas*, 1 (1943), 47–50; "Edgar Poe's Tradition," *SR*, 52 (1944), 24–33; "Poetic vs. Rhetorical Exegesis," *SR*, 52 (1944), 266–76; "Wyndham Lewis," *St. Louis U St in Honour of St. Thomas Aquinas*, 2 (1944), 58–72; "Kipling and Forster," *SR*, 52 (1944), 332–43; "An Ancient Quarrel in Modern America," *CJ*, 41 (1945–6), 156–62; "The New York Wits," *KR*, (1945), 12–28; "The Analogical Mirrors," in *Gerard Manley Hopkins* (New York, 1945), 15–27; "Footprints in the Sands of Crime," *SR*, 54 (1946), 617–34; "The Southern Quality," *SR*, 55 (1947), 357–83, reprinted in Allen Tate, ed., *A Southern Vanguard* (New York, 1947), 100–21; " 'Time', 'Life' and 'Fortune,' " *View* (spring, 1947), 33–7; Introduction, in Hugh Kenner, *Paradox in Chesterton* (New York, 1947), xi–xxii; "American Advertising," *Horizon*, No. 93–94 (Oct., 1947), 132–41, reprinted in B. Rosenberg and D. M. White, eds., *Mass Culture: The Popular Arts in America* (Glencoe, Illinois, 1957), 435–42; "Henry IV, a Mirror for Magistrates," *UTQ*, 17 (1947–8), 152–60; "Mr. Eliot's Historical Decorum," *Ren*, 2 (1949–50), 9–15; "The 'Color-Bar' of BBC English," *Can For*, 29 (1949–50), 9–10; "The Folklore of Industrial Man," *Neurotica*, No. 8 (spring, 1951), 3–20; "Pound's Critical Prose," in P. Russell, ed., *An Examination of Ezra Pound* (London, 1951), 165–71; "Tennyson and Picturesque Poetry," *EIC*, 1 (1951), 262–82, reprinted in J. Killham, ed., *Critical Essays on the Poetry of Tennyson* (London, 1960), 67–85; "John Dos Passos: Technique vs. Sensibility," in H. C. Gardiner, ed., *Fifty Years of the American Novel: A Christian Appraisal* (New York, 1951), 151–64; "Joyce, Aquinas, and the Poetic Process," *Ren*, 4 (1951–2), 3–18; "Technology and Political Change," *Int J*, 7 (1951–2), 189–95; "Advertising as a Magical Institution," *Commerce J* (Jan., 1952), 25–9; "The Esthetic Moment in Landscape Poetry," in A. S. Downer, ed., *English Institute Essays, 1951* (New York, 1952), 168–81; "Comics and Culture," in *Sat N*, 68 (Feb. 28, 1953), 1, 19–20, reprinted in Malcolm Ross, ed., *Our Sense of Identity: A Book of Canadian Essays* (Toronto, 1954), 240–6; "James Joyce: Trivial and Quadrivial," *Thought*, 28 (1953), 75–98; "The Later Innis," *QQ*, 60 (1953), 385–94; "The Age of Advertising," *C'weal*, 58 (1953), 555–7; "Culture without Literacy," *Explorations*, No. 1 (Dec., 1953), 117–27; "Joyce, Mallarmé, and the Press," *SR*, 62 (1954), 38–55; "Sight, Sound, and the Fury," *C'weal*, 60 (1954), 168–97, reprinted in B. Rosenberg and D. M. White, eds., *Mass Culture: The Popular Arts in America* (Glencoe, Illinois, 1957), 489–95; "Five Sovereign Fingers Taxed the Breath," "Media Log," "Space, Time and Poetry," all in *Explorations*, No. 4 (Feb., 1955), 31–3, 52–5, 56–62; "Radio and TV vs. the ABCED-minded," *Explorations*, No. 5 (June, 1955), 12–18; "The Psychopathology of 'Time' & 'Life,' " in C. Brossard, ed., *The Scene Before You* (New York and Toronto, 1955), 147–60; "The Media Fit the Battle of Jericho," *Explorations*, No. 6 (July, 1956), 15–19; (with Edmund Carpenter) "The New Languages," *Chicago R*, 10 (1956–7), 46–52; "The Effect of the Printed Book on Language in the 16th Century," *Explorations*, No. 7 (March, 1957), 99–108; "Third Program in *The Human Age*," *Explorations*, No. 8 (Oct., 1957), 16–18; "Why the CBC Must be Dull," *Sat N*, 72 (Feb. 16,

1957), 13–14; "Coleridge As Artist," in C. D. Thorpe, C. Baker, and B. Weaver, eds., *The Major English Romantic Poets: A Symposium in Reappraisal* (Carbondale, Illinois, 1957), 83–99; "The Subliminal Projection Project," *Can For*, 37 (1957–8), 196–7; "The Electronic Revolution in North America," in J. Wain, ed., *Int Lit'y Annual*, No. 1 (London, 1958), 165–9; "Myth and Mass Media," *Daedalus*, 88 (1959), 339–48, reprinted in H. A. Murray, ed., *Myth and Mythmaking* (New York, 1960), 288–99; "New Media and the New Education," in J. S. Murphy, ed., *Christianity and Culture* (Baltimore, 1960), 181–90; "Tennyson and the Romantic Epic," in J. Killham, ed., *Critical Essays on the Poetry of Tennyson* (London, 1960), 86–95; Report on Project in Understanding New Media, presented and published by the Nat Ass of Educational Broadcasters, for the Office of Education, U.S. Dept. of Health, Educ., and Welfare (1960), 170-plus pp.; "The Humanities in the Electronic Age," *HAC Bull*, 12, No. 1 (fall, 1961), 3–11; "Inside the Five Sense Sensorium," *Can Archit*, 6 (June, 1961), 49–54; "The Electronic Age—The Age of Implosion," in J. A. Irving, ed., *Mass Media in Canada* (Toronto, 1962), 179–205; "Prospect," *Can Art*, 19 (1962), 363–6.   (C) *DR, Explorations, KR, Ren, SR, UTQ*.   (D) *Understanding Media*, on various modes of communication (almost ready for publication).

MADDEN, JOHN F.: (A) (with Francis P. Magoun, Jr.) *A Grouped Frequency Word-List of Anglo-Saxon Poetry* (Harvard U. Dept. of English, 1957), xii + 52 pp. (second corrected printing, 1960).

MARION, SISTER M.: (D) A biography of Thomas Sprat, D.D., F.R.S. (almost complete).

SCHOECK, R. J.: (A) (ed., with Jerome Taylor) *Chaucer Criticism: 'The Canterbury Tales'* (Notre Dame, Ind., 1960), x + 310 pp.; (ed., with Jerome Taylor) *Chaucer Criticism*, volume II: *'Troilus and Criseyde' & The Minor Poems* (Notre Dame, Ind., 1961), x + 293 pp.   (B) "Sir Thomas More and Lincoln's Inn Revels," *PQ*, 29 (1950), 426–30; "Rhetoric and Law in Sixteenth-Century England," *SP*, 50 (1953), 110–27; "A Legal Reading of Chaucer's *House of Fame*," *UTQ*, 23 (1953–4), 185–92; "Acton on Dickens," *Dickensian*, 52 (1956), 77–80; "Chaucer's Prioress: Mercy and Tender Heart," *Bridge*, 2 (1956), 239–55, reprinted in R. J. Schoeck and J. Taylor, eds., *Chaucer Criticism* (Notre Dame, Ind., 1960), 245–58; "Early Anglo-Saxon Studies and Legal Scholarship in the Renaissance," *S Ren*, (1958), 102–10; "Law French," *Kentucky Foreign Lang Q*, 6 (1959), 132–9; "The Date of the *Replication*," *Law Q R*, 76 (1960), 500–3; "The Use of St. John Chrysostom in Sixteenth-Century Controversy," *Harvard Theol R*, 54 (1961), 21–7; "The *Cronica Cronicarum* of Sir Thomas More," *Bull Inst Hist Research*, 35 (1962), 84–6.   (C) *JEGP, Manuscripta, RN, Speculum, Thought, UTQ*.   (D) An edition of More's *Debellation* for the Yale edition of the Works of St. Thomas More (to be published 1963–4); a history of the Inns of Court (in progress); an edition of Dramatic Records in the Inns, for the Malone Soc. (in progress); a biography of Thomas More (in progress).

SHOOK, L. K.: (A) (trans.) Etienne Gilson's *Héloïse and Abélard* (Chicago, 1951), xvi + 194 pp.; (trans.) Etienne Gilson's *The Christian Philosophy of St. Thomas Aquinas* (New York, 1956), x + 502 pp.

(B) "St. Michael's College: The Formative Years," *Can Cath Hist Ass Report* (1951), 59–73; "Old English Riddle 28: Testudo (Tortoise-Lyre)," *MS*, 20 (1958), 93–7; "The Burial Ground in *Guthlac A*," *MP*, 58 (1960–1), 1–10; "The Prologue of the Old English *Guthlac A*," *MS*, 23 (1961), 294–304; "Newman's Correspondence with Two Canadians," *Dub R*, No. 485 (1960), 205–21.   (C) *Can Cath Hist Ass Report, MLN, MP, MS, UTQ*.   (D) An edition and study of the Old English Guthlac materials (almost complete); a historical study of Canadian Catholic colleges and universities (English-speaking) as part of a large NCCU project on Higher Education in Canada (to be completed in 1964).

UNIVERSITY OF VICTORIA

CUOMO, GEORGE: (A) *Becoming a Better Reader* (1960).   (B) "Of Children and Idiots," *Nation*, 184 (1957), 482–4; "How Fast Should a Person Read?" *Sat R*, 45 (April 21, 1962), 13–14.

HADDOCK, NEVILLE: (A) *Practice in Spoken English* (Cambridge, 1959). (B) "Syntax of the Lindisfarne Gospels," in R. Bruce-Mitford, *et al.*, eds., *The Lindisfarne Gospels* (Lausanne, 1957), Book II, 44 ff.; "The Tones of Bariba," *Phonetica*, 3 (1959), 90–4.   (C) *English and Germanic St, Math Gaz*.   (D) Completed articles on Anglo-Saxon palaeography, on variant forms in the Lindisfarne Gospels, and on speech aphasia.

KURTH, BURTON O.: (A) *Milton and Christian Heroism: Biblical Epic Themes in Seventeenth Century England* (Berkeley and Los Angeles, 1959), 152 pp.; (with Richard A. Condon) *Writing from Experience* (New York, 1960).   (D) A study of the decline of allegory and the development of realistic forms in the seventeenth and eighteenth centuries in relation to the changing concepts of the nature (psychology) of man and the presentation of human experience (in research stages).

LAWRENCE, ROBERT G.: (A) (an anthology) *Early Seventeenth Century Drama* (London, 1962).   (B) "Dr. Johnson and the Art of Flying," *N&Q*, NS, 4 (1957), 348–51; "A Bibliographical Study of Middleton and Rowley's *The Changeling*," *Library*, fifth series, 16 (1961), 37–43.   (C) *Victoria Daily Times*.   (D) Articles on Heywood's *Woman Killed*, and on D. H. Lawrence.

PETER, J. D.: (A) *Complaint and Satire in Early English Literature* (Oxford, 1956), 323 pp.; *A Critique of 'Paradise Lost'* (London and New York, 1960), 172 pp.   (B) "A New Interpretation of *The Waste Land*," *EIC*, 2 (1952), 242–66; "Reflections on the Milton Controversy," *Scrutiny*, 19 (1952), 2–15; "The Fables of William Golding," *KR*, 19 (1957), 577–92. (C) *EIC, KR, MLR, RES*.

SADDLEMYER, E. ANN: (D) A definitive edition, in two volumes, of the plays of J. M. Synge; a definitive bibliography of the works of J. M. Synge; a critical study of the early plays of W. B. Yeats.

UNIVERSITY OF WATERLOO

McCUTCHAN, J. WILSON: (A) *'31 Plus Twenty-five* (Charlotte, N.C., 1956); *Macbeth: A Complete Guide to the Play* (New York, 1963).   (B) "Similarities between Falstaff and Gluttony in Medwall's *Nature*," *Shakespeare Ass Bull*, 24 (1949), 214–19; " 'Noseled' and 'Snotty-nose,' " *MLN*,

65 (1950), 541–2; "Covetousness in *The Castle of Perseverance*," in F. Bowers, ed., *English Studies in Honor of James Southall Wilson* (Charlottesville, Va., 1951), 175–91; " 'He Has No Children,' " *McNeese R*, 8 (spring, 1956), 41–52; "Justice and Equity in the English Morality Play," *JHI*, 19 (1958), 404–10; " 'A Solempne and a Greet Fraternitee,' " *PMLA*, 74 (1959), 313–17. (C) *Amer Speech, Globe and Mail, J Christian Educ, N&Q, NY Times Mag, North Carolina Eng Teacher.* (D) Am general editor for Shakespeare volumes in Barnes and Noble's Focus Books series.

STONE, JAMES S.: (B) "Meredith and Goethe," *UTQ*, 21 (1951–2), 157–66; "Humanities and Social Sciences for Canadian Engineering Students," *QQ*, 68 (1961–2), 402–10. (D) "Humanistic Values in the Literature of Ideas" (to appear in *ACUTE Report* for 1962).

THOMAS, W. KEITH: (A) *Form and Substance: A Guide to the Research Paper* (Toronto, 1963), 102 pp. (B) "Canadian Political Oratory in the Nineteenth Century," *DR*, 39 (1959–60), 377–89; "The Flavour of Crabbe," *DR*, 40 (1960–1), 489–504. (C) *DR*. (D) As Truth Will Paint It: Essays on the Descriptive Poetry of George Crabbe (almost ready for publication).

UNIVERSITY OF WESTERN ONTARIO—UNIVERSITY COLLEGE AND MIDDLESEX COLLEGE

ATKINSON, W. E. D.: (D) Edition of Gilielmus Grapheus' *Acolastus* (1529), with an English translation and a critical introduction (complete; scheduled for publication in the series University of Western Ontario Studies in the Humanities, probably in 1964).

BATES, RONALD G. N.: (B) "Notes on Sidney Keyes," *Can For*, 28 (1948), 180–2; "Donner un sens plus pur aux mots de la tribu," *N&Q*, 198 (1953), 493–4; "Shakespeare's 'The Phoenix and Turtle,' " *SQ*, 6 (1955), 19–30; "A Note on Sentimentality," *DR*, 41 (1961), 215–21. (C) *Alphabet, Can For, DR, QQ*. (D) "Downdolphinry" (article on Hopkins); "A Topic in 'The Waste Land' "; "Some Structural Imagery in the 'Prelude' "; "Some Versions of Poetic Sense and Non-Sense"; "The Feast is a Flyday" (article on *Finnegans Wake*); a number of other articles on Joyce.

BERRY, H.: (A) *Sir John Suckling's Poems and Letters from Manuscript*, U.W.O. monograph (London, Ontario, 1960). (B) "Three New Poems by Davenant," *PQ*, 31 (1952), 70–4; (with E. K. Timings) "Lovelace at Court and a Version of Part of His 'The Scrutinie,' " *MLN* (1954), 396–8; (with E. K. Timings) "Spenser's Pension," *RES*, 11 (1960), 254–9. (D) "Hugh Helland" (accepted by *N&Q* for publication in fall of 1964); "Suggestions about the Stage at Blackfriars" (in negotiation with *SQ*); a life of Sir John Suckling (about three-quarters complete).

CONRON, A. B.: (A) (Latin ed.) of *The Literary Works of Matthew Prior* (ed. H. Bunker Wright and Monroe K. Spears; Oxford, 1959). (D) (with G. Sylvestre and C. F. Klinck) Canadian Writers: Ecrivains canadiens—a dictionary of Canadian writers (in press); two chapters on "The Essay" in C. F. Klinck, *et al.*, eds., A Literary History of Canada (to be published in 1964 by University of Toronto Press); a book on Morley Callaghan for Twayne World Authors series (to be completed by September, 1964).

DEAN, CHRISTOPHER: (A) *The Dialect of George Meriton's "A Yorkshire Dialogue"* (1683), Yorkshire Dialect Society, 3 (Leeds, 1962); *Some Arguments for and against Reforming English Spelling* (Kingston, Ontario, 1962) (for the Canadian Conference on Education). (B) "Joseph's Speech in *Wuthering Heights*," *N&Q* (Feb., 1960). (D) A study of the syntax of Chaucer's poetry using the methodology of modern structural linguistics.

DEVEREUX, E. J.: (B) "Early Printing in Newfoundland," *DR*, 43 (1963), 57–66; "The English Editions of Erasmus's *Catechismus*," *Library*, 17 (1962), 154–5; "Some Lost English Translations of Erasmus," *Library*, 17 (1962), 255–9. (C) *Library.* (D) English translations of Erasmus to 1700 (MS. needs revision and typing before being submitted to Oxford Bibliographical Society); Richard Taverner's translations of Erasmus—an article for *Library*; more lost English translations of Erasmus—an article for *Library*.

GRAHAM, JOHN W.: (B) "Time in the Novels of Virginia Woolf," *UTQ*, 18 (1949), 186–201; "The 'Caricature Value' of Parody and Fantasy in *Orlando*," *UTQ*, 30 (1960), 345–66. (C) *UTQ*. (D) A critical study of Virginia Woolf (to be completed (d.v.) in 1965).

HAUSER, D. R.: (B) "Medea's Strain and Hermes' Wand: Pope's Use of Mythology," *MLN*, 76 (1961), 224–9; "Otway Preserved: Theme and Form in *Venice Preserved*," *SP*, 55 (1958), 481–93; "The Date of John Heywood's *The Spider and the Flie*," *MLN*, 70 (1955), 15–18. (C) *ELH, MLN, PMLA, SP.* (D) "Pope's Windsor Forest and 'Albion's Golden Days': The Prophetic Mode" (accepted for publication in *PMLA*, probably in 1964); "Pope's 'Silvan Strains' " (being revised for *ELH*); a book-length study of Pope's use of classical mythology; a book-length study of S. T. Coleridge's theological perspective (publication of both rather distant).

KLINCK, C. F.: (A) *Wilfred Campbell, A Study in Late Provincial Victorianism* (Toronto, 1942); (with H. G. Wells) *Edwin J. Pratt: The Man and His Poetry* (Toronto, 1947); (ed., with R. E. Watters) *Canadian Anthology* (Toronto, 1955–7); (ed., with introduction) *Major Richardson's "Kensington Gardens in 1830"*; (ed., with introduction and notes) *William "Tiger" Dunlop, "Blackwoodian Backwoodsman"* (Toronto, 1958); (ed., with introduction) *Tecumseh: Fact and Fiction in Early Records* (Englewood Cliffs, N.J., 1961); (ed., with introduction) Frances Brooke's *The History of Emily Montague* (Toronto, 1961); (ed., with introduction) Susanna Moodie's *Roughing It in the Bush* (Toronto, 1962). (B) "Early Creative Literature of Western Ontario," *OH*, 45 (1953), 155–63; "Major Richardson's 'Kensington Gardens in 1830,' " *OH*, 48 (1956), 101–7; "Some Anonymous Literature of the War of 1812," *OH*, 49 (1957), 49–60; "John Galt's Canadian Novels," *OH*, 49 (1957), 187–94; "Adam Kidd: An Early Canadian Poet," *QQ*, 65 (1958), 495–506; "The Cacique of Ontario," *UTQ*, 29 (1959), 21–32; "The Canadian Chief and 'Tiger' Dunlop," *Wat R*, 2 (1959), 43–51; "The *Charivari* and Levi Adams," *DR*, 40 (1960), 34–42. (C) *DR, OH, QQ, UTQ, Wat R.* (D) General editor of Literary History of Canada, for University of Toronto Press; articles and essays for a book on early Canadian writers; Canadian Taste in Literature (in preparation).

MCKEEN, D.: (B) "The Carew Family and Its Connections," *N&Q*, 10 (1963), 54.

MacKinnon, M. H. M.: (B) "School Books Used at Eton College about 1600," *JEGP*, 56 (1957), 429–33; "Parnassus in Newfoundland," *DR*, 32 (1952), 110–19; "An Unpublished Letter of Sir Thomas Browne," *Bull Hist Medicine*, 27 (1953), 503–11; "Sir John Harington and Bishop Hall," *PQ*, 37 (1958), 80–6. (C) *RN, UTQ*. (D) The Letters of Sir John Harington (to be published in 1964 in the University of Western Ontario series Publications in the Humanities); The Life and Writings of Sir John Harington (1560–1612) (may be completed by 1965); bibliography of writings of A. S. P. Woodhouse (to be included in Essays in English Literature from the Renaissance to the Victorian Age, presented to A. S. P. Woodhouse, University of Toronto Press, 1964).

Rans, G.: (B) "English Literary Magazines," *Hud R*, 5 (1952), 111–15; "London Letter: Shakespearean Production," *Hud R*, 5 (1952), 423–31; "Mr. Wilkinson on *Comus*," *EIC*, 10 (1960), 364–9; "The Novels of Saul Bellow," *REL* (Oct., 1963). (C) *Higher Educ J, Hud R, Yorkshire Post.* (D) Edgar Allan Poe (expected publication in 1964); The Puritan Heritage of American Literature (thesis—publication under negotiation); article on A. M. Klein; article on Poe and the Apocrypha; work on Henry Francis Keenan (1850–1928), novelist, journalist, man of letters—possibly a biography; a book on J. F. Cooper, Scott, and Major John Richardson; the poetry and poetic theory of Emerson.

Reaney, James: (A) (ed.) *Alphabet*. (B) "The Canadian Poet's Predicament," *UTQ*, 26 (1957), 284–95; "The Condition of Light: Henry James—*The Sacred Fount*," *UTQ*, 31 (1962), 136–50; "The Third Eye: Jay MacPherson's *The Boatman*," *Can L*, 3 (1960), 23–34; "Isabella Valancy Crawford," in *Our Living Tradition*, Second and Third Series (Toronto, 1959), 268–88. (C) *Alphabet, Can For, Can L, Tam R, UTQ.* (D) Work on Henry James; the relationship between diagram and metaphor.

Stratford, Philip: (B) "Graham Greene," in *Les Ecrivains célèbres*, 4: *Ecrivains contemporains* (Paris, 1963); (trans.) Mauriac's "Commencements d'une vie," *Tam R* (spring, 1963). (C) *Can For, KR, Sat N, Tam R.* (D) Translating all of Jean LeMoyne's essays, *Convergences*, for Oxford University Press; translating three of LeMoyne's essays for *Tam R* (fall, 1964); translating *Mauriac on the Art of the Novel*; "Chalk and Cheese" (a comparative essay on Greene and Mauriac); "Two Forgotten Greenes" (article on two early Greene novels); Faith and Fiction: A Comparative Study of François Mauriac and Graham Greene (in press, University of Notre Dame Press).

Woodman, Ross G.: (A) *The Apocalyptic Vision in the Poetry of Shelley* (Toronto, 1964), xviii + 209 pp. (B) "Shelley's Changing Attitude to Plato," *JHI*, 21 (1960), 497–510; "Shelley's Prometheus," *Alphabet* (Sept., 1961), 25–9; "Literature and Life," *QQ*, 67 (1962), 621–32. (D) The Romantics as Critics of Each Other (research completed—publication 1966?).

UNIVERSITY OF WESTERN ONTARIO—HURON COLLEGE

Blissett, William: (A) (ed.) Reid MacCallum's *Imitation and Design* (Toronto, 1953). (B) "I. A. Richards," *UTQ*, 14 (1944), 58–66; "The Argument of T. S. Eliot's *Four Quartets*," *UTQ*, 15 (1946), 115–26; "Pater and Eliot," *UTQ*, 22 (1953), 261–8; "Synge's Playboy," *Adam* (1954); "Poetic Wave and Poetic Particle," *UTQ*, 24 (1954), 1–7; "Robert Graves," *Can For* (June, 1954), 59–61; "Dylan Thomas," *QQ*, 63 (1956), 44–58; "Lucan's Caesar and the Elizabethan Villain," *SP*, 53 (1956), 553–75; "Caesar and Satan," *JHI*, 18 (1957), 221–32; "Samuel Daniel's Sense of the Past," *Eng St*, 38 (1957), 1–15; "Bernard Shaw, Imperfect Wagnerite," *UTQ*, 27 (1958), 185–99; "Despots of the Rings," *SAQ*, 58 (1959), 448–56; "The Secret'st Man of Blood," *SQ*, 10 (1959), 396–408; "Ernest Newman and English Wagnerism," *Music and Letters*, 40 (1959), 311–23; "Thomas Mann, the Last Wagnerite," *Germanic R* (Feb., 1960), 50–76; "George Moore and Literary Wagnerism," *Comp Lit*, 13 (1961), 52–71; "Wagnerian Fiction in English," *Criticism*, 5 (1963), 239–60. (C) *Alphabet, Can For, Eng St, JHI, QQ, RN, UTQ*. (D) A book on literary Wagnerism; studies in Spenser, Shakespeare, and other writers of the English Renaissance.

UNIVERSITY OF WESTERN ONTARIO—BRESCIA COLLEGE

SHARP, SISTER M. CORONA: (A) *The Gifts of God* (St. Paul, Minn., 1942), 88 pp.; *The Confidante in Henry James: Evolution and Moral Value of a Fictive Character* (Notre Dame, 1963), 350 pp. (B) "Christian Marionettes," *America* (Aug. 12, 1939), 426–7; "The Secret of Swiss Freedom," *Cath World* (August, 1941), 542–6; "Dialogue in the Religious Life," *Benedictine R* (summer, 1960), 120–5 (winter, 1961), 27–32; "The Archetypal Feminine in *Our Mutual Friend*," *U Kansas City R* (June, 1961), 307–11 (Oct., 1961), 74–80; "The Theme of Masks in *Geneva*: An Example of Shaw's Later Technique," *Shaw R* (Sept., 1962), 82–91; "Sympathetic Mockery: A Study of the Narrator's Character in *Vanity Fair*," *ELH* (Sept., 1962), 324–36. (D) Symbolism of the house in the novels of Elizabeth Bowen—a critical essay for periodical publication (in advanced stage).

UNIVERSITY OF WESTERN ONTARIO—COLLEGE OF CHRIST THE KING

WIEDEN, F.: (D) Coleridge as a student of German literature.

YORK UNIVERSITY

MACLEAN, HUGH NORMAN: (A) (ed., with others) *The Critical Reader* (New York, 1962). (B) "The Structure of *A Passage to India*," *UTQ*, 23 (1952–3), 157–71; "Fulke Greville: Kingship and Sovereignty," *HLQ*, 16 (1952–3), 237–71; "Conservatism in Modern American Fiction," *CE*, 15 (1953–4), 315–25; "Hawthorne's *Scarlet Letter*: 'The Dark Problem of this life,' " *Amer Lit*, 27 (1955–6), 12–24; "Milton's Fair Infant," *ELH*, 24 (1957), 296–305; "Fulke Greville on War," *HLQ*, 21 (1957–8), 95–109; "Disguise in *King Lear*: Kent and Edgar," *SQ*, 11 (1960), 49–54. (C) *Can For, DR, UTQ*. (D) "Greville's 'Poetic' " (to appear in *SP*); a critical study of Fulke Greville.

THOMAS, CLARA: (A) *Canadian Novelists, 1920–1945* (Toronto, 1946), 141 pp. (D) (with E. Sanborn), R.M.S. *Titanic* and the Nature of Tragedy; Anna Jameson: A Biography (an expansion of Ph.D. thesis).

ROMANCE LANGUAGES

ACADIA UNIVERSITY

BENTLEY, CHARLES ANDREW: (B) "Ein Brief Rilkes an Annette Kolb," *MDU*, 44 (1952), 159–60; "Rilke's 'Sonette an Orpheus' and Max Dauthendey," *MLN*, 68 (1953), 393–5; "Rilke and André Maurois," *MLN*, 69 (1954), 340–3. (C) *QQ*. (D) Rilke and the French (to be completed in the fall of 1963).

RAYSKI-KIETLICZ, KONSTANTY: (A) *L'Esthétique de Proust* (Paris, 1939), xi + 95 pp. (B) "Stylografia M. Prousta," *Cath U at Lublin* (1933); "Styl emocionalny u Prousta," *Cath U at Lublin* (1934); "Metody badan stylu," Przeglad Filologiczny (1937); "Literatura zacisnietych zebów" (Literature behind the Iron Curtain), *Orzel Bialy*, 5 (1945), No. 239; "Listy Conrada" (Conrad's Letters), *Orzel Bialy*, 16 (1947), No. 250 (April 19); "Spotkanie z Archaniolem Smierci" (Essay on Malraux), *Orzel Bialy*, 20 (1947), No. 254 (May 17); "Literatura krajowa po wojnie" (Polish Literature after 1945), *Orzel Bialy*, 27 (1947), No. 261 (July 5); "G. B. Shaw," *Orzel Bialy*, 31 (1947), No. 265 (Aug. 2); "Podróz do Otchlani Piekla" (Essay on W. Faulkner), *Orzel Bialy*, 31 (1947), No. 271 (Sept. 13); "Cywilizacja," *Orzel Bialy*, 40 (1947), No. 274 (Oct. 4); "Cervantes," *Orzel Bialy*, 44 (1947), No. 278 (Nov. 1); "Swiat Malego Przypadku" (Essay on Kafka), *Wiadomosci*, 42 (1948), No. 133 (Nov. 17); "The Canadian Cultural Pattern," *DR*, 30 (1950), 170–8.

UNIVERSITY OF ALBERTA, CALGARY

BRESKY, DUSHAN: (A) *Bez Konce Json Lesy* (Prague, 1943), 123 pp.; *Hory Lyze Snih* (Prague, 1947), 201 pp. (B) "Schiller's Debt to Montesquieu and Adam Ferguson," *Comp Lit*, 13 (1961), 239–53. (D) "Rhythm and Rhyme in France's Prose" (article; ready for publication); The Art of Anatole France (Ph.D. thesis; to be submitted for publication).

BREUGELMANS, R.: (B) "Een blik op de Engelse Literatuur in Oorlogstyd," *Gentsche Bladen*, 1 (1945), 26–30; "Les Alurs du Congo Belge et des possessions anglaises," *Int Africa Inst* (1949), 114 pp.; "Les Logo," *Int Africa Inst* (1949), 32 pp.; "Hamlet, a Modern Character," *La Termitière* (1950), 1–2; "Enkele ethnologische wetenswaardigheden," *La Termitière*, 1 (1952), 7 pp.; "The Social Theory of a Good-Natured Hyper-Individualist," *Athenaion* (1955), 31–61; "The Dislikes of Oscar Wilde, Self-Conscious Fin-de-Siècle Artist," *Athenaion*, 3 (1956), 19–28; "Ernest Renan and Oscar Wilde," *Athenaion*, 4 (1956), 20–7; "An Outline of Wilde's Philosophy" (Antwerp, 1956), 16 pp.; "Wilde's Views on Aestheticism, Criticism and Amoralism in Their Relationship with the French Symbolists and 'Decadents'" (Antwerp, 1956), 16 pp.; "The Integration of Relatively Recent Authors into Literary History" (Antwerp, 1956), 8 pp.; "A Short Study in Comparative Literature; (Oscar Wilde and Sainte-Beuve)," *Rev Kesho*, 2 (1956), 14–18; "Charles Baudelaire and Oscar Wilde," *Spieghel Historiael*, 1 (1959), 27–34; "George Moore et la France," *Rev Belge de Philol et d'Hist*, 38 (1960), 479–84; "De grondslagen van de toestand in Kongo en de rol van het humanistisch hoger onderwijs," *Sociale Standpunten*, 7

(1960), 27–37; "Oscar Wilde's Weerklank in Nederland en in Vlaanderen," *Studia Germanica* (1962), 91 pp.

JENSEN, F.: (D) A book on the syntax of the subjunctive in Old French (nearly finished).

OYLER, J. E.: (B) "A German Grammar for the High School Level," *Lang Learning*, 10, 15–23; "The Noun and Adjective in German," *Can MLR*, 18 (1962), 41–2; "Your Own Ear is the Secret to Learning Languages Well," *Can High News*, 23 (1962). (D) "Harsdörffer and the Compound Noun" (article; to appear in *Can MLR* in 1963); a German grammar for high schools (completed); a study of Georg Schottel (nearly completed); dictionary of German idio-structures (in early stages).

ASSUMPTION UNIVERSITY OF WINDSOR

ALMAZAN, VINCENT: (A) *Portugisiska för nyborjare* (Stockholm, 1954); (trans.) *Eberhard Munck of Rosenschöld* (Stockholm, 1954). (B) "La 'bacina del barber' y el Altas Lingüistico de Cataluña," *Boletín de la Sociedad Castellonense de cultura*, 39 (1963). (C) *Boletín de la Sociedad Castellonense de cultura*. (D) "Carte linguistique française du Nouvel-Ontario" (completed); Die Lucan-Uebersetzung in dem GE Alphons des Weisen. Ein Beitrag zur Geschichte des frühen spanischen Prosa (Ph.D. thesis; completed); "Manual de conversacion basado en el refranero espanol" (completed); "An Introduction to Linguistic Geography" (advanced).

MCCARTHY, LILLIAN: (C) *Ren.* (D) Translation of a text submitted for publication; critical edition of a French MS on alchemy (to be completed by September, 1964).

SKAKOON, WALTER S.: (C) *Philosophy.* (D) Sartre's theory of imagination; Sartre's theory of the work of art.

THIBAULT, ALBERT A.: (A) *La France et la littérature française dans l'œuvre de G. K. Chesterton; Zola vu par ses contemporains.*

BISHOP'S UNIVERSITY

YARRILL, E. H.: (B) "Browning's 'Roman Murder Story' as recorded in a hitherto unknown MS," *Baylor Bull*, 42 (1939); "The French Summer School," *Educ Record*, 66 (1950); "French in School and College: Questions of Continuity and Direction," *FR*, 27 (1954), 280–6. (C) *Erasmus, Speculum, Scientiarum.*

UNIVERSITY OF BRITISH COLUMBIA

BONGIE, LAWRENCE L.: (B) "David Hume and the Official Censorship of the 'Ancien Régime,' " *FS*, 12 (1958), 234–46; "Hume, 'Philosophe' and Philosopher in Eighteenth-Century France," *FS*, 15 (1961), 213–27; "Crisis and the Birth of the Voltairian *conte*," *MLQ*, 23 (1962), 53–64. (C) *FS, HAC Bull, MLQ.* (D) Book on the political theories of D. Hume in eighteenth-century France (barely past document-gathering stage).

DALLAS, DOROTHY: (A) *Le Roman Français de 1660 à 1680* (Paris, 1932), 289 pp. (B) "The 'précieux' Novel," in *A Critical Bibliography of French Literature*, 3 (Syracuse, 1961). (D) Life under the French Régime in Canada from 1700 to 1763, as described in some personal letters of the period (work about half completed).

GREGG, ROBERT J.: (A) *A Student's Manual of French Pronunciation* (Toronto, 1960), 155 pp.; (with W. S. Avis, C. J. Lovell, M. H. Scargill) *Dictionary of Canadian English (The Beginning Dictionary)* (Toronto, 1962). (B) "Notes on the Pronunciation of Canadian English as Spoken in Vancouver, B.C.," *JCLA*, 3 (1957); "Neutralization and Fusion of Vocalic Phonemes in Canadian English as Spoken in the Vancouver Area," *JCLA*, 3 (1957); "Notes on the Phonology of a County Antrim Scotch-Irish Dialect," *Orbis*, 7 (1958), 392–406, and 8 (1959), 400–24. (C) *JCLA, Orbis*. (D) The second and third volumes of the *Dictionary of Canadian English* (to be published in Jan., 1963 and Jan., 1964); The Boundaries of the Scotch-Irish Dialects in Ulster—a monograph (to be published in 1964?).

HARDEN, ARTHUR ROBERT: (B) "François Villon and his Monetary Bequests," *Speculum*, 33 (1958), 345–50; four other published articles. (C) *Renaissance Papers, Romance Notes, Speculum, SP*. (D) Critical edition of the life of St. Alban for the Anglo-Norman Text Society (almost completed).

LIVERMORE, H. V.: (A) *A History of Portugal* (Cambridge, 1947); (ed., with W. J. Entwistle) *Portugal and Brazil, an Introduction* (Oxford, 1953); *A History of Spain* (London, 1958, New York, 1959, Milan, 1962); (trans.) L. del Corral's *The Rape of Europe* (London, 1960). (B) "El Caballero Salvaje," *Revista Filología Española*, 34 (1950), 166–83; "An Early English Play Described by a Spanish Visitor," *Atlante*, 1 (1953), 28–30; "Privileges of an Englishman in the Kingdoms and Dominions of Portugal," *Atlante*, 2 (1954), 57–77. (C) *Atlante, Br J Aesthetics, Bull Hisp St, Can History, History, TLS*. (D) A New History of Portugal—for Cambridge (in MS.); The Nasrid Kingdom of Granada (in type); From the Congo to Goa (in process); A History of Spanish Civilization (contracted for Allen & Unwin some time ago); The Royal Commentaries of the Inca Garcilasso de la Vega (translation delivered to Indiana Press in 1956, fate unknown).

NIEDERAUER, DAVID J.: (B) "Louys, Pierre," and "Maurice Maeterlinck," in *Lexicon der Weltliteratur im 20. Jahrhundert* (1961). (D) Pierre Louys, Poet and Moralist (being revised for submission to University of California Press).

PRIMEAU, MARGUERITE A.: (A) (with R. R. Jeffels and K. T. Brearley) *Contes et Scenarios* (New York, 1960). (B) "Gratien Gélinas et le théâtre populaire au Canada français," *Can L*, 4 (1960), 31–9. (D) A series of articles on the theatre of Montherlant (first is almost completed).

CANADIAN SERVICES COLLEGE, ROYAL ROADS

GRIFFITHS, DAVID A.: (B) "Les Caprices de Rachel," *Rev d'Hist du Théâtre*, 11 (1959), 7–20; "Un confrère de Victor Hugo à l'Académie: Ernest Legouvé," *Rev des Sciences Humaines* (1960), 203–11. (D) "Un ouvrage inconnu de Pierre Leroux: *Cours de Phrénologie* (1853)" (article; in press); "Au dossier des 'Annees sombres' d'Alphonse de Lamartine" (article; in press); "Victor Hugo et Victor Schoelcher au ban de l'Empire" (article; submitted for publication); La vie et l'œuvre de Jean Reynaud

(1806–1863) d'après sa correspondance inédite (doctoral thesis; submitted for publication).

OLDHAM, RONALD: (D) "Albert Camus: The Humanist" (article submitted to *DR*); "Molière: son théâtre et son époque" (completed); "Où va le roman français?" (in preparation).

DALHOUSIE UNIVERSITY

CHAVY, PAUL: (B) "Copenhague," in *L'Ame des Cités* (Paris, 1946), 275–300. (D) "Traduction automatique et enseignement des langues étrangères" (accepted for publication by *FR*—should appear in Dec., 1962); Français au travail, an anthology of 250 pp. (should be ready for publication in 1963).

JOURNOUD, S.: (A) (under René Lorain) *Petite Anthologie des Poètes Latins Erotiques* (Nice, 1948); (with Maurice Vittone) *Vie de Molière* (Nice, 1950).

THOMAS, PETER H.: (A) *La Double Mort de Frédéric Belot* (teaching aid for professors of second-year college French) (Toronto, 1962), 24 pp. (B) "The Will to Power in Nineteenth-Century Literature," *Yearbook Amer Philos Soc* (1959), 629–32. (C) *BA*. (D) Heinrich Mann et ses orientations étrangères (doctoral dissertation; to be published in spring, 1963); On the Social Psychology of Modern Formal and Familiar Speech (submitted for publication); "Jean-Paul Sartre" (review article to appear in *DR*); On Immorality in Literature (book in process of being written).

LAURENTIAN UNIVERSITY

BOUCHARD, DENIS: (B) "La Mystique de l'Action dans Saint-Exupéry," *RUL*, 16 (1961), 228–52. (C) *Rev Dominicaine*. (D) Saint-Exupéry et l'homme d'action (thesis being considered for publication by the Canada Council); a book of poetry (should be ready for publication within a year).

UNIVERSITÉ LAVAL

BOUCHARD, PAUL: (A) *La Province de Québec sous l'Union Nationale, 1936–39, 1944–56* (Québec, 1956), xiv + 280 pp. (B) "Deux siècles sans monnaie, Le Paraguay colonial," *Economie et Commerce*, 2 (1960), 3–5; "La religion en Amérique latine," *Tradition et Progrès*, 3 (1960), 18–25 (also in English in *Amer Eccles R* (1961) and in *Report of the Twenty-Ninth Couchiching Conference* (Toronto, 1960), 25; "L'Amérique hispanique, ses origines et son destin," *RUL*, 15 (1961), 894–912; "Formacion de la América Hispanica," *El Siglo*, 12 (1961); "La lutte pour l'Amérique Latine," *Nouvelles de Chrétienté* (1961) (also in *Tradition et Progrès*, 4 (1961); "Canada: Producción histórica," *Anuario de Estudios Americanos* (1961). (C) *AC, Amer Eccles R, Anuario de Estudios Americanos, Le Devoir, Economie et Commerce, La Nation, Nouvelles de Chrétienté, Presbyt J, Revista de Indias, RUL, El Siglo, Le Temps, Tradition et Progrès*. (D) Un ouvrage sur l'évolution économique de l'Amérique Latine.

LAFORGE, LORNE: (D) Manuel d'exercices grammaticaux en laboratoire (en préparation) avec enregistrements de 70 leçons.

MACKEY, ILONKA SCHMIDT: (A) (with I. A. Richards, C. Gibson, and

W. F. Mackey) *German through Pictures* (New York, 1953), 254 pp.; *German Workbook I* (Boston, 1954), 86 pp.; *German Workbook II* (Boston, 1955), 108 pp.; *Lou Salomé: inspiratrice et interprète de Nietzsche, Rilke et Freud* (Paris, 1956), 210 pp. (D) La programmation de l'alphabet cyrillique; L'alphabet russe; Manuel de phonétique de l'allemand contemporain.

MACKEY, WILLIAM FRANCIS: (A) *English Pronunciation Drills* (Montreal, 1951), 125 pp.; (with A. V. P. Elliott and J. A. Noonan) *Listen and Speak*, 1, 2 (6 vols., London, 1953), first published as a bilingual edition in Paris, 1, 155 pp., other bilingual editions (1953–8) in Italian, Norwegian, Dutch, Spanish, Modern Greek, Burmese, Siamese, Malay, etc.; (with I. S. Mackey and I. A. Richards) *German through Pictures* (New York, 1953), 254 pp.; *Textbooks for the Teaching of English as a Foreign Language* (London, 1956); *English for Migrants* (Geneva, 1957), 178 pp.; *Reading Materials in Controlled Vocabularies* (Ottawa, 1957), 30 pp.; *Teaching Manual to "English for Migrants"* (2 vols., Geneva, 1958), 225 pp.; *Graded Conversation with Differential Phonetic Guides in German, Dutch, Italian, Hungarian, French, and English* (Ottawa, 1958); *Teaching Guide to "Graded Conversation,"* 1 (Ottawa, 1958); *Language Laboratories: Their Nature, Use, and Design* (multigraphed) (Québec, 1958); *Allegemeine Englische Redewingen* and *Espressini Comuni Inglesi* (Ottawa, 1961); *Language Teaching Analysis* (London, 1963), 822 pp. (B) "The Meaning of Method," *Eng Lang Teaching*, 5: 1; "What to Look for in a Method," "Selection," "Grading," "Presentation," *Eng Lang Teaching*, 7: 3, 8: 2, 9: 2; "English Teaching in Puerto Rico," *Eng Lang Teaching*, 8: 1; "Shipboard Language Teaching," *Eng Lang Teaching*, 10: 2; "An Experiment in Bilingual Education," *Eng Lang Teaching*, 6: 4; "Rola gradacji wnauczaniu jezykow obcych," *Wiadomosci Nauczycielskie*, 5: 2; "English to Large Numbers," *West Africa*, 33; "Bilingualism and Education," *Pedagogie-Orientation*, 6: 2; "Bilingualism and Linguistic Structure," *Culture*, 14; "Bilingualism," *Enc Br* (1958); "Lingua Franca," *Enc Br*; "Slang," *Enc Br*; "Jespersen," *Enc Br*; "Toward a Redefinition of Bilingualism," *JCLA*, 2: 1; "Orientation: a Guide to the Culture Maze," *Amer Student Abroad* (1956–7); "The Oslo Congress: A Critical Report," *JCLA*, 3: 2; "Bilingualism in the Americas" (criticism of Haugen's Survey), *JCLA*, 4: 2; "A Theory of Structural Gradation," *Proc Eighth Int Congress of Linguists*; (with P. Drysdale and H. Scargill) "Pitch and Stress as Phonemes: Analysis or Synthesis?"; "What Bilingualism Means to the Newcomer," *Citizen*, 4; "Les Exigences du Bilinguisme pour l'Immigrant," *Citoyen*, 4; "The Description of Bilingualism," *JCLA*, 7: 2; "Language Didactics and Applied Linguistics," *Vuosikirja*, 4; "Contemporary Demands in Foreign Language Teaching," *Modern Language Instruction in Canada* (Ottawa, 1963); "A Framework for the Analysis of Language Theories," *Preprints of the Ninth Int. Congress of Linguists* (Cambridge, 1962); "L'étude du bilinguisme: problèmes et méthodes," *Congrès de l'ACCA* (1962); "Un calcul de la productivité," *Annales de l'Acfas*, 24; "Fonction d'un schéma de dichotomies croisées comme cadres des plans opératifs dans la comparaison des théories linguistiques," *Annales de l'Acfas*, 27; "Cadres d'analyses fonctionnelles pour servir de base à la mensuration du bilinguisme," *Annales de l'Acfas*, 28. (C) *Can J Linguistics, Citizen, Enc Br, Eng Lang Teaching, Vuosikirja: Uusien Kielten Opettajien Liitto.* (D) La Mensuration de l'Interférence: l'effet de deux systèmes phonologiques (intonation, rythme, caténation, articulation), grammaticaux, lexiques, sémantiques, stylistiques, et culturels sur le comportement de l'individu bilingue (pour juin 1963); Le Bilinguisme acadien: enquêtes sur le terrain durant l'été—questionnaires—archives sonores—enquêtes enregistrées auprès de 35 informateurs en 1962 (projet dans son deuxième année); La Mesure en didactique analytique: mensuration de facteurs de l'enseignement des langues (recherches complexes, en cours depuis douze ans bien avancées); Parameters of Restrictability (the analysis of factors that permit a language to limit itself, theoretical section completed); Les Ressources linguistiques du Canada: à base de questionnaires envoyés aux collèges, aux écoles, et aux journaux de langues étrangères (deuxième questionnaire déjà rentré, compilation en mai 1963); Le Vocabulaire disponible (direction de ce projet du département de linguistique de Laval depuis 1962, en panne); completed MSS., etc.: "Aspects sociaux du bilinguisme," 32 pp.; "L'art de la traduction," 26 pp.; "Problèmes linguistiques des peuples en contact," 12 pp.; "Language Teaching through Radio and Television," 16 pp.; "L'origine des anglo-saxons," 15 pp.; "Language Laboratories and Language Learning," 25 pp.; An Analytical Survey of Courses for Teaching English as a Second Language: 1. Great Britain and Canada, 115 pp.; "The Use of Special Phrase and Word Lists in Trades and Industry," 15 pp.; "Seven Types of Language Games" (mimeo), 12 pp.; "Modern Theories of Language: A Comparative Analysis" (mimeo), 37 pp., "Birkas Géza's Grammaire française à l'usage des Hongrois," 7 pp.; "Analysis of Vers la France," 5 pp.; "Toward a National Policy on the Training of Language Teachers," 10 pp.; "An Analysis of Palmer's New Method English Practice," 11 pp.; "Diagnostic Tests in English Pronunciation," 12 pp.; "The Second Phase of the Sopron Experiment," 7 pp.; "The Literacy Problem of Adult Immigrants," 12 pp.; "Analysis of 'Let's Learn English,'" 28 pp.; "The Language Problem of Reserve Indians: Preliminary Survey," 16 pp.; "Outline Revision of Learning the English Language," 102 pp.; "An Appraisal of Tan-Gau," 5 pp.; "Recruiting Canadian Language Personnel for Atlantic Sailings," 6 pp.; "The Canadian Scene in Basic," 75 pp.; "Bilingualism in Canadian Education," 27 pp.; "Preliminary Report on the International Seminar on Bilingualism," 14 pp.; "Bohlens Bild und Ton im neusprachlichen Unterricht," 12 pp.; "Prerequisites for an Evaluation of Language Teaching Texts," 28 pp.; "Language Teaching on Television: A Critical Analysis of Contemporary Practices," 18 pp.; "Language Teaching Methods in Israel," 10 pp.

MORICE, LOUIS: (A) *Verlaine, le drame religieux* (Paris, 1946), 557 pp.; *"Sagesse" de Verlaine* (édition critique commentée) (Paris, 1948), 529 pp. (B) "Le Drame de la Poésie moderne," *RUL*, 7 (1953), 582–97; "Chateaubriand, l'homme des songes," *RUL*, 7 (1953), 764–89; "Autour de Verlaine," *RUL*, 8 (1954), 442–57; "Le Catholicisme de Baudelaire," *RUL*, 8 (1954), 626–38; "La Vision de Paul Valéry," *RUL*, 17 (1962), 3–31; "Rimbaud et la conversion de Claudel," *ESC* (1962), 11–24. (C) *RUL*. (D) Editions critiques et commentées des recueils

"Amour" et "Liturgies Intimes" de Paul Verlaine; nombreuses analyses de textes (rédigées); projet: Initiation à la poésie.

MCGILL UNIVERSITY

HENRY, ROBINA E.: (A) (ed., with introduction, footnotes, vocabulary, "cuestionarios," selected bibliography, with Enrique Ruiz-Fornells) Joaquín Calvo-Sotelo's *La Muralla* (Spanish play in three acts) (New York, 1962), 112 pp.

JONES, HENRI: (B) "Du Classicisme," *Proc. Third Int. Congress on Aesthetics* (Venice, 1956); "Myths of the Romantic Attitude," *Proc. Fourth Int. Congress on Aesthetics* (Athens, 1960). (C) *Maintenant, Vie des Arts.* (D) Cybernetics and Mechanology; De l'Esthétique classique (Essai sur le Portrait et le Nu, almost finished).

MCMASTER UNIVERSITY

CONLON, P. M.: (A) *Voltaire's Literary Career from 1728 to 1750*, Studies on Voltaire and the Eighteenth Century, 14 (Geneva, 1961). (B) "Voltaire's Election to the Accademia della Crusca," in *Studies on Voltaire and the Eighteenth Century*, 6 (Geneva, 1958), 133–9; "A Bicentenary: Voltaire's 'Candide' 1759–1959," *J Australian U Mod Lang Ass*, 12 (1959), 20–9. (C) *J Australian U Mod Lang Ass, Studies on Voltaire and the Eighteenth Century.* (D) Chronology of the Age of Enlightenment in France, 1680–1789.

STOCK, MARIE: (D) Poullain de la Barre: A Seventeenth-Century Feminist (a monograph should be finished by the end of August).

UNIVERSITY OF MANITOBA

DIXON, J. E. G.: (B) "T. E. Lawrence and 'The Mint,' " *Roundel* (Sept., 1955), 41–5; "The Choice is Yours," *Canada Month* (Jan., 1962), 23–6. (D) A monograph on French nouns and their gender (an attempt to formulate rules, based on meaning, etymology, or termination, for the determination of the gender of French nouns, almost completed).

JENSEN, CHRISTIAN A. E.: (A) L'Evolution du romantisme: l'année 1826 (Geneva and Paris, 1959), viii + 359 pp. (D) "The Romanticism of Ferdinand d'Eckstein" (finished); "The Romanticism of the *Annales de la littérature et des arts*" (being revised); "Influence of the Saint-Simonians on Stendhal, Vigny, and Hugo" (in preparation); (in collaboration with Meredith Jones) anthology of French literature (for publication by Macmillan of Canada, in progress).

JOUBERT, A.: (B) "La Philosophie de Leon Bronschweg: Théorie de la raison" (Paris, 1947), 110 pp.; "La Théorie de l'imagination dans la philosophie de Gaston Bachelard" (Winnipeg, 1961), 14 pp. (D) "La caractérologie littéraire" (article, from Colloques du Département de Français de l'Université de Manitoba); Recherche sur le temps (from thèse de doctorat).

LEATHERS, VICTOR: (A) *British Entertainers in France* (Toronto, 1959), viii + 179 pp. (B) "Visit with Two Giants," *Winnipeg Free Press* (Sept. 5, 1961). (C) *Winnipeg Free Press.* (D) A book discussing the contribution made to French civilization from 1750 to 1850 by noted Creoles of the French Antilles (writing should be finished next summer).

MEMORIAL UNIVERSITY OF NEWFOUNDLAND

HARE, J.: (D) A critical study of Mallarmé (book; begun).

HEWSON, JOHN: (B) "The Language Laboratory," *Gage's Educ Pamphlets*, 4, 95–99. (D) French laboratory workbook and French pattern practice (both accepted for publication).

STOKER, JOHN T.: (A) *William Pitt et la Révolution Française: 1789–1793* (Paris, 1935), 222 pp.; (ed.), François Mauriac's *Noeud de Vipères* (1959). (B) "Fénelon's Errors Concerning Molière's *l'Avare*," *MLR*, 49 (1954), 472–3; "Molière, Writer of Comedies," *Mod Lang*, 37 (1956), 59–61; "Toinette's Age and Temperament," *Mod Lang*, 37 (1956), 102–3. (C) *Mod Lang, MLR.* (D) Edition of Molière's *Les Fourberies de Scapin* (material assembled); "Molière—l'auteur malgré lui" (article; completed); "The Question of Grace in Mauriac's Novels" (article; completed); notes and filmstrips in progress: Racine's *Andromaque*, Corneille's *Le Cid*, and *Macbeth*.

WILKINS, NIGEL EDWARD: (D) "The Codex Reina: A Revised Description" (article; to appear in *Musica Disciplina* in 1963); "Some Notes on Philipoctus de Caserta (*c.* 1360?–*c.* 1435)" (article; to appear in *Nottingham Medieval St* in 1963); a critical edition of the French and Italian texts and music contained in the *Codex Reina* (Bibl. Nat., Paris, MS. n.a. fr. 6771) (completed).

MOUNT ALLISON UNIVERSITY

BOUSQUET, JEAN: (A) *Salut ô Reine* (Montréal, 1938), 127 pp.; *Soyez Prêts* (Montréal, 1939), 126 pp.; *Les Jours et les Heures* (diary) (Montréal, 1940), 141 pp., *Comment éduquer vos enfants* (Montréal, 1942), 160 pp. (2nd ed., 1943); *Venez vous reposer* (Montréal, 1944), 63 pp.; *Notre-Dame du Rosaire de Fatima* (Montréal, 1945), 94 pp. (2nd and 3rd ed., 1946); *Vie de Saint Thomas d'Aquin* (Montréal, 1947), 77 pp.; *Comment j'élèverais mes enfants* (Montréal, 1948), 64 pp.; *Saint Vincent Ferrier* (Montréal, 1949), 133 pp.; *Lacordaire* (Montréal, 1951), 143 pp.; *Sainte Catherine de Sienne* (Montréal, 1953), 130 pp.; "Lourdes et Fatima devant l'O.N.U.," in *Les Tracts marials mensuels* (Nicolet, P.Q., 1956), 31 pp.; *Trois notices nécrologiques* (Montréal, 1962), 43 pp. (B) A series of nineteen articles published in *La Voix Nationale* (Montréal) on Christian education in the home. (D) Le secret de tante Rosanna (novel) and Ma sœur Lise (novel) (both should be ready at the end of next year).

UNIVERSITY OF NEW BRUNSWICK

HERISSON, CHARLES D.: (A) *Le Contrôle du Crédit par la Banque d'Angleterre* (Paris, 1932), 462 pp.; *Les Nations Anglo-Saxonnes et la Paix* (Paris, 1936), 200 pp.; *Autarcie Economie Complexe et Politique commerciale rationnelle* (Paris, 1937), 202 pp.; *La Politique économique internationale des Etats-Unis après la Guerre* (Paris, 1939), 760 pp.; *Les Problèmes économiques et raciaux de l'Union Sud-Africaine* (Paris, 1940), 172 pp.; (trans., with notes and introduction) J. Williams and H. May's *I Am Black* (Brussels, 1951). (B) "Le machinisme et l'agriculture française," *Rev d'Economie Politique*, 4 (1932), 1382–96; "Fondement du droit de punir," *Littérature, Philosophie et Pédagogie* (avril 1933), 550–3;

"Le national-socialisme et l'économie dirigée," *Rev. Politique et Parlementaire*, 151 (1933), 34–44; "Le capitalisme en Allemagne," *Esprit*, 1 (1933), 687–94; "Mutualité et assurances sociales en France," *Actualité Economique*, 10 (1934), 231–52; "Les coopératives de consommation en Algérie," *Annales du Droit et des Sc Soc*, 4 (1934), 301–26; "Le national-socialisme et la protection des classes moyennes," *Rev Economique Int*, 26 (1934), 446–79; "Le national-socialisme et l'organisation corporative," *Actualité Economique*, 9 (1934), 553–64; "Le drame autrichien," *Actualité Economique*, 10 (1934), 446–65; "Sismondi, réformateur social," *J de Statistique et Rev Economique Suisse*, 3 (1935), 435–9; "La structure économique et sociale de la France," *CF*, 23 (1935), 172–7; "Conte Sibérien: Les Trois Petits Pains," *CF*, 24 (1936), 119–26; "Conte Sibérien: Cemiletka," *CF*, 25 (1937), 204–10; "Le problème de la progressivité de l'impôt," *Actualité Economique*, 12 (1937), 355–73; "La conception française et l'organisation de la paix," *Littérature, Philosophie et Pédagogie* (mars 1937), 518–22; "L'artiste et l'écrivain devant la vie, un cas tragique: Gustave Flaubert," *Littérature, Philosophie et Pédagogie* (fév. 1939), 10–19; "La division du travail et l'éducation," *RTC*, 25 (1939), 83–92; "Le matérialisme historique," *CF*, 26 (1939), 644–66; "Problèmes raciaux en Afrique du Sud," *Actualité Economique*, 15 (1939), 427–36; "L'Afrique du Sud et le problème indigène," *CF*, 27 (1939), 20–9; "Le rôle et la formation des élites au Canada Français," *CF*, 27 (1940), 925–32; "Les Saints-Simoniens et la propriété privée," *Actualité Economique*, 16 (1940), 37–53; "La coopération de l'Union Sud-Africaine avec les Alliés," *CF*, 28 (1940), 131–44; "L'Union Sud-Africaine et le conflit européen," *Rev des Deux Mondes*, 57 (1940), 253–67; "L'Union Sud-Africaine et la France," *Rev des Deux Mondes*, 57 (1940), 339–51; "La vie politique et sociale de l'Inde," *CF*, 29 (1941), 54–63; "L'Inde et la guerre actuelle," *CF*, 29 (1941), 121–6; "Le Portugal, puissance colonisatrice," *Actualité Economique*, 17 (1941), 126–38; "L'Afrique, chantier européen," *Actualité Economique*, 17 (1941), 25–38; "La Route du Cap: 1486–1940," *Rev des Deux Mondes*, 58 (1941), 72–82; "L'Union Sud-Africaine et la production des matières premières," *RTC*, 27 (1941), 201–10; "L'agriculture de l'Union Sud-Africaine," *RTC*, 27 (1941), 311–25; "L'industrie sud-africaine," *RTC*, 27 (1941), 433–49; "Le Problème des races en Afrique du Sud: les métis," *CF*, 29 (1942), 520–31; "Les routes de l'Afrique du Sud," *RTC*, 28 (1942), 338–52; "L'Afrique, chantier européen: les Rhodésies et le Nyassaland," *Actualité Economique*, 19 (1943), 43–59; "La coopération africaine et le problème de communication," *France* (Nov., 1943); "Les chemins de fer de l'Afrique du Sud," *RTC*, 29 (1943), 406–24; "Le problème humain et psychologique de la coopération africaine," *France* (Jan., 1944); "Veterinary Cooperation in Africa," *France* (April, 1944); "La guerre et la métamorphose de l'économie sud-africaine," *RTC*, 30 (1944), 254–65; "Le pauperisme en Afrique du Sud," *Actualité Economique*, 20 (1944), 1–26; "French Literary Homage to Constantia Wine," *Libertas* (March, 1945); "Le problème hygiénique et médical en Afrique du Sud," *Actualité Economique*, 21 (1945), 151–66; "Le problème médical et vétérinaire en Afrique: La coopération pan-africaine," *RTC*, 31 (1945), 139–59; "Plea for a pan-African Bureau of Research," *Forum*, 103 (1945); "L'économie et les problèmes raciaux des

Rhodésies," *Actualité Economique*, 22 (1946); 515–31; "Le problème de l'éducation en Afrique du Sud," *RTC*, 32 (1946), 329–44; "Le problème agricole en Afrique: la coopération agricole pan-Africaine," *RTC*, 33 (1947), 319–46; "Le problème des recherches et de l'information en Afrique," *RTC*, 33 (1948), 397–409; "Julien Benda et l'éthique sociale," *AU*, 15 (1949), 52–61; "Le Vin de Constance: souvenirs littéraires franco-sud-africains," *RUL*, 3 (1949), 777–89; "Stendhal, peintre des mœurs et romancier politique et social," *RTC*, 35 (1949), 131–9; "Les écrivains français en Afrique du Sud: Bernardin de Saint Pierre au Cap," *RTC*, 35 (1950), 430–40; "Le drame de la création littéraire: la vie de Balzac," *RTC*, 36 (1950), 275–84; "La littérature de la révolte: Jules Vallés," *RUL*, 5 (1950), 219–31; "L'influence française en Afrique australe: 1685–1950," *RTC*, 36 (1951), 52–75; "La contribution des réfugiés huguenots français à la civilisation Sud-Africaine," *Bull Hist de la Soc de l'Hist du Protestantisme Français*, 98 (1951), 69–90; "Magie du verbe" (a study of the symbiosis of the sound and meaning of words for artistic effects), *AU*, 18 (1951), 60–75; "Présence française en Afrique du Sud," *RTC*, 37 (1952), 159–86; "Les réfugiés huguenots du XVIIe siècle et la survivance française en Afrique du Sud," *Bull Hist de la Soc de l'Hist du Protestantisme Française*, 100 (1953), 57–93; "A Libertine French Poet: Parny," *Standpunte* (Dec., 1953), 33–43; "Nature: Intégration et Virtuosité," *Universitas* (April, 1954), 8–9; "Le Vaisseau Fantomatique," *Universitas* (Sept., 1954); "L'hypocoristique 'petit' et les titres de journaux," *Français Moderne*, 22 (1954), 49–58, and 119–29; "L'hypocoristique 'petit' en français moderne: étude séman-tique," *Française Moderne*, 24 (1956), 35–47; "Le langage et les mœurs: l'hypocoristique 'petit' au cours des siècles," *Français Moderne*, 24 (1956), 113–24; "Les voyages du Chevalier de Parny," *L'Essor* (mai-juin 1956), 17–30; "Le voyage de Baudelaire dans l'Inde, Histoire d'une legende," *Mercure de France*, 327 (1956), 273–95; "L'influence française en Afrique du Sud au XVIIIe siècle," *L'Essor* (jan.-avril 1957), 17–25, and (juillet–oct. 1957), 13–23; "Langue et psychologie nationale," *RUL*, 13 (1958), 60–73; "Leconte de Lisle at the Cape," *Q Bull S African Lib* (March, 1959), 76–86; "Le voyage de Baudelaire," *Mercure de France*, 335 (1959), 637–73; "Quelques autres usages de l'hypocoristique 'petit,' " *Français Moderne*, 27 (1959), 298–307, and 28 (1960), 25–36; "A propos de Baudelaire en 1841 et 1842," *Mercure de France*, 338 (1960), 449–75; "Mauriac: essai de mise au point," *RUL*, 15 (1960), 121–30; "A propos de 'Gigi': Littérature et Sociologie," *FR*, 35 (1961), 42–9; "La jeunesse de Leconte de Lisle: 1822–1832," *Rev d'Hist Littéraire de la France* (oct.–dec. 1961), 55–63, and (jan.–mars 1962), 59–73; "The English-speaking Maritimers and Bilingual-ism," *Atlantic Advocate* (May, 1962), 152–61. (C) *Mercure de France*, *Rev de l'Hist Littéraire de la France*, RUL. (D) Les sources du poème "Les Hurleurs" de Leconte de Lisle; a semantic study on the hypocoristic in modern French (parts of this book have already been published in the form of seven articles in periodicals).

McANDREW, W. A. G.: (A) *Louis Hémon: sa vie et son œuvre* (Paris, 1936), 255 pp. (B) "Maria Chapdelaine chez elle," *UTQ*, 15 (1945), 76–85; "A Canadian Disciple of François Mauriac: Robert Charbonneau," *UTQ*, 16 (1946), 42–50; "The Survival of French," *Can MLR*, 3 (1946),

10–13.   (D) Arsène Houssaye—his relations with representative figures of his time: Gautier, Baudelaire, *et al.* (documentation yet to be done).

SIMAIKA, RAOUF: (A) *L'Inspiration épique dans les romans de V. Hugo* (Geneva, 1962), 232 pp.

UNIVERSITY OF OTTAWA

CELESTE, SISTER MARIE: (A) *Le Sens de l'Agonie dans l'œuvre de George Bernanos* (Paris, 1962), 190 pp.; "Lettre-préface" de Lucien Guissant, illustré de quatre hors texte, deux facsimilés et sous couverture originale.   (B) "L'Apostolat du Curé d'Ambricourt," *RUL*, 14 (1960), 536–47; "Bernanos: A Man of Spirit," *Culture*, 21 (1960), 413–18.   (C) *Rev Dominicaine*.   (D) "Le Rôle de l'Eglise dans l'œuvre de Bernanos" (part of a collection of essays entitled Thèmes et portraits de la spiritualité bernasienne).

MÉNARD, JEAN: (A) L'œuvre de Boylesne (Paris, 1956), 272 pp.; *De Corneille à Saint-Denys-Garneau* (Montreal, 1957), 217 pp.; Les Mythes (poèmes), (Montréal, 1963), 68 pp.   (B) "Madame de Staël et Roederer avec des documents inédits," *RUO*, 30 (1960), 150–84; "Madame de Staël et la musique avec des documents inédits," *RUO*, 31 (1961), 420–35, 552–63. (C) *Arch des Lettres Can, Le Droit, Rev Dominicaine, RUL, RUO.*   (D) Xavier, Marmier, et le Canada, avec des documents inédits (collection Vie des Lettres Canadiennes).

ROBIDOUX, RÉJEAN: (B) " 'Les soirées canadiennes' et 'Le Foyer canadien' dans le mouvement littéraire québecois de 1860," *RUO*, 28 (1958), 411–52; "Fortunes et infortunes de l'abbé Casgrain," *Arch des Lettres Can*, 1 (1961), 209–29.   (C) *RUO*.   (D) Roger Martin du Gard et la religion (thèse de doctorat, sera publiée à Paris, 1963); une étude sur le *Traité du Narcisse d'André Gide*: étude d'histoire littéraire et explication de texte (la documentation est à peu près achevée—reste à entreprendre la rédaction); article sur les tendances du jeune roman canadien pour les *Archives des Lettres canadiennes*, 3 (stade de la documentation).

WYCZYNSKI, PAUL: (A) *Emile Nelligan: sources et originalité de son œuvre* (Ottawa, 1960), 347 pp.; directeur et rédacteur-en-chef de la collection *Arch des Lettres Can*, 1, *Mouvement littéraire de Québec 1860* (Ottawa, 1960), 351 pp., 2, *L'Ecole littéraire de Montréal* (Montréal, 1963), 383 pp.   (B) "Perspectives du Symbolisme," *RUO*, 25 (1955), 34–58; "Adam Michieurir ou l'expression polonaise de l'époque romantique," *RUO*, 25 (1955), 436–56; "Emile Nelligan," *Les Lectures*, 6 (1959), 37–9; "Charles Gill Intime," *RUO*, 29 (1959), 447–72; "Les origines de l'école littéraire de Montréal," *Thought from the Learned Societies of Canada* (Toronto, 1960), 211–25; "Jean Charbonneau," *La Presse* (5 nov. 1960), 34; "Charles Gill," *Les Lectures*, 7 (1960), 163–5; "Dans les coulisses du Théâtre de Fréchette," *RUO*, 31 (1961), 230–58; "La littérature dans la perspective de ses valeurs veritables," dans *La Littérature par elle-même*, 2, (Montréal, 1962), 7–20; "Emile Nelligan: Poète de l'inquiétude," *Can L*, 10 (1961), 40–50; "L'école littéraire de Montréal," dans *Arch des Lettres*, 2 Montréal, 1963), 11–36.   (C) *Cahiers AGEUM, Can L, Lectures, RUO, Thought.*   (D) Histoire de la littérature canadienne-française; Horizon des lettres canadiennes; Emile Nelligan (pour la collection Ecrivain canadien d'aujourd'hui); Symbole en la dimension verticale de la poésie; Initiation à la recherche littéraire.

QUEEN'S UNIVERSITY

BESSETTE, GÉRARD: (A) *Poèmes Temporels* (Monte-Carlo, 1954), 64 pp.; *La Bagarre* (novel) (Montréal, 1958), 232 pp.; *Le Libraire* (novel) (Paris, 1960), 174 pp.; *Les Images en poésie canadienne-française* (Montréal, 1960), 282 pp.; *Les Pédagogues* (novel) (Montréal, 1961), 310 pp.; (introduction) *Anthologie d'Albert Laberge* (Montréal, 1963), xxxv + 310 pp. (B) "Analyse d'un poème de Nelligan," *AU*, 15 (1948), 62–79); "L'Evolution des images en poésie canadienne-française," *Culture*, 20 (1959), 3–14; "Bonheur d'occasion," *AU*, 18 (1952), 53–74; "French-Canadian Society as Seen by Contemporary Novelists," *QQ*, 49 (1962), 177–97; "Nelligan et les remous de son subconscient," *Arch des Lettres Can*, 2 (1963), 131–49. (C) *Arch des Lettres Can, Can L, Culture, QQ*. (D) La Commensale (a novel); (in collaboration) Histoire de la littérature française et canadienne-française par les textes.

HILBORN, H. W.: (A) *A Chronology of the Plays of D. Pedro Calderon de la Barca* (Toronto, 1938), vi + 119 pp. (B) "The Versification of *La Selva Confusa*," *MLN*, 53 (1938), 193–4; "Calderón's *Agudos* in Italianate Verse," *HR*, 10 (1942), 157–9; "Calderón's *Silvas*," *PMLA*, 58 (1943), 122–48; "Calderón's *Quintillas*," *HR*, 16 (1948), 301–10; "Comparative *Culto* Vocabulary in Calderón and Lope," *HR*, 26 (1958), 223–33. (C) *Can MLR, HR, QQ*. (D) *Leísmo* and *Loismo* in modern Spanish (about half completed); Calderón's *Culteranismo* (investigation almost completed); (trans.) Martinez, ed., *El ensayo mexicano moderno*.

UNIVERSITY OF SASKATCHEWAN

BUJILA, BERNARDINE: (A) (ed.) Rutebeuf's *La Vie de Sainte Marie l'Egyptienne*, Contributions in Modern Philology, 12 (Ann Arbor, 1949), vii + 92 pp. (B) "Michel Bibaud's *Encyclopédie canadienne*," *Culture*, 21 (1960), 117–32.

RIDGWAY, R. S.: (A) *La propagande philosophique dans les tragédies de Voltaire*, Studies on Voltaire and the Eighteenth Century, 15 (Geneva, 1961), 260 pp. (B) "*Athalie*, vue par Voltaire," *Bull de liaison racinienne*, 6 (Uzès, 1958).

ST. FRANCIS XAVIER UNIVERSITY

MacLEAN, CECIL: (A) *La France dans l'œuvre de R. L. Stevenson* (Paris, 1936), viii + 224 pp.

SAINT MARY'S UNIVERSITY

DEVINE, FRANCIS J.: (B) "Emile Baumann et le réalisme chrétien," *RUL*, XVII (1963), 806–19.

UNIVERSITY OF TORONTO (FRENCH)—UNIVERSITY COLLEGE

DEMBOWSKI, P. F.: (A) *La Chronique de Robert de Clari: Etude de la langue et du style* (Toronto, 1963), 142 pp. (B) "En marge du vocabulaire de R. de Clari," *RP*, 15 (1961), 12–18; "Corrections à l'édition de la chronique de R. de Clari, de Ph. Lauer," *Romania*, 82 (1961), 134–8. (C) *RP*. (D) Critical edition of *Jourdain de Blaye* (near completion).

FLINN, JOHN F.: (A) *Le* Roman de Renart *dans la littérature française et dans les littératures au Moyen Age* (Toronto, 1963), xii + 271 pp. (D) A work on the iconography of the *Roman de Renart*, with illustrations (most of the photographic research in Europe completed, text has to be completed and reworked, will take another year at least); an article on some verses in a branch of the *Roman de Renart* (to be sent off shortly to *Romania*).

GRAHAM, VICTOR E.: (A) (Edition critique suivie du commentaire de Malherbe) Philippe Desportes' *Cartels et Masquarades, Epitaphes*, Textes littéraires français, 78 (Geneva, 1958), 119 pp.; (édition critique suivie du commentaire de Malherbe) Philippe Desportes' *Les Amours de Diane*, 1, 2, Textes littéraires français, 85, 86 (Geneva, 1959), 194, 137 pp.; (édition critique) Philippe Desportes' *Les Amours d'Hippolyte*, Textes littéraires français, 93 (Geneva, 1960), 174 pp.; (édition critique) Philippe Desportes' *Les Elégies*, Textes littéraires français, 97 (Geneva, 1961), 226 pp.; (ed.) *Representative French Poetry* (Toronto, 1962), xiv + 114 pp. (B) "Some Undiscovered Sources of Desportes," *FS*, 10 (1956), 123–32; "Desportes and the Civil Wars," *RN*, 9 (1956), 195–201; "Supplément à la Bibliographie des œuvres de Desportes," *Bibliothèque d'Humanisme et Renaissance*, 19 (1957), 485–8; "Wanted: More Organists," *Presbyt Record*, 83, No. 5 (reprinted in the *Diapason*, the *Church Musician*); "French or Anglais *à la mode*," *J des Traducteurs*, 3 and 4 (1959), 25–9; "How Can We Teach French? *Can Educ*, 14 (1959), 3–11; "Water Imagery and Symbolism in Proust," *RR*, 50 (1959), 118–28; "Sputnik and Student Aid," *J Higher Educ.*, 30 (1959), 331–4; "Religion and St. Exupéry's *Le Petit Prince*," *Can MLR*, 15 (1959), 9–11; "Let's Sing Carols," *Presbyt Record*, 84, No. 10; "Quelques vues sur Desportes," *Rev d'Hist Littéraire de la France*, 60 (1960), 47–52; "Improving the Teaching of French," *Can MLR*, 16 (1960), 11–19; Hymns and Hymn-Singing," *Presbyt Record*, 86 (1961), 6–7; "Jodelle's *Eugène ou La Rencontre* Again," *RN*, 15 (1962), 161–4; "The Pelican as Image and Symbol," *Rev de Litt Comp*, 36 (1962), 235–43. (C) *Can MLR, FS, Presbyt Record, RN, RR*. (D) Final volume of the critical edition of the works of Philippe Desportes (in press); general study of French poetry (1575–1610) (just begun under grant from Canada Council); "Philemon Clasquin's 'Sonnets des vertus intellectuelles et morales' (1609)" (to appear in *ZRP*).

HAYNE, DAVID M.: (B) "Recent Aids to French-Canadian Literary Studies," *FS*, 9 (1957), 333–6; "A Forest of Symbols: An Introduction to Saint-Denys Garneau," *Can L*, 3 (1960), 5–16; "Les lettres canadiennes en France," *RUL*, 15 (1960), 222–30, 328–33, 420–6, 507–14, 716–25, 16 (1961), 140–8; "Sur les traces du préromantisme canadien," *RUO*, 31 (1961), 137–57. (C) *Bull des Recherches Hist, Can L, Can MLR, Enc Br, RUL, RUO*. (D) Completing Bibliographie critique du roman canadien-française, 1837–1900; engaged upon a study of Nicolas Boileau-Despreaux.

JOLIAT, EUGENE: (A) *Smollett et la France*, Bibliothèque de la Revue de littérature comparée, 105 (Paris, 1935), 280 pp. (B) "Millin's Use of

Smollett's *Travels*," *Rev de Litt Comp*, 18 (1938), 510–14; "Smollett, Editor of Voltaire," *MLN*, 54 (1939), 429–36; (with Ernest F. Haden) "Le Genre grammatical des substantifs en franco-canadien empruntés à l'anglais," *PMLA*, 55 (1940), 839–54; "L'Auteur malgré lui [Saint-Evremond]," *UTQ*, 25 (1956), 154–66. (C) *BA, Can MLR* (assoc. ed.), *JEGP*, PQ. (D) Work on the text of Saint-Evremond (continuing); (in collaboration with Robert Finch) anthology of eighteenth-century poetry.

KAYE, E. F.: (A) *Charles Lassailly (1806–1843)* (Geneva, 1962). (D) Editing the "journal intime" of Xavier Marmier; book on Regnier-Destourbet; book on Hippolyte Tampucci.

ROUILLARD, C. D.: (A) *The Turk in French History, Thought, and Literature* (1520–1660), Etudes de Littérature Etrangère et Comparée, 13 (Paris, 1940), 700 pp.; (ed., with H. L. Humphreys) Georges Duhamel's *Le Notaire du Havre* (Toronto, 1954), xxii + 309 pp.; (ed.) *Souvenirs de jeunesse: an anthology* (New York, 1957), 332 pp. (B) "Montaigne et les Turcs," *Rev de Litt Comp*, 70 (1938), 235–51; "[Theatre as a Reflection of Society in] the Age of Molière," *TRSC*, 3rd series, s. 2, 51 (1957), 15–22. (C) *Comp Lit, FS, MP*. (D) A book on the relations between the France of Louis XIV and Turkey (and Persia?), with emphasis on the impact which that increased familiarity with the Muslim world had upon French thought and literature from 1660 to 1700 or 1715 (hope to write and publish by 1967).

SANOUILLET, MICHEL E.: (A) *Rions ensemble* (Toronto, 1955), 225 pp. (London, 1956, 240 pp.); (éd.) *Marchand du Sel*, collected writings of Marcel Duchamp (Paris, 1958), 235 pp.; (édition critique) Francis Picabia's periodical, *391* (Paris, 1960), 156 pp.; (édition critique) Alfred Kubin's *L'Autre côté* (Paris, 1962), 318 pp.; *Le Séparatisme québecois et nous* (Toronto, 1962), 56 pp. (C) *Can Art, Beaux Arts, GL&L, Les Nouvelles Françaises, Les Nouvelles Littéraires, Syntheses*. (D) Histoire du Mouvement Dada (600–700 pp., in final stage); Francis Picabia et *391* (500–600 pp., in final stage); Le Mammifère amnésique (working title, collected writings of Erik Satie, writing stage); (éd.) René Crevel ou le Quatorzième convive (planning stage).

UNIVERSITY OF TORONTO (FRENCH)—VICTORIA COLLEGE

RATHÉ, CHARLES EDWARD: (D) A series of articles on Innocent Gentillet, Protestant "jurisconsulte" in sixteenth century, who wrote an *Anti-machiavel* (articles will be drawn from doctoral thesis for Syracuse University presented Nov., 1959).

RICKETTS, PETER T.: (D) Edition critique des *Poésies* de Guilhem de Montanhagol (under consideration for publication); critical edition of the *Breviari d'Amor* of Matfre Ermengaud of Béziers (in early stage of deciphering: years of preparation ahead).

RIÈSE, LAURE: (A) *L'Ame de la Poésie Canadienne-Française* (Toronto, 1955), 263 pp. (paperback); *Les Salons Littéraires Parisiens du Second Empire à nos jours* (Toulouse, 1962), 272 pp. (B) "Parisian Literary Salons: Defenders of a Vanishing Art," *QQ*, 64 (1957), 76–86; "La Femme du Nouveau Monde," *Age Nouveau*, 107–8 (1960), 68–85; "Proche et lointain Canada: et leur patrie lointaine," *Rev des Forces Françaises de l'Est* (15 avril 1958), 231–40. (C) *Acta Vic, Can For, Can MLR, Le Cerf Volant, Culture Française, School, Union Nationale des Femmes.* (D) Working on counterpart of book on French Salons, probably to be called Cénacles et dîners littéraires (still collecting material).

Ross, A. C. M.: (A) (trans.) Pierre Bourdieu's *The Algerians* (Boston, 1962), 208 pp. (D) Translation of Gaston Bachelard, *La Psychanalyse du feu* (for April, 1963).

TRETHEWEY, WILLIAM HILLIARD: (A) (ed.) *La Petite Philosophie, an Anglo-Norman Poem of the Thirteenth Century*, Anglo-Norman Text Society, 1 (Oxford, 1939), lxv + 159 pp.; (ed.) *The French Text of the Ancrene Riwle* (from Trinity College Cambridge MS. R. 14.7), Early English Text Society, 240 (London, 1958), xxxiii + 271 pp. (B) "The Seven Deadly Sins and the Devil's Court in the Trinity College Cambridge French Text of the *Ancrene Riwle*," *PMLA*, 65 (1950), 1233–46. (C) *FS, PMLA, ZRP.* (D) A study of the relation of the Trinity Text of the *Ancrene Riwle* to the Middle English MS. Cotton Titus D.xviii (about half completed).

WOOD, J. S.: (A) *René Bazin, sa vie et son œuvre* (Paris, 1934), 199 pp.; *French Prose Composition* (London, 1936), 128 pp.; (with R. Niklaus) *French Unseens* (London, 1940), 166 pp.; (ed.) Henri Trojat's *La Tête sur les épaules*, Textes Français Classiques et Modernes (London, 1961), 176 pp. (B) "Buvat to Barbier: the French Middle-Classes and Public Opinion, 1715–63," *Politica*, 4 (1939); "Les Goncourt et le réalisme, 1860–70," *RR*, 40 (1947), 18–34; "Taine and the Goncourt Brothers," *St in Fr Lang, Lit, and Hist* (Cambridge, 1949); "Sondages dans le roman français du point de vue social (1789–1830)," *Rev d'Hist Littéraire de la France*, 54 (1954), 32–48; "Marcel Proust," *Can For*, 34 (1954), 125–7; "Roger Martin du Gard," *FS*, 14 (1960), 129–40. (C) *Chamber's Enc.* (D) Le Roman français, 1830–48: Thèmes et techniques chez les écrivains mineurs (MS. submitted to Humanities Research Council).

UNIVERSITY OF TORONTO (FRENCH)—TRINITY COLLEGE

BASSAN, FERNANDE: (A) *Les Carnets d'Orient de Caignart de Saulay* (Paris, 1955); *Chateaubriand et la Terre-Sainte* (Paris, 1959), 278 pp. (B) "Les Dangers du voyage de Chateaubriand en Terre-Sainte," *Bull de la Soc Chateaubriand*, 1954 (Paris); "Education in France," *Goucher Weekly* (1959); "Trois lettres inédites de Chateaubriand," *Mercure de France* (1962). (C) *Bull de la Soc Chateaubriand.* (D) Edition critique de la *Correspondance adressée à la famille Pastoret* (de 1788 à 1856) par des contemporains célèbres (Chateaubriand, Fontanes, Joubert, Talleyrand, *et al.*) (almost finished).

UNIVERSITY OF TORONTO (FRENCH)—ST. MICHAEL'S COLLEGE

BONDY, LOUIS JOSEPH: (A) *Le Classicisme de Ferdinand Brunetière* (Paris, 1930), vii + 167 pp. (B) "Claudel and the Catholic Revival," in *The Maritain Volume of the Thomist* (New York, 1943); "The Legacy of Baudelaire," *UTQ*, 14 (1945), 414–30; "Trois poètes français (Baudelaire, Mallarmé, Claudel)," *Can. MLR* (fall, 1961). (D) Section on Brunetière in The Cabeen Bibliography of French Literature, Nineteenth Century (ready for press).

DONOVAN, RICHARD B.: (A) *The Liturgical Drama in Medieval Spain* (Toronto, 1958), 229 pp. (D) "Coluccio Salutati, Francis Petrarch, and French Medieval Culture" (article; submitted for publication in *S Ren*).

LAJEUNESSE, E. J.: (A) (ed., with introduction) *The Windsor Border Region: Canada's Southernmost Frontier*, Champlain Society, Ontario Series, 4 (Toronto, 1960), cxxix + 374 pp. (D) Strawberry Island in Lake Simcoe, a local history project (ready for the press) (private publication).

SISTER MARY OLGA: (B) "Le confident dans la tragédie de Racine," *RUL*, 8 (1953), 59–81. (C) *RUL*. (D) "Introduction à une étude sur l'esthétique du confident chez Racine" (article; accepted by *RUL*); a small book on the Esthétique du confident chez Racine (preparatory work on Racine practically completed, presently investigating the practice of Racine's contemporaries in the use of the "confident"; research should be finished by end of year, writing completed in the next year).

UNIVERSITY OF TORONTO (ITALIAN AND SPANISH)

CHANDLER, S. B.: (B) "La fortuna del Tasso epico in Inghilterra, 1650–1800," *Studi Tassiani*, 5 (1955), 69–105; "Man, Emotion, and Intellect in the *Decameron*," *PQ*, 39 (1960), 400–12; "The Movement of Life in Verga," *Italica*, 35 (1958), 91–100; "La figura poetica di Lorenzo de' Medici," *Letterature moderne*, 7 (1957), 70–6; "An Italian Life of Margaret, Queen of James III," *Scottish Hist R*, 32 (1953), 52–7; "A Renaissance News Correspondent," *Italica*, 29 (1952), 158–63 (on Giovanni Sabadino degli Arienti). (C) *Bibliofilia, Giorn Storica della letteratura italiana, Italica, PQ.* (D) Manzoni's approach to the reader in *I Promessi Sposi* (in early stages of preparation).

CORRIGAN, BEATRICE: (A) (Ed. and trans.) *Curious Annals: New Documents Relating to Browning's Roman Murder Story* (Toronto, 1956), 1 + 142 pp.; *Catalogue of Italian Plays, 1500–1700, in the Library of the University of Toronto* (Toronto, 1961), 134 pp.; (trans., with J. A. Molinaro) Vittorio Alfieri's *Of Tyranny* (Toronto, 1961), xxxvi + 120 pp. (B) "Sforza Oddi and his Comedies," *PMLA*, 49 (1934), 719–42; "Scenario by a Dictator," *QQ*, 54 (1947), 215–22; "An Annotated Commedia Erudita: G. B. Sogliani's *L'Uccellatoio*," *Italica*, 26 (1949), 188–97; "New Documents on Browning's Roman Murder Case," *SP*, 49 (1952), 520–33; "The Opposing Mirrors," *Italica*, 33 (1956), 165–79; "Guerrazzi, Boswell, and Corsica," *Italica*, 35 (1958), 25–37; "The Byron-Hobhouse Translation of Pellico's *Francesca*," *Italica*, 35 (1958), 235–41; "*Il Capriccio*: an unpublished Italian Renaissance Comedy," *S Ren*, 5 (1958), 74–86; "Browning's Roman Murder Story," *Eng Misc*, 11 (1960), 333–400; "Antonio Fogazzaro and Wilkie Collins," *Comp Lit*, 13 (1960), 39–51; "An Unrecorded Manuscript of Machiavelli's *La Clizia*," *Bibliofilia*, 63 (1961), 73–87. (C) *Comp Lit, Eng Misc, Italica.* (D) "The Correspondence of Giovanni Ruffini with Vernon Lee" (to be published in *Eng Misc*, 1963); "Leopardi in Victorian England" (to be published in *Eng Misc*, 1964); "An Italian Version of Con-

172   THE HUMANITIES IN CANADA

greve's *The Mourning Bride*" (to be published in 1962 in *Annali sezione romanza* of the Istituto Universitario Orientale); revising an article on Tasso for *Italica*; working on the Italian dramatic versions in the sixteenth and seventeenth centuries of the Erminia-Tancredi episode.

GULSOY, J.: (B) "El sentido del valenciano *atzucac*," *RP*, 14 (1961), 195–200; "El origen de cat. *corruixa (r)*," *RP*, 15 (1962), 284–92; (with J. H. Parker) "*El Príncipe Constante*: drama barroco de la contrarreforma," *Hispanófila*, 9 (1960), 15–23.   (C) *HR, Indice Histórico Español, MP, RP, Revista Valenciana de Filología*.   (D) *Diccionario Valenciano-Castellano* de Manuel Joaquim Sanelo (edición, estudio de fuentes e investigación lexicológica; being published in Spain); article (in collaboration with Neale H. Tayler); articles on the contribution of Gustavo A. Bécquer to Spanish romantic *leyenda*, on "Lexicografia valenciana," on toponomastic research (all three to appear soon); two articles on further Catalan phonologic problems (nearly completed); study on remnants of Old Spanish sibilants, *ç, z,* and *s,* in eastern Spain (quite advanced); textbook for intermediate and advanced Spanish composition (in preparation).

LEVY, KURT L.: (A) *Vida y obras de Tomás Carrasquilla* (Medellín, 1958), 397 pp.   (B) "New Light on Tomás Carrasquilla," *PMLA*, 68 (1953), 65–74; "Revuelta y tradición: dos valores del mosaico cultural iberoamericano," in Luis Monguió, *et al.*, *La Cultura la literatura iberoamericanas* (Berkeley, 1957), 69–79; "Some Patterns in Latin American Prose," in D. L. B. Hamlin, ed., *The Latin Americas* (Toronto, 1960), 82–8.   (C) *BA, Can MLR, Enc Br, Enc Br Yearbooks* (yearly summary of Latin American literature), *Erasmus, Hispania, MLN, MLQ, PMLA, Revista Iberoamericana*.   (D) A critical account of the prose fiction of Antioquia, Colombia (to be accompanied by an anthology of the genre; sections of the critical work are already completed, others are as yet in the research stage).

MCCREADY, WARREN T.: (A) (with J. A. Molinaro) *Angélica y Medoro de Cañizares*, Collana di testi e studi, 3 (Torino, 1958), 88 pp.; *La heráldica en las obras de Lope de Vega y sus contemporáneos* (Toronto, 1962), xii + 470 pp.   (B) "A Volume of Rare *Sueltas*," *Bull of the Comediantes*, 6 (1954), 4–8; "*Empresas* in Lope de Vega's Works," *HR*, 25 (1957), 79–104; "Cervantes and the 'Caballero Fonseca,'" *MLN*, 73 (1958), 33–5; "Lope de Vega's Birth Date and Horoscope," *HR*, 28 (1960), 313–18; (with J. A. Molinaro) "La *Relación breve* . . . de Cubillo de Aragón y la Paz de los Pirineos," *Bull Hispanique*, 62 (1960), 438–43.   (D) Bibliografía de la literatura periódica (1850–1950) sobre el teatro antiguo español (gathering of data is about nine-tenths done; should be in print by 1964).

MARIN, DIEGO: (A) (ed., with introduction, notes, vocabulary) *Artículos escogidos de Larra* (London, 1948), 199 pp.; *La vida española* (London, 1949), 197 pp. (rev. ed., New York, 1955); *Poesía española: Estudios y textos (siglos 15–20)* (Studium, Mexico, 1958), 500 pp.; *La intriga secundaria en el teatro de Lope de Vega* (Toronto and Mexico, 1958), 197 pp.; *La civilización española: Panorama histórico* (New York, 1961), lxii + 250 pp.   (B) "Los ensayos críticos de Larra," *Can MLR*, 7 (1950–51), 17–20; "El valor de época de A. López de Ayala," *Bull Hisp St*, 39 (1952),

131–8; "The Spanish Puzzle," *UTQ*, 22 (1953), 237–43; "El elemento oriental en D. Juan Manuel: Síntesis y revaluación," *Comp Lit*, 7 (1955), 1–15; "Culteranismos en *La Filomena* de Lope," *Revista Filología Española*, 39 (1955), 315–23. (C) *Hispania, Hispanófila, Revista Filología Española, Revista Hispaníca Moderna.* (D) Critical edition of Lope de Vega's *El galán de la Membrilla* (in press); the dramatic use and function of versification in Lope de Vega (to be published in 1962–3).

MOLINARO, JULIUS A.: (A) (with W. T. McCready) *Angélica y Medoro de Cañizares* (Torino, 1958), 88 pp.; (with J. H. Parker and Evelyn Rugg) *A Bibliography of Comedias Sueltas in the University of Toronto Library* (Toronto, 1959), viii + 149 pp.; (trans. and ed., with introduction, with Beatrice Corrigan) Vittorio Alfieri's *Of Tyranny* (Toronto, 1961), xxxvi + 120 pp. (C) *BA, Bull Hispanique, Italica, Quaderni Ibero-Americani.* (D) A Boiardo bibliography (in advanced stage of preparation); bibliography of Italian studies in America—to collaborate with Beatrice Corrigan to produce this four times a year for *Italica* (first to appear in March, 1963).

PARKER, J. H.: (A) (with Emilio Goggio and Beatrice Corrigan) *A Bibliography of Canadian Cultural Periodicals in Canadian Libraries* (Toronto, 1955), 45 pp.; *Breve historia del teatro español* (Mexico, 1957), 213 pp.; (with J. A. Molinaro and Evelyn Rugg) *A Bibliography of Comedias Sueltas in the University of Toronto Library* (Toronto, 1959), viii + 149 pp. (B) "Some Aspects of the Portuguese Contribution," *Can MLR*, 5 (1948), 11–17; "The Versification of the *Comedias* of Antonio de Solís y Rivadeneyra," *HR*, 17 (1949), 308–15; "The Chronology of the Plays of Juan Pérez de Montalván," *PMLA*, 67 (1952), 186–210; "Lope de Vega, the *Orfeo* and the *estilo llano*," *RR*, 44 (1953), 3–11; "Gil Vicente: A Study in Peninsular Drama," *Hispania*, 36 (1953), 21–5; "Almeida Garrett and Camões," *Hispania*, 38 (1955), 18–22; "The Present State of *Comedia* Performances," *Hispania*, 39 (1956), 408–11; "Lope de Vega and Juan Pérez de Montalván: Their Literary Relations (a preliminary survey)," in F. W. Pierce, ed., *Hispanic Studies in Honour of I. González Llubera* (Oxford, 1959), 225–35; (with J. Gulsoy) "*El príncipe constante*: Drama barroco de la Contrarreforma," *Hispanófila*, 9 (1960), 17–23; "Henry the Navigator: Hero of Peninsular Renaissance Fiction," *Hispania*, 44 (1961), 277–81. (C) *Can MLR, Hispania, HR, Hispanófila, PMLA, RR.* (D) "La Gitanilla de Montalván; enigma literario del siglo XVII" (in press, for *Actas*, First Int. Congress of Hispanists, Oxford, 1962); Spain of 1620–35: The Literary Relations of Lope de Vega and Juan Pérez de Montalván (a monograph; notes have been collected from local, U.S.A., and European libraries; writing yet to be done); The Present State of Lope de Vega Studies: A Survey of Lope Scholarship to 1962 (for the Quadricentennial of the dramatist's birth; monograph to be published by committee, MLA; research completed, by twelve MLA members, editing remains to be done).

ROMEO, LUIGI: (B) "*Pizza, pinza*, and *pitta*," *RP*, 16 (1962), 22–9. (D) "A Theory of Structural Pressures and Paradigmatic Diphthongization in East Romance" (submitted to *Word*); "Sul significato di *pialica* nell' *Inventario di Fondi*" (submitted to *Romanische Forschungen*); "Considerazioni linguistiche sul latino maccheronico" (first draft ready); (in collaboration with Prof. J. Gulsoy) The critical edition of *Liber Elegantiarum* (fifteen per cent ready); Graphemes and Phonemes in Early Italian Rhymes (first draft almost completed).

RUGG, EVELYN: (A) (with J. A. Molinaro and J. H. Parker) *A Bibliography of Comedias Sueltas in the University of Toronto Library* (Toronto, 1959), viii + 149 pp.; (trans. with Diego Marin) José Ortega y Gasset's *Meditations on Quixote* (New York, 1961), 192 pp. (C) *Hispania, Revista Interamericana de Bibliografía.* (D) (in collaboration with Diego Marin) A critical edition of Lope de Vega's *El galán de la Membrilla* (in press).

STAGG, GEOFFREY: (B) "La primera salida de don Quijote: imitación y parodia de sí mismo," *Clavileño*, 4 (1953), No. 22, 4–10; "The Date and Form of *El trato de Argel*," *Bull Hisp St*, 30, 181–92; "Castro del Río, ¿cuna del *Quijote*?," *Clavileño*, 6 (1955), No. 36, 1–11; "El sabio Cide Hamete Venengeli," *Bull Hisp St*, 33, 218–25; "Revision in *Don Quixote*, Part I," in F. W. Pierce, ed., *Hispanic Studies in Honour of I. González Llubera* (Oxford, 1959), 347–66; "Plagiarism in *La Galatea*," *Filologia Romanza*, 6, 255–76. (D) The composition of *Don Quixote*, Part I (a book to consist largely of articles already published or in preparation and papers already read); The Elaboration of Persiles y Sigismunda (a book, first draft being prepared).

UNIVERSITY OF WATERLOO

McKEGNEY, JAMES C.: (A) *A Survey of Graduate Studies in the Arts, Humanities, and Social Sciences in Canadian Universities* (Ottawa, 1954). (B) "Buenos Aires in the Poetry of Jorge Luis Borges," *Hispania*, 37 (1954), 162–6 (also in *Revista Iberoamericana*). (C) *BA, Hispania.* (D) The Useless Life of Pito Perez, a translation of *La Vida Inutil de Pito Perez*, by José Rubén Romero, and Female Characters in the Novels of José Rubén Romero and Gregorio López y Fuentes, a Comparative Study (both submitted to publishers).

RALSTON, ZACHARY T.: (A) *Gabriel Marcel's Paradoxical Expression of Mystery: A Stylistic Study of La Soif* (Washington, 1961), v + 102 pp.

WATERLOO LUTHERAN UNIVERSITY

BERMAN, LORNA: (D) "The Critics of Sade" (submitted to *PMLA*); "Sade and Religion" (submitted to *Studi francesi*); "The Concept of Evil in Sade" (in preparation for *Alphabet*).

TAYLER, NEALE H.: (A) *Las fuentes del teatro de Tamoyo y Baus* (Madrid, 1959), 211 pp. (C) *Hispania, Romance Notes.* (D) Latin-America: An Interpretation (revision of final MS.).

UNIVERSITY OF WESTERN ONTARIO—UNIVERSITY COLLEGE AND MIDDLESEX COLLEGE

CASAUBON, T. J.: (A) (ed.) *Conteurs Modernes* (an anthology of French short stories with exercises). (B) "A New Concept in Language Learning," *Educ. Forum.* (C) *Ontario MLR.* (D) A manual for French conversation.

CREIGHTON, DOUGLAS G.: (B) "Man and Mind in Diderot and Helvétius," *PMLA*, 71 (1956), 705–24. (C) *FR, PMLA.* (D) An anthology of French literature (choice completed, editing of texts at early stage).

HELLER, LANE: (B) "Diderot et la *Correspondance littéraire* de Grimm," *Proc. Tenth Pacific Northwest Conf Foreign Lang Teachers* (1959), 26–32. (D) The Apocalyptic fragments in Pascal's *Pensées* (nearly completed); Melchior Grimm's Early Months in Paris (submitted for publication).

OREA, TOMAS RAMOS: (A) *Coagulo* (Poems) (Madrid, 1954), 95 pp.; *La Fuente O Ella* (Poems) (Alcalá de Henares, 1962), 65 pp.; (co-author) *La Conversación al Dia: Aspectos de la Civilización Hispanica* (Toronto, 1964), 225 pp. (B) "La Mujer Americana" (series of eight articles), *Nuevo Alcalá* (1961–2); "Diez Dias en Finlandia," in *Programa de festejos de Alcalá de Heneres* (1961); "De Alcalá a U.S.A. con Vuelta: Aspectos," *Nuevo Alcalá* (1963); "La Idea del Amor en Tres Poetas Neorromanticos Ingleses Actuales," *Filologia Moderna* (1963). (C) *Filologia Moderna*.

SANDERS, JAMES B.: (A) (ed., with notes, vocabulary, with R. W. Torrens) *Contes de Nos Jours* (Toronto, 1956, and Boston, 1958), 312 pp.; (ed., with vocabulary, with R. W. Torrens) Claude Aveline's *La Double Mort de Fréderic Belot* (Toronto, 1958), 249 pp. (English edition, 1961); (ed., with notes, vocabulary, with R. W. Torrens) *La Communale* (New York, 1959), 334 pp.; (ed. with vocabulary, with R. W. Torrens) *Contes d'Aujourd'hui* (New York, 1963), 281 pp. (B) "Saint-Claude, French Citadel in Western Canada," *JCLA*, 1 (1954), 9–12. (D) "Camaret, havre de pêcheurs et d'artistes" (Bretagne) (to appear in *RUL*); "Henrik Ibsen's Introduction into France: *Ghosts*" (to appear in *FS*, autumn, 1963); A travers les siècles (anthology of French literature, in collaboration with D. G. Creighton); "The Influence of Mary, Queen of Scots upon Ronsard" (article; to be completed in summer, 1964).

SHERVILL, R. N.: (A) *Panorama Económico e Industrial de Hispanoamérica* (London, 1954), 54 pp; *The Phonological and Morphological Development of Old Spanish* (London, 1956), 40 pp.; *The Phonological and Morphological Development of Old French* (London, Ont., 1958), 52 pp. (B) "Lope de Vega's Female Characterization," *Bull of the Comediantes*, 12 (1960), 7–10. (D) Vida y obras de Felipe Godínez (reading original MSS. on micro-reader; only two plays exist in print).

TORRENS, ROBERT W.: (A) (ed.) Gabrielle Roy's *La Petite Poule d'Eau* (Toronto, 1956); (ed., with J. B. Sanders) *Contes de Nos Jours* (Toronto, 1956), 312 pp.; (ed.) *Lectures Variées* (Toronto, 1958); (ed., with J. B. Sanders) Claude Aveline's *La Double Mort de Fréderic Belot* (Toronto, 1958), 249 pp.; (ed., with J. B. Sanders) Jean L'Hôte's *La Communale* (New York, 1959), 334 pp.; (ed.) Jules Romains' *Donogoo* (New York, 1962); (ed., with J. B. Sanders) *Contes d'Aujourd'hui* (New York, 1963), 281 pp.

WALTERS, ROBERT L.: (D) Book on Voltaire and Science (most of reseach done; writing should be finished within a year).

WARWICK, JACK: (B) "Les pays d'en haut," *Culture*, 21 (1960), 246–65.

UNIVERSITY OF WESTERN ONTARIO—COLLEGE OF CHRIST THE KING

LENARDON, DANTE: (B) "An Annotated List of Articles dealing with Italian Literature appearing in the *Journal Encyclopédique* from 1756 to 1793," *Italica*, 40, 52–61. (D) *Le Journal Encyclopédique*: Index des

Auteurs et des Matières, 1756–1793 (in final stages, should be completed by spring, 1964).

UNIVERSITY OF WESTERN ONTARIO—HURON COLLEGE

METFORD, DEBORAH A. K.: (A) *La Metaphore dans l'œuvre de Stéphane Mallarmé* (Paris, 1938), viii + 210 pp. (B) "Le Rêve de Stéphane Mallarmé,"*PMLA*, 56 (1941), 874–84.

YORK UNIVERSITY

PRONGER, LESTER J.: (A) (ed., with introduction and notes, with J. G. Andison) Albert Husson's *La Cuisine des Anges* (New York, 1954), 160 pp. (B) "Marmontel as a source of Stendhal," *MLN*, 56 (1941), 433–5; "Stendhal Today," *Proc Second Pacific Northwest Conference of Foreign Language Teachers* (Vancouver, 1951, mimeo.). (D) La Poésie de Tristan Klingsor (an expanded revision of Ph.D. thesis, almost completed).

OTHER MODERN LANGUAGES

Celtic Studies

ST. FRANCIS XAVIER UNIVERSITY

MACLEOD, C. I. N.: (A) *An t-Eilthireach: Original Gaelic Poems and Melodies* (Glace Bay, N.S., 1952), 43 pp. (B) "The Gaelic Tradition in Nova Scotia," in A. Sommerfelt, ed., *Lochlann: A Review of Celtic Studies* (Oslo, 1958), I, 235–40. (C) *An Gaidheal* (Glasgow, Scotland), *Atlantic Advocate, Casket* (Antigonish, N.S.), *Food for Thought* (Toronto), *Gairm* (Glasgow, Scotland). (D) (with Helen Creighton) Gaelic Songs of Nova Scotia (Gaelic texts, English translations, and notes, of ninety-two Gaelic songs recorded on tape in Nova Scotia; in press).

German

ACADIA UNIVERSITY

WASEEM, GERTRUD: (D) On Robert Mune's "Der Mann ohne Eigenschaften" (progress very slow).

UNIVERSITY OF BRITISH COLUMBIA

HALLAMORE, G. JOYCE: (A) *Das Bild Laurence Sternes in Deutschland von der Aufklärung bis zur Romantik*, Germanische Studien, 72 (Berlin, 1936), 86 pp.; (with M. R. Jetter) *Am Kreuzweg: A Textbook Anthology of German Short Stories* (New York, 1957), 285 pp. (B) "Das Problem des Zwiespaltes in den Künstlernovellen E. T. A. Hoffmanns und Thomas Manns," *MDU*, 36 (1944), 82–94; "The Symbolism of the Marble Muse in Stifter's *Nachsommer*," *PMLA*, 74 (1959), 398–405; "Zur Siebenzahl in Thomas Manns *Zauberberg*," *Ger Q*, 35 (1962), No. 1.

MCNEELEY, JAMES A.: (B) "Historical Relativism in Wieland's Concept of the Ideal State," *MLQ*, 22 (1961), 269–82. (D) Monograph on political literature of the German enlightenment (research complete); Articles on Goethe's *Iphigenie* and Schiller's *Die Braut von Messina* (both to be completed in 1962).

MCGILL UNIVERSITY

ARNOLD, ARMIN: (A) *D. H. Lawrence and America* (London, 1958 and New York, 1959), 252 pp.; *Heinrich Heine in England and America: A Bibliographical Checklist* (London, 1959), 80 pp.; (ed., with introduction and notes) D. H. Lawrence's *The Symbolic Meaning* (London, 1962), 264 pp.; *James Joyce*, Köpfe des 20. Jahrhunderts (Berlin, 1963), 95 pp. (B) "Georg Kaiser in der Schweiz. Seine letzten Jahre nach den Briefen an Caesar von Arx," *Schweizer Rundschau*, 58 (1958), 514–30; "Der Status Heinrich Bölls," *Civitas*, 16 (1961), 349–55. (C) *Civitas, Comp Lit, Midway, MP, Neue Zürcher Zeitung, PQ, Schweizer Rundschau, Texas St in Lit and Lang, TLS, Vaterland.* (D) Die Dekadenz des amerikanischen Romans (to be published in 1965); Bernard Shaw, Köpfe des 20. Jahrhunderts (to be published in 1964); (ed.) D. H. Lawrence and Germany (to be published in July, 1963).

REISS, HANS SIEGBERT: (A) (ed.) *The Political Thought of the German Romantics, 1793–1815* (Oxford, 1955), 211 pp.; *Franz Kafka, eine Betrachtung seines Werkes* (Heidelberg, 1952), 195 pp. (2nd enlarged ed., 1956, 223 pp.); *Goethes Romane* (Berne and Munich, 1963), 320 pp.; (ed., with Herbert Wegener) *Emanuel Geibel: Briefe an Henriette Nölting, 1838–1855* (Lübeck, 1963), 103 pp. (B) "The Problem of Fate and of Religion in the Work of Arthur Schnitzler," *MLR*, 40 (1945), 300–8; "Zwei Erzählungen Franz Kafkas, eine Betrachtung," *Trivium*, 8 (1950), 218–42; "Zum Stil und zur Komposition in der deutschen Prosaerzählung der Gegenwart," *Studium Generale*, 8 (1955), 19–31; "Kant and the Right of Rebellion," *JHI*, 17 (1956), 179–92; "The Concept of the Aesthetic State in the Work of Schiller and Novalis," *Pub Eng Goethe Soc*, 26 (1957), 26–51; "The Study of Heinrich Heine: Retrospect of and Prospect," *Ger Q*, 20 (1959), 81–96; "Style and Structure in Modern Experimental Fiction," in Paul Böckmann, ed., *Stil- und Formprobleme in der Literatur* (Heidelberg, 1959), 419–24; "Fichte als politischer Denker," *Arch für Rechts- und Sozialphilos*, 48 (1962), 159–78. (C) *Akzente, Arch für Rechts- und Sozialphilos, Br J Sociology, Enc Br, Erasmus, GL&L, Hermathena, JHI, Mitteilungen des Deutschen Germanisten-Verbandes, MLQ, MLR, MP, Pub Eng Goethe Soc, Studium Generale, Universities Q.* (D) Goethe's Novels (an English version) (first draft done); a history of German political thought, 1780–1830 (still at an early stage of preparation).

MCMASTER UNIVERSITY

DENNER, K.: (C) *GL&L*. (D) Reception of Greek proper names in Gothic (trying to show how the form in which Greek words appear in Wulfila is determined by the sounds and sound combinations available in Gothic; not ready for publication).

PRAGER, JUTTA: (B) "Wesen und Ausdrucksformen des Modus im Neuhochdeutschen," *Wirkendes Wort*, 12 (1962), 274 ff. (D) Structural analysis of two grammatical categories in German and English: tense and moods (article; hope to submit it for publication in a German periodical by end of summer 1963); stylistic function of the adjective in different periods of German literature (still collecting material: should be ready early in

1964); language studies on the linguistic mixture of German and English used by German settlers in Ontario (if possible to collect material in Canada; in mere planning stage, hope to start work in summer).

UNIVERSITY OF MANITOBA

MAURER, K. W.: (A) (trans.) Rilke's *Letters to a Young Poet* (2nd ed., London, 1958), 46 pp.; Edward Friedrich Mörike, *Gedichte* (selected and edited) (3rd ed., London, 1958), 176 pp.; (trans. and ed., with introduction) *Death and the Ploughman* (from Johann Tepl's *Der Ackermann aus Böhmen*) (London, 1948), 42 pp.   (B) "Goethe's 'elective affinities,' " *MLR*, 42 (1947), 342–52; "Valéry and Goethe," *Pub Eng Goethe Soc*, 17 (1948), 74–100; "On the Appreciation of Paintings: Hints to the Layman," *QQ*, 65 (1958), 104–17; "Goethe's Novels," *Universitas* 4 (1959), 375–81; "Rainer Maria Rilke, A Selection of Poems" and "Hans Carossa's Mysterious Landscape," *Universitas*, 4 (1961), 251–63, and 274; "Friedrich Hölderlin, a Selection of Poems in Translation," *Universitas*, 4 (1961), 385–95; "Hermann Hesse: A Tribute on the Occasion of His Eighty-Fifth Birthday," *Universitas*, 5 (1962), 43–52; "Some Observations on Translating," *Actes*, *FILLM* (1961), 201–3.   (C) *Can Poetry Mag, Delta, Fiddlehead, GL&L, MLR, QQ, Universitas*.   (D) An anthology of German poems in translation, from Goethe to the present day; the University of Manitoba's Festival of the Arts, 1955 to 1962 (a critical report).

THIESSEN, JACK: (C) *Deutsche Philologie im Aufriss, Mennonite Life, Neue Schau, PMLA*.   (D) The Origin and Development of the Low German Spoken by the Canadian Mennonites (dissertation, in press).

QUEEN'S UNIVERSITY

EICHNER, HANS: (A) (ed., with introduction, commentary) Friedrich Schlegel's *Literary Notebooks 1797–1801* (London, 1957), 342 pp.; (with Hans Hein) *Reading German for Scientists* (London and New York, 1959), 207 pp.; (ed.) *Kritische Friedrich Schlegel-Ausgabe*, 4, 5, 6 (Paderborn, 1959 ff.); *Thomas Mann: Eine Einführung in sein Werk* (Bern, 1953), 123 pp. (2nd revised ed., 1961).   (B) "Aspects of Parody in the Works of Thomas Mann," *MLR*, 47 (1952), 30–48; "Friedrich Schlegel's Theory of Romantic Poetry," *PMLA*, 71 (1956), 1018–41; "Friedrich Ast und die Wiener Allgemeine Literatur-Zeitung," *Jahrbuch der Deutschen Schiller-Gesellschaft*, 4 (1960), 343–57.   (C) *Jahrbuch der Deutschen Schiller-Gesellschaft, JEGP, QQ*.   (D) A book on Friedrich Schlegel's literary criticism and poetry, and a critical edition of Schlegel's writings on literary subjects and of his literary notebooks (1797–1803), which will constitute vols. 2, 3, and 16 of the *Kritische Friedrich Schlegel-Ausgabe* (extensive work has been done on both projects, which should be completed by 1966).

HEIN, HANS R.: (A) (with H. Eichner) *Reading German for Scientists* (London and New York, 1959), 207 pp.

UNIVERSITY OF SASKATCHEWAN

GUNVALDSEN, K. M.: (B) "The Master Builder" and "Die versunkene Glocke," *MDU*, 33 (1941), 153; Gerhart Hauptmann's Dramatic Conception of the Artist, University of Wisconsin Summaries of Doctoral Dissertations

(1950); "Franz Kafka and Psychoanalysis," *UTQ*, 32 (1963), 266–81. (D) "The Plot of Kafka's *Trial*" (will be submitted to a journal in January, 1963); "The Plot of Kafka's *Castle*" (nearing completion); a book on Kafka (can be completed in 1963).

UNIVERSITY OF TORONTO—UNIVERSITY COLLEGE

BOESCHENSTEIN, HERMANN: (A) *Das literarische Goethebild der Gegenwart in England* (Breslau, 1933), 100 pp.; *Hermann Stehr* (Breslau, 1935), v + 92 pp.; *Kanadische Lyrik* (Bern, 1938), 69 pp.; *Gottfried Keller* (Bern, 1938), 178 pp.; (with V. Lange) *Kulturkritik und Literaturbetrachtung in Amerika* (1938); *The German Novel, 1939–1944* (Toronto, 1949), vii + 189 pp.; *Der neue Mensch* (Heidelberg, 1958), 130 pp.; *Gotthelf: Hans Joggeli der Erbvetter* (1961).

FAIRLEY, BARKER: (A) *Die Eneide Heinrichs von Veldeke und der Roman d'Eneas: Eine vergleichende Untersuchung* (Jena, 1910), 92 pp.; (trans.) *Three Plays*, by Frederic Hebbel (London, 1914), xxiv + 237 pp.; *Der Grüne Heinrich, Roman von Gottfried Keller, Erster Teil* (Oxford, 1925), 240 pp.; *Charles M. Doughty, a Critical Study* (London, 1927), 256 pp.; *Goethe as Revealed in His Poetry* (London, 1932), 210 pp.; (ed.) *Selected Passages from* The Dawn in Britain *of Charles Doughty* (London, 1935); (trans.) Hebbel's *Maria Magdalene* (Everyman's Library); *A Study of Goethe* (Oxford, 1947), 280 pp. (trans. by Franz Werneke, Munich, 1953); (ed.) *Der Landvogt von Greifensee von Gottfried Keller* (Oxford, 1948), 200 pp.; (ed.) *Goethe, Selected Letters, I, 1770–86* (Oxford, 1949), xviii + 205 pp.; *Goethe's Faust: Six Essays* (Oxford, 1953), 132 pp.; *Heinrich Heine: An Interpretation* (Oxford, 1954), 176 pp.; *Goethe, Selected Poems* (London, 1954), xxviii + 221 pp.; (ed.) *Goethe, Selected Letters, II, 1788–1832* (Oxford, 1955), xviii + 231 pp.; *Pfisters Mühle: Ein Sommerferienheft by Wilhelm Raabe* (London, 1956); *Wilhelm Raabe: An Introduction to His Novels* (Oxford, 1961), 275 pp. (trans. by H. Boeschenstein, Munich, 1961); (trans.) Laura Hofrichter's *Heine* (Oxford, 1963), xvi + 174 pp. (B) "The German National Spirit," *U Mag*, 14 (1915), 469–83; "Heinrich von Kleist," *MP*, 14 (1916), 65–84; "Literature and Actuality," *U Mag*, 17 (1918), 409–23; "Canadian War Pictures," *Can Mag*, 54 (1919), 2–11; "John Masefield," *QQ*, 26 (1919), 272–87; "Notes on the Form of *The Dynasts*," *PMLA*, 34 (1919), 401–15; "Masefield's Reynard the Fox," *Can Bookman*, 2 (1920), 14–15; "The New Conrad—and the Old," *Can Bookman*, 2 (1920), 26–9; "A Peep at the Art Galleries," *Can For*, 1 (1920), 19–21; "Some Canadian Painters: Lawren Harris," *Can For*, 1 (1920), 275–8; "Thomas Hardy's 'Lyrical Poems,' " *Can Bookman*, 2 (1920), 18–22; "Charles M. Doughty: Traveller and Poet," *Can Bookman*, 3 (1921), 17–19; "The Native Tradition in Contemporary English Literature," *QQ*, 29 (1921), 46–59; "F. H. Varley," *Can For*, 2 (1921), 594–6; "A Real Critic," *Can For*, 3 (1922), 50–2; "Joseph Conrad, 1857–1924," *Can For*, 5 (1924), 19–20; "The Modern Consciousness in English Literature," in *Essays and Studies*, 9 (Oxford, 1924), 126–44; "Cotman's Watercolours," *Can For*, 4 (1924), 113–15; "The Group of Seven," *Can For*, 5 (1925), 144–7; "Shaw and Saint Joan," *J Religious Thought*, 2 (1925), 197–210; "Four Poets," *Can For*, 5 (1926), 370; "Two of Our Conquerors," *Can*

For, 9 (1929), 130–1; "Nietzsche," *QQ,* 37 (1930), 259–75; "Open Letter to Professor Irving Babbitt," *Can For,* 11 (1931), 136–8; "Goethe and Mr. Babbitt," *Can For,* 11 (1931), 276–7; "Goethe the Poet," *DR,* 13 (1932), 143–58; "Goethe and Wordsworth, a Point of Contrast," *Pub Goethe Soc,* 10 (1934), 23–42; "Heine's Vaudeville," *UTQ,* 3 (1934), 185–207; "Nietzsche and Goethe," *Bull John Rylands Lib,* 18 (1934), 3–19; "Charles Doughty and Modern Poetry," *London Mercury,* 32 (1935), 128–37; "Nietzsche and the Poetic Impulse," *Bull John Rylands Lib,* 19 (1935), 1–18; "Goethe's Attitude to Science," *Bull John Rylands Lib,* 20 (1936), 3–17; "Canadian Art: Man versus Landscape," *Can For,* 19 (1939), 284, 286; "Rainer Maria Rilke: An Estimate," *UTQ,* 11 (1941), 1–14; "John Steinbeck and the Coming Literature," *SR,* 50 (1942), 145–61; "Charles Doughty (1843–1926)," *UTQ,* 13 (1943), 14–24; "Art: Canadians for the Use of (Qu'est-ce que l'art?)," *Can Aff,* 1 (Dec. 1, 1944); "The Chameleon Image: A Note on Goethe's animula vagula," *MDU,* 37 (1945), 25–30; "What is Wrong with Canadian Art?" *Can Art,* 6 (1948), 24–9 (also *Gallery Notes,* Buffalo Fine Arts Academy, Albright Art Gallery (spring, 1948), 27–31); "Goethe and the World of Today," in W. Rose, ed., *Essays on Goethe* (London, 1949); "Goethe: The Man and the Myth," *GL&L,* NS, 2 (1949), 265–76 (also in *Partisan R,* 16 (1949), 1063–76); "Inspiration and Letter Writing: A Note on Goethe's Beginnings as a Poet," *Ger R,* 24 (1949), 161–7; "J. E. H. MacDonald," in (catalogue) *A Loan Exhibition of the Work of J. E. H. MacDonald,* October 30–November 13, Mellors Galleries, Yonge St., pp. 3–6; "The 'Universal Goethe,'" *Listener,* 153 (1950), 385–8 (also *Can MLR* (spring, 1950), 3–7); "Helena in Goethe's Faust," in M. E. White, ed., *Studies in Honour of Gilbert Norwood* (Toronto, 1952), 255–60; "Literature and Society," *Zeitschrift für Anglistik und Amerikanistik,* 3 (1955), 261–73; "The Modernity of Wilhelm Raabe," *German Studies presented to Leonard Ashley Willoughby by pupils, colleagues, and friends on his retirement* (Oxford, 1952), 66–81 (also "Das Moderne an Wilhelm Raabes Erzähltechnik," *Mitteilungen der Raabe Gesellschaft,* 42 (1955), 74–89); "Heine, Goethe, and the Divan," *GL&L,* 9 (1956), 166–70; "'The Dawn in Britain' after Fifty Years," *UTQ,* 26 (1957), 149–64; "Faust," *Enc Br* (1958); "F. H. Varley," in R. L. McDougall, ed., *Our Living Tradition* (Toronto, 1959), 151–69; "A Misinterpretation of Raabe's *Hastenbeck,*" *MLR* (Oct. 1, 1962), 575–8; "Two Coincidences," *Jahrbuch der Raabe Gesellschaft* (1962), 74–7. (D) Heine, Selected Poems (should be completed in 1963).

MILNES, HUMPHREY: (B) "Kitchener German: a Pennsylvania German Dialect, Part 1, Phonology," *MLQ,* 14 (1953), 184–98, and (with Henry Kratz) "Part 2, Morphology," *MLQ,* 14, 274–83; "German Folklore in Ontario," *J Amer Folklore,* 67 (1954), 35–43; "Gesprochenes Deutsch in Kanada," *Mitteilungen des Instituts für Auslandsbeziehungen,* 7 (1957), 184–6; "Aba Bayefsky's Trip to India," *Can Art,* 16 (1959), 200, 201, 209; "The Play of Opposites in 'Iwein,'" *GL&L,* 16 (1961), 241–56; "The Concept of Man in Bertolt Brecht," *UTQ,* 32 (1963), 217–28. (D) "Aba Bayefsky's Mural" (accepted by *Can Art*); "Ulrich von Lichtenstein and the Minnesang" (accepted by *GL&L*); a study of the Minnesang (in process of being written).

SINDEN, MARGARET: (A) *Gerhart Hauptmann: The Prose Plays* (Toronto, 1957), viii + 238 pp. (D) A second volume on Hauptmann, on the verse plays (about one-quarter done).

UNIVERSITY OF TORONTO—VICTORIA COLLEGE

FIELD, GEORGE WALLIS: (B) "Schiller's Theory of the Idyl and *Wilhelm Tell*," *MDU*, 42 (1950), 13–21; "The Past Speaks for Germany," *UTQ*, 20 (1951), 357–68; "Music and Morality in Thomas Mann and Hermann Hesse," *UTQ*, 24 (1955), 175–90; "Hermann Hesse: A Neglected Nobel Prize Novelist," *QQ*, 65 (1958), 514–20; "Schiller's *Maria Stuart*," *UTQ*, 29 (1960), 325–40; "Hermann Hesse as Critic of English and American Literature," *MDU*, 53 (1961), 147–58. (C) *GL&L, MDU, QQ, UTQ.* (D) Translating Hermann Hesse into English.

MOWATT, D. G.: (A) (trans., with introduction and notes) *The Nibelungenlied*, Everyman's Library, 312 (London, 1962), 225 pp. (B) "In the Beginning was The First Version," *GL&L*, 12 (1959), 211–21; "Studies towards an Interpretation of the *Nibelungenlied*," *GL&L*, 14 (1961), 257–70. (D) (in collaboration with Hugh Sacker) a commentary to the *Nibelungenlied* (nearly finished).

UNIVERSITY OF TORONTO—ST. MICHAEL'S COLLEGE

MUELLER-CARSON, VICTORIA: (D) Work at Hermann Stehr Archiv in Wangen, Allgäu, West Germany: a complete bibliography, with comment and description (now in typed MS., needs final check with Archiv Directors before publication).

VICTORIA UNIVERSITY

MACLEAN, JAMES BEATTIE: (B) "Hartmann von Aue's Religious Attitude and Didacticism in his *Gregorius*," Rice Institute Pamphlet, 39 (1952), 1–17. (C) *MLQ, QQ.* (D) College text condensation of H. G. Konsalik's novel, *Strafbataillon 999* (to be ready in 1963).

UNIVERSITY OF WATERLOO

DYCK, J. W.: (A) *Mozart* (Boston, 1963), 96 pp. (B) "Mennonites in Josef Ponten's Novels," *Mennonite Life*, 12 (1957), 135–7; "Joseph Ponten's Visit to America," *Amer Ger R*, 24 (1958), 23–5; "Josef Pontens Stil und Sprache," *Muttersprache*, 71 (1961), 182–4; "The Fate of the Russo-Germans," *Can-Ger Folklore*, 1 (1961), 32–47; "Thomas Mann and Joseph Ponten," *Ger Q*, 35 (1962) 24–33; "Zum Motiv der Umwertung von Kulturgütern: Ponten," *Heimatbuch* (Landsmannschaft der Deutschen aus Russland) (Stuttgart, 1962), 110–18; "Doctor Zhivago: A Quest for Self-Realization," *SEEJ*, 6 (1962), 117–24. (C) *BA.* (D) Series of graded German readers.

HEIER, EDMUND: (B) "The Immigration of the Russo-German Catholics and Lutherans into Canada," *CSP*, 5 (1960), 160–75; "Russo-German Place Names in Russia and in North America," *Names*, 11 (1961), 260–8; "Wieland's Most Loyal Imitator, L. H. Nicolay," *MDU*, 54 (1962), 1–8; "A Note on the Pashkovites and L. N. Tolstoy," *CSP*, 5 (1962), 114–21; "William Robertson and L. H. Nicolay, His German Translator at the

Court of Catherine II," *Scottish Hist R*, 41 (1962), 135–40; "The Encyclo-
pedists and L. H. Nicolay (1737–1820)," *Rev de Litt Comp*, 36 (1962),
495–509.   (C) *CSP*.   (D) "L. H. Nicolay and His Contemporaries" (research completed); William Robertson's (Scottish historian) reception in
Russia (initial stages); A Russian reference and review grammar (first draft
completed).

UNIVERSITY OF WESTERN ONTARIO

ANDERSON, ALEX R.: (D) Article on the novels of Friedrich Spielhagen
(rough draft completed).

KALBFLEISCH, H. K.: (A) *German Grammar for Science Students*
(Toronto, 1957), viii + 124 pp.   (B) "German or Canadian?" *Fortieth
Annual Rep of the Waterloo Hist Soc* (1953), 18–29; "Pennsylvania German
in Ontario German Newspapers 1835–1918," *Amer Ger R*, 23 (1956), 31–3;
"German Literature as Represented in Two German Language News-
papers of Ontario, Canada," *Kentucky FLQ*, 3 (1956), 184–91; "John A.
Rittinger," *Amer Ger R*, 23 (1957), 18–20; "Ein Echo des Kulturkampfes in
Ontario 1872–1873," *Zeitschrift für Kulturaustausch*, 13 (1963), 10–14.
(D) A history of the German newspapers of Ontario, 1835–1918 (further
revision needed).

TRACY, G. L.: (A) (ed., with Frederick Kriegel) *Deutsche Gedichte*
(New York, 1963), xii + 100 pp.   (C) *MDU*.   (D) Bertolt Brecht's
lyric poetry (early stages).

Slavic Studies

UNIVERSITY OF ALBERTA

KATZ, M.: (D) Paper on Mikhail N. Katkov, Russian publicist (1818–
1887), for presentation to Ass of Can Slavists in summer of 1964 (in
preparation).

UNIVERSITY OF BRITISH COLUMBIA

CZAYKOWSKI, BOGDAN: (A) (with B. Sulik) *Polacy w W. Brytanii* (Paris,
1961), 586 pp.   (B) "Polski Osrodek Naukowy" (History of Polish Research Centre), *Nauka Polska* (London, 1962).   (C) *Kultura, Kontynenty*.
(D) The Poetics of Tadeusz Peiper (part of M.A. thesis, for *SEER*);
"Polish Poetry between the Two World Wars" (a long essay, about one-fifth
written); Karol Irzykowski as critic (collecting material).

PECH, STANLEY Z.: (B) "Pravda Reports," *QQ*, 59 (1951), 189–99; "Dr.
Benes and the Communists," *QQ*, 59 (1952), 1–14; A translation from
German of "Recent Hungarian Renaissance Scholarship," by Andrew
Angyal, *MH*, 8 (1954), 71–94; "F. L. Rieger: The Road from Liberalism
to Conservatism," *JCEA*, 17 (1957), 3–23; "Frantisek Ladislav Rieger:
Some Critical Observations," *CSP*, 2 (1957), 57–69; "Passive Resistance of
the Czechs, 1863–1879," *SEER*, 36 (1958), 434–52; "A Marxist Interpre-
tation of the Hussite Movement," *CSP*, 4 (1960), 199–212; "Manners and
Morals behind the Iron Curtain," *DR*, 42 (1962).

SCHWENCKE, C. G.: (A) (trans.) Dostoevsky's *De Krokodil*; *N. S. Ljeskov Over Zijn Romans en Varhelen* (Amsterdam, 1957). (B) article on Ljeskov, Philological Congress (Utrecht, 1962). (D) Thesis on Leskov.

ST. CLAIR-SOBELL, J. O.: (A) (ed., abridged, trans. by Joel Carmichael) N. M. Sukhanov's *The Russian Revolution, 1917, A Personal Record* (London and New York, 1955), 691 pp. (B) "The Historical Approach to Slavonic Languages," *Sl R*, 26 (1947), 187–96; "Russian Language Problems," *Proc Western Conference of Aatseel* (1948); "Post-war Czechoslovakia," *Int J*, 3 (1948), 356–61; "Problemy Russkogo Yazyka," *Russian Pedagogical J*, 13 (1949), 1–15; "The Animate and Inanimate Accusative in the Indo-European Languages," *Proc Pacific Northwest Conf Foreign Lang Teachers*, 2 (1951), 44–7; "An Early Approach to Linguistics," *Proc Pacific Northwest Conf Foreign Lang Teachers*, 4 (1953), 15–21; (with G. L. Hall) "Animate Gender in Slavonic and Romance Languages," *Lingua* (1954); "Slavonic Studies in Canadian Universities," *External Aff*, 6 (1954), 363–6; "Phonology and Language Teaching," *JCLA*, 1 (1955); "Phoneme Distribution and Functional Yield," *JCLA*, 1 (1955); "Notes on Spelling Pronunciation with Special Reference to Modern Standard Russian," *CSP*, 1 (1956), 66–75; "The Linguistic Calque, Some Observations on Its Character and Use," *Proc Pacific Northwest Conf Foreign Lang Teachers*, 8 (1957), 27–34; (trans.) B. V. Gnedenko's "Mathematical Education in the U.S.S.R.," *Amer Math Monthly*, 64 (1957), 389–408; "Some Remarks on the Pronunciation of Russian Surnames in the English-speaking World," *Three Papers in Slavonic Studies*, presented at the Fourth International Congress of Slavists (1958), 21–34; "Pronunciation of Russian" (University of British Columbia, 1959); (with I. M. Carlson) "The Structure of Russian Surnames," *CSP*, 4 (1960), 42–61; "Notes on Russian Grammar," 1, 2 (University of British Columbia, 1960–61); "Slavyanovedenie v. Kanada," *Mezhdunarodnij Sjezd Slavistov*, 4 (1960), 52–3; "Nakotorije zamechanija o proiznoshenii russkiz familij v anglijskom yazike," *IV Mezhdunarodnij Sjezd Slavistov*, 2 (1962), 320–1. (C) *CSP, SEER*. (D) Study of contemporary Russian orthography.

WAINMAN, ALEXANDER W.: (B) Collaborated in U.B.C. Research Committee's Report on Doukhobors, 1950–52; "Yugoslavia and the Balkan Pact," *Int J* (spring, 1955); "Some Peculiarities of the Dialects of Serbo-Croat" (University of British Columbia, 1958); "Nekotorije Osobennosti Serbsko-Xorvatskix Dialektov," *IV Mezhdunarodnij Sjezd Slavistov*, 2 (1962), 395–6.

MCGILL UNIVERSITY

LITWINOWICZ, V. N.: (D) Some aspects of Russian selenographic onomastics (to be published shortly); Russian literary pseudonyms (60 per cent prepared); research in Russian terminology (historical, morphological, and etymological aspects).

MCMASTER UNIVERSITY

SHEIN, LOUIS J.: (B) "An Analysis of Kierkegaard's view of Sin and Despair," *Crisis Christology*, 2 (1944); "Religious Freedom in Russia,"

Presbyt Record, 74 (1949); "Christianity and Communism," *Victory*, 22 (1961); "Soviet Education," *Teacher*, 29 (1961); "Soviet Youth Today," *Victory* (1962); "The Philosophy of N. O. Lossky," *Enc Philos*; "Adult Education in the Soviet Union on University Level," *Int Congress for Adult Educ J* (1963). (C) *Personalist, PhR, Presbyt Record, Religion and Life, Russian Rev, Scottish J Theol, Teacher, Victory*. (D) Nineteenth-century Russian Philosophy (book; most of the material assembled, in process of translating it into English); "S. N. Trubetskoy's Epistemology" (article; to be published in a book of essays on the theme "The Silver Age in Russia"); "N. O. Lossky's Theory of Knowledge" (article; to be submitted to *Dialogue*); "A. S. Khomyakov's Concept of Unity in his Ecclesiology" (article); "The Nature of Man in Soviet Literature" (article).

UNIVERSITY OF MANITOBA

RUDNYCKYJ, J. B.: (For a full bibliography see M. I. Mandryka, *Bio-Bibliography of J.B.R.*, Ukrainian Free Academy of Sciences, Winnipeg, 1961, 72 pp., which lists 751 items—only a few of the most important can be given here.) (A) *Ukrajinska mova ta jiji hovory* (L'viv, 1937), 78 pp.; (with B. Romanencuk) *Novyj ukrajinskyj pravopys iz slovnyckom dlja scodennoho vzytku* (L'viv, 1938), 160 pp.; *Narys hramatyky staro-cerkovno-slovjanskoji movy* (Munich, 1947), 172 pp.; (with G. Luckyj) *A Modern Ukrainian Grammar* (Minneapolis, Minn., 1949), 186 pp. (2nd ed., 1950, 3rd ed., Winnipeg, 1958); *An Etymological Dictionary of the Ukrainian Language*, 1 (Winnipeg, 1962). (B) "Ukrajinskyj naholos jak funkcijna problema," *Naukovyj Zbirnyk UVU* (Praha), 3 (1942), 316–30; "Slovo j nazva Ukrajina," *Onomastica UVAN* (Winnipeg), 1 (1951), 132 pp.; annual bibliographies, 1953+ with D. Sokulsky in *Ukrainica Canadiana* (Winnipeg) and 1957+ with A. Salys and Z. Folejewski in *PMLA* (East European languages and literatures); articles on language and linguistics in V. Kubijovyc, ed., *Ukraine: A Concise Encyclopaedia* (Toronto, 1963).

UNIVERSITY OF SASKATCHEWAN

ANDRUSYSHEN, C. H.: (A) (with J. N. Krett) *Ukrainian-English Dictionary* (Toronto, 1955), xxx + 1163 pp.; (annotated, with dictionary) *Readings in Ukrainian Authors* (Winnipeg, 1949), iv + 240 pp.; (selected and trans., with Watson Kirkconnell) *The Ukrainian Poets, 1189–1962* (Toronto, 1963), xxx + 500 pp.; (trans., with Watson Kirkconnell) *The Poetical Works of Taras Shevchenko* (Toronto, 1964). (B) "Skovoroda, the Seeker of the Genuine Man," *Ukrainian Q*, 2 (1946), 317–30; "The Dumy: Lyrical Chronicle of Ukraine," *Ukrainian Q*, 3 (1947), 134–44; "The Ukrainian Theater as the Political Factor," *Ukrainian Q*, 3 (1947), 249–64; "Ukrainian Literature—A Mirror of the Common Man," *Ukrainian Q*, 4 (1948), 44–54.

BUYNIAK, VICTOR O.: (B) "Stendhal as Young Tolstoy's Literary Model," *SEES*, 5 (1960), 16–28. (C) *JCLA, Slavica Canadiana, SEES, Sl R*. (D) "Tolstoy and Dickens" (an article, about 60 per cent done); Ukrainian reader for university use (to be supplied with vocabulary and notes).

UNIVERSITY OF TORONTO

BEDFORD, C. H.: (B) "The Fulfilment of Ivan Bunin," *CSP*, 1 (1956), 31–44; "D. S. Merezhkovsky: The Forgotten Poet," *SEER*, 36 (1957), 159–80; "Dmitry Merezhkovsky, the Intelligentsia, and the Revolution of 1905," *CSP*, 3 (1959), 27–42. (C) *CSP*, *SEER*. (D) Monograph on Dmitry Sergeevich Merezhkovsky (about one-third written).

BOWMAN, HERBERT E.: (A) *Vissarion Belinski (1811–1848): A Study in the Origins of Social Criticism in Russia*, Harvard Studies in Comparative Literature, 21 (Cambridge, 1954), viii + 220 pp. (B) "The Nose," *SEER*, 31 (1952), 214–21; "Intelligentsia in Nineteenth-Century Russia," *SEEJ*, 15 (1957), 5–21; "Literary and Historical Scholarship," in Cyril E. Black, ed., *The Transformation of Russian Society: Aspects of Social Change Since 1861*, Part 4, "Education, Scholarship, and Religion" (Cambridge, Mass., 1960), 371–85; "Postscript on Pasternak," *Survey*, 36 (1961), 106–10.

HUNTLEY, D. G.: (D) A manual for the study of Old Church Slavonic—grammar, texts, and glossary (in initial stages); verbs of motion in Old Church Slavonic (M.A. thesis in preparation: a summarized version to be read at Fifth Int. Congress of Slavists, Sept., 1963, later to be published as article or monograph).

LUCKYJ, GEORGE S. N.: (A) *Literary Politics in the Soviet Ukraine: 1917–34* (New York, 1956), 323 pp.; (ed.) Mykola Khvylovy's *Stories from the Ukraine* (New York, 1960); (ed.) Taras Shevchenko's *Poems* (Munich, 1961); (ed.) "Literature," in V. Kubijovyc, ed., *Ukraine: A Concise Encyclopaedia* (Toronto, 1963). (B) *CSP* (1956–61); "The Battle for Literature in the Soviet Ukraine," *HSS*, 3 (1957); "Multi-national Literature and Its Problems," *Survey*, 36 (1961), 56–64; "Shevchenko Studies One Century after the Poet's Death," *Slavic R* (Dec., 1962); "The Latest Debate in the Ukraine: Poetry," *Problems of Communism* (Nov.-Dec., 1962). (C) *BA*, *CSP*, *Slavic R*.

STRAKHOVSKY, LEONID I.: (A) *The Origins of American Intervention in North Russia, 1918* (Princeton, 1937), x + 140 pp.; *Intervention at Archangel: The Story of Allied Intervention and Russian Counter-Revolution in North Russia* (Princeton, 1944), viii + 336 pp.; *Alexander I of Russia, The Man Who Defeated Napoleon* (New York, 1947), 302 pp.; *Craftsmen of the Word: Three Poets of Modern Russia: Gumilyov, Akhmatova, Mandelstam* (Cambridge, Mass., 1949), 114 pp.; (ed.) *A Handbook of Slavic Studies* (Cambridge, Mass., 1949), xxii + 753 pp.; *American Opinion about Russia, 1917–1920* (Toronto, 1961), 135 pp. (B) "Three Sojourners in the Acmeist Camp," *Russian R*, 9 (1950), 131–45; "Peter Stolypin: Progressive Statesman," *UTQ*, 20 (1951), 239–53; "Boris Zaitsev —the Humanist," *Russian R*, 12 (1953), 95–9; "The Historianism of Gogol," *ASEER*, 12 (1953), 360–70; "Count Paul Ignatiev's Efforts to Save the Monarchy of Nicholas II," *UTQ*, 23 (1953), 64–83; "Was There a Kornilov Rebellion?—A Reappraisal of the Evidence," *SEER*, 33 (1955), 372–95; "Problems in Translating Russian Poetry into English," *SEER*, 35 (1956), 258–67; "Pushkin and the Emperors Alexander I and Nicholas I," *CSP*, 1 (1956), No. 1; "General Count N. P. Ignatiev and the Pan-Slav Movement," *JCEA*, 17 (1957), 223–35; "Count P. N. Ignatiev, Reformer of Russian Education," *SEER*, 36 (1957), 1–26; "The Canadian Artillery Brigade in North Russia, 1918–1919," *CHR*, 39 (1958), 125–46; "The Statesmanship of Peter Stolypin: A Reappraisal," *SEER*, 37 (1959), 348–70; "The Silver Age of Russian Poetry: Symbolism and Acmeism," *CSP*, 4 (1959); "Stolypin and the Second Duma," *CSP*, 6 (1964), 3–17. (C) *CHR, CSP, JCEA, J Mod Hist, Russian R, SEER, Slavic R, UTQ.* (D) A study of Peter A. Stolypin and of the Russian Constitutional Experiment, 1906–1912 (three-quarters completed).

UNIVERSITY OF WESTERN ONTARIO

IGNATIEFF, L.: (B) "American Literature in the Soviet Union," *DR* (spring, 1955), 56–66; "Rights and Obligations in Russia and the West," *CSP*, 2 (1957), 26–37. (C) *CSP*.

YORK UNIVERSITY

HARJAN, GEORGE: (B) "Jan Parandowski: A Contemporary Polish Humanist," *BA*, 34 (1960), 223–6. (C) *BA*. (D) Critical biography of Jan Parandowski.

NEAR EASTERN STUDIES

ROYAL ONTARIO MUSEUM

DALES, GEORGE F.: (B) "A Search for Ancient Seaports," *Expedition*, 4 (winter, 1962); "Harappan Outposts on the Makran Coast," *Antiquity*, 36 (1962), 86–92; (with Donald P. Hansen) "The Temple of Inanna, Queen of Heaven at Nippur," *Archaeology*, 15 (1962), 75–84. (C) *Amer Anthropologist, Antiquity, Archaeology, RA.* (D) "The Role of Natural Forces in the Ancient Indus Valley and Baluchistan" (to appear in the Anthropology Papers of the University of Utah); "Necklaces, Bands, and Belts on Mesopotamian Figurines" (MS. sent to *RA*); working on a long-range programme with the Oriental Institute, Chicago, and the American Schools of Oriental Research for the publication of the small finds from the recent series of excavations at Nippur, Iraq (in the initial information-gathering stage, but should be completed within the next two years).

NEEDLER, WINIFRED: (A) *Palestine Ancient and Modern: A Handbook and Guide to the Palestinian Collection of the Royal Ontario Museum* (Toronto, 1949), xii + 116 pp., 35 plates, 20 figs., 3 maps; *An Egyptian Funerary Bed of the Roman Period*, Roy. Ont. Mus., Art and Archaeology Div., Occasional Papers, No. 6 (Toronto, 1962). (B) "Some Ptolemaic Sculptures in the Yale University Art Gallery," *Berytus*, 9 (1949), 129–42; "A Thirty-Square Draughtboard in the Royal Ontario Museum," *J Egyptian Archaeology*, 39 (1953), 60–75; "A Flint Knife of King Djer," *J Egyptian Archaeology*, 42 (1956), 41–4; "Mourning Women at the Funeral of Maya," *ROMB*, 26 (1957), 10–16. (C) *Amer J Archaeology, Archaeology, J. Egyptian Archaeology,* Periodicals of the ROM. (D) "The Functions of Two-Dimensional Art in the Old Kingdom" (paper read at the Oriental Club of Toronto, intended for publication in *JNES*, or as monograph).

UNIVERSITY OF TORONTO—UNIVERSITY COLLEGE

McCULLOUGH, W. S.: (A) (co-author) *Psalms* in *The Interpreter's Bible*, IV (New York, 1955); (ed.) *The Seed of Wisdom: Essays in Honour of T. J. Meek* (Toronto, 1964). (B) About 180 short articles in *The Interpreter's Dictionary of the Bible* (4 vols., New York, 1962). (C) *JBL, Expository Times.* (D) Aramaic Incantation Texts, preserved in the Royal Ontario Museum (about one-third completed).

MEEK, THEOPHILE J.: (A) *Cuneiform Bilingual Hymns, Prayers, and Penitential Psalms* (Leipzig, 1913), 127 pp., with 62 plates; *Old Babylonian Business and Legal Documents* (doctoral dissertation) (Chicago, 1917), 48 pp., with 26 plates; *The Song of Songs: An American Translation* (Chicago, 1927), 19 pp.; *Old Akkadian, Sumerian, and Cappadocian Texts from Nuzi* (Cambridge, Mass., 1935), 60 pp., with 54 plates; *The Old Testament: An American Translation* (Chicago, 1935), 883 pp.; *Ancient Oriental Seals in the Royal Ontario Museum* (New York), 16 pp., with 6 plates; *Hebrew Origins* (New York and London, 1936), x + 231 pp. (2nd ed., 1950, xiv + 246 pp.; 3rd ed., 1960, xvi + 240 pp.); *The Song of Songs: Introduction and Exegesis,* in Nolan B. Harmon, ed., *The Interpreter's Bible,* V (New York and Nashville), 98–148; *The Book of Lamentations: Introduction and Exegesis,* in *The Interpreter's Bible,* VI (New York), 1–38; JOINT AUTHOR OF THE FOLLOWING: Wilfred H. Schoff, ed., *The Song of Songs: A Symposium* (Philadelphia, 1924), 120 pp.; *The Religion of the Bible* (Chicago, 1925), 130 pp.; *The Old Testament: An American Translation* (Chicago, 1927), 1725 pp.; *In the Beginning God: A Series of Biblical Views of Creation* (Chicago, 1927), 32 pp.; *The Story of Ruth* (Chicago, 1928), 22 pp.; *The Bible: An American Translation* (Chicago, 1931), 2158 pp.; Lewis Gaston Leary, ed., *From the Pyramids to Paul* (New York and London, 1935), 318 pp.; Goodspeed and Smith, eds., *The Short Bible* (Chicago, 1933), 585 pp. (Random House ed., 1940); Elihu Grant, ed., *The Haverford Symposium on Archaeology and the Bible* (New Haven, 1938), 236 pp.; Smith and Goodspeed, eds., *The Complete Bible: An American Translation* (Chicago, 1939), 1356 pp.; James B. Pritchard, ed., *Ancient Near Eastern Texts* (Princeton, 1950), 526 pp. (2nd ed., 1955, 594 pp.); James B. Pritchard, ed., *The Ancient Near East* (Princeton, 1958), 380 pp.; CONTRIBUTOR TO THE FOLLOWING: *The Master Bible* (Chicago, 1926); *Readings in Sociology* (New York, 1930), 689 pp.; *The Jewish Caravan* (London, 1935), 779 pp.; *The Junior Bible* (New York, 1936), 294 pp.; *A Selected and Annotated Bibliography of Books and Periodicals in Western Languages Dealing with the Near and Middle East* (Washington, 1952), *Supplement* (1954); *The New Schaff-Herzog Encyclopedia of Religious Knowledge,* supplementary volumes (1953); *Enc Can* (Ottawa, 1958); *Enc Amer* (New York and Chicago, 1958); F. M. Russell, ed., *This is My Concern: A Symposium* (Cobourg, 1962); *Hastings One-Volume Dictionary of the Bible* (1963). (B) "A Hymn to Ishtar, *AJSL*, 26 (1910), 156–61; "The Sabbath in the Old Testament," *JBL*, 33 (1914), 201–12; "Critical Notes in Assyriology," *AJSL*, 31 (1915), 286–7; "A Votive Inscription of Ashurbanipal," *JAOS*, 38 (1918), 167–75; "Some Bilingual

Religious Texts," *AJSL*, 35 (1919), 134–44; "Explanatory List Rm. 2, 588," *AJSL*, 36 (1920), 154–60; "Some Explanatory Lists and Grammatical Texts," *RA*, 18 (1920), 117–205; "A Proposed Reconstruction of Early Hebrew History," *AJT*, 24 (1920), 209–16; "Some Religious Origins of the Hebrews," *AJSL*, 37 (1921), 101–31; "Canticles and the Tammuz Cult," *AJSL*, 39 (1922), 1–14; "Was Jeremiah a Priest?" *Expositor*, 8th Series, 25 (1923), 215–22; "Babylonica," *JAOS*, 43 (1923), 353–7; "The Poetry of Jeremiah," *Jewish Theol R*, new series, 14 (1924), 281–91; "Babylonian Parallels to the Song of Songs, *JBL*, 43 (1924), 245–52; "Light from the Old Testament on Primitive Religion," *CJRT*, 2 (1925), 32–6; "The Interpenetration of Cultures as Illustrated by the Character of the Old Testament Literature," *JR*, 7 (1927), 244–62; "The Trials of an Old Testament Translator," *CJRT*, 4 (1927), 290–304; "Translating the Old Testament," *Press Impressions*, V (1928), 1–9; "Aaronites and Zadokites," *AJSL*, 45 (1929), 149–66; "The Co-ordinate Adverbial Clause in Hebrew," *JAOS*, 49 (1929), 156–9; "Some Emendations in the Old Testament," *JBL*, 48 (1929), 162–8; "The Structure of Hebrew Poetry," *JR*, 9 (1929), 523–50; "Some Old Testament Problems in the Light of Recent Archaeological Discoveries," *CJRT*, 6 (1929), 374–81; "The Co-ordinate Adverbial Clause in Hebrew," *AJSL*, 47 (1930), 51–2: "The Translation of *Gêr* in the Hexateuch and its Bearing on the Documentary Hypothesis," *JBL*, 49 (1930), 172–80; "Report from the Nuzi Expedition in Iraq," *BASOR*, No. 41 (1931), 25–7; "On the Map Found at Nuzi," *BASOR*, No. 42 (1931), 7–10; "The Akkadian and Cappadocian Texts from Nuzi," *BASOR*, No. 48 (1932), 2–5; "Some Gleanings from the Last Excavations at Nuzi," *Annual Amer Schools Oriental Res*, 13 (1933), 1–12; "A Visit to Satan," *Can Geog J*, 7 (1933), 116–26; "Translation Difficulties in the Old Testament," *Religion in Life*, 3 (1934), 491–506; "The Iterative Names in the Old Akkadian Texts from Nuzi," *RA*, 32 (1935), 51–5; "Ali's Holy Shrines," *Asia*, 35 (1935), 349–51; "The Israelite Conquest of Ephraim," *BASOR*, No. 61 (1936), 17–9; " 'Bowsprit' in the Oxford Dictionary," *Words*, 3 (1936), 8–10; "The Orientation of Babylonian Maps," *Antiquity*, 10 (1936), 223–6; "Notes on the Early Texts from Nuzi," *RA*, 34 (1937), 59–66; "Magic Spades in Mesopotamia," *UTQ*, 7 (1938), 228–48; "Lapses of Old Testament Translators," *JAOS*, 58 (1938), 122–9; "Moses and the Levites," *AJSL*, 56 (1939), 113–20; "Bronze Swords from Luristan," *BASOR*, No. 74 (1939), 7–11; "Hebrew Poetic Structure as a Translation Guide," *JBL*, 59 (1940), 1–9; "Primitive Monotheism and the Religion of Moses," *R of Religion*, 4 (1940), 286–303; "The Hebrew Accusative of Time and Place," *JAOS*, 60 (1940), 224–33; "The Accusative of Time in Amos 1:1," *JAOS*, 61 (1941), 63–4; "The Metrical Structure of II Kings 19:20–28," *Crozer Q*, 18 (1941), 126–31; "Again the Accusative of Time in Amos 1:1," *JAOS*, 61 (1941), 190–1; "The Beginnings of Writing," *UTQ*, 11 (1941), 15–24; "The Next Task in Old Testament Studies," *JR*, 21 (1941), 398–411; "Monotheism and the Religion of Israel," *JBL*, 61 (1942), 21–43; "Four Syrian Cylinder Seals," *BASOR*, No. 90 (1943), 24–7; "The Challenge of Oriental Studies to American Scholarship," presidential address, *JAOS*, 63 (1943), 83–93; "Ancient Oriental Seals in the Redpath Library," *BASOR*,

No. 93 (1944), 2–13 (also reprinted in pamphlet form as McGill University Publications, Series VII, Library, No. 28); "The Syntax of the Sentence in Hebrew," presidental address, *JBL*, 64 (1945), 1–15; "The Asyndeton Clause in the Code of Hammurabi," *JNES*, 5 (1946), 64–72; "Recent Trends in Old Testament Scholarship," *Religious Educ*, 41 (1946), 70–6; "A New Interpretation of Code of Hammurabi 117–119," *JNES*, 7 (1948), 180–3; "Old Testament Notes," *JBL*, 67 (1948), 233–9; "Archaeology and a Point in Hebrew Syntax," *BASOR*, No. 122 (1951), 31–3; "The Explicative Pronoun su/sa in the Code of Hammurabi," in *Symbolae ad studia orientis pertinentes Frederico Hrozny dedicatae*, Pars quinta (1951), 78–81; "Some passages bearing on the date of Second Isaiah," *Hebrew Union College Annual*, 23 (1950–1), 173–84; "The Standard Revised Version of the Old Testament: An Appraisal," *Religion in Life*, 23 (1954), 70–82; "Job 19:25–27," *Vetus Testamentum*, 6 (1956), 100–3; "Result and Purpose Clauses in Hebrew," *Jewish QR*, 46 (1955), 40–3; "I Kings 20:1–10," *JBL*, 78 (1959), 73–5; "Translation Problems in the Old Testament," *Jewish QR*, 50 (1959), 43–54; "Translating the Hebrew Bible," *JBL*, 79 (1960), 328–35; "Old Testament Translation Principles," *JBL*, 81 (1962), 143–54. (C) *AJSL, JAOS, JBL, JNES*. (D) A thorough revision of *the Old Testament: An American Translation* (almost completed); Hebrew Syntax (partly written).

REDFORD, DONALD B.: (B) "Some Observations on 'Amārna Chronology," *J Egyptian Archaeology*, 45 (1959), 34–7. (C) *J Egyptian Archaeology, JNES, Vetus Testamentum*. (D) "The pronunciation of *pr* in late Toponyms," *JNES*, 22 (1963) (in press); "Exodus 1:11" (to be published in 1963 in *Vetus Testamentum*).

WEVERS, JOHN WILLIAM.: (A) (with R. H. Robinson and D. F. Theall) the series *Let's Speak English* (Toronto, 1960)—*Sound Studies* (1960), 127 pp., *Basic Lessons 1* (1960), 224 pp., *Basic Lessons 2* (1961), 214 pp., *Basic Guide* (interim teacher's manual) (1961), 122 pp., translation books in Danish, Dutch, Swedish, German, Italian, French, Spanish, Portugese, Japanese, Greek, Hungarian, Finnish, Serbo-Croatian, Ukrainian, and Polish (app. 50 pp. each, 1960–62); *The Way of the Righteous: Psalms and the Books of Wisdom* (Philadelphia, 1961), 96 pp. (B) "A Study in the Hebrew Variants in the Books of Kings," *Zeitschrift für die alttestamentliche Wissenschaft*, 61, 43–76; "Exegetical Principles Underlying the Septuagint Text of I Kings ii 22 – xxi 43," *Oudtestamentische Studien*, 8 (Leiden, Brill, 1950), 300–22; "Evidence of the Text of the John H. Scheide Papyri for the Translation of the Status Constructus in Ezekiel," *JBL*, 70 (1951), 211–16; "Principles of Interpretation Guiding the Fourth Translator of the Book of Kingdoms," *Cath Bibl Q*, 14 (1952), 40–56; "A Study in the Exegetical Principles Underlying the Greek Text of 2 Sm 11:2– 1 Kings 2:11," *Cath Bibl Q*, 15 (1953), 30–45; "Septuaginta-Forschungen, *Theologische Rundschau*, N.F., 22 (1954), 85–138, 171–90; "A Study in the Form Criticism of Individual Complaint Psalms," *Vetus Testamentum*, 6 (1956), 80–96; "Semitic Bound Studies," *Can J Linguistics*, 7 (1961), 9–14; "Proto-Septuagint Studies," in W. S. McCullough, ed., *The Seed of Wisdom* (Toronto, 1964). (C) *Bibliotheca Orientalis, Can J. Linguistics* (editor in chief), *CJT, JBL, Vetus Testamentum, Zeitschrift für die alt-testamentliche Wissenschaft*.   (D) (with R. H. Robinson and D. F. Theall) A Short English Grammar, for the *Let's Speak English* series (almost ready for press); A Theology of Israel's Faith (to be about 600 pp., first draft about two-thirds finshed).

WILLIAMS, RONALD J.: (B) "On Certain Verbal Forms in Demotic," *JNES*, 7 (1948), 223–35; "Theodicy in the Ancient Near East," *CJT*, 2 (1956), 14–26; "The Literary History of a Mesopotamian Fable," *Phoenix*, 10 (1956), 70–7; "The Fable in the Ancient Near East," in E. C. Hobbes, ed., *A Stubborn Faith* (Dallas, 1956), 3–26; "Ancient Egyptian Folk Tales," *UTQ*, 27 (1958), 256–72; "Archaeology and Biblical Studies," in R. C. Chalmers and J. A. Irving, eds., *Challenge and Response: Modern Ideas and Religion* (Toronto, 1959), 1–22; "The Alleged Semitic Original of the *Wisdom of Amenomope*," *J Egyptian Archaeology*, 47 (1961), 100–6; "Reflections on the Lebensmüde," *J Egyptian Archaeology*, 48 (1962); "Inscriptions" and "Writing and Writing Materials," in *The Interpreter's Dictionary of the Bible* (New York, 1962), vol. 3, 706–12, vol. 4, 909–21; "Literature as a Medium of Political Propaganda in Ancient Egypt," in W. S. McCullough, ed., *The Seed of Wisdom* (Toronto, 1964).   (C) *CJT, J Cuneiform St, J Egyptian Archaeology, JNES, Phoenix, UTQ*.   (D) A volume of Coptic papyri and ostraca from Giessen University (almost completed); contributions to Vol. 2 of *Aesopica* by B. E. Perry (Vol. 1 published Urbana, 1952) (translation of Arabic material completed, a couple of chapters still to be written); A Syntax of Classical Hebrew (in its preliminary stages at present); a corpus of Egyptian Wisdom Texts (critical texts ready; translations largely completed; introduction and notes still to be prepared).

WINNETT, F. V.: (A) *A Study of the Lihyanite and Thamudic Inscriptions*, University of Toronto Studies, Oriental Series, No. 3 (Toronto, 1937), 55 pp.; *The Mosaic Tradition*, University of Toronto Press, Near and Middle East Series, No. 1 (Toronto, 1949), xii + 219 pp.; *Safaitic Inscriptions from Jordan*, University of Toronto Press, Near and Middle East Series, No. 2 (Toronto, 1957), x + 220 pp.   (B) The Place of the Minaeans in the History of Pre-Islamic Arabia," *BASOR*, No. 73, 3–9; "Excavations at Dibon in Moab, 1950–51," *BASOR*, 125 (1952), 7–20. (D) The MS. of a new collection of Safaitic inscriptions (about 4,000 in number) from Jordan (completed, but needing revision).

UNIVERSITY OF TORONTO—VICTORIA COLLEGE

CLARKE, ERNEST GEORGE: (A) *The Selected Questions of Ishō bar Nūn on the Pentateuch* (Leiden, 1962), 28 pp.   (D) A critical edition of the Syriac text of the Book of Ruth from the Peshitta for the International Peshitta Project (to be ready December, 1963).

REVELL, E. J.: (B) "The Order of the Elements in the Verbal Statement Clause in 1 Q Sereq," *Rev de Qumran*, 3 (1962), 559–69.   (D) Edition, translation, and analysis of some unpublished "Palestinian" liturgical MSS. from the Taylor-Schechter Collection of the Cambridge University Library in collaboration with Dr. Dietrich of the University of Münster (preparation has only begun).

UNIVERSITY OF TORONTO—TRINITY COLLEGE

NEWBY, MATTHEW T.: (D) Critical edition of the Syriac (Peshitta) version of the Book of Esdras using all the known manuscripts (part of the critical edition of the Old Testament being prepared under the direction of the Peshitta Institute, Leiden (should be completed in about a year's time).

UNIVERSITY OF WESTERN ONTARIO—HURON COLLEGE

JACKSON, JARED J.: (B) "The Deep," G. A. Buttrick, et al., eds., The Interpreter's Dictionary of the Bible, I (New York, 1962), 813–14.

ISLAMIC STUDIES

UNIVERSITY OF TORONTO

AHMAD AZIZ: (A) Nasl aur Saltanat (Delhi, 1941), 189 pp.; Tarraqī Pasand Adab (Hyderabad, 1945); Iqbāl (Karachi, 1950). (B) "Sayyid Ahmad Khān, Jamāl al-dīn al-Afghānī and Muslim India," Studia Islamica, 13 (1960), 55–78; "El Islam Español y la India musulmana moderna," Foro Internacional, 1 (1960), 560–70; "Iqbāl et la théorie du Pakistan," Orient, 17 (1960), 81–92; "Mongol Pressure in an Alien Land," Central Asiatic J, 6 (1961), 182–93; "Moghulindien und Dār al-Islām," Saeculum, 12 (1962), 266–90; "Akbar, hérétique ou apostat?" J Asiatique (1961), 21–38; "Religious and Political Ideas of Shaikh Ahmad Sirhindī," Rivista degli Studi Orientali, 36 (1961), 259–70; "Political and Religious Ideas of Shāh Walī-Ullāh of Delhi," Muslim World, 52 (1962), 22–30. (C) Bull School Or and Afr St, Orient, Studia Islamica. (D) Islamic Modernism (collecting material); Studies in Islamic Culture in the Indian Environment (in press).

KENNY, LORNE M.: (D) "The Khedive Ismā'īl's Dream of Civilization" (article; at revision stage).

MARMURA, MICHAEL E.: (B) "The Logical Role of the Argument from Time in the Tahāfut's Second Proof for the World's Pre-eternity," Muslim World, 49 (1959), 296–314; "Avicenna and the Problem of the Infinite Number of Souls," MS, 22 (1960), 232–9; "Avicenna's Psychological Proof of Prophecy," JNES, 22 (1963), 49–56; (trans.) Avicenna's Healing: Metaphysics X, in Ralph Lerner and Muhsin Mahdi, eds., Medieval Political Philosophy (New York, 1963), pp. 99–100; "Avicenna's Theory of Prophecy in the Light of Ash'arite Theology," in W. S. McCullough, ed., The Seed of Wisdom (Toronto, 1964). (C) Amer J Or St, JNES, MS, Muslim World. (D) "Some Aspects of Avicenna's Theory of God's Knowledge of Particulars" (article; to appear in Amer J Or St); (with John Rist) "Al-Kindi on the Existence and Oneness of God" (article; submitted for publication); translation Avicenna's treatise On the Proof of Prophecies (in the press); "Al-Ghazali on Scientific Demonstration" (to be finished in June, 1963); an edition of Avicenna's Fī Ithbāt al-Nubuwwāt (begun).

SAVORY, ROGER M.: (B) "Persia since the Constitution," in D. Grant, ed., The Islamic Near East (Toronto, 1960), 243–61; "The Principal Offices of the Safawid State during the reign of Isma'īl I (907–30/1501–24)," Bull School Or and Afr St, 23 (1960), 91–105; "The Principal Offices of the

Safawid State during the reign of Tahmāsp I (930–84/1524–76)," *Bull School Or and Afr St*, 24 (1961), 65–85. (C) *Bull School Or and Afr St*, *Der Islam*, *Enc of Islam*, *Grolier Enc.* (D) Two articles accepted by *Der Islam* for publication early in 1963; article submitted for publication in the *Bull School Or and Afr St*; translation of the *Futuwwat-nāma* of Husain Vā'iz Kāshifī (two-thirds completed).

WICKENS, G. M.: (A) (ed.) *Avicenna Scientist and Philosopher* (London, 1952), 128 pp.; *First Readings in Classical Arabic* (Toronto, 1961), 36 pp.; *Booklist on Asia for Canadians* (Toronto, 1961). (B) "Religion," in *Legacy of Persia* (Oxford, 1953), 148–73; "Nāsir-i Khusrau's Sa'ādapnāmeh," *Islamic Q*, 2 (1955), 117–32, 206–21; "Al-Jarsifī on the Hisba," *Islamic Q*, 3 (1956), 176–87; "The Chronology of Nāsir-i Khusrau's *Safarnāma*," *Islamic Q*, 4 (1957), 66–77; "Sa'dīs Pandnāmeh," *Annals Or Res* (1957), 1–26; "Bozorg Alavi's 'Portmanteau,' " *UTQ*, 28 (1959), 116–33; "Poetry in Modern Persia," *UTQ*, 29 (1960), 262–81; "Nasīr ad-Dīn Tūsī on the Fall of Baghdad," *J Semitic St*, 7 (1962), 23–35; "Mamluk Egypt at the Eleventh Hour: Some Eyewitness Observations," in W. S. McCullough, ed., *The Seed of Wisdom* (Toronto, 1964). (C) *Bull School Or and Afr St*, *Enc of Islam*, *Islamic Q*, *JAOS*, *J Semitic St.* (D) The Nasirean Ethics (in press); Concise Oxford Dictionary of Modern Arabic (nearly ready for press); A Modern Social History of Persia (material still being collected).

ASIAN STUDIES

UNIVERSITY OF BRITISH COLUMBIA

CHU, TUNG-TSU: (A) *Law and Society in Traditional China* (Paris and The Hague, 1961), 308 pp.; *Local Government in China under the Ching* (Cambridge, Mass., 1962), 360 pp.

HOWES, JOHN F.: (A) (trans.) Hideo Kishimoto's *Japanese Religion in the Meiji Era* (Tokyo, 1956); (with Otis Cary) *Japan's Modern Prophet*, (Amherst, 1962). (B) "The Non-church Christian Movement in Japan," *TASJ* (1956), 119–37; "The Chijinron of Uchimura Kanzô," *Trans Int Conference of Orientalists in Japan*, 5, 116–26. (C) *Pacific Aff.* (D) A study of the life and works of the Japanese religious leader, Uchimura Kanzô.

ROYAL ONTARIO MUSEUM

SHIH, HSIO-YEN: (B) "I-nan and Related Tombs," *Artibus Asiae*, 22 (1959), 277–311; "Han Stone Reliefs from Shensi Province," *Arch Chinese Art Soc of Amer*, 14 (1960), 49–64; "Arts of the Han Dynasty," *Oriental Art*, 8 (1962), 20–8. (C) *Arch Chinese Art Soc of Amer*, *Artibus Asiae*, *JAS*, *Monumenta Serica*, *Oriental Art.* (D) A translation of the *Li-tai ming-hua chi* of Chang Yen-yuan (project in third draft).

TRUBNER, HENRY: (A) *Chinese Ceramics from the Prehistoric Period through Ch'ien-lung* (Los Angeles, 1952), 120 pp.; *The Arts of the T'ang Dynasty* (Los Angeles, 1957); *The Arts of the Han Dynasty* (New York, 1961). (B) "Three Important Buddhist Bronzes of the T'ang Dynasty," *Artibus Asiae*, 20 (1957), 103–10; "The Arts of the T'ang Dynasty," *Ars Orientalis*, 3 (1959), 147–52; "A Bronze Dagger Axe," *Arti-*

bus Asiae, 22 (1959), 170–8; "The Arts of the Han Dynasty," *Arch Chinese Art Soc of Amer*, 14 (1960); "An Unusual Chinese Tomb Figure," *Arch Chinese Art Soc of Amer*, 16 (1962). (C) *Arch Chinese Art Soc of Amer*; *Artibus Asiae, JAOS*. (D) "Aspects of Han Pictorial Representation" (article; to be published in March or April, 1963, in *Trans Or Ceramic Soc*).

UNIVERSITY OF TORONTO

DOBSON, WILLIAM ARTHUR CHARLES HARVEY: (A) *Late Archaic Chinese* (Toronto, 1959), xxviii + 254 pp.; *Early Archaic Chinese* (Toronto, 1962), xxxi + 288 pp.; (trans.) *Mencius* (Toronto, 1963), 240 pp. (B) Studies in the Grammar of Early Archaic Chinese: I, the Particle *Wei*," *T'oung Pao*, 46 (1958), 339–68; "Towards a Historical Grammar of Archaic Chinese: I, Early Archaic *Yüeh* becomes Late Archaic *Chi*," *HJAS*, 21 (1958); "Studies in the Grammar of Early Archaic Chinese: II, the Word *Jo*," *T'oung Pao*, 47 (1959), 281–93. (C) *HJAS, T'oung Pao*. (D) Tso's Commentary on the Spring and Autumn Annals (about half completed).

SHIH, C. C.: (B) "A Study of 'Cheng' and 'Pao' Recorded in The Tso Chuan," *Chinese Culture Mag*, 1 (1958); "Notes on a Phrase in The Tso Chuan: 'The Great Affairs of a State are Sacrifice and War,' " *Chinese Culture Mag*, 2 (1959); "The Origin of the Six-Minister Official System in China," *Continental Mag*, 25 (1962); "A Study of Ancestor Worship in Ancient China," in W. S. McCullough, ed., *The Seed of Wisdom* (Toronto, 1964). (C) *Int J*. (D) A study of ancestor worship in ancient China, based mainly on the evidence of oracle bone and bronze vessel inscriptions (ready for publication).

SMITH, R. MORTON: (B) "Contrasts in Indian and Western Ways of Thought," *Art and Letters* (1952); "The Birth of Thought" (3 parts), *Annals Bhandarkar Or Res Ins* (1953, 1954, 1955); "India in the 6th century B.C.," *Art and Letters* (1954); "Temporal Technique in Story-telling, Illustrated from India," *J Behar Soc* (1954); "Story of Amba in the Mahabharata," *Adyar Bull* (1955); "Contrasting Factors in Indian and Western History," *Art and Letters* (1957); "Power in Ancient India" (2 parts), *Annals Bhandarkar Or Res Inst* (1958); "Why is India Neutral?" *Can For*, 37 (1958), 274–6; "On the Ancient Chronology of India," Part I, *JAOS*, 77 (1957), 116–29, Part II, *JAOS*, 77 (1957), 266–80, Part III, *JAOS*, 78 (1958), 174–92; "Story of Nala in the Mahabharata," *J Or Inst of Baroda* (1960); "Slokas and Vipulas," *Indo-Iranian J* (1961); "Tradition and Modernization in India," *UTQ*, 31 (1962), 378–91; "Techniques of Disintegration," *Culture*, 23 (1962), 368–88. (C) *Archaeology, CJEPS, JAOS, JAS, JRAS, Pacific Aff*. (D) Dates and Dynasties of Ancient India: Part I, The Kings (ready for publication); Part II, The Vedas (undergoing final revision); Part III, The Brahmans (first draft completed).

UEDA, MAKOTO: (A) *The Old Pine Tree and Other Noh Plays* (Lincoln, 1962), xxvi + 63 pp. (B) "Chikamatsu and his Ideas on Drama," *Educ Theatre J*, 12 (1960), 107–12; "The Implications of the Noh Drama," *SR*, 69 (1961), 367–74; "Zeami on Art," *JAAC*, 20 (1961), 73–9; "Japanese Literature since World War II," *Literary Rev*, 6 (1962), 1–22. (D) Major Japanese Aestheticians (book; draft of several chapters completed).

WALMSLEY, L. C.: (A) (trans., with Chang Yin-nan), *Poems by Wang Wei* (Tokyo and Rutland, 1958), 159 pp. (D) Paintings by Wang Wei (material mostly collected; partly written in collaboration with C. C. Shih).

PHILOSOPHY

UNIVERSITY OF ALBERTA

HEINTZ, JOHN: (D) "Existence Statements and Existence Claims" (revised version of paper read at McMaster meetings last summer for *Dialogue*).

ASSUMPTION UNIVERSITY OF WINDSOR

ALLEN, ELLIOTT B.: (B) "Hervaeus Natalis: An Early 'Thomist' on the Notion of Being," *MS*, 22 (1960), 1–14.

DE ALVAREZ, HELEN: (D) Translation of "Principles and Causes," by Etienne Gilson, an article that appeared in the *Rev Thomiste*, 1952 (probably for *Philos Today*).

NELSON, RALPH: (D) Jacques Maritain, the Philosopher and the Man (MS. completed and accepted for publication in fall of 1963).

UNIVERSITY OF BRITISH COLUMBIA

MULLINS, WARREN J.: (D) The Political Philosophy of David Hume (a book to be completed some time in 1963).

REMNANT, PETER: (B) "Moral Facts," *Philosophy*, 32 (1957), 148–57; "God and the Moral Law," *CJT*, 4 (1958), 23–9; "Kant and the Cosmological Argument," *Australasian J Philos*, 37 (1959), 152–5; "Is Everything I See Really Inside My Head?" *UTQ*, 30 (1960), 86–94; "Red and Green All Over Again," *Analysis*, 21 (1961), 93–5; "Marx's Manifesto," *QQ*, 70 (1963), 114–25; "Incongruent Counterparts and Absolute Space," *Mind*, 72 (1963), 393–9. (C) *Analysis, Mind, PhR, Philosophy*. (D) A study of the concept of reason in the philosophy of the seventeenth and eighteenth centuries, with particular emphasis on Descartes, Hume, and Kant (in early stages).

STROLL, AVRUM: (A) *The Emotive Theory of Ethics* (Berkeley and Los Angeles, 1954), ii + 91 pp.; *Philosophy Made Simple* (New York, 1956), 192 pp.; *Introduction to Philosophy* (New York, 1961), iv + 421 pp.; *Reason and Religious Belief* (Vancouver), 42 pp. (B) "Is Everyday Language Inconsistent?" *Mind*, 63 (1954), 219–25; "Believing the Meaningless," *Analysis* (Dec., 1955); "On 'The,'" *JPPR*, 16 (1956), 496–504; "Uses of Analytic Sentences in Ordinary Discourse," *Mind*, 66 (1957), 541–2; "Meaning, Referring, and the Problem of Universals," *Inquiry*, 2 (1961). (C) *Analysis, Inquiry, JAAC, J Aesthetics, JPPR, Mind, PhR*. (D) A book on statements (still in outline stage); three articles forthcoming.

CARLETON UNIVERSITY

TALMAGE, R. S.: (D) An inquiry into the possibility of formalizing certain types of philosophical argument (to be published as one or more articles); a short introductory logic text (should be completed by spring of 1964).

THOMPSON, J. M.: (D) Short introductory text on epistemology (to be completed probably late 1963).

WAND, BERNARD: (B) "A Note on Sympathy in Hume's Moral Theory," *PhR*, 64 (1955), 275–9; "Hume's Account of Obligation," *PhQ*, 6 (1956), 155–68; "Hobbes," in *Encyclopaedia of Morals* (New York, 1956), 224–8; "The Origin of Causal Necessity," *JP*, 56 (1959), 493–500; "Evolution and the Basis of Moral Principles," in *Darwin in Retrospect* (Toronto, 1960), 35–47; "The Content and Function of Conscience," *JP*, 58 (1961), 765–72; "Intelligibility and Free Choice," *Dialogue*, 1 (1962), 239–58. (C) *Dialogue, JP, PhR*. (D) "Grace and Moral Motivation" (research about completed: should be ready for publication September, 1963).

WERNHAM, JAMES C. S.: (D) Two Russian Thinkers: An Essay in Berdyaev and Shestov (a short book, completed for publication); a short introductory text on ethics (expected to be completed late this year).

DALHOUSIE UNIVERSITY

VINGOE, ROBERT H.: (D) F. H. Bradley's Critique of Pragmatism (the first draft is finished: most of the revision will be done in the summer of 1963).

UNIVERSITÉ LAVAL

BLANCHET, L. EMILE: (D) Comment presenter un manuscrit philosophique (le manuscrit est presque terminé); L'infini chez les anciens et chez les mathématiciens modernes (thèse de doctorat, rédaction des premiers chapitres terminée).

GAUDRON, EDMOND: (B) "L'expérience dans la morale aristotélicienne," *LTP*, 3 (1947), 243–61; "L'émancipation de l'homme et son explication scientifique," *Culture*, 8 (1947), 173–83; "La hiérarchie des biens," *Culture*, 14 (1953), 64–71; "Bien commun et justice sociale," *Culture*, 15 (1954), 61–70; "A propos de doctrine et de faits," *Culture*, 15 (1954), 175–82; "Education morale et civique," *Culture*, 17 (1956), 284–91; "Humanisme et science," *Culture*, 18 (1957), 175–82; "French Canadian Philosophers" in Julian Park, ed., *The Culture of Contemporary Canada* (Ithaca, 1957), 274–92; "Mémoire présenté à la Commission Royale d'Enquête sur les Publications," *Culture*, 21 (1960), 419–24; "Sur l'objet du Sophiste," *LTP* (1960), 70–93; "Notre public et son élite intellectuelle," *Culture*, 22 (1961), 99–108; "Le fait canadien-français," *Culture*, 22 (1961), 220–7. (C) *Culture, Dialogue, LTP*. (D) La preuve, dans le Phédon, de l'existence des formes séparées (article à paraître prochainement); Les premières distinctions entre la sensation et l'intelligence, chez les derniers Présocratiques, et l'âme connaissant par elle-même, tel que, dans la suite, Platon le conçoit, et Le signe du réel chez Parménide (ces deux études seront terminées dans un avenir prochain).

GODIN, GUY: (B) "La Notion d'Admiration," *LTP*, 17 (1961), 40 pp.; "L'Admiration, principe de la recherche philosophique," *LTP*, 17 (1961), 30 pp. (C) *Can League, Rev St. Grégoire, RUL*. (D) "Le langage courant et le mot recherche" (un article, à paraître dans *LTP* en 1963).

SIMARD, EMILE: (A) *La Nature et la portée de la méthode scientifique* (Québec et Paris, 1956), 400 pp. (version espagnole, *Naturaleza y alcance del método cientifico* (Madrid, 1961), 400 pp.); *Communisme et science* (Quebec, 1963), 528 pp. (B) "M. Julian Huxley et la pensée communiste," *LTP*, 18 (1962). (C) *LTP*. (D) Recherches sur les rapports de la science expérimentale aux autres disciplines intellectuelles.

MCGILL UNIVERSITY

HENDERSON, T. G.: (B) "Santayana Awaiting Death," *JP*, 50 (1953), 201–6; "Whitehead: Philosophy as Approximation" and "Santayana: A Departed Guest," in R. Klibansky, ed., *Philosophy in the Mid-Century*, 4 (Firenze, 1959). (C) *Can For, JP, UTQ*. (D) The Withness of the Body: A Whiteheadian Exploration (working title) (a book, slightly more than half finished in lecture form).

KLIBANSKY, R.: (A) *Carolus Bovillus, Liber de Sapiente* (Leipzig, 1927), 120 pp.; *Ein Proklus-Fund und seine Bedeutung* (Heidelberg, 1929), 41 pp.; (ed.) *Cusanus-Texte I, Predigten, "Dies Sanctificatus"* (Heidelberg, 1929), 56 pp.; (ed.) *Nicolai de Cusa Opera omnia iussu et auspiciis Academiae Heidelbergensis edita, II, Apologia Doctae Ignorantiae* (Leipzig, 1931–2), xii + 249 pp.; (ed., with E. Hoffmann) *Nicolai de Cusa Opera Omnia,* I (Leipzig, 1932), xx + 181 pp.; (ed.) *Magistri Eckardi Opera Latina, Fasc. I, Super oratione dominica* (Leipzig, 1934), xviii + 17 pp.; (ed.) *Magistri Eckardi Opera Latina, Fasc. XIII, Commentariolum de Eckardi magisterio* (Leipzig, 1936), 35 pp.; (ed., with H. J. Paton) *Philosophy and History* (Oxford, 1936), xii + 360 pp. (reprint of rev. ed., New York, 1963); *The Continuity of the Platonic Tradition* (London, 1939) (2nd ed., London, 1950, rev. ed. in preparation, Oxford and Montreal, 1964); (ed.) *Corpus Platonicum Medii Aevi. Auspiciis Academiae Britannicae. . . : Plato Latinus I* (London, 1940), xxii + 92 pp.; *Lat. II* (1950), xx + 156 pp.; *Arabus I* (1951), xii + 118 pp.; *Arab. II* (1943), xxii + 33 + 23 pp.; *Arabus III* (1952), xiv + 37 + 47 pp.; *Lat. III* (with preface and notes, with Carlotta Labowsky) (1953), xlii + 139 pp.; *Lat. IV* (1962), clxxxii + 436 pp.; (ed., with R. W. Hunt) *Mediaeval and Renaissance Studies*: Vol. I, 1 (London, 1941), 149 pp.; Vol. I, 2 (1943), pp. 150–334; Vol. II (1951), 189 pp.; Vol. III (1954), 251 pp.; Vol. IV (1958), 284 pp.; Vol. V (1961), 272 pp.; Supp., Vol. I (1951), 164 pp.; Supp., Vol. II (1952), 184 pp.; Supp., Vol. III (1956), 135 pp.; *Leibniz's Unknown Correspondence with English Scholars and Men of Letters* (London, 1941), 17 pp.; (ed., with commentary) *Mussolini's Memoirs* (London, 1949), xx + 320 pp.; (ed.) *Benedetto Croce: Essays on the Moral and Political Problems of Our Time* (London and New York, 1949), 240 pp. (reprint, New York, 1962, 254 pp.); (ed., with E. C. Mossner) *New Letters of David Hume* (Oxford, 1954), xxxiv + 253 pp. (second, enlarged ed. in preparation); (general ed.) *Nelson Philosophical Texts*: Vols. I, II (Edinburgh, 1951), xxvi + 256 pp., xxx + 246 pp.; Vol. III (1952), xxv + 278 pp.; Vols. IV, V (1953), xxxii + 308 pp., xlii + 330 pp.; Vol. VI (1954), lvi + 303 pp.; Vol. VII (1957), lxix + 308 pp.; Vol. VIII (1962), xxiii + 300 pp.; (ed., with H. Bascour) *Nicolaus de Cusa, De pace fidei* (London, 1956), lviii + 135 pp., republished (ed.) *Nicolai de Cusa, Opera Omnia,* Vol. VII (Hamburg, 1959); (rev. and ed., with co-operation of G. Calogero, trans. by A. E. Taylor) *Plato's Philebus and Epinomis* (Edinburgh, 1956), vi + 272 pp.;

(ed.) *Philosophy in the Mid-Century—La Philosophie au Milieu du Vingtième Siècle* (Firenze, 1958–9): Vol. I, *Logic and Philosophy of Science*, xii + 336 pp.; Vol. II, *Metaphysics and Analysis*, 218 pp.; Vol. III, *Values, History, Religion*, 232 pp.; Vol. IV, *History of Philosophy—Contemporary Thought in Eastern Europe and Asia*, 330 pp. (2nd ed. of the four vols., with added preface, 1961–2); (ed., with E. Anscombe, trans. by A. E. Taylor) *Plato, Sophist and Statesman* (Edinburgh, 1961), viii + 344 pp.;(ed., premessa) *John Locke, Lettera sulla Tolleranza* (testo latino e versione italiana), Filosofia e Comunità Mondiale, 3 (Firenze, 1961); (Prologo) *John Locke, Carta sobre la tolerancia* (Latin: Castellano), Filosofia y Comunidad Mundial (Montreal, 1962), xl + 124 pp.; (ed., with foreword) *La Philosophie Médiévale* (Montréal and Fiesole, 1962), viii + 62 pp.; (ed., introduction, of Latin text) *John Locke, List o tolerancji*, in Polish series, Philosophy and World Community (Warsaw, 1963), 131 pp. (B) Annual Reports on the Progress of Cusanus Studies, in *Jahresberichte der Heidelberger Akademie* (1929–31); (with E. Hoffmann) Nicolaus de Cusa's *Adumbratio Cosmologica* (Heidelberg, 1930); "An Unknown Letter by Peter Abailard," in *Jahresberichte der Heidelberger Akademie* (1930); "'Directio Speculantis,' the Last Work of Nicholas of Cusa," in *Jahresberichte der Heidelberger Akademie* (1931); "Niccolo da Cusa," *Enciclopedia Italiana* (Rome, 1932); "Nicholas of Cusa's MS. of Scotus Eriugena: A Tenth Century Versification of Scotus Eriugena's De divisione naturae," *Deutsche Literaturzeitung*, 52 (1935); (with W. Solmitz) "Bibliography of Ernst Cassirer's Writings," in Klibansky and Paton, eds., *Philosophy and History* (Oxford, 1936); "Standing on the Shoulders of Giants," *Isis*, 26 (1936), 147–9; "The Philosophical Character of History," in H. J. Paton, ed., *Philosophy and History* (Oxford, 1936); "De dialogis De vera sapientia Francisco Petrarcae addictis" (Leipzig, 1937); rapports annuels sur le progrès du Corpus Platonicum, *Acad Royale de Belgique* (1937, 1938, 1939, 1953, 1958, 1959, 1961, 1962); "New Letters of David Hume," *TLS* (Jan. 21, 1939); *The Continuity of the Platonic Tradition during the Middle Ages, Outlines of a Corpus platonicum medii aevi* (London, 1939), 58 pp.; *Plato's Parmenides in the Middle Ages and the Renaissance* (London, 1943), 50 pp.; "The Rock of Parmenides: Mediaeval Accounts of the Origins of Dialectic," *MRS*, 1 (1943), no. 2; annual reports on Platonic Studies, *Annual Rep of the Warburg Inst* (1943–59); "La Lettre de Bérenger de Poitiers contre les Chartreux," *Rev de Moyen Age Latin*, II (Lyons et Strasbourg, 1946); "An International Dictionary of the Basic Terms of Philosophy and Political Thought," *Proc Third Interamerican Congress of Philos* (Mexico, 1950) (also in Spanish); "Copernic et Nicolas de Cues," in *Leonard de Vinci et l'esprit scientifique au XVIe siècle*, Etudes publiées par le Centre National de la recherche scientifique (Paris, 1953); "Descartes: A Selected Bibliography," reprinted from *Descartes: Philosophical Writings*, Nelson Philosophical Texts (Edinburgh, 1954), xlix–liv; *Bibliography of Philosophy—Bibliographie de la Philosophie*, Introduction, Vol. I, pp. 9–12 (Paris, 1954); Premessa, *Gli Editti de Asoka*, Filosofia e Comunità Mondiale, 1 (Firenze, 1960); Premessa, *Sebastiano Castellione*, Filosofia e Comunità Mondiale, 2 (Firenze, 1960); "The School of Chartres," in *Twelfth-Century Europe and the Foundations of Modern Society* (Madison,

Wis., 1961); "Peter Abailard and Bernard of Clairvaux," *MRS*, 5 (1961), 1–27; "Nicholas of Cues," in *La Philosophie Médiévale* (Montreal and Fiesole, 1962). (C) *MRS*. (D) (with F. Saxl and E. Panofsky) Saturn and Melancholy: Studies in the History of Religion, Art, and Natural Philosophy (to appear before the end of 1963); History of Platonism (in MS. stage).

McCALL, STORRS: (B) "A Simple Decision Procedure for One-Variable Implication/Negation Formulae in Intuitionist Logic," *Notre Dame J Formal Logic*, 3 (1962). (C) *Dialogue, J Symbolic Logic, Notre Dame J Formal Logic*. (D) Aristotle's Modal Syllogisms (to be published in June, in Amsterdam); editing Polish Logic, a collection of translations of Polish logical papers (publication at some time in the future).

McKINNON, ALASTAIR: (B) "God, Humanity, and Sexual Polarity," *Hibbert J* 52 (1954), 337–42; "Christianity and Existentialism," *Anglican Outlook* (May, June, July, 1957); "The Meaning of Religious Assertions," *Encounter* (Oct., 1960); "Søren Kierkegaard," in *Architects of Modern Thought* (Toronto, 1962). (C) *Christian Outlook, Dialogue, Hibbert J, QQ*. (D) Miracles and Paradoxes, a major work attempting to separate religious belief from certain traditional mythological wrappings (completion expected this year); Falsification and Belief, a brief refutation of two current charges against religious belief (nearly complete).

MILLER, JAMES W.: (A) *The Structure of Aristotelian Logic* (London, 1938), 97 pp.; *Exercises in Introductory Symbolic Logic* (Ann Arbor, 1955); *Logic Workbook* (New York, 1958), 88 pp. (B) "Logical Dualism," *JP*, 47 (1950), 341–53; "Descartes's Conceptualism," *RM*, 4 (1950), 239–46; "The Logic of Terms," in P. Henle, H. Kallen, S. Langer, eds., *Structure, Method and Meaning: Essays in Honor of Henry M. Sheffer* (New York, 1951), 35–41; "The Development of the Philosophy of Socrates," *RM*, 6 (1953), 551–61; "Plato and Scoon," *RM*, 7 (1953), 128–31; "The Socratic versus the Platonic Order of the Dialogues," *First Session, Pakistan Philosophical Congress* (Karachi, 1955), 115–31. (C) *J Symbolic Logic, RM*. (D) A book on the philosophy of Socrates (about two-thirds written).

MCMASTER UNIVERSITY

DULMAGE, H. A.: (B) "A Philosopher's View of Psychology," *Ontario Psych Ass Q*, 12 (1959), 21–5. (D) A re-examination of process philosophy (including Whitehead) from the standpoint of linguistic analysis (preliminary formulation of one aspect in a paper to be delivered at the C.P.A. meetings at Laval in June, 1963); "Intuition and Language in Mascal, I. T. Ramsey, and Whitehead"; also in prospect, a restatement of a contextualistic theory of value in terms of normative discourse.

UNIVERSITY OF MANITOBA

GLASSEN, PETER: (B) "Some Questions about Relations," *Analysis*, 17 (1957), 64–8; "A Fallacy in Aristotle's Argument about the Good," *PhQ*, 7 (1957), 319–22; "Reds, Greens, and the Synthetic A Priori," *Philos St*, 9 (1958), 33–8; "Moore and the Indefinability of Good," *JP*, 55 (1958), 430–5; "Is Man a Physical Object?" *Proc Twelfth Int Congress of Philos*

(1958), 2, 169–74; " 'Charientic' Judgments," *Philosophy*, 33 (1958), 138–46; "The Cognitivity of Moral Judgments," *Mind*, 68 (1959), 57–72; "The Classes of Moral Terms," *Methodos*, 11 (1959), 223–44; "The Senses of 'Ought,' " *Philos St*, 11 (1960), 10–16; "Are There Unresolvable Moral Disputes?" *Dialogue*, 1 (1962), 36–50. (C) *Analysis, Dialogue, JP, Methodos, Mind, PhQ, Philos St, Philosophy.*

HUGGETT, WILLIAM J.: (B) "The Fundamental Question of Ethics," *Mind*, 67 (1958), 538–41; "Paradox Lost," *Analysis*, 19 (1958/9), 21–3; "On Not Being Gulled by Ravens," *Australasian J Philos*, 38 (1960), 48–50; "Losing One's Way in Time," *PhQ*, 10 (1960), 264–7; "The 'Proslogion' Proof Re-examined," *Indian J Philos*, 2 (1961), 193–202; "The Non-existence of Ontological Arguments," *PhR*, 71 (1962), 377–9. (C) *Analysis, Australasian J Philos, Dialogue, Indian J Philos, Mind, PhQ, PhR, QQ.*

SIBLEY, W. M.: (B) "Does Naturalism Leave Obligation Out of Ethics?" *JPPR*, 8 (1947), 269–75; "The Pragmatic Theory of Scientific Objects," *PhR*, 57 (1948), 248–59; "The Rational Versus the Reasonable," *PhR*, 62 (1953), 554–60. (C) *Dialogue, JPPR, PhR, QQ, UTQ.*

VINCENT, R. H.: (B) "A Note on Some Quantitative Theories of Confirmation," *Philos St*, 12 (1961), 91–2; "The Paradox of Ideal Evidence," *PhR*, 71 (1962), 497–503; "Popper on Qualitative Confirmation and Disconfirmation," *Australasian J Philos*, 40 (1962), 157–66. (C) *Australasian J Philos, Dialogue, Mind, PhR, Philos St, Philos of Sc.* (D) Four articles accepted for publication in *Mind, Dialogue,* and *Philos of Sc* some time in 1963.

MOUNT ALLISON UNIVERSITY

BAXTER, CLAYTON A.: (B) "Some Reflections on Thirty Years of Psychology," *Bull Maritime Psych Ass*, 1, No. 2; "A Meta-Psychological Approach to Mental Health," *Bull Maritime Psych Ass*, 3, No. 2, 30–40; "Some Limitations of Gestalt Psychology," *Bull Maritime Psych Ass*, 6, No. 2, 8–18; "Doctrines of Science and Their Influence in Psychology," *Bull Maritime Psych Ass*, 8, No. 2, 60–71; "The Existence and Definition of Consciousness," *Bull Maritime Psych Ass*, 9, No. 22, 56–62. (C) *CJEPS, QQ.* (D) The Nature and Conditions of Abstracting (practically finished); Existence as a Predicate (half done).

UNIVERSITY OF OTTAWA

WOJCIECHOWSKI, JERZY A.: (B) "Le Problème du Mouvement," *RUO*, 27 (1957), 145–88; "La Relation Sujet-Objet et la Physique Quantique," *RUO*, 29 (1959), 88–99; "The Epistemological Problems of De-Anthropomorphization of Modern Science," *PACPA*, 33 (1959), 58–64; "Analytic Philosophers' View of Science: An Appraisal," *PACPA*, 34 (1960), 194–200; "The Philosophy of Communism," *Fulcrum*, 21 (1960), no. 5; "Philosophy in the Science Curriculum," *Culture*, 22 (1961), 55–61; "Science and the Notion of Reality," *RUO*, 31 (1961), 25–38; "Measurement and Understanding," *RUO*, 32 (1962), 88–104; "Remarques sur la Notion de Cause dans la Physique Contemporaine," *Dialogue*, 1 (1962), 81–92. (C) *Dialogue, PACPA, RUO.* (D) "What Kind of Knowledge Does Physical Science Give Us?" (to be published in *Int Philos Q*); "Scientific

Laws and Indetermination of Matter" (to be included in the *Proc Int Congress of Philos*); A larger study in the Philosophy of Science.

QUEEN'S UNIVERSITY

DUNCAN, A. R. C.: (A) *Practical Reason and Morality* (New York, 1957), 182 pp.; (trans.) H. J. De Vleeschauwer, *The Development of Kantian Thought* (New York, 1962), 200 pp. (B) "The Stoic View of Life," *Phoenix*, 6 (1952), 123–38. (C) *Enc Br, Philosophy*. (D) An Introduction to Philosophy (not a textbook, should be completed by fall, 1963).

ESTALL, H. M.: (A) (ed.) *Rights and Liberties in Our Time* (Toronto, 1947), viii + 108 pp. (B) "John Dewey," in *Architects of Modern Thought* (Toronto, 1955), 49–56; "Hume's 'Ruling Passion,' " *QQ*, 46 (1959), 46–55; "Existentialism as a Philosophy," *UTQ*, 29 (1960), 297–309. (C) *Dialogue* (ed.).

WHEATLEY, JON: (B) "The Logical Status of Meta-Ethical Theories," *Theoria*, 1 (1960); "Some Notes on John Wisdom's Position," *Mind*, 70 (1961), 351–61; "The Logical Presuppositions of Language," *PhQ*, 11 (1961), 256–9; "On Inadequate Definitions: Their Inadequacy," *Analysis*, 22 (1961), 15–18; "Like," *Proc Aristotelian Soc*, 62 (1962), 99–116; "Virtue: An Analysis and a Speculation," *Analysis*, 22 (1962), 70–2; "Hampshire on Human Freedom," *PhQ* (July, 1962). (C) *Analysis, Mind, PhQ, Theoria*. (D) Working on the theory of language—articles will be appearing fairly soon.

ST. FRANCIS XAVIER UNIVERSITY

GATTO, EDO P.: (D) A Latin and English text of the *opusculum De Natura Generis*, attributed to St. Thomas Aquinas; seven philosophical *opuscula* attributed to St. Thomas Aquinas: a palaeographical, historical, and doctrinal study (about a year to publication).

MONAHAN, EDWARD J.: (B) "Human Liberty and Free Will According to John Buridan," *MS*, 16 (1954), 72–86. (C) *Dialogue, Mod Schoolman, Thomist*. (D) Research on natural law (two articles, in preparation); anthology on ethics (part of projected five-volume series intended for undergraduate use, volume on ethics should be ready for mimeograph use by mid-winter 1964).

SAINT MARY'S UNIVERSITY

MARSHALL, ROWLAND COLLINGE: (D) The Notion of Historicity in the Philosophy of Hegel.

MONAHAN, ARTHUR P.: (B) "The Subject of Metaphysics for Peter of Auvergne," *MS*, 16 (1954), 118–30; "Selected Texts from Peter of Auvergne," in J. R. O'Donnell, ed., *Nine Mediaeval Thinkers* (Toronto, 1955); "Catholicism in the Hamilton Area before the Establishment of the Diocese in 1856," *Can Cath Hist Ass Rep* (1956), 29–39; "A Politico-Religious Incident in the Life of Thomas d'Arcy McGee," *Can Cath Hist Ass Rep* (1957), 39–51; "Bishop Farrell of Hamilton as a Participant in the Political Life of His Day," *Can Cath Hist Ass Rep* (1960), 25–34. (C) *Can Cath Hist Ass Rep, MS*. (D) A short history of Irish contributions to the Roman Catholic Church in Canada; an intellectual history of the development of Roman Catholicism in English Canada.

UNIVERSITY OF SASKATCHEWAN

JACK, HENRY HOWARD: (B) "On the Analysis of Promises," *JP*, 55 (1958), 597–604; "Logical Truth and the Law of Excluded Middle," *Mind*, NS, 68 (1959), 93–7; "Reply to Barker's Criticism of Formalism," *Philos of Sc*, 26 (1959), 355–61. (D) A textbook in philosophy of science (first draft mostly completed).

MILLER, LEONARD G.: (A) (with Arthur Smullyan, Paul Dietrichson, David Keyl) *Introduction to Philosophy* (an anthology) (Belmont, Calif., 1962), x + 418 pp. (B) "Rules and Exceptions," *Ethics*, 66 (1956), 262–70; "Descartes, Mathematics, and God," *PhR*, 66 (1957), 451–65; "Moral Scepticism," *JPPR*, 22 (1962), 239–45. (C) *Ethics, JPPR, PhR*. (D) Several articles on Descartes, ethics, in preparation.

SIR GEORGE WILLIAMS UNIVERSITY

FRASER, WILLIAM ROSS: (A) *A White Stone* (philosophical novel) (New York, 1955), 183 pp.; (with Oldbury, Tinsley, and Tom Wiswell) *International Draughts and Checkers* (London and New York, 1959), 191 pp.; *The Inferno of Checkers* (Los Angeles, 1959), 212 pp.; "Canadian Reactions," in *Edward Bellamy Abroad* (with Sylvia Bowman, *et al.*) (New York, 1962), 543 pp. (B) "Reflections on Chess and Checkers," *Elam's Checker Board* (June-July, 1952); "Aesthetic Reflections on the Modern Novel," *JPPR*, 19 (1959), 518–23. (C) *California Checker Chatter, Elam's Checker Board*. (D) (with T. Wiswell) The Art of Checkers (probably to be published in 1964); another philosophical novel, Not Looking Back (should be published by 1965 at the latest).

UNIVERSITY OF TORONTO

ANDERSON, F. H.: (A) *The Argument of Plato* (London, 1935), 216 pp.; *The Philosophy of Francis Bacon* (Chicago, 1948), viii + 312 pp.; (ed., with introduction) *The Symposium of Plato* (New York, 1948), vi + 51 pp.; (ed., with introduction) *The Meno of Plato* (New York, 1949), xiv + 38 pp.; (ed., with introduction) *The Phaedo of Plato* (New York, 1951), xii + 74 pp.; *Francis Bacon's New Organon and Related Writings* (New York, 1960), xl + 292 pp.; *Francis Bacon: His Career and His Thought* (Los Angeles, 1962), ix + 367 pp. (B) "The Influence of Contemporary Science on Locke's Methods and Results" (Toronto, 1923), 31 pp.; "Causality and Cognition," *Proc Seventh Int Congress of Philos* (1931), 357–460; "On Interpreting Locke," *UTQ*, 6 (1935), 24–33; "Notes on Plato's Aesthetic," *PhR*, 48 (1939), 65–70; "On a Certain Revival of Enthusiasm," *UTQ*, 12 (1941), 182–96; "Bacon on Platonism," *UTQ*, 13 (1942), 154–66; "Introduction," *Philosophy in Canada* (Toronto, 1952), 1–5; "Plato's Phaedrus," *JP*, 49 (1952), 532–7; "Francis Bacon," *The New Century Encyclopedia of Names*, I (New York, 1954); "Poetry as Knowledge," *TRSC*, 3rd series, s. 2, 48 (1954), 47–58; "Plato's Aesthetics Reconsidered," *UTQ*, 25 (1956), 425–36; "Platonic Elements in Epistemology,"

PACPA, 33 (1959), 21–7.   (D) A book on the aesthetical problems of Plato, Aristotle, and Plotinus (first draft completed); book on the philosophy of John Locke (half done); studies in the Platonic elements in Coleridge.

DRAY, W. H.: (A) *Laws and Explanation in History* (London, 1957), 174 pp.   (B) "R. G. Collingwood and the Acquaintance Theory of Knowledge," *Rev Int de Philos*, 42 (1957), 420–33; "Historical Understanding as Rethinking," *UTQ*, 27 (1958), 200–16; "Toynbee's Search for Historical Laws," *History and Theory*, 1 (1960), 32–54; "Choosing and Doing," *Dialogue*, 1 (1962), 129–52; "The Historian's Problem of Selection," in E. Nagel, ed., *Logic, Methodology and Philosophy of Science* (Stanford, 1962), 595–603; "Some Causal Accounts of the American Civil War," *Daedalus*, 91 (1962), 578–98.   (C) *Analysis, Daedalus, Dialogue, History and Theory, JP, Mind, UTQ*.   (D) An Introduction to Philosophy of History (about 120 pp., to be submitted to publisher next summer); The Concept of Objectivity in History (about 200 pp., to be submitted to publisher in the summer of 1964).

DRYER, DOUGLAS POOLE: (B) "Ethical Reasoning," *Amer Philos Ass*, 2 (University of Pennsylvania Press, 1953); "Metaphysics and Christian Faith," *RM*, 10 (1957), 666–74.   (C) *Can For, CJEPS, UTQ*.   (D) Kant's Solution for Verification in Metaphysics (over 800 pp. MS., nine-tenths ready for publisher).

FACKENHEIM, EMIL L.: (A) *Paths to Jewish Belief* (New York, 1960), 157 pp.; *Metaphysics and Historicity* (Milwaukee, 1961), 100 pp.   (B) "The Conception of Substance in the Philosophy of the 'Ikhwan as-Safa' (Brethren of Purity)," *MS*, 5 (1943), 115–22; "Ibn Sina's Treatise on Love," *MS*, 7 (1945), 208–28; "The Possibility of the Universe in Al Farabi, Ibn Sina, and Maimonides," *Proc Amer Acad for Jewish Res*, 16 (1947), 39–70; "Medieval Jewish Philosophy," in Fenn, ed., *A History of Philosophical Systems* (New York, 1950), 171–84; "Self-realization and the Search for God," *Judaism*, 1 (1952), 291–306; "Schelling's Philosophy of Religion," *UTQ*, 22 (1952), 1–17; "Schelling's Conception of Positive Philosophy," *RM*, 7 (1954), 563–82; "Schelling's Philosophy of the Literary Arts," *PhQ*, 4 (1954), 310–26; "Kant and Radical Evil," *UTQ*, 23 (1954), 339–53; "Kant's Concept of History," *Kant-Studien*, 48 (1956/7), 381–98; "The Dilemma of Liberal Judaism," *Commentary*, 30 (1960), 301–10; "Apologia for a Confirmation Test," *Commentary*, 31 (1961), 401–10.   (C) *CCAR J, Commentary, Judaism, PhR, RM*.   (D) A study of the philosophy of religion of Kant, Fichte, Schleiermacher, Schelling, Hegel, and Kierkegaard (about three-quarters complete); a theological analysis of the concept of "covenant" in contemporary Jewish theology.

GALLOP, DAVID: (B) "Determinism and Character," *UTQ*, 29 (1960), 152–61; "True and False Pleasures," *PhQ*, 10 (1960), 331–42; "Justice and Holiness in Plato's *Protagoras*," *Phronesis*, 6 (1961), 86–93; "On Being Determined," *Mind*, NS, 71 (1962), 181–96.   (D) "Plato and the Alphabet" (an article, a critical discussion of a paper by G. Ryle, "Letters and Syllables in Plato"; completed, to be published in *PhR*); a study in key analogies in Plato's dialogues, to illustrate his epistemology and moral theory (in early stages).

GOUDGE, T. A.: (A) (ed., with introduction) *Bergson's Introduction to Metaphysics* (New York, 1949), xx + 51 pp. (2nd ed., 1955); *The Thought of C. S. Peirce* (Toronto, 1950), xiv + 360 pp.; *The Ascent of Life: A Philosophical Study of the Theory of Evolution* (London and Toronto, 1961), 235 pp. (B) "Some Realist Theories of Illusion," *Monist*, 44 (1934), 108–25; "The Views of Charles Peirce on the Given in Experience," *JP*, 32 (1935), 533–44; "Further Reflections on Peirce's Doctrine of the Given," *JP*, 33 (1936), 289–95; "Peirce's Treatment of Induction," *Philos of Sc*, 7 (1940), 56–68; "The Spectator Fallacy," *JP*, 39 (1942), 14–21; "Science and Symbolic Logic," *Scripta Mathematica*, 9 (1943), 69–80; "Charles Peirce: Pioneer in American Thought," *UTQ*, 12 (1943), 403–14; "Philosophical Trends in Nineteenth-Century America," *UTQ*, 16 (1947), 133–42; "The Conflict of Naturalism and Transcendentalism in Peirce," *JP*, 44 (1947), 365–75; "The Function of Reason," *DR*, 27 (1948), 329–38; "The Future of Materialism," *PhR*, 59 (1950), 107–12; "Peirce's Theory of Abstraction," in Frederic H. Young and Philip P. Wiener, eds., *Studies in the Philosophy of Charles Sanders Peirce* (Cambridge, Mass., 1952), 121–32; "Organismic Concepts in Biology and Physics," *RM*, 7 (1953), 282–9; "Physical Cosmology and Philosophical Physics," *RM*, 7 (1954), 444–51; "The Concept of Evolution," *Mind*, NS, 63 (1954), 16–25; "Some Philosophical Aspects of the Theory of Evolution," *UTQ*, 23 (1954), 386–401; "What is a Population?" *Philos of Sc*, 22 (1955), 272–9; "Progress and Evolution," in E. G. D. Murray, ed., *Studia Varia: Royal Society of Canada Literary and Scientific Papers* (Toronto, 1957), 86–94; "Is Evolution Finished?" *UTQ*, 26 (1957), 430–42; "Causal Explanations in Natural History," *Br J for Philos of Sc*, 9 (1958), 194–202; "Explorations across the Great Divide," *UTQ*, 29 (1959), 85–90; "Darwin's Heirs," *UTQ*, 30 (1961), 245–50; "The Genetic Fallacy," *Synthese*, 13, 1, 41–8; "The Evolutionary Vision of Teilhard de Chardin," *UTQ*, 32 (1962), 70–80. (C) *JP, Mind, PhR, QQ, UTQ*. (D) A systematic investigation of problems associated with the evolution of mind in the light of recent scientific and philosophical doctrines (still in preparatory stage).

HUNTER, J. F. M.: (D) "Conscience" (accepted for publication in *Mind*); articles on "Responsibility" and on "Evil, Wickedness, and Sin" (nearing completion); an introductory ethics textbook (about half finished).

LONG, MARCUS: (A) *Introduction to Systematic Philosophy* (Toronto, 1948), 127 pp.; *The Spirit of Philosophy* (New York, 1953), viii + 306 pp. (B) Innumerable articles. (C) *Alberta Teachers' Ass Mag, Can Commentator, Courier, QQ, RCAF Staff J, UTQ*, etc. (D) Revision of *The Spirit of Philosophy* (largely at the level of intention).

McRAE, ROBERT: (A) *The Problem of the Unity of the Sciences: Bacon to Kant* (Toronto, 1961), x + 148 pp. (B) "Criticism and Fixed Species," *JP*, 37 (1940), 297–302; "Phenomenalism and J. S. Mill's Theory of Causation," *JPPR*, 9 (1948), 237–50; "Final Causes in the Age of Reason," *UTQ*, 19 (1950), 247–58; "Hume as a Political Philosopher," *JHI*, 12 (1951), 285–90; "The Two Moralities of Spinoza," *UTQ*, 24 (1955), 60–9; "The Unity of the Sciences: Bacon, Descartes, and Leibniz," *JHI*, 18 (1957), 27–48 (published also in Philip P. Wiener and Aaron Noland, eds., *Roots of Scientific Thought,* New York, 1957); "How Can Berkeley be Refuted?" *UTQ,* 28 (1959), 223–32. (D) The concept "causa sine ratio" in the metaphysics of the seventeenth century (still in early stage).

PAYZANT, GEOFFREY: (B) "The Presbyterian Organ," *Organ Institute Q,* 5 (1955), 2–7, and 6 (1956), 29–34; "The Actual Need," *CMJ,* 1 (1957), 20–32; "The Competitive Music Festivals," *CMJ,* 4 (1960), 35–46. (C) *CMJ* (editor for its six years), *DR.* (D) Art Invention as Discovery and Elaboration (doctoral thesis being revised for publication); Obstacles to Faith (a small book in the philosophy of religion, searching for a publisher who will not want it expanded to twice its present length).

SAVAN, DAVID: (A) *Newcomers from Israel* (Toronto, 1955, mimeo, bound), 43 pp. (B) "John Dewey's Conception of Nature," *UTQ,* 17 (1947), 18–28; "On the Origins of Peirce's Phenomenology," in P. P. Wiener and F. H. Young, eds., *Studies in the Philosophy of Charles Sanders Peirce* (Cambridge, Mass., 1952); "John Dewey, 1859–1952," *Can For,* 32 (1952), 103–5; "Spinoza and Language," *PhR,* 67 (1958), 212–25; "Peirce as Man and Philosopher," *Can For,* 39 (1959), 87–8. (D) C. S. Peirce's Infallibilism; Poetry, Myth, and Dialectic in Plato's *Protagoras;* Self-Predication in *Protagoras 330–331;* and *Sophrosune* and *Sophia: Protagoras 332–333* (all four papers completed); Frege and Spinoza (work in progress).

WHEATLEY, J. M. O.: (B) "Deliberative Questions," *Analysis,* 15 (1955), 49–60; "Wishing and Hoping," *Analysis,* 18 (1958), 121–31; Bacon's Redefinition of Metaphysics," *Personalist,* 42 (1961), 487–99; "Knowledge, Empiricism, and ESP," *Int J Parapsych,* 3 (1961), 7–23. (C) *Analysis, J Amer Soc for Psychical Res.* (D) Analysis of extra-sensory cognition, etc. (in progress).

UNIVERSITY OF TORONTO—VICTORIA COLLEGE

SPARSHOTT, F. E.: (A) *An Enquiry into Goodness* (Toronto, 1958), xiv + 304 pp.; *The Structure of Aesthetics* (Toronto, 1963), 471 pp. (B) "Plato and Thrasymachus," *UTQ,* 27 (1957), 54–61; "The Central Problem of Philosophy," *UTQ,* 31 (1961), 1–19; "Avowals and Their Uses," *Proc Aristotelian Soc,* NS, 62 (1961/2), 63–76; "The Concept of Purpose," *Ethics,* 72 (1961/2), 157–70. (C) *Ethics, PhR, Phoenix, UTQ.* (D) Looking for Philosophy: An Enquiry into the Nature of Philosophical Enquiry (looking for a publisher).

For JOHN A. IRVING, see page 245.

UNIVERSITY OF TORONTO—ST. MICHAEL'S COLLEGE

KENNEDY, L.: (B) "The Middle Ages and Scepticism," *Culture,* 20 (1959), 160–71; "The Nature of the Human Intellect According to St. Albert the Great," *Mod Schoolman,* 37 (1960), 121–37; "St. Albert the Great's Doctrine of Divine Illumination," *Mod Schoolman,* 40 (1963), 23–37. (D) Article on "Averroists and the Agent Sense" (close to being completed).

WINGELL, ALBERT E.: (B) "*Vivere viventibus est esse* in Aristotle and St. Thomas," *Mod Schoolman,* 38 (1961), 85–120.

UNIVERSITY OF VICTORIA

DE LUCCA, JOHN: (C) *Philos of Sc.* (D) A textbook in the philosophy of science (initial stages, planning and outlining, some parts in rough draft); a textbook of readings in the theory of knowledge (preliminary planning); article entitled "Spinoza's Mode of Philosophizing and His Literary Mode of Exposition" (near completion).

UNIVERSITY OF WATERLOO

ARMOUR, LESLIE: (A) *The Rational and the Real* (The Hague, 1962), 97 pp. (B) "The Duty to Seek Agreement," *JP*, 56 (1959), 985–92; "The Ontological Argument and the Concept of Completeness and Selection," *RM*, 14 (1960), 280–91; "Value Data and Moral Rules," *PhQ* (1962); "Morality, Objectivity, and Time," *Indian J Philos* (1962); "Rationality, Goodness, and Immortality," *Theoria*, 29 (1963), 1–11. (C) *Indian J Philos, JP, PhQ, RM, Theoria.* (D) A book "God and Argument" (final version should be complete late 1963 or early 1964).

BURGENER, R. J. C.: (B) "The Problem of Origin in a Eudaemonist Theory of Beauty," 245 pp. (typescripts available from the U. of T. library, 1955); "The Problem of Origin . . . an abstract, 6 pp. (Toronto, 1955); "Price's Theory of the Concept," *RM*, 11 (1957), 143–59; "Remarks on Price's 'Comment,'" *RM*, 12 (1959), 649–53; "An Inspective Theory of Thinking," *RM*, 13 (1959), 175–84. (C) *Philos of Sc, RM.* (D) A book tentatively entitled "Reason and Will" (well under way).

UNIVERSITY OF WESTERN ONTARIO—UNIVERSITY COLLEGE AND MIDDLESEX COLLEGE

BLOCK, IRVING: (B) "The Order of Aristotle's Psychological Writings," *AJP* (1961), 50–77; "Truth and Error in Aristotle's Theory of Sense-Perception," *PhQ* (Jan., 1961), 1–9; "Aristotle and the Physical Object," *Philos and Phenomenological Res* (Sept., 1960), 93–101; "The Desired and Desirable in Dewey's Ethics," *Dialogue* (Sept., 1963), 170–81; "Plato, Parmenides, Ryle and Exemplification," *Mind* (Oct., 1963). (C) *Philos and Phenomenological Res.* (D) Book on Aristotle's theory of sensory cognition and its relationship to his theory of science (about half done); "Three German Commentators on the Individual Senses and the Common Sense in Aristotle's Psychology" (to appear in *Phronesis*).

BRONAUGH, RICHARD: (C) *Analysis, Dialogue, Ethics, Mind, PhQ, PhR.* (D) "The Argument from the Elliptical Penny" (accepted by *PhQ*); "Uncertainty and Free Choice" (accepted by *Dialogue*); "Freedom as the Absence of an Excuse" (submitted to publisher).

BUTTS, ROBERT E.: (B) "Rationalism in Modern Science: D'Alembert and the *Esprit Simpliste*," *Bucknell R*, 8 (1959), 127–39; "Hume's Scepticism," *JHI*, 20 (1959), 413–19; "Husserl's Critique of Hume's Notion of Distinctions of Reason," *Philos and Phenomenological Res*, 20 (1959), 213–21; "Does 'Intentionality' Imply 'Being'? A Paralogism in Sartre's Ontology," *Kant-Studien*, 52 (1960/61), 426–32 (abstract of same in *JP*, 55 (1958), 911–12); "Hypothesis and Explanation in Kant's Philosophy of

Science," *Arch für die Gesch der Philos*, 43 (1961), 153–70; "Kant on Hypotheses in the 'Doctrine of Method' and the *Logik*," *Arch für Gesch der Philos*, 44 (1962), 185–203; " 'Indoctrination *in*', 'Indoctrination *with*', and 'Indoctrination *into*,' " *Bucknell R*, 10 (1962), 347–63. (C) *Arch für Gesch der Philos*. (D) "Necessary Truth in Whewell's Theory of Science" (to appear in *Amer Philos Q*); review article on a new Berlin Academy edition of Kant's lectures on physics and philosophical encyclopedia (to appear in *Arch für Gesch der Philos*); "Comment: On Walsh's Reading of Whewell's View of Necessity" (submitted to *Philos of Sc*); Necessity and Induction: An Essay on William Whewell's Philosophy of Science (book in early stages of writing).

DAVIS, JOHN W.: (B) "Berkeley's Doctrine of the Notion," *RM* (March, 1959); "The Molyneux Problem," *JHI* (Sept., 1960); "The Permanent Element in Empiricism," *Philosophical Forum* (June, 1962); "Berkeley's Phenomenalism," *Dialogue* (June, 1962). (C) *JHI, RM*. (D) A book entitled Berkeley's Design (first draft of MS. should be completed by summer of 1964).

FRENCH, STANLEY G.: (A) *The North-West Staging Route* (Ottawa, 1957). (B) "Conceptual Meaning," *Southern Soc for Psych and Philos* (April, 1958); "Locke and the Philosophy of Language," *Can Philos Ass* (June, 1960); "The Hume's Hurdle Paradox," *Amer Philos Ass* (Dec., 1961); "Hume's Hurdle," *Dialogue*, 1 (1963), 390–9; "The Spirit of French-Canadian Philosophy," *Can Philos Ass* (June, 1963). (D) The Spirit of French-Canadian Philosophy (a book, completed, soon to be published as a University of Western Ontario monograph); "Atheism" (an article, in progress).

JOHNSON, A. H. (A): (ed., with an introduction) *The Wit and Wisdom of Whitehead* (Boston, 1947), vi + 102 pp.; (ed., with introduction) *The Wit and Wisdom of John Dewey* (Boston, 1949), x + 111 pp.; (ed.) *Whitehead and the Modern World* (Boston, 1950), viii + 54 pp.; *Whitehead's Theory of Reality* (Boston, 1952), x + 263 pp. (rev. ed., New York, 1962); *Whitehead's Philosophy of Civilization* (Boston, 1958), xii + 211 pp. (rev. ed., New York, 1962); (ed.) *Whitehead's American Essays in Social Philosophy* (New York, 1959), xii + 206 pp.; *Whitehead's Interpretation of Science* (Indianapolis, 1961), xliv + 274 pp. (B) "A Criticism of D. Bidney's 'Spinoza and Whitehead,' " *PhR* (July, 1938), 410–14; "Modern Realistic Epistemology and the 'Man in the Street,' " *JP*, 39 (1942), 414–18; "The Intelligibility of Whitehead's Philosophy," *Philos of Sc*, 10 (1943), 47–55; "The Social Philosophy of Alfred North Whitehead," *JP*, 40 (1943), 261–71; " 'Truth, Beauty and Goodness' in the Philosophy of A. N. Whitehead," *Philos of Sc*, 11 (1944), 9–29; "Whitehead's Theory of Actual Entities: Defense and Criticism," *Philos of Sc*, 12 (1945), 237–95; "Whitehead and the Making of Tomorrow," *Philos and Phenomenological Res*, 5 (1945), 398–406; "The Psychology of Alfred North Whitehead," *J Gen Psych*, 32 (1945), 175–212; "Whitehead's Philosophy of History," *JHI*, 7 (1946), 234–49; "Whitehead's Discussion of Education," *Education* (June, 1946), 653–71; "Alfred North Whitehead," *UTQ*, 15 (1946), 373–83; "A. N. Whitehead's Theory of Intuition," *J Gen*

Psych, 37 (1947), 61–6; "Recent Discussions of Alfred North Whitehead," *RM*, 5 (1951), 293–308; (contributor) *Philosophy in Canada* (Toronto, 1952), 40–3; "Hartshorne and the Interpretation of Whitehead," *RM*, 7 (1954), 495–8; "A. N. Whitehead," *Enc Br* (1957); "The Philosophical Foundation for Democracy," *Ethics*, 68 (1958), 281–5; "Leibniz and Whitehead," *Philos and Phenomenological Res*, 19 (1959), 285–305; "Francis Hutcheson and the 'Moral Sense,'" *TRSC*, 3rd series, s. 2, 53 (1959), 11–17; "Leibniz's Method and the Basis of his Metaphysics," *Philosophy*, 35 (1960), 51–61; "Modes of Being According to Paul Weiss," *Philos and Phenomenological Res*, 21 (1960), 114–22; "Whitehead on the Use of Language," in I. Leclerc, ed., *The Relevance of Whitehead* (London, 1961), 125–41; "A. N. Whitehead," in *Architects of Modern Thought* (Toronto, 1962), 41–50; "Some Aspects of Whitehead's Social Philosophy," *Philos and Phenomenological Res*, 24 (1963), 61–72. (C) *Philos and Phenomenological Res*, *RM*. (D) An introduction to philosophy for the general reader (almost complete); a philosophical system (just begun).

JOHNSON, HAROLD J.: (D) The Logic of Politics and the Politics of Logic in Hobbes—monograph in University of Western Ontario series (further work needed); four articles: "Three Ancient Meanings of Matter: Democritus, Plato, Aristotle" (nearly completed); "Aristotle's Four Causes and Thomas's Five Ways"—one brief article stating thesis on relations of "causes" and "ways," and a longer, more technical one examining the literature in the field, and debating rival interpretations (research completed); "Science and Ethics: Positive and Negative Analogies" (outlined).

WILLIAMS, M. E.: (B) "Hegel's Philosophy of History," *RM*, 16 (1962), 139–44. (D) "Kant's Two Concepts of the Synthetic a Priori" (paper delivered in June, 1963, to Can. Philos. Ass., almost ready for submission to *Kant-Studien*).

UNIVERSITY OF WESTERN ONTARIO—HURON COLLEGE

COMBER, GEOFFREY J.: (D) (with Dr. M. Emmet Wilson) a book on music appreciation (virtually completed—330–350 pp.); an article on the concept of aesthetic logic as a category for art criticism (probably for *JAAC*, hope to complete in two months).

GIVNER, DAVID AARON: (B) "Scientific Preconceptions in Locke's Philosophy of Language," *JHI*, 23 (1962), 340–54.

MORRIS, WILLIAM S.: (A) (ed.) *The Unity We Seek* (Toronto, 1962). (B) "The Reappraisal of Edwards," *NEQ*, 30 (1957), 515–25. (C) *CH*, *Hibbert J*, *JR*.

TRENTMAN, JOHN: (B) "Intervju med amerikansk religionsfilosof," *Tro och liv*, no. 5 (1959), 213–16; "The Philosophy Student in Sweden," *Graduate R of Philos*, 2 (1959), 11–18; "Ockham on Concepts," *Graduate R of Philos*, 4 (1961), 17–28; "Nagra reflektioner över nutida amerikansk teologi," *Tro och liv*, no. 2 (1962), 70–5; "A Note on *Tractatus* 4.12 and Logical Form," *Graduate R of Philos*, 4 (1962), 29–33. (D) A dissertation on simple supposition in fourteenth-century logical theory (about half written); translation of a Pär Lagerkvist short story, for *Minnesota R* (begun).

UNIVERSITY OF WESTERN ONTARIO—BRESCIA COLLEGE

ST. MICHAEL, MOTHER M.: (B) "A Basic Doctrine Overlooked by Thomistic Existentialists," *Proc Fourth Int Thomistic Congress* (*Sapientia Aquinatis*), 1 (1955), 525–7; "Similitudo Amoris," *LTP*, 11 (1955), 221–3; "Of Stars and the Children of Light" (on the need for good teachers), *Ont Eng Cath Teachers' Ass R*, 11 (1955), 6–12; "Roman Catholic Women's Communities: A History," *Enc Can* (1958), 9, 71–82; "Existential Analysis and the Human Condition," *PACPA* (1961), 125–41. (C) *Amer Cath Sociological R, UNESCO R.* (D) A study of the philosophy and psychology of work—a Thomistic view (research about three-quarters done; one chapter written; another six months' steady work needed).

YORK UNIVERSITY

HARRIS, H. S.: (A) *The Social Philosophy of Giovanni Gentile* (Urbana, Ill., 1960), 387 pp.; (trans., with introduction, notes, bibliography) G. Gentile's *Genesis and Structure of Society* (Urbana, Ill., 1960), 228 pp. (B) "Studi sull'attualismo e influenza di Gentile sulla cultura anglosassone," *Giorn. crit. della filosofia italiana*, 38 (1959), 312–52; "Hegelianism of the Right and Left," *RM* 11 (1958), 603–9. (C) *PhR, Philos of Sc.* (D) Several articles on Italian philosophy and philosophers for the *Enc of Philos* (New York) (one completed, the rest to be done in 1963).

HISTORY

ACADIA UNIVERSITY

MACINTOSH, ALAN: (D) The policital career of Sir Charles Tupper— extension of Ph.D. thesis (considerable research ahead).

UNIVERSITY OF ALBERTA

BROWN, R. C.: (B) "Goldwin Smith and Anti-Imperialism," *CHR*, 43 (1962), 93–105; "Canadian Nationalism in Western Newspapers," *Alberta Hist R*, 10 (1962), 1–7. (C) *Alberta Hist R, Can For, CHR.* (D) The National Policy and Canadian-American Relations, 1883–1900 (to be published in 1964); (co-editor with M. E. Prang), Documents in Canadian History, 1867–1945 (to be published in 1964).

EVANS, B. L.: (D) Diplomacy on the South China Frontier 1855–85 (final draft due summer of 1964).

HERTZMAN, LEWIS: (A) *DNVP: Right-Wing Opposition in the Weimar Republic 1918–1924* (Lincoln, Nebraska, 1963). (B) "The Founding of the German National People's Party (DNVP), November 1918–January 1919," *J Mod Hist*, 30 (1958), 24–36; "Conservative Nationalists under the Weimar Régime," *Wiener Lib Bull*, 14 (1960), 50–1; "Gustav Stresemann: The Problem of Political Leadership in the Weimar Republic," *Int R of Soc Hist*, 5 (1960), 361–77; "The Course of German Nationalism," *QQ*, 69 (1963), 579–92. (C) *AHR, CHR, J Mod Hist, QQ.*

HEYMANN, F. G.: (A) *John Zizka and the Hussite Revolution* (Princeton, 1955), x + 521 pp. (B) Chapters on "Germany and her Satellites," in Sir J. Hammerton and Maj.-Gen. Sir C. Gwynn, eds., *The Second Great War, A Standard History* (7 vols., London, n.d.); "The

National Assembly of Cáslav," *MH*, 8 (1954), 32–55; "The Role of the Towns in the Bohemia of the Later Middle Ages," *J World Hist* (1955), 326–46; "John Rokycana, Church Reformer between Hus and Luther," *CH* 28 (1959), 240–80; "The Death of King Ladislav: Historiographical Echoes of a Suspected Crime," *CHA Rep* (1961), 96–111; "City Rebellions in 15th-Century Bohemia and their Ideological and Sociological Backgrounds," *SEER*, 40 (1962), 324–40.   (C) *CHA Rep, CHR, CH, JCEA, J World Hist, MH, SEERS, SLR, Speculum.*

JONES, W. J.: (B) "Elizabethan Marine Insurance: The Judicial Undergrowth," *Business Hist*, 2 (1960), 53–66; "Conflict or Collaboration? Chancery Attitudes in the Reign of Elizabeth I," *Amer J Legal Hist*, 5 (1961), 12–54; "Chancery and the Cinque Ports in the Reign of Elizabeth I," *Archaeologia Cantiana*, 76 (1961), 143–51; "Due Process and Slow Process in the Elizabethan Chancery," *Amer J Legal Hist*, 6 (1962), 123–50. (C) *Amer J Legal Hist, Archaeologia Cantiana, Business Hist, Calif Law R, CHR, National Lib of Wales J.*   (D) Completing a book on the Elizabethan Chancery; monograph on Tudor-Stuart bankruptcy statutes and commissions (draft work and research completed); biography of Lord Chancellor Ellesmere (1540–1617) (considerable research done over the last few years).

LIEBEL, HELEN P.: (A) *The Bourgeois Reform Movement in West Germany: Enlightened Bureaucracy vs. Enlightened Despotism in Baden, 1750–1792* (Ann Arbor, Mich., 1959), 317 pp. (on microfilm); in the U.S. National Archives series of *Guides to Captured German War Documents* (Washington, D.C.): (co-author) No. 10, *Records of the Reich Ministry for Armaments and War Production* (1959), 109 pp.; No. 15, *Records of Former German and Japanese Embassies and Consulates, 1890–1945* (1960), 63 pp.; No. 20, *Records of the National Socialist German Labor Party (Part 2)* (1960), 45 pp.; No. 21, *Records of the Deutsches-Ausland-Institut, Stuttgart* (Part 2: *The General Records*) (1961), 180 pp.; No. 23, *Records of Private Austrian, Dutch, and German Enterprises, 1917–1946* (1961), 119 pp.; (joint ed. and trans.) Source Book for Hist. 2.1, History of Western Civilization, 2 (Brooklyn, N.Y., 3rd rev. ed., 1963), 559 pp.   (B) "Idealist Logic in the Historische Zeitschrift, 1859–1914," *History and Theory*, 3 (1963), 1–15.   (C) *Amer J Economics and Sociology, Jahrbuch für die Geschichte Mittel- und Ostdeutschlands, History and Theory, Wiener Lib Bull.*   (D) "Veblen's Positive Synthesis" (to appear in *Amer. J. Economics and Sociology*, Jan., 1965); revision of *Enlightened Bureaucracy vs. Enlightened Despotism in Baden, 1750–92* (in press); "Middle-Class Leadership and the Rise of Hamburg in the European Economy in the Eighteenth Century" (about 100 pages, needs retyping); "The Bourgeoisie, Southwestern Germany, 1500–1789—A Rising Class?" (64 pp., being considered for publication in journal; "Event, Prediction, and History: A Comment on Gale" (10 pp., under consideration); "The Plague and the Decline of the Ottoman Empire, 1700–1841" (39 pp., under consideration); "History and the Limitations of Science," (20 pp., needs retyping).

TOEWS, J. B.: (D) "Emperor Frederick III and Pope Pius II" (to be published by Dec., 1963).

WIEDNER, D. L.: (A) *A History of Africa South of the Sahara* (New York, 1962), xii + 579 pp.; *L'Afrique noire avant la colonisation* (Paris, 1963), 219 pp.   (B) "Forced Labour in Colonial Peru," *Americas*, 16 (1960), 357–83; "Background to Africa," *Mount Holyoke Alumnae Q*, 44 (1960), 74–84.   (C) *Africa Rep*, AHR, CHR.   (D) Money and Accounts in Western Europe and Overseas Expansion, 1450–1936 (revising and checking MS.).

ASSUMPTION UNIVERSITY OF WINDSOR

BOLAND, F. J.: (A) (ed.) *Canadian American Studies* (1960–2).   (B) "Father Soulerim, CSB, Founder and Administrator," *Can Cath Hist Ass Rep.* (1956), 13–27; "The Attitude of the American Hierarchy toward the Doctrine of Papal Infallibility at the Vatican Council, *Can Cath Hist Ass Rep* (1960), 35–49.   (C) *Can Cath Hist Ass Rep*, CHR.   (D) Behring Sea Controversy (research largely completed).

FARRELL, J. K.: (B) "Some Opinions of Christian Europeans Regarding Negro Slavery in the Seventeenth and Early Eighteenth Centuries," *Can Cath Hist Ass Rep* (1958), 13–22; "Schemes for the Transplanting of Refugee American Negroes from Upper Canada in the 1840's," *OH*, 52 (1960), 245–9.

VUCKOVIC, M. N.: (B) "The Suppression of the Religious Houses in France, 1880, and the Attitude of Representative British Press," *Can Cath Hist Ass Rep* (1961).

BISHOP'S UNIVERSITY

MASTERS, D. C.: (A) *The Reciprocity Treaty of 1854, Its History, Its Relation to British Colonial and Foreign Policy and to the Development of Canadian Fiscal Autonomy* (London, 1937), xxiv + 267 pp.; *The Rise of Toronto, 1850–1890* (Toronto, 1947), xii + 239 pp.; *The Winnipeg General Strike* (London, Toronto, 1950), xvi + 159 pp.; *Bishop's University: The First Hundred Years* (Toronto, 1950), xii + 253 pp.; *A Short History of Canada* (Princeton, N.J., and Toronto, 1958), 191 pp.; *Canada in World Affairs 1933–1955* (Toronto, 1959).   (B) "The Nicolls Papers: A Study in Anglican Toryism," *CHA Rep* (1945), 42–8; "Toronto vs. Montreal, the Struggle for Financial Hegemony, 1860–1875," CHR, 22 (1941), 133–46; "Bishop's University and the Ecclesiastical Controversies of the Nineteenth Century (1845–1878)," *CHA Rep* (1951), 36–42; "The Establishment of the Decimal Currency in Canada," *CHR*, 33 (1952), 129–47.   (C) *CHA Rep*, CHR, DR, QQ.   (D) Volume based on the correspondence of Jasper Hume Nicolls (first principal of Bishop's University) and his wife, giving a picture of Quebec English-speaking society of middle part of the nineteenth century (to be completed 1963); volume on Protestant church colleges in the history of higher education (to be completed in 1963 or 1964).

UNIVERSITY OF BRITISH COLUMBIA

BOSHER, J.: (D) The Single Duty Project: A Study of the Movement for a French Customs Union in the Eighteenth Century (a monograph to be published in 1964); "French Administration and Public Finance in their European Setting" (a chapter to be published in 1964).

HANRAHAN, J.: (C) *MS*. (D) The School of Laon in the Twelfth Century (thesis, being written); "New MSS of the School of Laon" (being written).

HARNETTY P.: (B) "British and Indian Attitudes to the Indian Problem at the End of the 19th Century," *CHA Rep* (1959), 48–62; "The Indian Cotton Duties Controversy, 1894–1896," *EHR* (1962), 684– 702. (C) *CHR, Can For, JAS, Pacific Aff, Pacific Hist R*. (D) The Impact of the Cotton Famine on India, 1861–66 (a monograph research begun in summer of 1962).

HEADLEY, J. M.: (D) Luther's View of Church History (a revision of doctoral dissertation, to be published in 1963); Complete Works of St. Thomas More (volume 5: "Responsio ad Lutherum") in progress.

HILL, L. E.: (D) Ernst von Weizsaecker, 1882–1951 (book-length, almost completed); "Another Look at the German Foreign Office in the Nazi Era" (article, being revised); "Resistance from the German Foreign Office on the Eve of Munich, 1938" (article, only introduction remains to be written).

MACDONALD, A. N.: (B) "The Business Leaders of Seattle 1880–1910," *Pacific Northwest Q*, 50 (1959), 1–13. (C) *CHA Rep, Pacific Northwest Q*.

NORRIS, J.: (A) *Shelburne and Reform* (London, 1963), xiv + 325 pp. (B) "The Policy of the British Cabinet in the Nootka Crisis," *EHR*, 70 (1955), 562–80; "Samuel Garbett and the Early Development of Industrial Lobbying in Great Britain," *Economic HR*, 10 (1958), 450–60. (C) *CHR, Economic Hist R, EHR*. (D) The Home Front: The Mobilization of the British Economy for War, 1793–1818 (being written).

SOWARD, F. H.: (A) *Moulders of National Destinies* (Toronto, 1938–40), x + 203 pp.; (co-author) *Canada in World Affairs, 1935–1939* (Toronto, 1941); *Twenty-Five Troubled Years, 1918–1943* (Toronto, 1943), x + 437 pp; (co-author) *Canada and the Pan-American System* (Toronto, 1947), viii + 47 pp.; *Canada in World Affairs, 1944–1946* (Toronto, 1950); (ed.) *The Changing Commonwealth* (Toronto, 1950), xiv + 268 pp.; *The Adaptable Commonwealth* (Toronto, 1950), 54 pp.; (co-author) *Canada and the United Nations* (New York, 1957), xii + 285 pp.; (co-author) *Evolving Canadian Federalism* (Durham, N.C., 1958). (C) *Amer J Int Law, CHR, Can Fortnightly, Int J, Int St, Pacific Hist R, Pacific Aff, Political Q, QQ, Round Table, World Politics*.

CANADIAN SERVICES COLLEGE, ROYAL ROADS

BURCHILL, C. S.: (B) "The Eastern Irrigation District," *CJEPS*, 5 (1939), 206–15; "The Origins of Canadian Irrigation Law," *CHR*, 29 (1948), 353–62. (C) *DR, QQ*. (D) Two articles and one textbook submitted to publishers.

RODNEY, WILLIAM: (B) "John George 'Kootenai' Brown," *Enc Can*, 2 (Ottawa, 1962), 127; "Canada," booklet published by British Society for International Understanding, London (for NATO). (C) *Br Survey*,

RCMP Q. (D) A book on Brown (possible publication 1963); (Can. ed.), Bibliography of World Communism and Soviet Foreign Relations.

CARLETON UNIVERSITY

BOWEN, D.: The Idea of the Church in England, 1833–1889 (Ph.D. thesis being edited for publication).

COUSE, G. S.: (D) The Historical Spirit in the French Doctrinaires (a book being written).

FARR, D. M. L. (A) *The Colonial Office and Canada, 1867–1887* (Toronto, 1955), xii + 362 pp. (B) "Sir John Rose and Imperial Relations: An Episode in Gladstone's First Administration," *CHR,* 33 (1952), 19–38; "Lord Dufferin: A Viceroy in Ottawa," *Culture,* 19 (1958), 153–64; "John S. Ewart," in R. L. McDougall, ed., *Our Living Tradition,* second and third series (Toronto, 1959), xvi + 288 pp. (C) *CHR, J Commonwealth Polit St.* (D) Relations between Canada and Great Britain since 1867 (for Century of Canada Series, ed. by D. G. G. Kerr (being written).

GIBSON, JAMES A.: (A) (with D. G. G. Kerr) *Sir Edmund Head: A Scholarly Governor* (Toronto, 1954), xii + 259 pp. (B) "Sir Edmund Head's Memorandum, Containing Reasons for Fixing the Seat of Government for Canada at Ottawa," *CHR,* 16 (1935), 411–17; "The 'Persistent Fallacy' of the Governors Head," *CHR,* 19 (1938), 295–7; "The Life of Sir Edmund Walker Head, Bart." (abstract of D. Phil. thesis, Oxford, 1939), 11, 74–9; contributor to: *Canada in Transition* (Toronto, 1944), *Canada and the Four Freedoms* (Toronto, 1944), *The Story of Our Time* (Toronto, 1948); "Canada and Foreign Affairs," *CHR,* 29 (1948), 183–94; "Canadian Foreign Policy: A Forward View," *Int J,* 4 (1949), 109–18; "Mr. Mackenzie King and Canadian Autonomy, 1921–1946," *CHA Rep* (1951), 12–21; (contributor) R. A. MacKay and S. A. Saunders, *The Modern World* (Toronto, 1951), chaps. 23 and 24; "The Development of Canadian Foreign Policy," *Current Aff,* 2 (1952), 20 pp.; "Canadian Foreign Policy," *QQ,* 58 (1951/2), 477–85; "Mr. Mackenzie King and the Blunt Pencil," *DR,* 32 (1952), 19–24; "The Queen's Realms," *Can Geog J,* 46 (1953), 220–6; "The Commonwealth Nations and NATO," data paper for British Council Study Conference on the British Commonwealth (1953) (mimeo); "How Ottawa Became the Capital of Canada," *OH,* 46 (1954), 213–22 (reprinted in centenary issue of *Ottawa Citizen,* Aug. 18, 1954); "The Colonial Office View of Canadian Federation, 1858–1868," *CHR,* 35 (1954), 279–313; "At First Hand: Recollections of a Prime Minister," *QQ,* 61 (1954), 13–20; "The Choosing of the Capital of Canada," *BC Hist Q,* 17 (1954), 75–85; "Canada and the Council of Europe," data paper for Nobel Institute Conference on *Western Democracies and World Problems* (Oslo, 1955) (mimeo); "The Oslo Conference, 1955," *Int J,* 10 (1955), 262–6; "Each Man's Mind," an address broadcast in Religious Period (Ottawa, 1955) (mimeo); (contributor) *A Handbook for Commonwealth Servicemen* (London, 1956); "Mystery and Intention in Education," (Ottawa, 1956), 16 pp. (mimeo); "Canadian Foreign Policy: A Mid-Century View," *Current Aff for the Canadian Forces,* 11 (1957); "American Investment in the Canadian Economy," *Centennial R,* 1 (1957), 349–54; "Flags and Arms (Armorial Bearings)," *Enc Can,* 4, 168–70; "National

Songs," *Enc Can*, 7, 250–3; "The Abuse of Greatness," *BC Hist Q*, 21 (1958), 75–82; "Sir Robert Borden," in R. L. McDougall, ed., *Our Living Tradition*, third series (Toronto, 1959), 95–122; (introduction) Fred Landon's *An Exile from Canada to Van Diemen's Land* (Toronto, 1960), xii + 321 pp.; "International Resources for Tomorrow," *Can Welfare*, 38 (1962), 102–7; "The Duke of Newcastle and British North American Affairs, 1859–1864," *CHR*, 44 (1963), 142–56. (C) *BC Hist Q, CHR, DR, Int J, QQ*. (D) The Nature of Canadian Federalism (expected completion June, 1964); The Evolution of Canadian Self-Government (extensive materials assembled).

MEALING, S. R.: (A) (ed., with an introduction) *The Jesuit Relations and Allied Documents: A Selection* (Toronto, 1963), 157 pp. (B) "The Enthusiasms of John Graves Simcoe," *CHA Rep* (1958), 50–62; "L'Angleterre de 1760 et son influence sur le Canada," *RUL*, 15 (1961), 611–18. (C) *CHR, QQ*. (D) (with D. M. L. Farr and J. S. Moir) grade 13 history text, *Two Democracies* (publication planned for spring, 1963).

MOIR, J. S.: (A) *Church and State in Canada West: Three Studies in the Relation of Denominationalism and Nationalism, 1841–1867* (Toronto, 1959), xvi + 223 pp.; (ed.) *History of the Royal Canadian Corps of Signals, 1903–1961* (Ottawa, 1962), 366 pp. (B) "The Settlement of the Clergy Reserves, 1840–1855," *CHR*, 37 (1956), 46–62; "The Correspondence of Bishop Strachan and John Henry Newman," *CJT*, 3 (1957), 219–25; "The Origins of the Separate School Question in Ontario," *CJT*, 5 (1959), 105–18. (C) *CHR, OH*. (D) (co-author) Grade 13 history textbook, *Two Democracies* (publication planned for spring, 1963); History of the Christian Church in Canada, 1763–1867; Lord Sydenham in Canada: Portrait of a Proconsul; "Sectarian Tradition in Canada," Canadian Church Traditions (to be published in 1963).

DALHOUSIE UNIVERSITY

BURROUGHS, PETER: (D) Imperial Administration in Australia, 1831–1855 (Ph.D. thesis, in process of being rewritten and revised for publication).

FERGUSSON, C. BRUCE: (A) *Establishment of the Negroes in Nova Scotia* (Halifax, 1948), 140 pp.; *A Century of Service to the Public*, Centennial of Nova Scotia Savings, Loan and Building Society (Halifax, 1950), 40 pp.; (ed., with introduction, notes) Richard John Uniacke's *Sketches of Cape Breton; and Other Papers Relating to Cape Breton Island* (Halifax, 1958), x + 198 pp.; *A Directory of the Members of the Legislative Assembly of Nova Scotia, 1758–1958* (Halifax, 1958), viii + 519 pp.; (notes to) D. C. Harvey, ed., *The Diary of Simeon Perkins, 1780–1789* (Toronto, 1958), lviii + 531 + xvi pp.; (ed., with introduction, notes) *The Diary of Simeon Perkins, 1790–1796* (Toronto, 1961), xliv + 477 pp. (B) "Eighteenth-Century Halifax," *CHA Rep* (1949), 32–9; "The Rise of the Theatre at Halifax," *DR*, 29 (1949/50), 419–27; "Durells in Eighteenth-Century Canadian History," *DR*, 35 (1955/6), 16–30; "Charles Fenerty: The Life and Achievement of a Native of Sackville, Halifax County, N.S." (Halifax, 1955), 15 pp.; "The Origin of Representative Government in Canada," Committee on Bicentenary of Representative Government, Halifax (1958), 47 pp.; "Letters and Papers of Hon. Enos Collins" (Halifax, 1959), 64 pp.; "Mechanics' Institutes in Nova Scotia" (Halifax, 1960), 47 pp.; "The Life of Jonathan Scott" (Halifax, 1960), 63 pp.; "Early Liverpool and Its Diarist" (Halifax, 1961), 54 pp.; "Local Government in Nova Scotia" (Halifax, 1961), 18 pp.   (C) *Collections NS Hist Soc, DR, J Educ of NS.*

MacLean, Guy: (B): "The Canadian Offer of Troops for Hong Kong, 1894," *CHR*, 38 (1957), 275–83; "Yugoslavia: The 'Trojan Horse' of Communism," *Int J*, 13 (1958), 287–97; "Clio and the Tape-Recorder," *Culture*, 19 (1958), 177–81; "The Georgian Affair: An Incident of the American Civil War," *CHR*, 42 (1961), 133–44.   (C) *CHR.*   (D) "Imperial Federation Movement in Canada in the Nineteenth Century" (article, nearly ready for publication).

Waite, P. B.: (A) *The Life and Times of Confederation, 1864–1867* (Toronto, 1962), viii + 379 pp.; (ed.) *The Confederation Debates in the Province of Canada, 1865* (Toronto, 1963), xviii + 157 pp; *The Charlottetown Conference, 1864*, CHA Booklet, 15 (Ottawa, 1963), 28 pp.   (B) "The Struggle of Prerogative and Common Law in the Reign of James I," *CJEPS*, 25 (1959), 144–52; "*Le Courrier du Canada* and the Quebec Resolutions," *CHR*, 40 (1959), 294–303; "Edward Whelan Reports from the Quebec Conference," *CHR*, 42 (1961), 23–45; "Edward Cardwell and Confederation," *CHR*, 43 (1962), 17–41; "A Nova Scotian in Toronto, 1858," *OH*, 55 (1963), 155–9.   (C) *CHR, DR, Enc Amer, QQ.*   (D) Early Travellers in the Maritimes, 1784–1867 (1965); Documents of Canadian History, 1760–1867 (1964); Parliamentary Debates of the Dominion of Canada, 1867–1874 (1965–67); A history of Nova Scotia (1970?).

LAURENTIAN UNIVERSITY

Cadieux, Lorenzo: (A) *De l'aviron à l'avion: Joseph-Marie Couture,* Société historique du Nouvel-Ontario, document historique no 39–40 (Sudbury, 1942, Montreal, 1961), 138 pp.; *Au royaume de Nanabozho*, Société historique du Nouvel-Ontario, document historique no 37 (Sudbury, 1942, 1959); (with E. Comte) *Un héros du Lac Supérieur: Frédéric Baraga,* Société historique du Nouvel-Ontario, document historique no 27 (1954). (B) "Vers un régionalisme gaspésien," *AN*, 8 (1936), 127–30, 166–75, 236–47; "La canalisation du Saint-Laurent," *l'Entr'Aide*, 3 (1935/6); "Fondateurs du diocèse du Sault-Sainte-Marie," Société historique du Nouvel-Ontario (Sudbury, 1944), 47 pp.   (D) Le comte Frederic Romanet du Caillaud, pionnier de Sudbury.

Lemieux, Germain: (A) Société historique du Nouvel-Ontario (Sudbury): *Folklore franco-ontarien—Chansons I & II*, nos 17, 20 (1949, 1950), 48 pp. each; *Contes populaires franco-ontariens I*, no 25 (1953), 40 pp.; *Contes franco-ontariens II*, no 35 (1958), 60 pp.; *Index analytique de 35 documents*, no 36 (1959), 47 pp.   (B) "Folklore et folkloristes," *Relations*, 166 (1954), 280; "Nos paysans sont-ils des savants?" *Droit* (22 juin 1961); "Héritiers des Orientaux," *Droit* (13 juillet 1961); "De l'Egypte au Canada français," *Droit* (28 juillet 1961); "Nos conteurs inventent-ils?" *Droit* (12 août 1961).   (C) *Le Droit, L'Information, Folklore.*   (D) Le conte Placide-Eustache (thesis to be published next June at Les Presses de l'Université Laval); Romancero franco-ontarien (probably the next year).

UNIVERSITÉ LAVAL

GALARNEAU, CLAUDE: (A) *Edmond de Nevers, essayiste,* Cahiers d'Histoire no 2 (Québec, 1960), 95 pp. (B) "Histoire de l'Europe et histoire du Canada. Esquisse pour une histoire de la mentalité religieuse au Canada français," *CHA Rep* (1956), 26–37; "Aperçus sur la vie économique en France au XVIIIᵉ siècle," *Cahiers de l'Académie canadienne-française* (Montréal, 1957), 115–34; "Une lettre de l'abbé Linsolas," publication d'un document avec commentaire critique, *Cahiers d'histoire publiés par les Universités de Clermont-Lyon-Grenoble* (Lyon, 1959), 4, 3; "La Mentalité paysanne en France sous l'ancien régime (XVIᵉ–XVIIIᵉ siècle)," *Rev d'Hist de l'Amerique Française,* 14 (1960), 16–24; "Les Echanges culturels franco-canadiens," *Recherches et débats,* Cahier 34 (Paris, 1961), 68–78. (C) *Recherches Sociographiques, Rev d'Hist de l'Amérique Française, RUL.* (D) La France devant l'opinion publique canadienne, 1760–1860 (travail de recherches à long terme, commencé en 1953 et en bonne voie); histoire des collèges catholiques d'expression française au Canada (pour le compte de la Fondation des Universités Canadiennes.

LAMONTAGNE, LEOPOLD: (A) *La Gaspésie* (Rimouski, 1936), 56 pp.; *Les Archives régimentaires des Fusiliers du Saint-Laurent* (Rimouski, 1943), 244 pp.; (ed., with introduction and notes) *Royal Fort Frontenac* (trans. Richard A. Preston), Champlain Society, Ontario Series, 2 (Toronto, 1958), xxx + 503 pp.; (ed., with notes) *Arthur Buies (1840–1901)* (Montréal et Paris, 1959), 93 pp. (B) "Habits gris et chemise rouge," *CHA Rep* (1950), 20–9; "The Ninth Crusade," *CHR,* 32 (1951), 220–35; "Les poètes franco-canadiens devant les invasions américaines," *Bull de la Soc hist franco-américaine* (1953); "Kingston's French Heritage," *OH,* 45 (1953), 109–21; "Le roi du Nord et sa suite française à Winnipeg en 1885," *CHA Rep* (1954); "Ontario and the Two Races," in Mason Wade, ed., *Canadian Dualism: Studies of French-English Relations* (Toronto and Québec, 1960), xxvi + 427 pp. (C) *Chatelaine, QQ.* (D) Projet, pour 1967, d'une histoire de la littérature canadienne-française (collaboration entre les Universités Laval, de Montréal, et d'Ottawa—président du comité de rédaction).

SANFAÇON, ROLAND: (A) *Tableaux de phonétique historique du français* (Québec, 1962), 82 pp. (B) "Une dépendance de l'abbaye bénédictine de Nouaillé en Poitou: la seigneurie de Jouarenne du VIIIᵉ an XVᵉ siècle," *Bull de la Soc des Antiquaires de l'Ouest,* 6 (1961), 163–211. (C) *Cahiers de Civilisation médiévale, Cahiers de Géog de Québec, Culture, RUO.* (D) Les défrichements en Haut-Poitou du Xᵉ au XIIIᵉ siècle (environ 250 pp., à paraître sous peu).

SAVARD, PIERRE: (B) "Les débuts de l'enseignement de l'histoire et de la géographie au Petit Seminaire de Québec (1765–1830)," *Rev d'Hist de l'Amérique française,* 15 (1961), 509–25, 16 (1962), 43–62, 188–212. (C) *Bull de la Soc des Professeurs d'Hist, Culture, Rev d'Hist de l'Amérique française, Vie française.* (D) La France et les Etats-Unis dans la vie et l'œuvre de Jules-Paul Tardivel (1851–1905) (thèse de doctorat à soutenir en avril 1964).

SYLVAIN, ROBERT: (A) *La vie et l'œuvre de Henry de Courcy (1820–1861), premier historien de l'Eglise catholique aux Etats-Unis* (Québec, 1955), viii + 347 pp.; *Clerc, garibaldien, prédicant des deux mondes: Alessandro Gavazzi (1809–1889)* (2 vols., Québec, 1962), viii + 587 pp.

(B) "Un singulier historien du Canada," *RUL*, 3 (1948), 71–88, 145–66; "Louis XVII vint-il en Amérique?" *RUL*, 3 (1949), 743–61, 857–82; "Gaumisme en vase clos," *RUL*, 4 (1949), 252–7; "Lamartine et les catholiques de France et du Canada," *Rev d'Hist de l'Amérique française*, 4 (1950), 29–61, 233–49, 375–97; "Relations d'Alexis de Tocqueville avec les catholiques américains," *RUL*, 11 (1957), 471–86; "Un 'quarante-huitard' du Risorgimento au Canada," *RUL*, 11 (1957), 759–79, 878–90, continued in 12 (1957), 23–40; "Alessandro Gavazzi à New York," *Rev d'Hist de l'Amérique française*, 11 (1957), 56–92; "Séjour mouvementé d'un révolutionnaire italien à Québec," *Rev d'Hist de l'Amérique française*, 13 (1959), 183–229; "Le 9 juin 1853 à Montréal, encore l'affaire Gavazzi," *Rev d'Hist de l'Amérique française*, 14 (1960), 173–216; "Aperçu sur le prosélytisme protestant au Canada français de 1760 à 1860," *Mémoires et comptes-rendus de la Société royale du Canada*, 55 (1961), 65–77.   (C) *Rev d'Hist de l'Amérique française, RUL.*   (D) Histoire du protestantisme canadien-français, des origines à nos jours (encore deux ans avant d'être prêt à publier le résultat des recherches); La querelle des classiques paiens et chrétiens au Canada ou les origines de l'ultramontanisme québecois (devrait pouvoir être publiée dans environ un an).

MCGILL UNIVERSITY

BAYLEY, CHARLES CALVERT: (A) *The Formation of the German College of Electors in the Mid-Thirteenth Century* (Toronto, 1949), x + 237 pp.; *War and Society in Renaissance Florence: The "De Militia" of Leonardo Bruni* (Toronto, 1961), viii + 440 pp.   (C) *AHR, CHR, Speculum.* (D) (with J. I. Cooper) The Foreign Legions in the Crimean War (MS. completed).

MLADENOVIC, MILOS: (A) *L'Etat Serbe au Moyen-Age: son caractère* (Paris, 1931), 222 pp.   (B) "The Osmanli Conquest and Islamization of Bosnia," *SEES*, 4 (1959), 210–28; "Die Herrschaft der Osmanen in Serbien im Lichte der Sprache," *Südost-Forschungen*, 20 (1961), 159–208; "Turkic Language Influence upon the Balkan Slavs," *SEES*, 7 (1962), 13–22.   (C) *SEES, Südost-Forschungen.*   (D) Economic and social conditions of the Christians in the Balkans under the Ottoman Rule according to the British Consular Reports (about half ready); War and Society in Russia.

REID, W. STANFORD: (A) *The Church of Scotland in Lower Canada* (Toronto, 1936), 190 pp.; *Economic History of Great Britain* (New York, 1954), x + 557 pp.; *Problems in European Intellectual History* (Montreal, 2nd rev. ed., 1958), 120 pp.; "The Triumph of the Reformation in Scotland," in *Reformed and Reforming* (Toronto, 1960), vi + 99 pp.; *The Scottish Reformation* (Toronto, 1960), 38 pp.; *Skipper from Leith: The History of Robert Barton of Over Barnton* (Philadelphia, 1962), 334 pp. (B) "The Lollards in Pre-Reformation Scotland," *CH* (Dec., 1942); "Scotland and the Church Councils of the Fifteenth Century," *Cath Hist R*, 28 (1943), 1–24; "The Origins of Anti-Papal Legislation in Fifteenth-Century Scotland," *Cath Hist R*, 29 (1944), 445–69; "The Douglasses at the Court of James X of Scotland," *Juridical R* (Edinb., Aug., 1944); "The Scottish

Counter-Reformation before 1560," *CH*, 14 (1945), 104–25; "Lutheranism in the Scottish Reformation," *Westminster Theol J* (May, 1945); "The Papacy and the Scottish War of Independence," *Cath Hist R*, 31 (1945), 282–301; "The Place of Denmark in Scottish Foreign Policy, 1470–1540," *Juridical R* (Dec., 1946); "An Early French Canadian Pension Agreement," *CHR*, 27 (1946), 291–4; "The Middle Class Factor in the Scottish Reformation," *CH*, 16 (1947), 137–53; "The Habitant's Standard of Living on the Seigneurie des Mille Isles, 1820–1850," *CHR*, 28 (1947), 266–78; "Clerical Taxation: The Scottish Alternative to Dissolution of the Monasteries, 1530–1560," *Cath Hist R*, 34 (1948), 129–53; "Robert Barton of Over Barnton, A Scottish Merchant of the Sixteenth Century," *MH* (1948), 46–61; "A Sixteenth-Century Marriage Contract between Sir James Sandilands of Calder and Robert Barton of Over Barnton," *Scottish Hist R*, 28 (1949), 58–62; "The Christian in the World, A Facet of Calvin's Thought," *Gordon R* (May, 1951); "The Stone of Scone: Fact or Fiction?" *DR*, 33 (1953), 50–9; "Trade, Traders, and Scottish Independence," *Speculum*, 29 (1954), 210–22; "Calvin and the Founding of the Academy of Geneva," *Westminster Theol J* (Nov., 1955); "Calvin's Interpretation of the Reformation," *Evangelical Q* (March, 1957); "The English Stimulus to Scottish Nationalism, 1286–1370," *DR*, 38 (1958), 189–206; "The Protestant Reformation: Third Dimension in Western Civilization," *Gordon R* (Jan., 1958); "The Scots and the English Wool Staple Ordinance of 1313," *Speculum*, 34 (1959), 598–610; "Historical Materialism: Empirical or Metaphysical," *Gordon R*, 5 (1959), 35–45; "The Settlement of a Canadian Seigneurie (1760–1855)," *Educ Record*, 85 (1959), 118–23; "Calvin and the Political Order," in Jacob T. Hoogstra, ed., *John Calvin, Contemporary Prophet* (Grand Rapids, Mich., 1959), 243–57; "The University's Social Task," *Free UQ*, (1959), 253–61; "Sea-Power in the Anglo-Scottish Wars, 1296–1328," *Mariner's Mirror* (Jan., 1960); "Historical Factors in the Development of Canadian Nationalism," *JRSA*, 109 (1961), 468–75. (D) At present working on the problem of social patterns and their relationship to the Reformation, with particular reference to Scotland: a study of the changes in class structure prior to 1560 and its influence on the Reformation being prepared; study of the relationship between Calvinism and sixteenth-century scientific thought.

MCMASTER UNIVERSITY

EVANS, JAMES A. S.: (A) *A Social and Economic History of an Egyptian Temple in the Greco-Roman Period*, Yale Classical Studies, 17 (New Haven, 1961), 143–283. (B) (with C. Bradford Welles) "The Archives of Leon," *J of Juristic Papyrology*, 7–8 (1953/4), 29–70; "Herodotus and the Gyges Drama," *Athenaeum*, 33 (1955), 333–6; "Cyprus," *Can For*, 35 (1955), 155, 157–8; "Cyprus in Hazard," *QQ*, 63 (1956), 366–74; "The Poll-Tax in Egypt," *Aegyptus*, 37 (1957), 259–65; "Athens, 1958," *Can For*, 38 (1958), 102–4; "The O'Leary Report," *Can For*, 41 (1961), 97–8; "Enter General Walker," *Can For*, 41 (1962), 267–8; "The Strange Case of Billy Sol Estes," *Can For*, 42 (1962), 80–2; "The Classical Tradition in Ontario Architecture," *Can Geog J* (Feb., 1962), 66–9; "Notes on Miltiades' Capture of Lemnos," *CP*, 58 (1963), 168–9. (C) *CJ, Classical World*, (literary ed.)

Can Commentator, Can For, (editor) *Vergilius.* (D) "Histiaeus and Aristagoras, Notes on the Ionian Revolt" (to appear in *AJP* in 1963); "Tyrtaios, Frag. 8, 1–2" (to appear in *Glotta*); (trans.) Sallust, *Catilinian Conspiracy* and *War with Jugurtha,* fragments of histories (partly completed).

JOHNSTON, CHARLES M.: (A) *The Head of the Lake: a History of Wentworth County* (Hamilton, 1958), 345 pp. (B) "An Outline of Early Settlement in the Grand River Valley," *OH,* 54 (1962), 43–67. (D) "Joseph Brant, the Grand River Lands, and the Northwest Crisis" (to be published shortly); The Valley of the Confederacy: The Indian Lands on the Grand River (volume VII in the Champlain Society's Ontario Series.

MCNEAL, ROBERT H.: (A) (comp.) *The Russian Revolution: Why Did the Bolsheviks Win?* (New York and Toronto, 1959), 62 pp.; *The Bolshevik Tradition: Lenin, Stalin, Khrushchev* (Toronto, 1963); (ed.) *Voices of Bolshevism: Lenin, Stalin, Khrushchev* (Toronto, 1963); (trans.) S. G. Pushkarev's *The Emergence of Modern Russia* (Toronto, 1963). (B) "Soviet Historiography on the October Revolution: A Review of Forty Years," *ASEER,* 17 (1958), 269–81; "Lenin's Attack on Stalin: Review and Reappraisal," *ASEER,* 18 (1959); "Khrushchev and Clio," *Int J,* 15 (1960), 49–58; "Trotsky's Interpretation of Stalin," *CSP,* 5 (1961), 87–97; "Stalin's Conception of Soviet Federalism," *Annals of the Ukrainian Acad of Sc in the US*; "The Conference of Jassy: An Early Fiasco of the Anti-Bolshevik Movement," in John S. Curtiss, ed., *Essays in Russian and Soviet History* (New York, 1963); "Roosevelt through Stalin's Spectacles," *Int J,* 18 (1963), 194–206. (D) An Annotated Bibliography of the Works of J. V. Stalin (should be finished this year for publication in bibliographical series of the Hoover Institution).

SALMON, EDWARD TOGO: (A) *A History of the Roman World from 30 B.C. to A.D. 138* (New York and London, 5th reprinting, 4th ed., 1963), xiv + 363 pp. (B) Over 80 articles on Roman history in *Oxford Classical Dictionary* (Oxford, 1949); over 20 articles on the Roman Republic in *Collier's Enc* (1962); over 140 articles on the Roman Empire in the *Grolier Enc*; "Sulmo Mihi Patria Est," in Niculae I. Herescu's *Ovidiana* (Paris, 1958), 3–20; "Strategy of the Second Punic War," *Greece and Rome,* 7 (1960), 131–42; "The End of Roman Imperialism," *Austral Hum Res Council,* Occasional Paper No. 4 (1961), 13 pp.; "Cause of the Social War," *Phoenix,* 16 (1962), 107–19; "The *Coloniae Maritimae*," *Athenaeum,* 41 (1963), 20. (C) *AJP, CP, JRS, Phoenix.* (D) A book on Samnium and the Samnites (first draft almost finished).

TRUEMAN, JOHN H.: (A) *The Enduring Past* (Toronto, 1959), x + 517 pp.; *Britain, the Growth of Freedom* (Toronto and Vancouver, 1960), x + 444 pp. (B) "The Statute of York and the Ordinances of 1311," *MH,* 10 (1956), 64–81; "The Privy Seal and the English Ordinances of 1311," *Speculum,* 31 (1956), 611–25; "The Personnel of Mediaeval Reform: The English Lords Ordainers of 1310," *MS,* 21 (1959), 247–71.

UNIVERSITY OF MANITOBA

FROST, RICHARD H.: (C) *CHR.* (D) The Mooney Case (two-thirds completed: to be published in 1965).

MCEWEN, J. M.: (B) "The Coupon Election of 1918 and Unionist Members of Parliament," *J Mod Hist*, 34 (1962), 294–306. (C) *J Mod Hist*. (D) "Canadians at Westminster, 1900–1950" (article, near completion); "Liberal M.P.'s in the British Parliament of 1906" (article, most of the material gathered, no writing done as yet).

MORTON, W. L.: (A) (ed.) *The Voice of Dafoe* (Toronto, 1945), xxvi + 293 pp.; (with Margaret Morton Fahrni) *Third Crossing: A History of the First Quarter Century of the Town and District of Gladstone in the Province of Manitoba* (Winnipeg, 1946), x + 118 pp.; *The Progressive Party in Canada* (Toronto, 1950), xiv + 331 pp.; (ed.) *Alexander Begg's Red River Journal & Other Papers Relative to the Red River Resistance of 1869–1870* (Toronto, 1956), xxiv + 636 pp.; (introduction) E. E. Rich and A. M. Johnson, eds., *London Correspondence Inward from Eden Colvile, 1849–1852* (London, 1956), cxvi + 300 pp.; *One University: A History of the University of Manitoba, 1877–1952* (Toronto, 1957), 200 pp.; *Manitoba: A History* (Toronto, 1957), xii + 519 pp.; *The Canadian Identity* (Madison, Wis., 1961), 125 pp.; (with Margaret A. MacLeod) *Cuthbert Grant of Grantown: Warden of the Plains of Red River* (Toronto, 1963), xiv + 174 pp.; *The Kingdom of Canada* (Toronto, 1963), 556 pp. (B) "The Red River Parish: Its Place in the Development of Manitoba," in University of Manitoba, *Manitoba Essays* (Toronto, 1937), 89–105; "Canada and the World Tomorrow: Opportunity and Responsibility" (Toronto, 1943), 65 pp.; "Building Post-War Canada" (Toronto, 1943), 72 pp.; "The Extension of the Franchise in Canada," *CHA Rep* (1943), 72–81; "Prepare for Peace: Canadian Foreign and Domestic Policy after the War" (Toronto, 1944), 39 pp.; "Direct Legislation and the Origins of the Progressive Movement," *CHR*, 25 (1944), 279–88; "Behind Dumbarton Oaks" (Toronto, 1945), 28 pp.; "Canada and Future Policy in the Pacific," *Int J*, 1 (1946), 55–64; "Clio in Canada: The Interpretation of Canadian History," *UTQ*, 15 (1946), 227–34; "The Western Progressive Movement and Cabinet Domination," *CJEPS*, 12 (1946), 136–47; "Marginal," *MAR*, 5 (1946), 26–31; "The Western Progressive Movement, 1919–1921," *CHA Rep* (1946), 41–55; "Canada's Far Eastern Policy," *Pacific Aff*, 19 (1946), 241–9; "The Social Philosophy of Henry Wise Wood, the Canadian Agrarian Leader," *Ag Hist*, 22 (1948), 114–23; "Agriculture in the Red River Colony," *CHR*, 39 (1949), 305–21; "The Significance of Site in the Settlement of the American and Canadian Wests," *Ag Hist*, 25 (1951), 97–104; "Manitoba Schools and Canadian Nationalism, 1890–1916," *CHA Rep* (1951), 51–9; "A Note on Palliser's Act," *CHR*, 34 (1953), 33–8; "The Formation of the First Federal Cabinet," *CHR*, 36 (1955), 113–25; "Canada, 1841–1931," *Current Hist* (July, 1955), 38–44; "The Bias of Prairie Politics," *TRSC*, 3rd series, 49 (1955), s. 2, 57–66; "The West and Confederation, 1857–1871," CHA Booklet, 9 (Ottawa, 1958), 19 pp.; "The History of Canada," *Enc Br* (1959); "The Art of Narrative," *Culture*, 20 (1959), 391–402; "The North in Canadian History," *Northern Aff Bull*, 7 (1960), 26–9; "British North America and a Continent in Dissolution, 1861–71," *History*, 47 (1962), 139–56. (C) *AHR, Can For, CHR, CJEPS, Culture, DR, EHR, History, QQ, UTQ*. (D) The Union of British America, 1857–1873 (half written).

OLESON, TRYGGVI, J.: (A) *Saga Islendinga í Vesturheimi* (History of the Icelanders in the Western Hemisphere), 4, 5 (Reykjavik, 1951, 1953), viii + 423 pp., viii + 480 pp.; *The Witenagemot in the Reign of Edward the Confessor* (Toronto, 1955), x + 187 pp.; *Early Voyages and Northern Approaches, 1000–1632* (Toronto, 1964), xii + 211 pp. (B) "The Literature of Iceland, 1000–1550," *Icelandic Canadian*, 1 (1943), 8–12, 2 (1943), 12–15; "Icelandic Pioneers in the Argyle District," *Icelandic Canadian*, 5 (1947), 5–8, 40–6; "Newfoundland," *Icelandic Canadian*, 7 (1949), 12–15; "Polar Bears in the Middle Ages," *CHR*, 31 (1950), 47–55; "Bishop Jon Arason," *Icelandic Canadian*, 9 (1951), 9–12, 41–6; "Hver er Mauttull sá?" (On the Image of Edessa), *Timarit*, 34 (1952), 53–6; "Bishop Jón Arason, 1484 –1550," *Speculum*, 28 (1953), 245–78; "A Note on Bishop Jón Arason," *Speculum*, 29 (1954), 535–6; "The Vikings in America—Some Problems and Recent Literature," *CHA Rep* (1954), 52–60; "Giraldus Cambrensis and Iceland," *Icelandic Canadian*, 12 (1954), 31–3; (trans.) K. Eldjarn's "The Chests of King Athelstan," *Icelandic Canadian*, 13 (1954), 14–19, (trans.) K. Eldjarn's "Valley of the Eastmen—A Mediaeval Settlement in Greenland," *Icelandic Canadian*, 13 (1954), 28–38; "The Vikings in America: A Critical Bibliography," *CHR*, 36 (1955), 166–73; "A Renaissance Fragment in Iceland," *RN*, 9 (1956), 192–4; "Edward the Confessor's Promise of the Throne to Duke William of Normandy," *EHR*, 72 (1957), 221–8; "Book Collections of Mediaeval Icelandic Churches," *Speculum*, 32 (1957), 502–10; "Book Donors in Mediaeval Iceland," *Nordisk Tidskrift för Bok'och Biblioteksväsen*, 44 (1957), 88–94, and 48 (1961), 10–22; "Römm er su taug," *Icelandic Canadian*, 16 (1958), 12–16; "Book Collections of Icelandic Churches in the Fourteenth Century," *Nordisk Tidskrift för Bok'och Biblioteksväsen*, 46 (1959), 111–23; (trans., with H. Thorgrimson) K. Eldjarn's "The Silver Hoard from Gaulverjaber," *Icelandic Canadian*, 18 (1959), 11–13, 37–41; "Edward the Confessor in History," *TRSC*, 3rd series, 53 (1959), s. 2, 27–35; "Book Collections of Icelandic Churches in the Fifteenth Century," *Nordisk Tidskrift för Bok'och Biblioteksväsen*, 47 (1960), 90–103; "þankar um Játvarð góða" (Reflections on Edward the Confessor), *Timarit*, 41 (1960), 41–8; "Bishop Gottskalk's Children," *Studia Islandica*, 18 (1960), 39–51; "The Viking Spirit," *Icelandic Canadian*, 19 (1960); "Pjóðsögur a pjóðsögur ofan" (Myths and More Myths), *Andvari*, 87 (1962), 107–12.

UPTON, L. F. S.: (A) (ed.) *The Diary and Selected Papers of Chief Justice Smith, 1784–1793*, I, *The Diary, January 24, 1784 to October 5, 1785* (Toronto, 1963), lvi + 295 + xv pp. (C) *CHR*. (D) Life of Chief Justice William Smith (being translated into French); The Diary and Selected Papers of William Smith, 1784–1793, vol. 2 (approaching final typescript form).

WEBSTER, T. S.: (D) Napoleon and Canada (Ph.D. thesis reworked, will be submitted to a publisher in December, 1962).

MEMORIAL UNIVERSITY OF NEWFOUNDLAND

ROTHNEY, GORDON OLIVER: (A) *Newfoundland: From International Fishery to Canadian Province*, CHA Historical Booklet, 10 (Ottawa, 1959),

28 pp. (B) "The Case of Bayne and Brymer: An Incident in the Early History of Labrador," *CHR*, 15 (1934), 264–75; "Quebec's Liberal Reveille," *Can For*, 20 (1940), 108–9; "Parties and Profits," *Can For*, 22 (1942), 204–6; "Leave Quebec Alone," *Can For*, 22 (1942), 178–80 (French tr., Montréal, 1942); (trans.) Lionel Groulx "Why We Are Divided," *AN* (Montréal, 1943), 32 pp.; "Canada Pattern for World Peace," *AN*, 26 (1945), 411–20; "Quebec: Watchful Waiting," *Can For*, 24 (1945), 254–6; "Quebec Saves Our King," *Can For*, 25 (1945), 83–4; "A Liberal Decade," *Can For*, 25 (1945), 203–4; "Les Vainqueurs [1760]," *AN*, 28 (1946), 289–307; "Newfoundland," *Enc Can*, 7 (Ottawa), 305–20; "Bilingual Canada and the World," *Culture*, 7 (1946), 129–39; "The Denominational Basis of Representation in the Newfoundland Assembly, 1919–1962," *CJEPS*, 28 (1962), 557–70. (C) *AN, Can For, CHR, CJEPS, Culture, Devoir, Int J, Rev d'Hist de l'Amérique française.* (D) History of Newfoundland (partially completed); Our World (a school history of the twentieth century, possible completion in twelve months).

SCHWARZ, G. M.: (B) "Deutschland und Westeuropa bei Ernst Troeltsch," *Historische Zeitschrift*, 191 (1960), 510–47. (C) *Historische Zeitschrift, J of Int Aff, Oxoniensia.* (D) A study of neo-liberalism in German social policy, 1871–1914 (initial stages, main thesis blocked out); biography of Chancellor Bethman-Hollweg (initial stages); a reinterpretation of social and political developments in nineteenth-century Germany (note-collecting stage).

MOUNT ALLISON UNIVERSITY

LOCKWOOD, P. A.: (D) "Milner's Entry into the War Cabinet, December 1916" (accepted for publication in the *Cambridge Hist J* for 1963); "A Sketch of British Politics 1906–26" (article, being written); the British Workers' League, an episode in British Labour politics (work begun).

UNIVERSITY OF NEW BRUNSWICK

BAILEY, ALFRED GOLDSWORTHY: (A) *The Conflict of European and Eastern Algonkian Cultures, 1504–1700: A Study in Canadian Civilization* (Saint John, 1937), 206 pp. (B) "Social Revolution in Early Eastern Canada," *CHR*, 19 (1938), 264–76; "Railways and the Confederation Issue in New Brunswick, 1863–1865," *CHR*, 21 (1940), 367–83; "The Basis and Persistence of Opposition to Confederation in New Brunswick," *CHR*, 23 (1942), 374–97; "Creative Moments in the Culture of the Maritime Provinces," *DR*, 29 (1949), 231–44; "Toynbee and the Problem of Climaxes in the Development of the Fine Arts," *TRSC*, 3rd series, 29 (1955), s. 2, 13–21; "Literature and Nationalism after Confederation," *UTQ*, 25 (1956), 409–24. (C) *CHR.* (D) The Canada First Movement (all material collected, but the writing less than half completed).

CHAPMAN, J. K.: (A) *The Career of Arthur Hamilton Gordon, First Lord Stanmore, 1829–1912* (Toronto, 1964), x + 387 pp. (B) "The Mid-nineteenth-century Temperance Movement in New Brunswick and Maine," *CHR*, 35 (1954), 43–60; "Arthur Gordon and Confederation," *CHR*, 37 (1956), 141–7.

CONDON, THOMAS J.: (B) "Politics, Reform, and the New York City

Election of 1886," *NY Hist Soc Q*, 44 (1960), 363–93; "New York's Dutch Period: An Interpretive Problem," *Halve Maen*, 26 (1961), 7–15. (C) *NEQ*.

MacNutt, W. S.: (A) *Days of Lorne*, from the private papers of the Marquis of Lorne 1878–1883 in the possession of the Duke of Argyll at Inveraray Castle, Scotland (Fredericton, 1955), x + 262 pp.; *The Making of the Maritime Provinces, 1713–1784*, CHA Historical Booklet, 4 (Ottawa, 1955), 20 pp.; *New Brunswick; A History, 1784–1867* (Toronto, 1963), xvi + 496 pp. (B) "Why Halifax Was Founded," *DR*, 12 (1932), 524–32; "The Beginnings of Nova Scotian Politics, 1758–1766," *CHR*, 16 (1935), 41–53; "The Politics of the Timber Trade in Colonial New Brunswick, 1825–1840," *CHR*, 30 (1949), 47–65; "New Brunswick's Age of Harmony: The Administration of Sir John Harvey," *CHR*, 32 (1951), 105–25; "The Coming of Responsible Government to New Brunswick," *CHR*, 33 (1952), 111–28; "New England's Tory Neighbours," Colonial Soc. of Massachusetts (April, 1959). (C) *CHR, DR, QQ*. (D) The Atlantic Provinces, 1713–1867 (vol. 8, Canadian Centenary Series) (commenced, to be published in 1966).

Young, Douglas MacMurray: (A) *The Colonial Office in the Early Nineteenth Century* (London, 1961), x + 310 pp.

QUEEN'S UNIVERSITY

Gundy, H. P.: (A) *Early Printers and Printing in the Canadas* (Toronto, 1957), 63 pp. (B) "Sir Wilfrid Laurier and Lord Minto," *CHA Rep* (1952), 28–38; "Molly Brant—Loyalist," *OH*, 45 (1953), 69–72; "A Kingston Surgeon in the American Civil War," *Historic Kingston*, 7 (1958), 64–7; "The Bliss Carman Centenary," *Douglas Lib Notes*, 10 (1961), 1–16; "A National Library for Canada—a Record and a Promise," *Can Lib*, 17 (1961), 170–7; "Publishing and Bookselling in Kingston since 1810," *Historic Kingston*, 10 (1962), 22–36; "Lorne Pierce: Friend and Benefactor," *Douglas Lib Notes*, 11 (1962), 1–6. (C) *Douglas Lib Notes, OH, QQ*. (D) Editing a work on publishing and bookselling in Canada sponsored by the Canadian Book Publishers' Council for possible publication in fall of 1963.

Leith, James A.: (B) "The Idea of Art as Propaganda during the French Revolution," *CHA Rep* (1959), 30–43. (C) *CHR, Fr Hist St.* (D) The Idea of Art as Propaganda in France 1750–1799 (MS. accepted for publication); a study of educational theories in France on the eve of the French Revolution (begun).

Lower, A. R. M.: (A) (with F. R. Scott, *et al.*) *Evolving Canadian Federalism* (Durham, N.C., 1958), xvi + 187 pp.; (ed., with H. A. Innis) *Select Documents in Canadian Economic History, 1783–1885* (Toronto, 1933), 846 pp.; *The Trade in Square Timber* (Toronto, 1933), pp. 40–61; *Settlement and the Forest Frontier in Eastern Canada* (with H. A. Innis's *Settlement and the Mining Frontier* in *Canadian Frontiers of Settlement*, 9) (Toronto, 1936), 424 pp.; (with W. A. Carrothers and S. A. Saunders) *The North American Assault on the Canadian Forest* (Toronto, 1938), xxviii + 377 pp.; *Canada and the Far East—1940* (New York, 1940), x + 152 pp.; *Colony to Nation; A History of Canada* (Toronto, 1946), 600 pp.

(new ed., Toronto, 1947; 3rd ed., Toronto, 1957, xxxii + 600 pp.); *Canada, Nation and Neighbour* (Toronto, 1952), 202 pp.; *Canadians in the Making: A Social History of Canada* (Toronto, 1958), 475 pp.   (B) "Determinism in Politics," *CHR*, 27 (1946), 233–48; "Two Ways of Life: The Spirit of Our Institutions," *CHR*, 28 (1947), 383–400; "Canada and the New, non-British World," *Int J*, 3 (1948), 208–21; "Europe Is Still Alive," *QQ*, 57 (1950), 1–20; "West and Western Germany," *Int J*, 6 (1951), 300–7; "The Canadian University," *TRSC*, 3rd series, 47 (1953), s. 2, 1–16; "Political 'Partyism' in Canada," *CHA Rep* (1955), 88–95; "Time, Myth, and Fact: The Historian's Commodities," *QQ*, 64 (1957), 241–9; "Canadians in the Making: A Social History of Canada" (Toronto, 1958), 475 pp.; "Some Angry Home Thoughts from Abroad," *Maclean's Mag*, 73 (1960), 10, 51–2; "The Growth of Population in Canada," *TRSC*, 3rd series, s. 2 (1961); "The Social Responsibilities of the Business Man," *University of Western Ontario Business Q*; "How Good are Canadian Universities?" *CAUT Bull* (fall, 1962); "Speaking to Each Other—En parlant l'un à l'autre," *TRSC*, 3rd series, s. 2 (1962); "Queen's, Yesterday and Today," *QQ*, 70 (1963), 69–75.   (C) *CHR, CJEPS, Maclean's Mag, QQ*.   (D) Elusive Quarry (a book on the English speaking or 'old' members of the Commonwealth; (MS. complete, but requiring much revision); It Was Not Too Unbearable (200 pp. completed on a species of autobiography).

PIERCE, RICHARD A.: (A) *Russian Central Asia, 1867–1917: A Selected Bibliography* (Berkeley, Calif., 1953), ii + 28 pp.; *Russian Central Asia, 1867–1917: A Study in Colonial Rule* (Berkeley, Calif., 1960), viii + 359 pp.; (with A. S. Donnelly) *Cities of Central Asia* (London, 1961).   (B) "Source Materials on a Project for Russian Colonization in South America (1735–1737)," *Calif Slavic Papers*, 1 (1960), 189–96; "Bulgaria," "Czechoslovakia," "Hungary," "Romania," "Yugoslavia," "Albania," for *Collier's Yearbook* (1958–62).   (C) *Can Hist J, QQ*.   (D) Soviet Rule in Central Asia (book slated for completion in late 1963).

ROYAL MILITARY COLLEGE

PRESTON, R. A.: (A) (with G. F. G. Stanley) *A Short History of Kingston as a Naval and Military Centre* (Kingston, 1950); *Gorges of Plymouth Fort: The Life of Sir Ferdinando Gorges* (Toronto, 1953), 495 pp.; (with S. F. Wise and H. O. Werner) *Men in Arms: A History of the Inter-relationship of Warfare and Western Society* (New York, 1956) (2nd ed., 1962), viii + 406 pp.; (ed., with L. Lamontagne) *Royal Fort Frontenac* (Toronto, 1958), xxx + 503 pp.; (ed.) *Kingston Before the War of 1812* (Toronto, 1959), cxvi + 428 pp.   (B) "Gibraltar, Colony and Fortress," *CHR*, 27 (1946), 402–23; "Sir William Keith's Justification of a Stamp Duty in the Colonies, 1739–42," *CHR*, 29 (1948), 168–82; "William Blathwayt and the Evolution of a Royal Personal Secretariat," *History*, 34 (1949), 28–43; "The Laconia Company of 1629: An English Attempt to Intercept the Fur Trade," *CHR*, 31 (1950), 125–44; "The Fate of Kingston's Warships," *OH*, 44 (1952), 85–100; "The History of the Port of Kingston," *OH*, 46 (1954), 201–11, 47 (1955), 23–38; "NATO—a New Departure in International Politics," *QQ*, 65 (1958), 365–77; "Broad

Pennants on Point Frederick," *OH*, 50 (1958), 81–90; "Can We Disarm?" Canadian Institute of International Affairs, Headline Booklets (Jan., 1958); "Presidential Address," *CHA Rep* (1962), 1–16. (C) *AHR, Army Q, Austral Army Q, Can Commentator, CHA Rep, CHR, Can Army J, Crow's Nest, DR, Enc Br, Enc Can, Historic Kingston, History, Int J, Mariner's Mirror, Military Aff, OH, Proc of the US Naval Inst, QQ, RCAF Roundel, RCAF Staff J, RMC of Can R, Sask H, UTQ.* (D) A history of the origin, development and operation of Commonwealth defence relationships.

SCHURMAN, DONALD M.: (B) "Esquimalt: Defence Problem," *BC Hist Q* (Jan.-April, 1955); (comp., with Brian Tunstall, P. M. Stanford) *Catalogue of the Corbett Papers* (Bedford, 1958); "King George Sound and Imperial Defence, 1870–1887," *U St in Western Austral Hist* (Oct., 1959); "Some Thoughts on Albert Camus," *QQ* (autumn, 1961); "Historical Materials and Comment," *Ontario Churchman* (Nov., 1962–May, 1963); "The Arrival of Archbishops in the Canadian Church," *Can Church Hist Soc J* (April, 1963); "Mutiny," *Enc Br* (Jan., 1963). (C) *CHR*, (ed.) *Ontario Churchman, QQ.* (D) The Pens behind the Fleet (a history of naval historians, MS. complete); articles on the Battles of Alma, Balaclava, Blenheim, Inkerman, Dettingen, Dunes, Malplaquet, Plassey, accepted by *Enc Br.*

STANLEY, GEORGE F. G.: (A) *The Birth of Western Canada: A History of the Riel Rebellions* (London, 1936) (2nd ed., Toronto, 1960, reprinted, 1963), xiv + 475 pp.; *Canada's Soldiers: The Military History of an Unmilitary People* (Toronto, 1954) (2nd ed., 1960), 449 pp.; *In Search of the Magnetic North: A Soldier-Surveyor's Letters from the North-West* (Toronto, 1955), xxviii + 171 pp.; *In the Face of Danger: The History of the Lake Superior Regiment* (Port Arthur, 1960), 357 pp.; (ed.) *For Want of a Horse: Being a Journal of the Campaigns against the Americans in 1776 and 1777 conducted from Canada* (Sackville, N.B., 1961), x + 194 pp.; *Louis Riel* (Toronto, 1963), 433 pp. (B) "Act or Pact," *CHA Rep* (1956), 1–25; "Louis Riel, Patriot or Rebel?" CHA Historical Booklet, 2 (Ottawa, 1954), 24 pp.; "French and English in Western Canada," in Mason Wade, ed., *Canadian Dualism: Studies of French-English Relations* (Toronto and Québec, 1960), 311–50; "The Canadian Militia during the War of 1812," in Philip P. Mason, ed., *After Tippecanoe: Some Aspects of the War of 1812* (Detroit and Toronto, 1963), 28–48. (C) *Beaver, CHR, OH, QQ, Rev d'Hist de l'Amérique française,* various encyclopedias. (D) The War of 1812 (in process of reading, making notes, and gathering data).

THOMPSON, FREDERIC F.: (A) *The French Shore Problem in Newfoundland, an Imperial Study* (Toronto, 1961), 222 pp. (B) "A Chapter of Early Methodism in the Kingston Area," *Historic Kingston*, 6 (1957), 32–45; "Reflections upon Education in the Midland District, 1810–1816," *Historic Kingston*, 11 (1963), 8–20.

ST. FRANCIS XAVIER UNIVERSITY

MACDONELL, MALCOLM: (B) "The Early History of St. Francis Xavier University," *Can Cath Hist Ass Rep* (1947), 81–90.

SAINT MARY'S UNIVERSITY, HALIFAX

BÓBR-TYLINGO, STANISLAW: (B) "Napoléon III et le problème polonais, 1830–1859," *Rev Int d'Hist politique et constitutionelle*, 19 (1955), 259–80; "La France et les rapports polono-russes 1860–62," *Antemurale*, 4 (1958), 91–135; "Napoléon III et la question polonaise, 1860–62," *Politique Rev Int des Doctrines et des Institutions* (avril-juin 1959), 165–81; "L'attentat de Berezowski, le 6 juin 1867," *Antemurale*, 6 (1960/61), 159–93.   (C) *Antemurale, Bellona, SEES, Teki Historyczne.*   (D) "Napoléon III, l'Europe et la Pologne en 1863" (for *Antemurale*).

HEALEY, J. E.: (B) "The Alliance of John of Gaunt and John Wyclif: A Revision," *Can Cath Hist Ass Rep* (1962).   (D) Church-state relations in later medieval England.

UNIVERSITY OF SASKATCHEWAN

FRY, M. G.: (B) "The Grand Army and the Invasion of Russia," *History Today*, 10 (1960), 255–65.   (C) *CHR*.   (D) Completing doctoral thesis: Anglo-American-Canadian Relations with Special Reference to Far Eastern and Naval Issues 1916–22.

GRAHAM, WILLIAM ROGER: (A) *Arthur Meighen: A Biography*, I, *The Door of Opportunity, 1874–1920* (Toronto, 1960), ix + 341 pp.; II, *And Fortune Fled* (Toronto, 1963), viii + 535 pp.   (B) "Sir Richard Cartwright, Wilfrid Laurier, and Liberal Party Trade Policy, 1887," *CHR*, 33 (1952), 1–18; "Arthur Meighen and the Conservative Party in Quebec: The Election of 1925," *CHR*, 36 (1955), 17–35; "Meighen and the Montreal Tycoons: Railway Policy in the Election of 1921," *CHA Rep* (1957), 71–85; "Some Comments on a Credible Canadian," *CHR*, 39 (1958), 296–311.   (C) *CHR*.   (D) Third volume of Meighen biography, to be published in 1964.

LAMBI, IVO N.: (A) *Free Trade and Protection in Germany, 1868–1879* (Wiesbaden, 1963), 269 pp.   (B) "The Agrarian-Industrial Front in Bismarckian Politics, 1873–1879," *JCEA*, 20 (1961), 378–96; "The Protectionist Interests of the German Iron and Steel Industry," *J Economic Hist*, 22 (1962), 59–70.   (C) *CHR, JCEA, J Mod Hist*.   (D) A major work on the role of economic and military considerations in European diplomacy, 1870–1914 (two years of research done; four or five years' more work yet to do).

MARSH, PETER: (D) A book on controversies about the character of the Church of England, 1868–74 (awaits final revision); "The Threat of Disestablishment of the Church of England, 1868–74" (an article, to be submitted early in 1963).

MITCHELL, HARVEY: (B) "Francis Drake and the Comte d'Antraiques: A Study of the Dropmore Bulletins, 1793–1796," *Bull Inst of Hist Res*, 29 (1956), 123–44; "Archives of Newfoundland," *Amer Archivist*, 21 (1958), 43–53; "The Constitutional Crisis of 1889 in Newfoundland," *CJEPS*, 24 (1958), 323–31; "Vendémiaire, a Revaluation," *J Mod Hist*, 30 (1958), 191–202; "A New Look at Canada's Negotiations with Newfoundland, 1887–1895," *CHR*, 40 (1959), 277–93; "Introduction: To Commission or not to Commission," *Can J Public Administration* (Sept., 1962), 253–60.

(D) Britain's Underground War against Revolutionary France (a book, to be submitted for publication in 1963).

THOMAS, LEWIS H.: *The Struggle for Responsible Government in the North-West Territories, 1870–97* (Toronto, 1956), viii + 276 pp.; *The University of Saskatchewan, 1909–1959* (Saskatoon, 1959), 64 pp. (B) "The Saskatchewan Legislative Building and Its Predecessors," *J Roy Archit Inst of Can* (July, 1955), 248–52; "The Hind and Dawson Expeditions 1857–58," *Beaver*, 289 (1958), 39–45. (C) *Beaver, CHR, QQ, Sask H*. (D) A high school text on Canadian history (about one-third completed).

UNIVERSITY OF TORONTO

BROWN, GEORGE W.: (A) *Building the Canadian Nation* (Toronto, 1942), 478 pp. (rev. ed., 1956, xi + 579 pp., new ed., 1959, 658 pp.); *Canadian Democracy in Action* (Toronto, 1945), vi + 122 pp. (new ed., 1959, viii + 148 pp.); (ed.) *Canada*; chapters by Edgar McInnis *et al.* (Berkeley, Calif., 1950), xviii + 621 pp.; *Canada in the Making* (Toronto, 1953), viii + 151 pp.; (with E. Harman and M. Jeanneret) *Canada in North America to 1800* (Toronto, 1960), xiv + 368 pp.; (with E. Harman and Marsh Jeanneret) *Canada in North America, 1800–1901* (Toronto, 1961), x + 371 pp.; (with Allen S. Merritt) *Canadians and Their Government* (Toronto, 1961), v + 113 pp. (B) "Canadian Nationalism: An Historical Approach," *J Int Aff*, 30 (1954), 166–74; "The 'Atlantic Alliance' in Perspective," *Int J* (1957), 79–82. (C) *CHR, Int J*. (D) (ed.) Dictionary of Canadian Biography/Dictionnaire Biographique du Canada, vol. I, persons who died in the period up to 1700. The French and English volumes are to be published simultaneously by Les Presses de l'Université Laval and the University of Toronto Press. About one hundred authors have contributed.

CAIRNS, JOHN C.: (A) (co-author) *The Foundations of the West* (Toronto, 1963). (B) "The Historian in the Western World," *SAQ*, 51 (1952), 504–14; "Acton: A Portrait," *UTQ*, 22 (1952), 72–89; "Politics and Foreign Policy: The French Parliament, 1911–1914," *CHR*, 34 (1953), 245–76; "International Politics and the Military Mind: The Case of the French Republic, 1911–1914," *J Mod Hist*, 25 (1953), 273–85; "Clio and the Queen's First Minister," *SAQ*, 52 (1953), 505–20; "Letters and International Politics, 1911–1914: The French Writer in a World Crisis," *UTQ*, 23 (1954), 122–42; "Carl Becker: An American Liberal," *J Politics*, 16 (1954), 623–44; "Morocco Forty Years After," *Can For*, 35 (1955), 146–7; "Great Britain and the Fall of France: A Study in Allied Disunity," *J Mod Hist*, 27 (1955), 365–409; "The Fall of France, 1940: Thoughts on a National Defeat," *CHA Rep* (1957), 55–70; "The Successful Quest of Henry Adams," *SAQ*, 57 (1958), 168–93; "Algeria Again: Progress of a War," *Can For*, 38, No. 447, 4–6; "De Gaulle au Pouvoir," *Int J*, 13 (1958), 179–83; "An Assembly for the Republic," *Can For*, 38 (1959), 221–3; "Along the Road Back to France, 1940," *AHR*, 64 (1959), 583–603; "The Fifth Republic's First Year," *Int J*, 14 (1959), 272–82; "The Quiet Frenchman," *Can For*, 39 (1960), 265–6; "General de Gaulle and the Salvation of France, 1944–1946," *J Mod Hist*, 32 (1960), 251–9; "Algerian Progress: Toward Reality and Negotiation," *Int J*, 16 (1961),

HISTORY 227

158–68; "France" and "French Community," in *Americana Annual* (1961, 1962, 1963); "Algeria: The Last Ordeal," *Int J*, 17 (1962), 87–97; "President de Gaulle and the 'Régime of Misfortune,' " *Int J*, 18 (1962/3), 58–66; "A Few Thoughts on President de Gaulle," *Can For*, 42, No. 504, 220–2. (D) (ed., with introduction) Sources of Western Civilization, 9, The Nineteenth Century (to be published in summer 1964); The Fall of France, 1940 (publication indefinite, possibly 1965–6); France (to be published in fall of 1964); "France" and "French Community" in *Americana Annual*, 1964.

CARELESS, J. M. S.: (A) *Canada; A Story of Challenge* (Toronto, 1953), xvi + 417 pp.; (with G. W. Brown, G. M. Craig, E. Ray) *Canada and the Commonwealth* (Toronto, 1953), x + 462 pp.; (ed., with G. W. Brown, C. R. MacLeod, E. Ray) *Canada and the World* (Toronto, 1954), x + 469 pp.; (with G. W. Brown, G. M. Craig, E. Ray) *Canada and the Americas* (Toronto, 1954), x + 486 pp.; *Brown of the Globe* (2 vols., Toronto, 1959–63), viii + 354 pp., x + 406 pp. (B) "The Toronto *Globe* and Agrarian Radicalism, 1850–67," *CHR*, 29 (1948), 14–39; "Mid-Victorian Liberalism in Central Canadian Newspapers, 1850–67," *CHR*, 31 (1950), 221–36; "History and Canadian Unity," *Culture*, 12 (1951), 117–24; "Frontierism, Metropolitanism, and Canadian History," *CHR*, 35 (1954), 1–21; "Canadian Nationalism—Immature or Obsolete?" *CHA Rep* (1954), 1–21; "George Brown," in R. L. McDougall, ed., *Our Living Tradition* (Toronto, 1959); "George Brown and the Mother of Confederation," *CHA Rep* (1960), 57–73. (C) *CHR, CJEPS, OH.* (D) The Rise of the City [in Canada], pamphlet for CHA series (MS. to be completed this fall); Canada, 1841–59 (volume in W. L. Morton, ed., Canadian Centenary Series, for publication by 1965); The Canadians, 1867–1967: The Record of Achievement (editing a series of essays in large volume for publication in 1967).

CIENCIALA, ANNA M.: (D) Polish Foreign Policy and the Western Powers, January 1938–April 1939: A Study in the Interdependence of Eastern and Western Europe (under consideration by a publisher); Danzig in Polish-German Relations, 1933–1939 (research just begun).

CLOUGH, CECIL H.: (B) "Cesare Anselmi: A Source for the Sack of Brescia and Battle of Ravenna," *Atti dell'Ateneo di Brescia* (1962); "La verità intorno la novella di Luigi da Porto," *Atti dell'Accademia Olimpica*, NS, 1, 43–52 (Vicenza, 1962); "Luigi da Porto's *Lettere Storiche* as a Source for Bembo's *Storia di Venezia*," *Nuovo Archivio Veneto* (winter, 1962); "More Light on Pandolfo and Ludovico Ariosto," *Italica*, 39 (1962), 195–6; "A Further Note on Pandolfo and Ludovico Ariosto," *Italica*, 40 (1963), 167–9. (C) *CHR, Italica, RN, Revista della Storia della Chiesa. . . .* (D) A critical edition of *Le Lettere Storiche* of Luigi da Porto (being published in two volumes by the Fondazione Giorgio Cini, Venice, 1962–3); Italian Renaissance Studies (accepted for publication by Storia e letteratura, Rome, 1963); a chronological index of P. Bembo's *Epistolario* and a bibliography of Italian letters printed 1450–1700 (both works nearing completion); a biography of Pietro Bembo (several years' work ahead).

CONACHER, J. B.: (A) (ed., with notes) Francois du Creux's *History of*

Canada, or New France (trans. by P. J. Robinson) (2 vols., Toronto, 1951, 1952), xxviii + 404 pp., viii + pp. 405–775.   (B) "The British Party System between the Reform Acts of 1832 and 1867," *CHA Rep* (1955), 69–78; "Peel and the Peelites, 1846–1850," *EHR*, 73 (1958), 431–52; "Party Politics in the Age of Palmerston," in P. Appleman, W. A. Madden, and M. Wolff, *1859: Entering an Age of Crisis* (Bloomington, Ind., 1959), 163–80, 302–4; "The Politics of the 'Papal Aggression' Crisis, 1850–1851," *Can Cath Hist Ass Rep* (1959), 13–27.   (C) *CHR*, (General ed.) Champlain Soc., 1951–62; *The Official History of the Canadian Army in the Second World War*.   (D) The Peelites: A Study in British Party Politics of the Mid-Nineteenth Century (a book, most of research completed, first draft more than half written).

Cook, Ramsay: (A) *The Politics of John W. Dafoe and the Free Press* (Toronto, 1963), xii + 305 pp.   (B) "Church, Schools, and Politics in Manitoba," *CHR*, 39 (1958), 1–23; "J. W. Dafoe at the Imperial Conference, 1923," *CHR*, 41 (1960), 19–40; "John W. Dafoe: Conservative-Progressive," *CHA Rep* (1961), 75–85; "Dafoe, Laurier, and the Formation of the Union Government," *CHR*, 42 (1961), 185–208.   (C) *AHR*, *Can Annual Rev*, *Can For*, *CHR*, *CJEPS*, *Int J*, *UTQ*.   (D) A volume in the Canadian Centenary Series covering the years 1897–1921 (research just begun); vol. 5 (1867–1914) in Canadian Historical Documents (just begun).

Craig, G. M.: (A) (ed., with introduction) *Early Travellers in the Canadas, 1791–1867* (Toronto, 1955), xxxvi + 300 pp.; *Upper Canada: The Formative Years, 1784–1841* (Toronto, 1963); (ed.) *Lord Durham's Report* (Toronto, 1963).   (B) "The American Impact on the Upper Canadian Reform Movement before 1837," *CHR*, 29 (1948), 383–52.   (C) *CHR*, *Int J*.   (D) The United States and Canada (for the American Foreign Policy Library); volume in projected Canadian Historical Documents series.

Creighton, D. G.: (A) *British North America at Confederation* (Ottawa, 1940); *Dominion of the North: A History of Canada* (Boston and Toronto, 1944) (rev. ed., 1957); *John A. Macdonald: The Young Politician* (Toronto, 1952) (new ed., 1956); *John A. Macdonald: The Old Chieftain* (Toronto, 1955); *The Empire of the St. Lawrence* (Toronto, 1956) (originally published as *The Commercial Empire of the St. Lawrence*, 1937); *Harold Adams Innis: Portrait of a Scholar* (Toronto, 1957); *The Story of Canada* (London and Toronto, 1959).   (B) "The Commercial Class in Canadian Politics, 1792–1840," *CHR*, 12 (1931), 120–44; "The Economic Background of the Rebellions of 1837," *CJEPS*, 3 (1937), 283–91; "The Victorians and the Empire," *CHR*, 19 (1938), 138–53; "Federal Relations in Canada Since 1914," in C. Martin, ed., *Canada in Peace and War* (Toronto, 1941), 25–57; "Economic Nationalism and Confederation," *CHA Rep* (1942), 44–51; "Sir John Macdonald and Canadian Historians," *CHR*, 29 (1948), 1–13; "The United States and Canadian Confederation," *CHR*, 39 (1958), 209–22; "Sir John Macdonald," in *Our Living Heritage* (Toronto, 1958).

Goffart, Walter: (B) "Byzantine Policy in the West under Tiberius II and Maurice: The Pretenders Hermenegild and Gundovald (579–585),"

Traditio, 13 (1957), 73–118; "The Privilege of Nicolas I for St. Calais: A New Theory," *Rev Bénédictine*, 71 (1961), 287–337. (C) *Speculum.* (D) "The Fredegar Problem Reconsidered" (to appear in *Speculum*, January, 1963); The Le Mans Forgeries: Date, Purpose, and Authorship (doctoral thesis being transformed into a book, will probably be submitted to a publisher in fall of 1963).

McNAUGHT, KENNETH: (A) *A Prophet in Politics: a Biography of J. S. Woodsworth* (Toronto, 1959), vi + 339 pp.; (with J. H. S. Reid and H. S. Crowe) *A Source-Book of Canadian History* (Toronto, 1959), xvi + 472 pp. (B) "J. S. Woodsworth and a Political Party for Labour, 1896 to 1921," *CHR*, 30 (1949), 123–43; "Ottawa and Washington Look at the U.N.," *Foreign Aff*, 33 (1955), 663–78; "Canadian Foreign Policy and the Whig Interpretation," *CHA Rep* (1957), 43–54; (with Andrew Brewin) "Debate on Defence" (pamphlet) Ontario Woodsworth Foundation (Toronto, 1960); "Canadian Foreign Policy," in M. Oliver, ed., *Social Purpose for Canada* (Toronto, 1961), 445–72. (C) *Can For, CHR, Foreign Aff, Int J, QQ.* (D) Canada in World Affairs, 1957–59 (for C.I.I.A) (in draft); A Source-Book of Canadian History, 2 (research under way); Grade 13 textbook: American history half (to be published in January, 1963).

NELSON, HAROLD I.: (A) *Land and Power: British and Allied Policy on Germany's Frontiers, 1916–1919* (London, 1963), xvi + 402 pp. (C) (ed.) *Int J.*

NELSON, WILLIAM H.: (A) (with Frank E. Vandiver) *Fields of Glory* (New York, 1960), 316 pp.; *The American Tory* (Oxford, 1961), 194 pp. (B) "The Last Hopes of the American Loyalists," *CHR*, 32 (1951), 22–42; "R. H. Tawney," chapter 20 in (Herman Ausubel, J. B. Brebner, and Erling M. Hunt, eds.), *Some Modern Historians of Britain.* (C) *CHR, J Southern Hist, Mississippi Valley Hist R, Pennsylvania Mag Hist and Biog.* (D) Background of the American Revolution, 1739–60.

PIEPENBURG, W. N.: (B) "Pests, Meddlers, and Regicides," *CHR*, 40 (1959), 137–42. (C) *Can For, CHR, Int J.* (D) The Cromwellian Church; Life of Charles Fleetwood (research on both in progress, publication at least five years off).

POWICKE, MICHAEL RHYS: (A) *Military Obligation in Medieval England* (Oxford, 1962), 263 pp. (B) "Distraint of Knighthood and Military Obligations under Henry III," *Speculum*, 25 (1950), 457–70; "Edward II and Military Obligation," *Speculum*, 31 (1956), 92–119. (C) *AHR, Speculum.* (D) Studies in war and society in the fifteenth century.

SENIOR, HEREWARD: (B) "The Character of Canadian Orangeism," in *Thought from the Learned Societies of Canada, 1961* (Toronto, 1962) (originally delivered before Canadian Historical Society, June 1961). (C) *CHR, Irish Hist St.* (D) The Character and Political Activities of the Orange Lodges in Ireland and Great Britain, 1795–1836 (accepted for publication by Routledge & Kegan Paul of London and Ryerson of Toronto); a study of the Canadian Orange Lodges in the Nineteenth Century (in preparation for Ryerson).

SPENCER, ROBERT: (A) *History of the Fifteenth Canadian Field Regiment, Royal Canadian Artillery, 1941–1945* (Amsterdam, 1945), 303 pp.;

Canada in World Affairs, 5, From UN to NATO, 1946–1949 (Toronto, 1959), xii + 447 pp.; (with E. McInnis, R. Hiscocks) "The Berlin Dilemma," in *The Shaping of Postwar Germany* (London and Toronto, 1960), 90–149. (B) "Farewell to German History? Revisionism versus Traditionalism," *CHA Rep* (1955), 51–61; "Triangle into Treaty: Canada and the Origins of NATO," *Int J*, 14 (1959), 87–98; "External Affairs and Defence," *Can Annual R 1960, 1961, 1962* (Toronto, 1961–63). (C) *Can For, CHR, Int J, J Mod Hist, QQ.* (D) Study of the German Confederation, 1815–66 (still at research stage).

STACEY, C. P.: (A) *Canada and the British Army, 1846–1871* (Toronto, 1936), xiv + 287 pp.; *Military Problems of Canada* (Toronto, 1940), viii + 184 pp.; *The Canadian Army, 1939–1945* (Ottawa, 1948), xvi + 354 pp.; *Official History of the Canadian Army in the Second World War*, 1, *Six Years of War* (Ottawa, 1955); *Quebec, 1759* (Toronto, 1959), xiv + 210 pp.; (ed., with introduction) *Records of the Nile Voyageurs, 1884–1885* (Toronto, 1959), x + 285 pp. (C) *AHR, Can For, CHR, Int. J, J Mod Hist.* (D) A Study of Canadian military policy, 1939–45, for the Department of National Defence (well advanced); general editor of a series of five volumes of Canadian historical documents to be published by Macmillan, and the editor of one of the volumes, dealing with the period 1914–57 (project only recently launched).

THORNTON, A. P.: (A) *West-India Policy under the Restoration* (Oxford, 1956), vi + 280 pp.; *The Imperial Idea and Its Enemies: A Study in British Power* (London, 1959), xiv + 370 pp. (B) "Some Statistics on West-India Produce, Shipping, and Revenue, 1660–1685," *Caribbean Hist R* (Oct., 1952); "The Modyfords and Morgan: Letters from Sir James Modyford on the Affairs of Jamaica, 1667–1672, in the Muniments of Westminster Abbey," *Jamaican Hist R*, 2 (1952), 36–60; "The Buccaneers of the Caribbean," *AUR*, 34 (1952), 209–16; "The English at Campeachy, 1670–1682," *Jamaican Hist R*, 2 (1953), 27–38; "The Argument about Africa," *Fortnightly R*, NS, 173 (1953), 22–6; "Colonial Policy and Colonial Politics," *Fortnightly R*, NS, 173 (1953), 376–81; "British Policy in Persia, 1858–1890," *EHR*, 69 (1954), 554–79, and 70 (1955), 55–71; "Afghanistan in Anglo-Russian Diplomacy, 1869–1873," *Cambridge Hist J*, 11 (1954), 204–18; "G. A. Henty's British Empire," *Fortnightly R*, NS, 175 (1954), 97–101; "Experts and Islanders: A View of the West Indies," *Corona* (Oct., 1955); "The Organization of the English Slave-Trade in the English West Indies, 1660–1685," *William and Mary Q*,12 (1955), 399–409; "Spanish Slave-Ships in the English West Indies, 1660–85," *HAHR*, 35 (1955), 374–85; "Realms of the Commonwealth, 1955," *Enc Br Yearbook* (1955); "The Century of the Common Man," "Wide Open Spaces," and "My Country, Right or Wrong," in Geoffrey Grigson, ed., *Ideas* (London, 1955); "The Reopening of 'the Central Asian Question,' 1864–1869," *History* (1956), 122–36; "The G. R. G. Conway MS. Collection in the Library of the University of Aberdeen," *HAHR*, 36 (1956), 345–7; "Charles II and the American Colonies," *History Today*, 6 (1956), 3–11; "The Commonwealth: The Major Nations, 1956," *Enc Br Yearbook* (1956); "The British in Manila, 1762–1764," *History Today*, 7 (1957), 44–53; "The Rights of Men," an inaugural lecture delivered at the University College of the West Indies. (Kingston, Jamaica, 1960); "Aspects of West Indian Society," *Int J*, 15 (1960), 113–21; "Sir Garnet Wolseley," *Enc Br* (1960); "Sir Evelyn Wood," *Enc Br* (1960); "The Idea of a University" (Kingston, Jamaica, 1961); "Rivalries in the Mediterranean, the Middle East, and Egypt, 1870–1901," *New Cambridge Modern History*, 11, chap. 22 (Cambridge, 1962). (C) *AHR, CHR, EHR, Victorian St.* (D) The Habit of Authority: Paternalism and Democracy in British History (a book, nearly completed).

WHITE, PATRICK C. T.: (A) (ed., with introduction) *Lord Selkirk's Diary* (Toronto, 1958), xxxii + 359 pp. (C) *CHR, CJEPS, Int J, Mississippi Valley Hist.* (D) A history of Canadian-American relations 1815–46 (research completed, in process of writing).

WILKINSON, B.: (A) *The Chancery under Edward III* (Manchester, 1929), xxxii + 242 pp.; *The Medieval Council of Exeter* (Manchester, 1931), xxxiv + 105 pp.; *Studies in the Constitutional History of the Thirteenth and Fourteenth Centuries*, Victoria University of Manchester Historical Series, No. 73 (Manchester, 1937, 2nd ed., 1952), 289 pp,; *The Constitutional History of England*, vols. 1–3 (London, 1948–58). (B) "The Authorization of Chancery Writs Under Edward III," *Bull John Rylands Lib*, 8 (1924), 107–39; "A Letter of Louis de Male Count of Flanders," *Bull John Rylands Lib*, 9 (1925), 177–87; "A Letter of Edward III to his Chancellor and Treasurer," *EHR*, 42 (1927), 248–51; "The Household Ordinance of 1279," *History*, NS, 12 (1927), 46–7; "The Protest of the Earls of Arundel and Surrey in the Crisis of 1341," *EHR*, 46 (1931), 177–93; "The Coronation Oath of Edward II," in J. G. Edwards, V. H. Galbraith, and E. F. Jacobs, eds. *Historical Essays in Honour of James Tait* (1933), 405–17; "Freeman and the Crisis of 1051," *Bull John Rylands Lib*, 22 (1938), 368–87; "The Deposition of Richard II and the Accession of Henry IV," *EHR*, 54 (1939), 215–39; "Northumbrian Separatism in 1065 and 1066," *Bull John Rylands Lib*, 23 (1939), 504–26; "The Peasants' Revolt of 1381," *Speculum*, 15 (1940), 12–35; "The Chancery," in Willard and Morris, eds., *The English Government at Work, 1327–37* (Cambridge, Mass., 1940), 162–205; "The Council and the Crisis of 1233–4," *Bull John Rylands Lib*, 27 (1942/3) 384–93; "The Coronation Oath of Edward II and the Statute of York," *Speculum*, 19 (1944), 445–69; "The Government of England during the Absence of Richard I on the Third Crusade," *Bull John Rylands Lib*, 28 (1944), 485–509; "Tendencies in Fourteenth-Century Constitutional Development," *CHA Rep* (1946), 18–29; "An Aspect of the Decline of Citizenship in the Later Roman Empire," *Phoenix*, supp. to Vol. 1 (spring, 1947), 19–29; "The Negotiations Preceding the 'Treaty' of Leake, 1318," in R. W. Hunt, W. A. Pantin, and R. W. Southern, eds., *Studies in Medieval History Presented to F. M. Powicke* (Oxford, 1948), 333–53; "The Sherburn Indenture and the Attack on the Despensers, 1321," *EHR*, 63 (1948), 1–28; "The 'Political Revolution' of the Thirteenth and Fourteenth Centuries in England," *Speculum*, 24 (1949), 502–9; *The Coronation in History*, EHA Pamphlets, G. 23 (London, 1953), 36 pp.; "English Politics and Politicians of the Thirteenth and Fourteenth Centuries," *Speculum*, 30 (1955), 37–48; "Notes on the Coronation Records of the Fourteenth Century," *EHR*, 70 (1955), 582–600;

"The Duke of Gloucester and the Council, 1422–8," *Bull Inst of Hist Res*, 31 (1958), 19–20.   (C) *Bull John Rylands Lib*, *CHR*, *EHR*, *Speculum*. (D) History of England, 1216–1485 (in its early stages); vol. 4 of *The Constitutional History of England*, Political and Constitutional History: the Fifteenth Century (in press).

VICTORIA COLLEGE—UNIVERSITY OF TORONTO

SISSONS, C. B.: (A) *Bilingual Schools in Canada* (London, 1917), 242 pp.; *Egerton Ryerson, His Life and Letters* (2 vols., Toronto, 1937–47), xi + 601 pp., x + 678 pp.; *A History of Victoria University* (Toronto, 1952), viii + 346 pp.; (ed.) *My Dearest Sophie: Letters from Egerton Ryerson to His Daughter* (Toronto, 1955), xxxvi + 350 pp.; *Church and State in Canadian Education, an Historical Study* (Toronto, 1959), x + 414 pp. (B) "Sycophant," *TRSC*, 3rd series, 43, s. 2 (1949), 137–41; "The Rights of Minorities in a Democracy," *TRSC*, 3rd series, 48, s. 2 (1954), 99–106; "Section 93," *TRSC*, 3rd series, 55, s. 2 (1961), 1–7.   (D) Memoirs (in press).

UNIVERSITY OF VICTORIA

OGELSBY, J. C. M.: (B) "British Columbia and the Near East Crisis, 1922," *Pacific Northwest Q*, 50 (1959), 108–14.   (C) *Historian, Pacific Northwest Q*.   (D) "Why Not Do Your Graduate Research in Europe?" (to be published in the *Historian* in 1963); "The British at Panama, 1742" (sent to *Caribbean St*); "Anglo-Spanish Rivalry in the Gulf of Honduras, 1740–48" (in preparation, for *Caribbean St*); "Admiral Vernon and General Wentworth in the West Indies—A Re-assessment" (partly completed).

PETTIT, SYDNEY G.: (B) "Dear Sir Matthew: A Glimpse of Judge Begbie," *BC Hist Q*, 11 (1947), 1–14; "Judge Begbie in Action: The Establishment of Law and Preservation of Order in British Columbia," *BC Hist Q*, 11 (1947), 113–48; "His Honour's Honour: Judge Begbie and the Cottonwood Scandal," *BC Hist Q*, 11 (1947), 187–210; "The Tyrant Judge: Judge Begbie in Court," *BC Hist Q*, 11 (1947), 273–94; "Judge Begbie's Shorthand: A Mystery Solved," *BC Hist Q*, 12 (1948), 293–6; "The Trials and Tribulations of Edward Edwards Langford," *BC Hist Q*, 17 (1953), 5–40; "Frontier Judge," in *British Columbia Anthology* (Toronto, 1958).   (C) *BC Hist Q*.   (D) A biography of William Windham, 1750–1810 (being written, after a year of research).

UNIVERSITY OF WATERLOO

CORNELL, PAUL G.: (A) *The Alignment of Political Groups in Canada, 1841–1867* (Toronto, 1962), x + 119 pp.   (B) "William Fitzwilliam Owen, R.N., Naval Surveyor," *Trans NS Hist Soc*, 32 (1959), 161–82. (C) *CHR, Can Public Administration, Int J, Northwest R*.   (D) Collaborating on bicultural monograph on Canadian history organized on sectional lines (MS. due for completion early in 1964).

MACKIRDY, KENNETH A.: (B) "Conflict of Loyalties: The Problem of Assimilating the Far Wests into the Canadian and Australian Federations," *CHR*, 32 (1951), 337–55; "Dominions History and the Comparative

Method," *Hist St: Austral and NZ*, 6 (1953), 379–85; "Problems of Adjustment in Nation Building: The Maritime Provinces and Tasmania," *CJEPS*, 20 (1954), 27–43; "Clio's Australian Accent: Main Trends of Recent Historical Writing in Australia," *CHA Rep* (1958), 77–98; "The First Australian Department of External Affairs, 1901–16," *CJEPS*, 25 (1959), 503–7; "The United Nations: Some Thoughts on Changing Perspectives," *QQ*, 67 (1961), 557–67.   (C) *AHR, Austral Q, CHR, CJEPS, Hist St: Austral and NZ, J Mod Hist, OH, Pacific Northwest Q, QQ*.   (D) "Australia," chapter in Robin Winks, ed., The British Empire-Commonwealth: Historiographical Reappraisals (to be published by Duke University Press, chapter with editor); Barriers to Nationhood: The Anatomy of Regionalism in Canada and Australia (MS. requires considerable editing); (collaborating with T. H. Qualter on monograph) Survey of the Coverage of 1962 General Election in the Ontario Daily Press (in final stages of preparation); (with T. H. Qualter) "Election Coverage in the Ontario Press," chapter for book on general election of 1962 being edited by John Meisel (first draft completed); gathering material for the new election—one more monograph can be written on material from the 1962 election and a larger book written on the 1963 election.

PATTERSON, E. PALMER, II: (C) *CHR, Northwest R*.   (D) Andrew Paull and Canadian Indian Resurgence (Ph.D. dissertation, being considered for publication by University of Washington Press); at present engaged in preliminary research on the life of the Rev. Arthur E. O'Meara, an Anglican clergyman who was active in the cause of Indian rights *c.* 1910–28.

RENISON COLLEGE—UNIVERSITY OF WATERLOO

REES, A. W.:   (A) (ed., with commentary) *Colenso Letters from Natal* (Pietermaritzburg, Natal, 1958), 440 pp.; *The Natal Technical College, 1907–1957* (University of Natal Press, 1958), 303 pp.   (C) *CHR*.

WATERLOO LUTHERAN UNIVERSITY

MONTGOMERY, JOHN WARWICK: (A) *A Union List of Serial Publications in Chicago-Area Protestant Theological Libraries* (Chicago, 1960), 284 pp.; *A Seventeenth-Century View of European Libraries* (Berkeley, Calif., and Cambridge, Eng., 1962), 181 pp.; *Chytraeus on Sacrifice: A Reformation Treatise in Biblical Theology* (St. Louis, Mo., 1962), 151 pp.; *The Shape of the Past: An Introduction to Philosophical Historiography*, History in Christian Perspective, Vol. 1 (Ann Arbor, Mich., 1962), 382 pp.   (B) "The Colonial Parish Library of Wilhelm Christoph Berkenmeyer," *Papers Biblio Soc Amer*, 53 (1959), 114–49; "Eros and Agape in the Thought of Giovanni Pico della Mirandola," *Concordia Theol Monthly*, 32 (1961), 733–46; "The Apologetic Approach of Muhammad Ali," *Muslim World*, 51 (1961), 111–22; "Luther and Libraries," *Lib Q*, 32 (1962), 133–47; "Wisdom as Gift: The Wisdom Concept in Relation to Biblical Messianism," *Interpretation*, 16 (1962), 43–57; "A Normative Approach to the Acquisition Problem in the Theological Seminary Library," *Amer Theol Lib Ass Proc*, 16 (1962), 65–95.   (C) *Christianity Today, Lib Q*.   (D) Editing and translating Louis Jacob de Saint-Charles's *Traicté des Plus Belles Bibliothèques du Monde* (Paris, 1644), the first comprehensive, book-length history of libraries (will be completed within three years); A History of Theological Bibliography in Western Christendom—the first such history (will be completed within three years); History in Christian Perspective (Vols. 2–5 of a five-volume series covering philosophical and methodological historiography, and the history of the West from the rise of Christianity to the close of the seventeenth century; the four volumes will be issued over the next eight years); "Sixtus of Siena and Roman Catholic Biblical Scholarship during the Reformation Period" (accepted for publication in *Archiv. für Reformationsgeschichte* in 1963).

UNIVERSITY OF WESTERN ONTARIO—UNIVERSITY COLLEGE

BALDERSTON, WALTER: (B) "Sir William Herschel and his Place in the History of Science," *J Royal Astronomical Soc Can*, 55, 1–8.   (D) Preparatory work on the structure of British science in the eighteenth century.

HILBORN, K. H. W.: (B) "The Social Responsibility of the Businessman," *Business Q*, 27 (1962), 15–16, 19–20; "Canada and the World," monthly department in *Canada Month*, starting April, 1963.   (C) *Canada Month*, *QQ*.   (D) "Anglo-German Relations in the Asia Minor Railway Question, 1892–93" (article, documentation complete, revision necessary); Canadian policy regarding Formosa since 1949, with special reference to view taken of island's legal status (article, research in progress).

HODGINS, BRUCE W.: (A) *Maritime Claims Relative to the Prairie Provinces "Land" Subsidy and to the Lands' Question* (Charlottetown, P.E.I., 1957), 53 pp.   (C) *Can For, CHR, OH*.   (D) Article for *OH* on an aspect of Political Career of John Sandfield Macdonald (thesis subject; in preparation).

KERR, D. G. G.: (A) *Sir Edmund Head, A Scholarly Governor* (Toronto, 1954), xii + 259 pp.; *A Historical Atlas of Canada* (Toronto, 1961), x + 120 pp.; *Canadian History Series* (16 wall maps) (Chicago, 1963). (C) *AHR, CHR, CJEPS, Collier's Enc, Grolier Enc*.   (D) Revised edition, and French edition, of *A Historical Atlas in Canada* (both in progress); Canada: Its Changing Frontiers (nine maps and articles; completed, for publication in 1964 by *World Book Year Book*).

OVERTON, RICHARD C.: (A) *The First Ninety Years: An Historical Sketch of the Burlington Railroad, 1850–1940* (Chicago, 1940), 40 pp.; *Burlington West: A Colonization History of the Burlington Railroad* (Cambridge, Mass., 1941); *Gulf to Rockies: The Heritage of the Fort Worth & Denver— Colorado & Southern, 1861–1898* (Austin, Texas, 1953); *Milepost 100: The Origin and Development of the Burlington Lines* (Chicago, 1949), 64 pp.   (B) "The Vermont Flood Control Issue," *Harvard Alumni Bull*, 41 (1939), No. 18; (with Joan Douglas) "Vermont Controls Flood Control," *Young Republican*, 4 (1939), No. 3; "Dickens' Brother and Western Railroad Publicity," *Bull Business Hist Soc*, 13 (1939), No. 6; "The Story of the Burlington," *Railroad Worker's J* (July, 1941); "Sources for Northwest History," *Minnesota History*, 23 (1942), No. 2; "How a Railroad Helped Settle the West," *American Life Historical Papers*; "Chicago, Railway Capital of the Nation," in *75th Anniversary Journal of the Western Society of Engineers* (Chicago, 1944); "Setting History Straight," *Railway Age*,

117 (1944), No. 27; "Scholars Get Access to Burlington Records," *Railway Age*, 114 (1944), No. 9 (also in *Bull Business Hist Soc*, 18 (1944), No. 3); "The Lexington Group," *Special Libraries* (Oct., 1945); "Railroad Records and Local History," *Vermont Q*, 14 (1946), No. 3; "Biography of Charles Elliott Perkins," *Iowa State Hist Soc Centennial Papers* (Aug., 1946); "Rails Uniting a Nation: Volumes that Tell of Their History," *Chicago Sun* (May 4, 1947); "Getting History Right on Railroads," *Railway Age*, 123 (1947), No. 5; "Problems of Writing the History of Large Business Units, with Special Reference to Railroads," *Bull Business Hist Soc*, 22 (1948), No. 1; "Private Car 200," *Trains*, 8 (1948), No. 5; "Good and Useful Railroad History," *Railway Age*, 124 (1948), No. 7; "The Lexington Group: Clio's Topsy," *History News*, 4 (1949), No. 8; "History of the Colorado and Southern Railway," *Colorado Mag*, 26 (1949), Nos. 2, 3; "Railroads: Weathervanes of Free Enterprise," *Railway Age*, 146 (1949), 77; "Railroadiana," *Trains*, 10 (1949), 60–1; "Westward Expansion since the Homestead Act," in H. F. Williamson, ed., *The Growth of the American Economy* (New York, 1944) (revised ed., 1950); "Can the Records Manager Help the Historian?" *Business Hist R*, 29 (1955), No. 3; "Hale Holden," in *Dictionary of Amer Biog*; "Ralph Budd: Railroad Entrepreneur," *Palimpsest*, 36 (1955), No. 11; "Charles Elliott Perkins," *Business Hist R*, 31 (1957), No. 3; "Railroad Regulation in the United States," *Enc Amer*; "Why Did the CB&Q Build to Denver?" *Nebraska History*, 40 (1959), No. 3; "The Burlington—A Citizen of the West," in *The American West—An Appraisal* (papers from the Second Conference on the History of the West) (Museum of New Mexico Press, 1963). (C) *AHR, Business Hist R, CHR, J Economic Hist, Minnesota Hist, Mississippi Valley Hist R, Railway Age*. (D) A general history of the Burlington Lines—Burlington Route (publication scheduled for 1964).

STOCKDALE, WILLIAM: (D) Book on period 1530–1640 in England (projected).

TUCKER, A. V.: (B) "W. H. Mallock and Late Victorian Conservatism," *UTQ*, 31 (1962), 223–41; "Disraeli and the Natural Aristocracy," *CJEPS*, 28 (1962), 1–15; "Army and Society in England, 1870–1900: A Re-assessment of the Cardwell Reforms," *J Br St*, 2 (1963), 110–41. (C) *CHR, Can L*. (D) A study of the relationship between the army and the social structure in England from the Crimean War to the First World War.

UNIVERSITY OF WESTERN ONTARIO—MIDDLESEX COLLEGE

ARMSTRONG, F. H.: (B) "Two Renaissance Testoons," *ROMB*, 17 (1951), 12–13; "The Plate Money of Sweden," *ROMB*, 18 (1952), 15–16; "The First Great Fire of Toronto," *OH*, 53 (1961), 201–21; "The Rebuilding of Toronto after the Great Fire of 1849," *OH*, 53 (1961), 234–49; "A Stormy Voyage in 1850," *Inland Seas*, 18 (1962), 219–24; "The Carfrae Family, a Study in Early Toronto Toryism," *OH*, 54 (1962), 161–81; "The York Riots of March 23, 1832," *OH*, 55 (1963), 61–72; "Ontario," *Americana Annual* (1964), 504–5; "Toronto," *Americana Annual* (1964), 683. (C) *OH*. (D) Article "The Ihnasyah Hoard Re-examined" (to appear in *Roy Ont Mus Div Art and Archaeology Annual*, 1964).

WILSON, ALAN: (B) "The Clergy Reserves: 'Economical Mischiefs' or Sectarian Issue?" *CHR*, 42 (1961), 281–99. (C) *Can For, Can L, CHR, DR*. (D) Administrative History of the Clergy Reserves of Upper Canada (to be published early in 1965); biography of John Northway (MS. within six weeks of completion); The Canada Company, 1824–64 (to be published as one of CHA Historical Booklets, fall, 1964).

UNIVERSITY OF WESTERN ONTARIO—HURON COLLEGE

HENDERSON, J. L. H.: (B) "The Founding of Trinity College, Toronto," *OH*, 49 (1952), No. 1; "The Anglican Church of Canada," in William G. Leidt, *Anglican Mosaic* (Seabury Press, 1963). (D) Monograph on John Strachan (1778–1867), Bishop of Toronto (in preparation).

ROWE, JOHN GORDON: (B) "Paschal II and the Latin Orient," *Speculum*, 32 (1957), 470–501; "The Papacy and the Greeks," *CH*, 28 (1959), 115–30, 310–27; "The Papacy and the Ecclesiastical Province of Tyre (1100–1187)," *Bull John Rylands Lib*, 43 (1960), 160–89; "Clio Observed: A Survey of Recent Literature in Ecclesiastical History," *CJT*, 6 (1960), 262–74; "The Tragedy of Aeneas Sylvius Piccolomini (Pope Pius II): An Interpretation," *CH*, 30 (1961), 288–313. (C) *Bull John Rylands Lib, CH, CHR, CJT, Speculum*. (D) A monograph on the papacy in the reign of Hadrian IV (first draft completed); two articles dealing with the papacy and the crusade in the twelfth century (should be published in 1965).

UNIVERSITY OF WESTERN ONTARIO—COLLEGE OF CHRIST THE KING

CRUNICAN, PAUL: (B) "Father Lacombe's Strange Mission: The Lacombe-Langevin Correspondence on the Manitoba School Question, 1895–96," *Can Cath Hist Ass Rep*, 26 (1959), 57–71.

YORK UNIVERSITY

BRÜCKMANN, J.: (B) "An Old French Poetic Version of the Life and Miracles of Saint Magloire (Part II)," *MS*, 21 (1959), 53–128. (D) Editing the mediaeval English coronation *ordines* (practically completed for the period 1216–1377; research for the earlier period should begin in summer, 1963; final appearance in book form probably in two or three years).

McINNIS, EDGAR: (A) *The War* (6 vols.) (London and Toronto, 1940–6); *The Unguarded Frontier: A History of American-Canadian Relations* (Garden City, 1942), 384 pp.; *North America and the Modern World* (Toronto, 1945), x + 478 pp. (rev. ed., 1954, xii + 438 pp.); *Canada, a Political and Social History* (New York, 1947), 574 pp. (rev. and enl. 2nd ed., 1959, 619 pp.); *The Atlantic Triangle and the Cold War* (Toronto, 1959), 163 pp. (C) *CHR, Int J, QQ*. (D) A study of the efforts at peacemaking after the second world war (first half in unrevised draft).

MURRAY, ALEX. L.: (B) "The Provincial Freeman: A New Source for the History of the Negro in Canada and the United States," *J Negro Hist*, 44 (1959), 123–35; "The Extradition of Fugitive Slaves from Canada: A Re-evaluation," *CHR*, 43 (1962), 298–314. (D) Just completing a study of Canada's role in the Anglo-American anti-slavery movement; just beginning a biography of Lewis Tappan, a New York merchant and philanthropist.

FINE ART AND VARIED TOPICS

Fine Art

UNIVERSITY OF BRITISH COLUMBIA

McNAIRN, IAN: (B) "Sir Thomas Brock," *Enc Br* (1958); "Frank Dobson," *Enc Br* (1958); "Sir Jacob Epstein," *Enc Br* (1958); "Charles Despiau," *Enc Br* (1958). (C) *Can Art.* (D) Critical essays and catalogue of the work of Lawren Harris (ready for publication in January, 1963).

MCGILL UNIVERSITY

GALAVARIS, GEORGE: (B) "The Symbolism of the Imperial Costume as Displayed on Byzantine Coins," *Museum Notes*, 8 (1958), 99–117; "Seals of the Byzantine Empire," *Archaeology*, 12 (1959), 264–70; "The Mother of God, 'Stabbed with a Knife,' " *Dumbarton Oaks Papers*, 13 (1959), 229–33; "The Representation of the Virgin and Child on a 'Thokos' on the Seals of the Constantinopolitan Patriarchs," *J Archaeological Soc Christian Antiquities of Greece*, 2 (1960–1), 153–81. (C) *Archaeology, Can Art, Dumbarton Oaks Papers, J Archaeological Soc Christian Antiquities of Greece, Museum Notes, Reallexikon zur byzantinischen Kunst.* (D) The Illustrations of the Liturgical Homilies of Gregory Nazianzenus (ready for publication).

MOUNT ALLISON UNIVERSITY

Dow, HELEN JEANNETTE: (B) "A Plea for Art History," *Bull HAC*, 19 (1956), 14–15; "The Rose-Window," *J Warburg and Courtauld Institutes*, 20 (1957), 248–97; "Two Italian Portrait-Busts of Henry VIII," *Art Bull*, 42 (1960), 291–4. (C) *Art Bull, Gazette des Beaux-Arts, J Warburg and Courtauld Institutes.* (D) The Sculptures of the Henry VII Chapel (book, submitted for publication); Alex Colville (book, submitted for publication); "Lawrence Emler" (article, accepted for publication by *Gazette des Beaux-Arts*); "Van Gogh, both Prometheus and Jupiter" (article, submitted for publication to the *Burlington Mag*); catalogue of the art collection in the Owens Museum at Mount Allison; a study of the sculptures at Winchester Cathedral (beginning stage); a study of the origin of Durham Cathedral (beginning stage).

HARRIS, LAWREN P.: (B) "Contemporary Maritime Art," *Food for Thought*, 15 (1955), 13–17. (C) *Food for Thought.* (D) The chapter on contemporary painting in *Arts of New Brunswick* (book in process of publication).

ST. MARY'S UNIVERSITY

CZAKO, AMBROSE: (A) *The Magic of Art* (New York, 1959), 138 pp.

UNIVERSITY OF SASKATCHEWAN

BORNSTEIN, ELI: (B) "Transition toward the New Art," *Structure*, 1 (1958), 30–45; "Structurist Art—its Origins," *Structurist*, 1 (1960–1), 2–12;

"The Window on the Wall," *Structurist*, 1 (1960–1), 52–64; "The Crystal in the Rock," *Structurist*, 2 (1961–2), 5–19. (C) *Structurist*. (D) "Conflicting Concepts in Art" (article, to be published in *Structurist*, January, 1963).

HUDSON, ANDREW: (B) "On Church and Art," *Old Palace*, 16 (1960). (C) *Can Art, Nor'wester, Prince Albert Daily Herald, Saskatoon R, Saskatoon Star-Phoenix*. (D) Further art reviews.

SIR GEORGE WILLIAMS UNIVERSITY

PINSKY, ALFRED: (B) "Picasso," in *Architects of Modern Thought* (Toronto, 1962); "Paul Cezanne," in *Architects of Modern Thought* (Toronto, 1962). (C) *Can Art*. (D) For *Can Art*, a review of the spring show at the Montreal Museum of Fine Art.

UNIVERSITY OF TORONTO

BROOKS, H. ALLEN: (B) "The Early Work of the Prairie Architects," *J Soc Archit Historians*, 19 (1960), 2–10; "Architectural Drawings by Frank Lloyd Wright," *Burlington Mag*, 104 (1962), 210–12. (C) *J Roy Archit Inst Can, J Soc Archit Historians*. (D) "The Midwest Contemporaries of Frank Lloyd Wright" (article, to be published in the collected papers of the Twentieth International Congress of the History of Art in 1963); The Prairie School, Frank Lloyd Wright and His Contemporaries (book, three-fourths written, to be published in 1964).

GRAHAM, J. WALTER: (A) *Palaces of Crete* (Princeton, 1962), 269 pp. (B) "Lamps from Olynthus, 1931," in D. M. Robinson, ed., *Excavations at Olynthus*, Part V, "Mosaics, Vases, and Lamps" (Baltimore, 1933); Part VIII, "The Hellenic House," in D. M. Robinson, ed., *Excavations at Olynthus* (Baltimore, 1938); "Olynthiaka, 1–6," *Hesperia*, 22 (1953), 196–207, and 23 (1954), 320–46; "The Phaistos 'Piano Nobile,' " *Amer J Arch*, 60 (1956), 151–7; "The Central Court as the Minoan Bull-Ring," *Amer J Arch*, 61 (1957), 255–62; "Auri Sacra Fames," *Phoenix*, 11 (1957), 112–20; "The Ransom of Hector on a new Melian Relief," *Amer J Arch*, 62 (1958), 313–9; "Light-Wells in Classical Greek Houses?" *Hesperia*, 27 (1958), 318–23; "The Residential Quarter of the Minoan Palace," *Amer J Arch*, 63 (1959), 47–52; "Windows, Recesses, and the Piano Nobile in the Minoan Palaces," *Amer J Arch*, 64 (1960), 329–33; "The Minoan Unit of Length, and Minoan Palace Planning," *Amer J Arch*, 64 (1960), 335–41; "Mycenaean Architecture," *Archaeology*, 13 (1960), 46–54; "The Minoan Banquet Hall," *Amer J Arch*, 65 (1961), 165–72. (C) *Amer J Arch, Archaeology, Hesperia, Phoenix*. (D) An article on the origins of Minoan palace architecture (to be published in a volume of papers delivered at the Wingspread Conference).

WINTER, F. E.: (B) "Hellenistic Fortifications in South Italy, Sicily, and Asia Minor," in *Yearbook Amer Philos Soc* (Philadelphia, 1958), 388–93; "Ikria and Katastegasma in the Walls of Athens," *Phoenix*, 13 (1959), 161–200. (C) *Amer J Arch, Phoenix*. (D) "The Chronology of the Euryalos Fort at Syracuse" (article, to be published in 1963 in *Amer J Arch*); "Ancient Corinth" (article, to be published late in 1963 or early in 1964 in *Phoenix*); Greek Fortifications from the Early Iron Age to Late Hellenistic Times (book, final draft nearly complete).

ROYAL ONTARIO MUSEUM

BURNHAM, HAROLD B.: (A) *Chinese Velvets* Roy Ont Mus Occasional Paper 2 (Toronto, 1959), 64 pp. (B) "Une armure gaze complexe chinois," *Bull de Liaison du Centre Int d'Etude des Textiles Anciens*, 9 (1959), 29–35; "Un velours impérial chinois d'époque Ming—Dossier de recensement," *Bull de Liaison du Centre Int d'Etude des Textiles Anciens*, 9 (1959), 53–60. (C) *Bull de Liaison du Centre Int d'Etude des Textiles Anciens, Royal Ont Mus Div Art and Arch Annual.* (D) International textile vocabulary (English version) for use in study of ancient textiles (to be completed in June, 1963); Persian personnage velvets—Safavid period (to be completed in January, 1964); Ainu Textiles (to be completed in 1964); Naskapi costume (to be completed in 1964).

SYMONS, SCOTT: (B) Series of eleven articles in *La Presse* (25 mars–10 avril 1961); weekly articles in *Le Nouveau J* (septembre 1961–mars 1962). (C) *Le Nouveau J, La Presse.* (D) Volume on French-Canadian and English-Canadian cultural history relations (second draft half finished); (collaborating with Mrs. Scott Symons) a comprehensive volume on French-Canadian and English-Canadian furniture and taste (still in research stage; probable publication, 1964).

Music

UNIVERSITY OF ALBERTA, CALGARY

CHURCHLEY, F. E.: (B) "The Piano in Canada," *Music J* (1961), 86.

UNIVERSITY OF BRITISH COLUMBIA

PROCTOR, GEORGE A.: (D) "Musical Style of Gaspé Songs" and "Old-time Fiddling in Ontario" (articles, to appear shortly in *Contributions to Anthrop*); "Nicola Matteis: A Review" (submitted for publication).

MOUNT ALLISON UNIVERSITY

ELLIOTT, CARLETON: (D) "Music in New Brunswick" (ready for publication).

UNIVERSITY OF TORONTO

BECKWITH, JOHN: (A) (ed. with Udo Kasemets) *The Modern Composer and His World* (Toronto, 1961), xii + 170 pp. (B) "Composers in Toronto and Montreal," *UTQ*, 26 (1956), 47–69; "Music," *The Arts in Canada* (Toronto, 1958); "Music," *The Culture of Contemporary Canada* (Ithaca, 1958); "Musical Education," *Enc Can* (1958); "Jean Papineau-Couture," *CMJ*, 3 (1959), 4–20; "Notes on a Recording Career," *Can For*, 40 (1961), 217–219; "Schoenberg: Ten Years After," *Can For*, 41 (1961), 180–82; "The Performing Arts," *Can Annual R for 1960* (Toronto, 1961), 328–36; "Music," *Can Annual R* (1962), 396–407; "A Stravinsky Triptych,"

CMJ (1962). (C) *Can Annual R, Can For, CMJ, UTQ.* (D) Material for the annual music report in the *Can Annual R for 1962.*

Art and Archaeology

ROYAL ONTARIO MUSEUM

BRETT, GERARD: (B) "The Mosaic of the Great Palace in Constantinople," *J Warburg and Courtauld Institutes,* 5 (1942), 34–43; "The Seven Wonders of the World in the Renaissance," *Art Q,* 12 (1949), 339–58; "East-West," *ROMB* (1952), 1–5; "West-East," *ROMB* (1953), 1–48; "King Solomon," *Ars Quatuor Coronatorum,* 66 (1954), 89–96; "Flemish Oak Reredos in the Royal Ontario Museum," *Gazette des Beaux-Arts* (1954), 75–7; "Automata in the Byzantine Throne of Solomon," *Speculum,* 29 (1954), 477–87; The Durham Rider section in *Relics of the Tomb of St. Cuthbert* (Oxford, 1956), 339–58; "A Sketchbook of Pietro da Cortona," *ROMB,* 26 (1957), 4–10; "The Archaeological Museum: its Past and Present," *Royal Ont Mus Div Art and Arch Annual* (1959), 12–23. (C) *Royal Ont Mus Div of Art and Arch Annual.* (D) English Furniture and its Setting, 1675–1825 (handbook, to be submitted for publication in 1963); book on the history of meals from about 900 or 1000 until the present (begun).

KIDD, KENNETH E.: (A) *The Excavation of Ste. Marie I* (Toronto, 1949), xiv + 191 pp.; (with Selwyn Dewdney) *Indian Rock Paintings of the Great Lakes* (Toronto, 1962), viii + 127 pp. (B) "The Identification of French Mission Sites in the Huron Country: A Study in Procedure," *OH,* 41 (1949), 89–94; "The Excavation and Historical Identification of a Huron Ossuary," *Amer Antiquity,* 18 (1953), 359–79; "Trade Goods Research Techniques," *Amer Antiquity,* 20 (1954), 1–8; "A Woodland Site near Chatham, Ontario," *Trans Roy Can Inst.* (C) *Amer Antiquity, Man.* (D) The ethnographic significance of the work of Paul Kane (in process of second writing); on the utility of glass trade beads for dating Indian sites, including a history of beads in the West (writing of first book nearly completed); on historical archaeology in Canada (begun).

LEIPEN, NEDA: (B) "A Greek Bronze Mirror," *ROMB,* 25 (1957), 4–6; "A Greek Bronze Patera," *ROMB,* 26 (1957), 18–21; "A Bronze Wall-bracket," *Royal Ont Mus Div Art and Arch Annual* (1960), 21–6; "A Clay Alabastron with Shield Decoration," *Royal Ont Mus Div Art and Arch Annual* (1961), 27–34. (C) *ROMB, Royal Ont Mus Div Art and Arch Annual.* (D) A study of the Athena Parthenos (ready for publication).

PARKER, HARLEY: (D) Collaborating with H. M. McLuhan on a study of concepts of space in poetry and painting.

ROGERS, EDWARD S.: (A) *The Round Lake Ojibwa,* Roy Ont Mus Occasional Paper 5 (Toronto, 1962). (B) (with Murray H. Rogers) "Archaeological Reconnaissance of Lakes Mistassini and Albanel, Province of Quebec, 1947," *Amer Antiquity,* 14 (1948), 81–90; "Archaeological Investigations in the Region about Lakes Mistassini and Albanel, Province of Quebec, 1948," *Amer Antiquity,* 15 (1950), 322–37; (with Roger Bradley) "An Archaeological Reconnaissance in South-Central Quebec, 1950," *Amer An-*

tiquity, 19 (1953), 138–44; (with Jean H. Rogers) "The Yearly Cycle of the Mistassini Indians," *Arctic*, 12 (1959), 130–8.   (C) *Amer Antiquity, Anthropologica, Arctic, Southwestern J Anthrop.*   (D) "Changing Settlement Patterns among the Cree-Ojibwa of Northern Ontario" (in press); "Indian-Eskimo Contacts in the Labrador Peninsula" (in press); "Analysis of the Hunting Group–Hunting Territory Complex among Mistassini Indians and Neighbouring Peoples" (in press); "The Material Culture of the Mistassini Indians" (almost ready for press).

TUSHINGHAM, A. D.: (A) *Natural Law in the Old Testament* (Chicago, 1948; on microfilm); (with Allan Fleming), *The Art of Fine Printing and Its Influence on the Bible* (Toronto, 1956), 51 pp.; (introduction) *Masks: The Many Faces of Man* (Toronto, 1959), 75 pp.   (B) "A Reconsideration of Hosea, Chapters 1–3," *JNES*, 12 (1953), 150–9; (with Kathleen Kenyon) "Jericho Gives up its Secrets," *National Geog Mag*, 14 (1953), 853–70; "Excavations at Dibon in Moab, 1952–53," *BASOR*, 133 (1954), 6–26; "An Inscription of the Roman Imperial Period from Dhiban," *BASOR*, 138 (1955), 29–34; "Archaeology and the Canadian," *QQ*, 62 (1956), 554–64; "The Men Who Hid the Dead Sea Scrolls," *National Geog Mag*, 114 (1958), 784–808.   (C) *BASOR, JNES, National Geog Mag, QQ.*   (D) A study of the Iron Age tombs at Jericho (completed and awaiting publication); "Dibon" (article, to be published in *Enc of Arch*); "Archaeology as a Career" (brochure for the Ontario Department of Education; nearly complete); "The Excavation of Dhiban" (about one-quarter completed).

ST. MARY'S UNIVERSITY

LOEWENSTEIN, JOHN: (A) *Chinesische Spiegel* (2 vols., Vienna, 1933), 300 pp.   (B) "Eine besondere Gruppe alter Metallspiegel aus Ostasien," *Ostasiatische Zeitschrift*, 10 (1934); "The Swastika, its History and Meaning," *Man*, 41 (1941), 49–55; papers for the Central Office of Information, London, England, published during 1946–47: "Aus der Fibel der Menschheit," "Grosstadtleben am Indus-Dreitausend Jahre vor Christus," "Wo liegt das Heilige Grab?" "Durchleuchtete Tiefen"; "Tulang Mawas re-examined," *J Malayan Branch Roy Asiatic Soc*, 26 (1953); "A Bronze Kettledrum (T'ung-ku) in the EU Collection," *Singapore Art Soc and China Soc* (1954); "Ancient Jewellery of Modern Design," *Argentor* (1952); "The Origin of the Malayan Metal Age," *J Malayan Branch Roy Asiatic Soc*, 29 (1956); "Neolithic Stone Gouges from the Malay Archipelago and their Northern Prototypes," *Anthropos*, 52 (1957), 841–9; "Evil Spirit Boats of Malaysia," *Anthropos*, 53 (1958), 203–11; "A Propos d'un Tableau de W. Schellinks s'inspirant des Miniatures Mogholes," *Ars Asiatiques*, 5 (1958); "Who first settled in Polynesia?—A New Theory," *Listener*, 61 (1959), 711–13; "Rainbow and Serpent," *Anthropos*, 56 (1961), 31–40; "An 'Ordos' Bronze Knife from Prehistoric Malaya," *Anthropos*, 56 (1961), 936–7; "Open Letter," *Current Anthrop*, 2 (1961), 406.   (C) *Anthropos, Ars Asiatiques, Current Anthrop, J Malayan Branch Roy Asiatic Soc, Man.*   (D) "Hollow Clay Stands from Neolithic Malaya" (article, to be published by *J Malayan Branch Roy Asiatic Soc*).

Varied Topics

ASSUMPTION UNIVERSITY OF WINDSOR

WATERMAN, RICHARD A. (Dept. of Anthropology): (B) *Bibliog. of Asiatic Music*, published serially in *Notes of Mus. Lib. Ass.* (1947–51); "African Influence on the Music of the Americas," in Sol. Tax, ed., *Acculturation in the Americas* (Chicago, 1952), 207–18; "Music," in *Handbook of Latin American Studies* (Hispanic Foundation, Lib. of Congress), Nos. 17–23 (1954–60); "Moral Values of the Aboriginals of Yirkalla, N.E. Arnhem Land, Australia," in Vergilius Ferm, ed., *Enc of Morals* (1956), 1–8; "The Role of Dance in Human Society," *Focus on Dance* (Washington, 1962).

CARLETON UNIVERSITY

EGGLESTON, WILFRID (Dept. of Journalism): (A) *The Road to Nationhood* (Toronto, 1946); *Scientists at War* (Toronto, 1950); *Canada at Work* (Montreal, 1953); *The Frontier and Canadian Letters* (Toronto, 1957); (ed.) *The Green Gables Letters* (Toronto, 1960); *The Queen's Choice* (Ottawa, 1961). (D) A book of memoirs (nearly complete); a history of nuclear energy in Canada (half finished); "The Press as an Agency in Canadian Life" (material assembled, not much writing done yet).

KESTERTON, WILFRED HAROLD (Dept. of Journalism): (B) "A History of Canadian Journalism from 1752 to *c.* 1900," in *Canada Year Book, 1957–8* (Ottawa, 1959); "A History of Canadian Journalism from *c.* 1900 to 1958," in *Canada Year Book, 1959* (Ottawa, 1960); "Source Materials for a History of Canadian Journalism," *Can Communications*, 1 (autumn, 1960); "Journalism," *Can Annual R for 1960* (Toronto, 1961); "The Confusing Criticisms of the Press," *QQ*, 69 (summer, 1962). (D) A history of Canadian journalism (last section being written).

MUNN, ALLAN (Dept. of Physics): (A) *Free-will and Determinism* (Toronto & London, 1960), 218 pp. (D) The mystical and other possible phenomena of sensory deprivation experiments.

SAINT MARY'S UNIVERSITY

BURKE-GAFFNEY, M. W. (Dept. of Astronomy): (A) *Kepler and the Jesuits* (Milwaukee, 1944); *Daniel Seghers, 1590–1661* (New York, 1961), 54 pp. (B) "Nicole Oresme and the Astrologers," *Traditio*, 8 (1952), 461–4; "Ireland's Ornament: Agnes Mary Clerke," *J RASC* (Jan.-Feb., 1956); "Mary in the Accounts of What Happened in New France," *Our Lady of the Cape* (1957), March, 22–5; Apr., 20–3; May, 22–4; June, 26–8; July, 26; (and other articles and reviews).

THEOLOGY AND HISTORY OF RELIGION

ASSUMPTION UNIVERSITY OF WINDSOR

McCANN, L.: (A) *The Doctrine of the Void* (Toronto and Rochester, 1955). (C) *Theol St* (Woodstock, Md.).

MURRAY, JOHN CLIFFORD: (C) *Cath World* (many reviews). (D) The infused knowledge of Christ in the Theology of the twelfth and thirteenth centuries (doctoral thesis ready for publication).

CANTERBURY COLLEGE, ASSUMPTION UNIVERSITY (DIVINITY)

HILL, HENRY GORDON: (D) "The Wesleys and Anglican Spirituality" (article completed); "Spiritual Experience," for symposium ed. Canon H. L. Puxley (article to be prepared).

KINGSTON, FREDERICK TEMPLE: (A) *French Existentialism: A Christian Critique* (Toronto, 1961), viii + 222 pp. (B) "Classical Culture and the Wholeness of Faith," *Anglican Theol R*, 40 (1958), 26 ff.; "Anglican Unity and the Ecumenical Movement, *Anglican Theol R*, 42 (1960), 246 ff.; "An Introduction to Existential Thought," *DR*, 40 (1960), 181 ff. (C) *Anglican Theol R, Can Churchman, CJT, DR*. (D) "Some Aspects of the Notion of Paradox" (accepted by *Anglican Theol R*); "Laws of Nature and the Natural Law" (submitted for publication).

RAYSON, ROBERT S.: (A) *A Firm Foundation* (Toronto, 1954). (B) "John Strachan, A Study in Biography," *Amer Church Monthly*; "Charles Inglis First Bishop of Nova Scotia," *QQ*.

BISHOP'S UNIVERSITY (DIVINITY)

CROUSE, ROBERT D.: (B) (tr. and notes) "Matthew of Aquasparta: Disputed Questions on Faith" in E. R. Fairweather, ed., *A Scholastic Miscellany: Anselm to Ockham* (Philadelphia and London, 1956), 402–27; "The Augustinian Background of St. Anselm's concept *justitia*," *CJT*, 4 (1958), 111–9; "The Hellenization of Christianity: A Historiographical Study," *CJT*, 8 (1962), 22–33. (C) *CJT, Harvard Divinity School Bull.*

JELLICOE, SIDNEY: (B) "Ezra-Nehemiah: A Reconstruction," *Expository Times* (Edin.), 59 (1947–8); "A Note on *al mûth* (Psalm 48.15)," *J Theol St*, 49 (1948); "The Prophets and the Cultus," *Expository Times*, 60 (1948–9); "The Interpretation of Psalm 73.24," *Expository Times*, 67 (1955–6); "St. Luke and the Seventy (-two)," *New Testament Studies* (Cambridge, 1960), vol. 6; "Aristeas, Philo, and the Septuagint *Vorlage*," *J Theol St*, NS, 12 (1961); "St. Luke and the Letter of Aristeas," *JBL*, 80 (1961). (C) *JBL, J Theol St.* (D) The Septuagint and modern study (ten of twelve chapters completed); a study of the text of the Greek O.T., with special reference to the *Vorlage*, history of textual transmission, chief recensions, relation to underlying Hebrew text and principal ancient versions; article, "The Hesychian recension reconsidered" (under final revision for *JBL*).

MCMASTER UNIVERSITY—DIVINITY COLLEGE

ALBAUGH, GAYLORD P.: (B) Six articles, "Anti-Missionary Movements," "Battle-Axe-Experiment," "Religious Journalism," "Religious Tract Movement," "Seamen's Movement," and "Sunday School Movement," in V. Ferm, ed., *Amer Enc of Religion* (New York, 1945); "Anti-Missionary Movement," in L. A. Loetscher, ed., *Twentieth Century Enc Religious Knowledge* (Grand Rapids, 1955); "Themes for Research in Canadian

Baptist History," *Foundations*, 6 (1963), 42–56.   (C) *Can Baptist, CJT, CH, Foundations* (Rochester), *Interpretation* (Richmond, Va.), *J Presbyt Hist*.   (D) A checklist of American Presbyterian periodicals begun before 1830, with library locations (to be published as a series of four articles in *J Presbyt Hist*); a two-volume history and annotated bibliography of American religious periodicals and newspapers, 1730–1830 (needs a sabbatical year to complete it).

ALDWINCKLE, R. F.: (B) "The Christian Conception of God," in E. A. Payne, ed., *Studies in History and Religion* (Lutterworth, 1942); "Myth and Symbol in Contemporary Theology and Philosophy," *JR*, 39 (1954); "Biblical Theology and Philosophy," *Religion in Life*, 24 (1955); "Infant Baptism or Believers' Baptism," *Foundations*, 2 (1959); "Much Ado about Words," *CJT*, 7 (1961); "Truly man: The Humanity of the God-Man," *CJT*, 8 (1962).   (C) *Baptist Q, CJT, Foundations, JR, Religion in Life, Review and Expositor*.   (D) Divine presence and human language: the nature of religious language and its ontological reference in the light of modern study of myth and symbol and philosophical analysis (near completion); introduction to Christian ethics (just started); studies in Christology (three chapters done).

CLIFFORD, PAUL ROWNTREE: (B) "Confronting the Episcopalian Theory of the Apostolic Ministry," *Foundations*, 2 (1959); "The Theology of Acceptance," *Pastoral Psych* (1961); "Omnipotence and the Problem of Evil," *JR* (1961).   (C) *CJT, Dialogue*.   (D) Interpreting metaphysics (book-length MS. being considered for publication); "Perception and judgment" (article accepted by *Dialogue*); other articles in preparation.

PARKER, N. H.   (D) Interpreting the Prophets (book-length MS. ready for submission for publication); God in History (book on historical section of O.T., more than half done).

MOUNT ALLISON UNIVERSITY

EBBUTT, A. J.: (A) *The Life, the Question, and the Answer* (Toronto), 165 pp + bibliog.; *The Bible and Christian Education* (Toronto), 44 pp. + bibliog.   (C) *United Church Observer*.   (D) Religion in the public schools of Canada (ready for publication).

ST. FRANCIS XAVIER UNIVERSITY

MACKINNON, GREGORY: (D) Abstract of thesis, "The Role of the Laity in the Church According to Cardinal Newman" (should be ready early in 1964).

SAINT MARY'S UNIVERSITY

FOGARTY, D. (Education): (A) *Roots for a New Rhetoric* (New York, 1958).   (B) "A Tentative Philosophy of Communication," *Can Communications* (1960); one chapter in F. Shoemaker, *et al.*, eds., *Communication in General Education* (Dubuque, 1961).

WATERLOO LUTHERAN SEMINARY

LEUPOLD, U. S. (A) (trans.) Vilmos Vajta's *Luther on worship* (Philadelphia, 1958).   (C) *Lutheran Q, Lutheran World, Response*.   (D) Vol. 53 of Luther's Works (final editing in progress).

ADDENDUM (for page 204)

IRVING, JOHN A.: (A) (ed. with an introductory essay, "Social Philosophy of E. J. Urwick") Urwick's *The Values of Life* (Toronto, 1948), 310 pp.; *Science and Values* (Toronto, 1952), xii + 148 pp.; (ed. and contributor) *Philosophy in Canada: A Symposium* (Toronto, 1952), 48 pp. (chap. I, "One Hundred Years of Canadian Philosophy," 6–26); (ed. with introduction, and contributor) *Architects of Modern Thought*, First and Second Series (Toronto, 1955), 98 pp. ("Bertrand Russell," 91–8); Third and Fourth Series (Toronto, 1959), x + 145 pp., Fifth and Sixth Series (Toronto, 1962), x + 154 pp. ("Herbert Spencer," 51–62); (ed. with R. C. Chalmers, and contributor) *The Light and the Flame* (Toronto, 1956), xiv + 143 pp. (Preface and chap. V, "Logical Analysis and Mysticism," 85–104); *The Social Credit Movement in Alberta* (Toronto, 1959), xiv + 369 pp.; (ed. with R. C. Chalmers, contrib.) *Challenge and Response* (Toronto, 1959), 140 pp. (Preface, chap. VII, "Ideological Differences and World Order," 113–30); (ed. and contributor) *Mass Media in Canada* (Toronto, 1962), viii + 236 pp. (Preface, chap. I, "The Development of Communications in Canada," 1–12, chap. X, "The Problems of the Mass Media," 221–35). (B) "Logical Positivism and Psychology," *Proc Amer Philos Ass* (Bryn Mawr) (Dec., 1932); "Toward Radical Empiricism in Ethics," in H. M. Kallen and Sidney Hook, eds., *American Philosophy Today and Tomorrow* (New York, 1935), 227–47; "The Social A Priori," *JP*, 33 (Dec. 3, 1936), 687–8; "Leibniz's Theory of Matter," *Philos of Sc*, 3 (1936), 208–14; "Consciousness and Behaviour," *Bull Can Psych Ass*, 5 (1945), 10–15; "The Achievement of George Sidney Brett," *UTQ*, 14 (1944–45), 329–65; "The Future of Philosophy," *UTQ*, 16 (1946–47), 188–98; "Psychological Aspects of the Social Credit Movement in Alberta," *Can J Psych*, 1 (1947), 17–27, 75–86, 127–40; "The Evolution of the Social Credit Movement," *CJEPS*, 14 (1948), 321–41; "Evolution and Ethics," *QQ*, 55 (1948–49), 450–63; "The Comparative Method and the Nature of Human Nature," Proceedings of the Second Inter-American Congress of Philosophy (New York, 1947), published in *Philos and Phenomenological Res*, 9 (1949), 544–57; "The Function of an Annual Conference on the Teaching of Philosophy," in F. P. Harris, ed., *The Teaching of Philosophy* (Cleveland, 1950), 26–30; "The Reconstruction of Humanity," *PhR*, 59 (1950), 115–23; "The Development of Philosophy in Central Canada from 1850 to 1900," *CHR*, 31 (1950), 252–87; "Philosophical Trends in Canada between 1850 and 1950, *Philos and Phenomenological Res*, 12 (1951), 224–45; "The Manifesto of Democracy," *QQ*, 58 (1951–52), 312–26; "General Happiness as an Ethical End," *QQ*, 57 (1950–51), 459–72; "The Sciences and Philosophy in Modern Culture," in R. C. Chalmers, ed., *The Heritage of Western Culture* (Toronto, 1952), 88–101; "Prairie Ideals and Realities," *QQ*, 63 (1956–57), 188–200; "Philosophy," in Julian Park, ed. *The Culture of Contemporary Canada* (Ithaca, 1957), 242–73; "Mysticism and the Limits of Communication," in A. P. Stiernotte, ed., *Mysticism and the Modern Mind* (New York, 1959), 99–112; "The Aesthetic Temper in Ethics," *Philos and Phenomenological Res*, 20 (1959), 56–62; "The Philosophy of John Dewey," *JP*, 57 (June 23, 1960), 442–50; "The Achievement of Thomas McCulloch," in Malcolm Ross, ed., Thomas McCulloch's *The*

Stepsure Letters (Toronto, 1960), 150–6; "Interpretations of the Social Credit Movement in Alberta," in B. R. Blishen, F. E. Jones, K. D. Naegele, and John Porter, eds., *Canadian Society* (Toronto, 1961), 314–25; "Social Credit," in H. G. Thorburn, ed., *Party Politics in Canada* (Toronto, 1963), 85–95.   (C) *Can For, CHR, CJEPS, Can J Psych, DR, Int J, JP, PhR, Philos and Phenomenological Res, Philos of Sc, Psych R, Public Opinion Q, QQ, Sat N, UTQ.*   (D) (ed.) The Meaning of Life in Five Great Religions (scheduled for publication, 1965); chapters on "Philosophy," in C. F. Klinck, ed., A Literary History of Canada (to be published 1964); The History of Philosophy in Canada, from the beginning to 1965; articles on Canadian philosophers for the Dictionary of Canadian Biography.